The Future of Entrepreneurship in Africa

For many years, entrepreneurship has been considered as one of the most important solutions to the three-pronged challenges, poverty, unemployment and inequality, of most African countries. A recent development that has undoubtedly compounded the challenges that African entrepreneurs face and further impede the economic growth impact is COVID-19. This pandemic has exerted severe damage to economies and businesses globally. For the African setting, the implications of COVID-19 on businesses and individuals would be enormous, as African societies are rarely equipped to absorb unexpected shocks of this magnitude as the social and welfare schemes are far below requirements.

This book illuminates entrepreneurship in the African setting, focusing on the prospects, challenges and the post-COVID-19 pandemic future. It aims to offer a rich repository of information on strategies and techniques for sustaining entrepreneurial activities that can enrich African nations and will be of relevance to academics, researchers, advanced students, entrepreneurs, governments and government agencies who are interested in understanding issues relating to entrepreneurship development within the African continent.

Anthony Abiodun Eniola is a Professor (Associate) in the Herbert Chitepo School of Law and Business Sciences, Graduate Business School, Great Zimbabwe University, Zimbabwe.

Chux Gervase Iwu is a Professor (Full) in the Faculty of Economic and Management Sciences at the University of the Western Cape, South Africa.

Abdullah Promise Opute is a Visiting Professor, Lecturer, PhD Supervisor and Examiner at University of Wales Trinity Saint David, UK and a Researcher with GPROM Academic and Management Consulting, Germany.

Routledge Studies in Entrepreneurship and Small Business

Edited by Robert Blackburn
University of Liverpool, UK

Small Business and Effective ICT: Stories and Practical Insights
Carmine Sellitto, Scott Bingley, David A. Banks, and Stephen Burgess

Motivating SMEs to Cooperate and Internationalize
A dynamic perspective
George Tesar and Zsuzsanna Vincze

How Small to Medium Enterprises Thrive and Survive in Turbulent Times: From Deconstructing to Synthesizing Organizational Resilience Capabilities
Yiu Hin Chu and Kosmas Smyrnios

Managing People in Small and Medium Enterprises in Turbulent Contexts
Alexandros Psychogios and Rea Prouska

Business Transfers, Family Firms and Entrepreneurship
Edited by Bérangère Deschamps, Audrey Missonier, Catherine Thévenard-Puthod, Paulette Robic, and Dominique Barbelivien

The Persistence of Entrepreneurship Myths: Reclaiming Enterprise
Simon Bridge

Corporate Volunteering, Responsibility and Employee Entrepreneurship
Aldona Glińska-Neweś and Beata Glinka

Entrepreneurial Communities and Ecosystems: Theories in Culture, Empowerment, and Leadership
Edited by Morgan R. Clevenger and Michael W-P Fortunato

Empowering Entrepreneurial Communities and Ecosystems: Case Study Insights
Edited by Michael W-P Fortunato and Morgan R. Clevenger

Entrepreneurship, Innovation, and Crisis: SME Responses to the COVID-19 Pandemic
Edited by Joanna Duda and Rafał Kusa

The Future of Entrepreneurship in Africa: Challenges and Opportunities Post-Pandemic
Edited by Anthony Abiodun Eniola, Chux Gervase Iwu, and Abdullah Promise Opute

The Future of Entrepreneurship in Africa

Challenges and Opportunities Post-Pandemic

Edited by
Anthony Abiodun Eniola, Chux Gervase Iwu, and Abdullah Promise Opute

Routledge
Taylor & Francis Group
NEW YORK AND LONDON

First published 2023
by Routledge
605 Third Avenue, New York, NY 10158

and by Routledge
4 Park Square, Milton Park, Abingdon, Oxon, OX14 4RN

Routledge is an imprint of the Taylor & Francis Group, an informa business

Library of Congress Cataloguing-in-Publication Data
Names: Eniola, Anthony Abiodun, editor, author. | Iwu, Chux Gervase, editor, author. | Opute, Abdullah Promise, editor, author.
Title: The future of entrepreneurship in Africa : challenges and opportunities post-pandemic / edited by Anthony Abiodun Eniola, Chux Gervase Iwu, and Abdullah Promise Opute.
Description: New York City : Routledge, 2022. | Includes bibliographical references and index.
Identifiers: LCCN 2022031628 | ISBN 9781032106670 (hardback) | ISBN 9781032106687 (paperback) | ISBN 9781003216469 (ebook)
Subjects: LCSH: Entrepreneurship--Africa, Sub-Saharan. | COVID-19 Pandemic, 2020---Economic aspects--Africa, Sub-Saharan. | Africa, Sub-Saharan--Economic conditions--21st century.
Classification: LCC HB615 .F8784 2022 | DDC 338.040967--dc23/eng/20220705
LC record available at https://lccn.loc.gov/2022031628

ISBN: 978-1-032-10667-0 (hbk)
ISBN: 978-1-032-10668-7 (pbk)
ISBN: 978-1-003-21646-9 (ebk)

DOI: 10.4324/9781003216469

Typeset in Bembo
by MPS Limited, Dehradun

Contents

Figures

Tables

Contributors

Dr Ogechi Adeola is an Associate Professor of Marketing and the Head of Department of Operations, Marketing and Information Systems at the Lagos Business School, Pan-Atlantic University, Nigeria. Her multi-dimensional research focuses on the advancement of knowledge across the intersection of marketing, entrepreneurship, tourism and gender. Her research has been published in top international journals, including *Annals of Tourism Research, Tourism Management, Journal of Business Research, Industrial Marketing Management, International Marketing Review,* and *Psychology and Marketing*. Adeola's international marketing consultancy experience spans Africa, Asia, the United Kingdom and the United States.

Isaiah Adisa is a management researcher and consultant based in Nigeria. He has co-edited book(s) with several other book chapters and journal articles in recognised outlets. He is affiliated with the Olabisi Onabanjo University, Ago-Iwoye, Ogun State, and his research interest cuts across human resources management, organisational behaviour, marketing and gender studies. His consultancy experience spans the education and health sectors. Isaiah was part of the Sector Master Plan Strategy (a team member of Tourism and Hospitality Industries Thematic Group – THITG) for the Nigeria Economic Summit Group.

Chukwuka Blessing is an enthusiastic researcher who is currently studying for her PhD in the field of management at Queens University Belfast. Her research interests span across development studies, entrepreneurial studies, gender studies, organisational and management studies. Prior to her doctorate studies, she worked as a research assistant at Lagos Business School, where she rendered her research expertise to the advancement of faculty research work.

Willie Chinyamurindi is a National Research Foundation (NRF) Rated Researcher (Y2) working at the University of Fort Hare as a Professor in the Department of Business Management. As a broad theme, his research is along aspects of human and organisational capabilities and how they contribute towards the theme of development. This entails aspects such as

(a) Human Resources Development (HRD) and Organisational Psychology covering sub-themes such as careers, employability, decent work, technology in HRD; (b) Interpretivist research methods within the management sciences; (c) Entrepreneurship and Strategic Management, especially the intersection of strategy in organisational behaviour.

Dr Oluwakemi Chukwuma-Nwuba is an Assistant Professor of entrepreneurship at the International Centre for Transformational Entrepreneurship (ICTE), Coventry university, United Kinfdom. She is an astute teacher and entrepreneur with a remarkable background in teaching entrepreneurship and related modules, and an outstanding knowledge in agribusiness. Kemi is a Ford Fellow. She holds a PhD in enterprise and entrepreneurship, and an MSc in innovation management and entrepreneurship from UK universities. Her passion for youths flows through in her teaching. In addition to being the course director of Add +vantage Programme, Kemi represents ICTE at the Faculty of Business and Law Global Engagement Committee.

Anthony Abiodun Eniola is a Professor (Associate) in the Munhumutapa School of Commerce, Graduate Business School at Great Zimbabwe University, Zimbabwe. He has a demonstrated history of working in the higher education industry. His research areas are in entrepreneurship, SME finance and social entrepreneurship. He has authored books in this area of research.

Ujunwa Perpetua Ezeachikulo is a researcher, who is keen on social issues. She is currently the Secretary of the OAAD women's Network and also the current Jiangsu coordinator of NIDO East China. She has contributed to research work and authored papers published in Elsevier, IJRP and as well published conference papers. She is currently working on a poverty alleviation project.

Dr Gebregziabher Gebreyesus Fiseha was born in Tigray, Ethiopia. He received his first degree in Accounting from the University of Gondar, Ethiopia. Dr Gebregziabher acquired honours and masters in development studies from the University of Fort Hare, South Africa. He holds a PhD in development studies from the University of Fort Hare in 2020. His PhD thesis focused on social entrepreneurship and poverty reduction. Dr Gebregziabher has published five articles in internal accredited journals from his masters and honours degrees work.

Dr Sirak Berhe Hagos is a freelance researcher and consultant offering acculturation and integrating solutions to academic and government units. In this connection, Dr Sirak Berhe Hagos works as Visiting Lecturer at Durham University where he delivers lectures occasionally on Culture Understanding, and also offers coaching on Culture and Inter-Cultural Understanding (through Investing in People and

Culture). Dr Hagos has been appointed severally in the UK to speak on the topic of cultural Adaptation and Integration of refugees and asylum seekers. Dr Hagos' research interest includes Cross-Cultural Management, Integration of Refugees and Asylum Seekers, Ethnic Minority Businesses, and Ethnic Conflict and Management.

Elona N. Ndlovu-Hlatshwayo (PhD candidate) is an emerging researcher with a keen interest in sustainable entrepreneurial development through entrepreneurial coaching and building sustainable entrepreneurial ecosystems. She is a Master Coach (ABCCCP), the Chair of Research for COMENSA (Coaches and Mentors of South Africa) and a lecturer in the Masters in Business & Executive Coaching programme at the Wits Business School as well as a Research Methodology at the Management and Entrepreneurship Department in Tshwane University of Technology. She supervises Masters' research in both entrepreneurship and coaching.

Dr Julius Irene is a Geologist with over 20 years' experience in the upstream sector of oil and gas industry, mainly in exploration and development assets across Africa, Middle East and Europe. Dr Irene primary research area examines spaces of contention in the energy transition in order to improve critical support for policy development, advance the diffusion of innovative energy technologies and sustainable approaches for decarbonisation. Furthermore, Dr Irene is interested in understanding how energy systems can be institutionalised, guided and fitted in a social and environmental context. Dr Irene also researches entrepreneurship and SMEs.

Chux Gervase Iwu is a Full Professor in the School of Business & Finance of the Faculty of Economic and Management Sciences, the University of the Western Cape, South Africa. He served as the Assistant Dean, Research and Innovation in the Faculty of Business and Management Sciences at the Cape Peninsula University of Technology, South Africa. He researches the broad area of socioeconomic issues of emerging economies.

Dr Kalu Ibe Kalu is an Agile Delivery & Transformation Coach expert. He works in a cross-functional team role in the private equity and venture capital industry, leading entrepreneurial business development and Agile technology transformation. Kalu has exceptional leadership and project management skills, honed through experiences, mentoring and coaching talent.

Tendai Makwara is a PhD (Business Management Science) candidate at Central University of Technology, Bloemfontein. He holds a Master of Philosophy degree and a Post-Graduate Diploma (Cum Laude) in (HIV and AIDS) Management from Stellenbosch University, South Africa. His research interests are in the broad areas of health, small business, social responsibility and entrepreneurship fields.

Dr Moshe Timothy Masonta is a Principal Research Technologist and Research Group Leader at the Council for Scientific and Industrial Research, South Africa. He is responsible for the development and implementation of the research, development and innovation strategy within the Networked Systems and Applications impact area. His research interests include frequency spectrum management, 5G radio access networks, and Fourth Industrial Revolution technologies supporting small, medium and macro enterprises development for the township and rural digital economy. He holds a Doctorate Degree in Electrical Engineering (Telecommunications) and a Programme for Management Development certificate from the University of Pretoria's Gordon Institute for Business Science.

Dr Motshedisi Mathibe is a Senior Lecturer at the University of Pretoria's Gordon Institute of Business Science (GIBS). Dr Mathibe has more than ten years of experience in academic institutions, lecturing at various universities such as the University of the Free State, Central University of Technology Free State and the University of Pretoria. Dr Mathibe is an emerging researcher. Her research focuses on the entrepreneurship context (Social and Women Entrepreneurship, Informal Sector, Township Economy and Base of the Pyramid markets). Motshedisi is also a mentor for United Nations' Global Impact Young Sustainable Development Goals (SDGs) Innovators Programme.

Kelechi Chinemerem Mezieobi is a Lecturer in the Department of Arts and Humanities Education, Faculty of Education, Alex Ekwueme Federal University Ndufu-Alike, Ikwo, Ebonyi State, Nigeria. He previously taught education management and social studies at the Imo State University Owerri Nigeria. Kelechi has published widely (nationally and internationally) in areas of social studies, education management and general education. His research interests include social studies education, inclusive education, educational management, climate change and environment management safety practices.

Dr Tonderai Muchenje is a Lecturer at the Tshwane University of Technology (South Africa), in the Department of Information Technology. He holds a PhD in Information Technology (Nelson Mandela University), MCom Computer Auditing (University of Johannesburg), MSc in Computer Science (University of Fort Hare), Certified Trainer CCNA1, Certified Trainer CCNA2: Routing, Switching and Wireless Essentials, Certified Trainer: CCNA Cybersecurity Operations, Advanced Business Analysis (University of Pretoria). Currently lecturing computing systems and information security and supervising masters at TUT and Mancosa. His research areas of interests are wireless security, internal control systems, information portfolio management and smart meter technologies.

Sayibu Muhideen is a researcher at the Department of Philosophy of Sci-Tech Communication Policy at the University of Science and Technology of China. Obtained his master's degree in Public Policy Management from that same university. His research interest is in innovative and technology-building phenomena toward digital mobile in health and education. The majority of my research focused on mobile-driven digital technology advancement in education and health.

Dr Alufheli Edgar Nesamvuni is the Executive Dean of the Faculty of Management Sciences at The Tshwane University of Technology which hosts the Centre of Entrepreneurship Development (CED) which develops student entrepreneurs. The CED sparked his interest in grassroots entrepreneurship development emerged through engagement with student entrepreneurs. He is passionate about self-starting SMEs and advocates for the contextualisation of Lean Start-up methodology for the African continent. He supervises entrepreneurship doctoral and master's students. He is a member of the Enterprise and Cooperatives Development Committee (ECDC) as well as the deputy chairperson of the Research Dialogue Technical Task Team (RDTTT) of the Services Seta. The focus at the Services Seta is to develop and implement an integrated Programme of Action (PoA) comprising innovative, relevant and impactful skills development products to better support entrepreneurs and cooperatives.

Fulufhelo Netswera is a Professor of Public Governance and the Executive Dean of management sciences at the Durban University of Technology. He is a former Director of the South African BRICS Think Tank, a former Erasmus fellow at Groningen University and current visiting professor at Lincoln International Business School. He researchers and writes in the areas of entrepreneurship, public governance and higher education policy, among other things.

Deborah Odu Obor obtained a PhD in Sociology from the University of Ibadan, Nigeria. She is currently a research fellow at the Institute for Peace and Conflict Resolution (IPCR), Abuja-Nigeria. Before joining IPCR, she worked nine years as a lecturer in the Department of Sociology, Bowen University, Iwo, Osun state. Her research interests include graduate employability, entrepreneurship education, industrial sociology and emerging technologies.

Ekene Francis Okagbue is a researcher and a member of the OAAD African research organisation. As an agent for positive change, he focuses on using his research works and knowledge to bring solutions to social issues most especially in the African context.

Dr Olugbenga Joseph Oluwole holds a PhD degree from the Department of Industrial Psychology at the University of Fort Hare, South Africa. While his bachelor and master's degree were obtained from the University of Ibadan, Ibadan in Nigeria.

Dr Solomon Omonona is a Postdoctoral Fellow in the Department of Business Management, University of Fort Hare, Eastern Cape South Africa. He has authored several scientific publications in reputable journals. In addition, Dr Omonona is currently working on the "revitalization of the rural and township economy in the Eastern cape region of South Africa".

Prof Olabanji Oni is an expert in the field of Business Management. He has supervised Masters and PhD students and published widely in the field of Business Management. His research areas are in Entrepreneurship, Small Business Management and Finance. He is a co-conveyer for the International Conference on Business and Management Dynamics as well as a reviewer and guest editor for various business management journals. He is a member of various committees in the university and has served in various leadership positions.

Dr Abdullah Promise Opute is a freelance academic and management consultant. Currently, he is a scholar at the Management School, University of Wales Trinity Saint David, UK. Dr Opute is academic consultant at several African and European universities. His research has been published in top international journals, including *Journal of Business and Industrial Marketing*, *International Journal of Entrepreneurship and Small Business*, *Journal of Entrepreneurship and Innovation in Emerging Economies*, *International Journal of Management Education*, *Team Performance Management*, amongst others. He researches inter-functional integration, relationship management, cross cultural management, consumer behaviour, entrepreneurship and SMEs, strategic marketing, strategic management accounting, etc.

Ibrahim Oluwapelumi Orekoya is a Doctoral Researcher and Associate Lecturer in the Department of Entrepreneurship and Strategy, Lancaster University Management School, Lancaster University, United Kingdom. He holds a bachelor's degree in Business Administration (first class honors) from Babcock University, Nigeria and a master's degree in Management from the University of Lagos, Nigeria. Prior to joining Lancaster University Management School, he worked as a Research Assistant at the Lagos Business School, Pan-Atlantic University, Lagos, Nigeria. He is a Graduate Member of the Nigerian Institute of Management (Chartered).

Lucky Sibanda holds a master's degree in Business Administration (Entrepreneurship), a BTech degree in Business Administration (cum laude) and a Diploma in Entrepreneurship (cum laude) from the Cape Peninsula University of Technology. Over the past eight years, he has taught face-to-face and distance learning modes in the higher education space. He has also co-authored several peer-reviewed academic articles.

Ndivhuho Tshikovhi is a Postdoctoral Fellow at the Durban University of Technology. He holds a doctorate in social and political sciences from the Université Libre de Bruxelles, Belgium and a master degree in entrepreneurship from the Tshwane University of Technology in South Africa. He also studied at Fudan University in China and at the University of Mannheim Center for Entrepreneurship and Innovation as a guest doctoral student in the Institute for SMEs Research and Entrepreneurship. His core research interest is anything related to entrepreneurship.

1 COVID-19 Effect on Human Resources for Entrepreneurship Development

Willie Chinyamurindi

Introduction

The world is currently experiencing challenges posed by the COVID-19 pandemic. Due to this, there has been a global government response (Park & Fowler, 2021). The COVID-19 pandemic appears to affect the business configurations. The literature defines business configurations as those elements that consist of (a) environments, (b) industries, (c) technologies, (d) strategies, (d) structures, (e) cultures, (f) ideologies and (g) practices (Meyer et al., 1993). In essence, the entire organisational architecture of business functions stands at the risk of being affected (Du et al., 2021). As a result of the COVID-19 pandemic, a need exists to build resilience against disruptions from such unexpected contingencies (Maruping et al., 2021). Such resilience can be in addressing cost and supply challenges imposed by the pandemic with intentional managerial strategies (Mishra et al., 2021). This has led some to posit that there is still much we do not know about the impact of the COVID-19 pandemic on the world of work (Hossain, 2021). Further, the role of the COVID-19 pandemic and the managerial response becomes also important (Ahlqvist et al., 2020).

In developing countries like South Africa, there is advocacy for dedicated attention to aspects related to entrepreneurship development (Shava & Chinyamurindi, 2022; Mkhonza & Sifolo, 2022). Quests for entrepreneurship growth are tied to improving countries' competitiveness while improving citizens' livelihood (Schiavone et al., 2021). Calls exist for studies that explore the role moments of crisis (like that of the COVID-19 pandemic) may have on small business enterprises and entrepreneurs (Doern, 2016; Galindo-Martin et al., 2021; Newman et al., 2022). While the devastation created by the pandemic in terms of loss of life is relatively documented (Walker et al., 2020), less is known about its impact on business continuity and survival (Baur, 2020). Further, there is a need to understand how the people aspect of the organisation, referred to here as the human resource function, is affected by all this (Bapuji et al., 2020). The focus is on understanding how businesses adjust to the new normal but also on understanding the people management aspect of this (Handfield et al., 2020; Trautrims et al., 2020).

DOI: 10.4324/9781003216469-1

Research purpose and objectives

Given the COVID-19 pandemic, calls exist to understand the impact of the pandemic on business functions (Handfield et al., 2020; Hudecheck et al., 2020; Trautrims et al., 2020). From the people side in organisations, arguments are made to understand the effect of the COVID-19 pandemic on business and aspects related to human resource development (Chinyamurindi et al., 2021). Based on a sample of entrepreneurs, this study sought to understand the challenges faced by entrepreneurs in light of the COVID-19 pandemic, especially on the human resources function. This fits into calls in understanding the influence of macro-events on the enterprise and its actors (Atiku et al., 2020; Cho, 2020).

Further, suggestions are made for entrepreneurship development based on the identified challenges. The following research question was explored: what are the challenges faced by entrepreneurs in light of the COVID-19 pandemic, especially on the human resources function? This question will also help set in motion solutions and policy implications for human resources and entrepreneurship development.

Literature review

Theoretical lens

To theoretically position this study, relevant foundations are underlined. First, theories need to exemplify aspects of interdependence rather than duality (Furnari et al., 2021). This means that the human resource function should not be seen as operating in isolation but as part of interaction with other business functions (Razmdoost et al., 2020). Second, quests for this argument for interdependence should be linked with systems thinking that is holistic (Kim et al., 2016). In embracing this holistic system thinking, there is also a need to understand the interacting role of multiple organisational actors (Nambisan et al., 2018). The challenge of the COVID-19 pandemic necessitates a response from management scholars (Wieland, 2021).

The study borrows from two primary theoretical considerations. First, the human capital theory. At the core of the human capital theory is the focus on human resources existing as a competitive advantage source (Bag & Gupta, 2019; Doern, 2016). This places importance on the existence of such resources and also on their management (Hoffmann & Rüsch, 2017). In response to challenges, organisations can use internal or external capabilities to their advantage (Barreto et al., 2017). This can include using technology, changes to organisational structure, and work plans to respond to the challenges experienced (Telukdarie et al., 2018). This can be a source of competitive advantage (Evans, 2019).

The second consideration to the study is the dynamic capabilities perspective (Teece & Pisano, 1994). The idea here is that dynamic capabilities exist as those competencies that assist the firm in responding to the rapid changes happening within the environmental context (Samsudin & Ismail, 2019). Given environmental uncertainty, dynamic capabilities allow one firm to perform better than the other (Abbady et al., 2019). In essence, dynamic capabilities can assist in forming a competitive advantage (Ragmoun & Alwehabie, 2020). Dynamic capability activities are framed as sensing and seizing opportunities, including reconfiguring internal opportunities given this (Semke & Tiberius, 2020). The thinking here is that small business owners will do everything to perform better despite challenges. The current challenge of the COVID-19 pandemic will merely be used as a stepping stone to rise above such a challenge. This will come in the form of the identified activities from the extant literature, as argued by Semke and Tiberius (2020). In achieving such, the role of resources is argued as key (Peterson et al., 2020) together with an organisational culture (Glyptis et al., 2021).

Impact of COVID-19 pandemic on human resources and entrepreneurship development

The COVID-19 pandemic has affected the human resources function within organisations. Due to challenges related to lockdown, this has led to changes in the way work is conducted, also affecting customers (Opute, 2022; Opute et al., 2020). A resultant effect of all this within small businesses is the loss of income (Bressan et al., 2021). An attribution of this identified in other sectors is a shrinking budget base (Mitra, 2020) and dwindling cash flow (Cowling et al., 2020). Due to this shrinkage, internal resources and capabilities are affected. This trickles into an organisation's activities (Matsa, 2010; Teece et al., 1997). Ultimately, as per the findings of Oni and Omonona (2020), COVID-19 negatively affects the performance of small businesses.

The COVID-19 pandemic also takes a toll on finance options available to enterprise development. Notably, this limits the amount of funding and financing options available to entrepreneurs (Brown et al., 2020). In some countries, women-owned businesses have less chance of business recovery and are most affected by the COVID-19 pandemic (Manolova et al., 2020).

For the small business sector, the COVID-19 pandemic stifles growth and limits resource commitments. The argument here is that resource components, i.e., strategic, physical, financial, human, and organisational resources, are constantly re-directed or re-prioritised given the pandemic (Lim et al., 2020). Such shifts pose challenges and may in themselves be periods of uncertainty not only in the way the small business is run but also for the entrepreneur (Nummela et al., 2020). Ultimately, due to the COVID-19, the idea of global firms emerging from the small business context may become an illusion (Korsgaard et al., 2020).

Another effect of the COVID-19 pandemic is the toll this has on the entrepreneurs running the small businesses and the employees (Yue & Cowling, 2021). This is no surprise, as the most affected by the pandemic are employees (Brown & Cowling, 2021).

Addressing challenges posed by the COVID-19 pandemic for human resources and entrepreneurship development

There is a need for systems to be in place, especially within small businesses, to address the challenges presented in the previous section (Iswanto, 2021). This can come in the form also of business-to-business synergies in addressing the impact posed by the COVID-19 pandemic (Cortez & Johnston, 2020). Scholars suggest how this can happen to curtail the devastation caused by disruptions such as the COVID-19 pandemic. Notably, this includes (a) *inter*-functional coordination (Ruiz-Alba et al., 2020), (b) *resource integration* (Kleinaltenkamp et al., 2012), (c) integration of finance and strategy capabilities (Puck & Filatotchev, 2020) and (d) small business relief schemes (Oni & Omonona, 2020).

Some solutions appear to have been put in place to assist the human resource component in responding to the effects of the COVID-19 pandemic. Technology is argued as one such tool. The role of technology should be seen because of the broader changes happening in a society driven by technology. This has allowed the usage of a range of digital tools to assist organisations and individuals (Hinings et al., 2018). Such tools have allowed the introduction of intelligent services for the business (Spicer et al., 2021). The role of technology in the pandemic also appears inevitable. Redda (2021) argues within a South African context that the pandemic accelerated the adoption of online retailing.

Given current social distancing measures imposed by the COVID-19 pandemic (Agostino et al., 2020), the usage of technology allows employees to be still engaged in work activities. This can affect aspects related to how employees learn and acquire skills within an organisational setting (Scull et al., 2020).

Despite the usage of such digital tools, some concerns can be flagged. Chief of these is how such innovations can promote further injustice and inequality (Wang et al., 2021). Others also caution against the psychological impact of technology usage, especially during the COVID-19 pandemic (Parker, 2020). A concern here is the mental health toll created by the continued use of technology, especially in response to the COVID-19 pandemic (Andrew et al., 2020). In essence, despite its benefit, technology may perpetuate continued divide and loneliness (Knudsen, 2020). The literature appears to argue for guided concern around the usage of technology. This should incorporate support mechanisms to assist organisations (Roper & Turner, 2020). Policies could be put in place around the usage of technology (Korsgaard et al., 2020). This could also equip the business owners in acquiring the requisite skills and competencies around the usage of technology and new ways of working (Kuckertz, 2021).

Research method

In answering the research question, an interpretivist research philosophy using a qualitative research approach was utilised in this study. The rationale for this stems from the praise given to this philosophy and approach in understanding the complexity that accompanies human experience (Bryman et al., 2018; Chinyamurindi, 2020). Such a philosophy and approach enables a subjective understanding of the meaning of social action and potential response sense-making (Bryman et al., 2018; Delport et al., 2018). In previous studies, such a philosophy and approach has been utilised to understand the impact of the COVID-19 pandemic within the human resource profession (Chinyamurindi et al., 2021).

Sampling and research participants

A non-probability sampling approach was utilised, relying on a purposive sampling technique because the participants were deemed as suitable that is, they would offer practical manifestations of the impact of the COVID-19 pandemic on a sample of small business owners in South Africa (Cohen et al., 2018; Rule & John, 2017). The aim was to narrow focus only to those characteristics needed in the sample based on their experience (Mooi et al., 2018; Morgan and Sklar, 2018; Nardi, 2018), i.e., experts within the entrepreneurial space. Twenty-five entrepreneurs operating within the Eastern Cape Province of South Africa took part in the study. The sample of entrepreneurs operated mainly within the engineering and construction spaces. Table 1.1 presents the demographic profiles of the participating entrepreneurs. The following inclusion and exclusion criteria were used to select participants: (a) a participant had to be an entrepreneur who had been in operation for a minimum of five years, and (b) a participant had to be running their small business within the Eastern Cape Province within the engineering and construction spaces.

Data collection and data recording

To achieve the objectives of this research, qualitative research approach was deemed suitable towards gaining in-depth understanding of the complexity that the COVID-19 pandemic has created. In achieving all this, semi-structured interviews were utilised with 25 entrepreneurs operating in the Eastern Cape Province of South Africa. The interviews were audio-recorded with permission. Each interview lasted between 30 and 50 minutes.

Table 1.1 Demographic characteristics of participants

Participant	*Gender & race*	*Years of business operation*	*Sector*
1	Male (B)	6	Construction
2	Male (B)	8	Construction
3	Male (W)	12	Engineering
4	Male (C)	10	Construction
5	Female (I)	9	Engineering
6	Female (I)	9	Engineering
7	Female (B)	10	Construction
8	Male (B)	11	Construction
9	Male (B)	8	Construction
10	Male (I)	8	Engineering
11	Male (W)	6	Engineering
12	Male (B)	16	Construction
13	Male (W)	12	Construction
14	Female (W)	11	Engineering
15	Male (C)	9	Engineering
16	Male (B)	13	Construction
17	Female (I)	15	Construction
18	Female (I)	9	Engineering
19	Male (B)	7	Engineering
20	Female (B)	8	Construction
21	Male (B)	9	Construction
22	Female (W)	15	Engineering
23	Male (W)	18	Engineering
24	Male (C)	14	Construction
25	Female (B)	6	Construction

B - Black; C - Coloured; I - Indian; W - White

Strategies to ensure data integrity

There is a need to ensure data quality and reporting, especially in qualitative research. The researcher paid attention to many strategies (Bryman et al., 2018; Silverman, 2021). Interviews conducted for the study were audio-recorded. After the recording, the transcription of data commenced. After the transcription process, interview transcripts were sent to the participants to verify the information in the transcripts. In also ensuring data integrity, data was collected over an eight-month period.

Data analysis

A qualitative thematic analysis approach was utilised (Braun et al., 2019; Silverman, 2021). Over the eight months of data collection, the interviews were transcribed soon after each interview. The transcripts were then entered into the QSR NVivo 9 data analysis and management software (Reuben & Bobat, 2014). The software was used to code each of the transcripts' paragraphs into themes and sub-themes. The coding was done using the participants' own words wherever possible. However, the researcher did not only rely on the software to develop the themes, it was also used as a complementary method to develop themes. Thematic analysis was utilised to analyse the qualitative data by identifying and examining common patterns within the data (Vaismoradi et al., 2013). In analysing the data through thematic analysis was utilised (Braun et al. 2019).

Ethical considerations

The research adhered to ethical guidelines. First, ethical clearance was applied for and granted by the participating institution where the researchers are based. Second, participants were assured that their identity and data collected would be handled confidentially (Devlin, 2018; Ferreira, 2018; Patten & Newhart, 2018). Third, the researchers also adhered to other ethical considerations that included informed consent (Pajo, 2018; Saunders & Lewis, 2018) and the right to withdraw from the research at any point (Neuman, 2014). Finally, after transcribing the interviews, copies were sent back to the participants as a way of verification. Participants were free to add or correct the transcriptions and return them to the researchers. All interviews were conducted in strict adherence to COVID-19 protocols. Physical interaction was avoided.

Findings

Two main findings emerged from the study regarding the effect of the COVID-19 pandemic on human resources for entrepreneurship development. First, the entrepreneurs reported a cutting back, especially on human resources activities. Second, the participating entrepreneurs suggested resultant cushions around the impact of the COVID-19 pandemic. These included (a) compliance with government employee assisted programs such as the unemployment insurance fund and financial assistance; (b) supporting employee well-being during the pandemic times; (c) formalised associations to help local entrepreneurs in cross-sharing ideas for small business survival and finally and (d) leveraging on the benefits of technology in assisting entrepreneurship development. These findings are discussed next.

Theme one: cutting back as a result of the pandemic

The participating entrepreneurs cited challenges of a cut-back nature attributed to the pandemic. This cutting back came from the need to stay afloat, given the limited cash flow to the business. The cutting back mainly was on two strands. First, cutting back on any unnecessary spending. Second, having to let go of some employees or innovative work arrangements around work rotation. One participant narrated the experience of cutting back on unnecessary spending:

> The pandemic has forced us to weigh what we need against what we think we need. I have had to be more circumspect in terms of spending. As a rule, all new purchases and orders are scrutinized more to avoid wastage. [Participant 24, Male Construction Sector]

A second participant also narrated challenges related to a spending cut-back directly attributed to the COVID-19 pandemic and the limited cash flow available to the enterprise. This participant also attributed the lockdown phases as having an impact as well:

> The start of the pandemic had untold suffering. What would emerge would also be uncertainty. For instance, the various lockdown also means periods of having little or no cash depending on the nature of the restriction. [Participant 17, Female Construction Sector]

Regrettably, the COVID-19 pandemic also affected the human resource component of the enterprise. Notably, it resulted in some of the small businesses releasing some of their staff in a bid to stay afloat.

> Having to let go of your staff members was the most difficult experience for us. Remember, the tender system was closed at the start of the pandemic due to the restrictions. So I had no work or projects from which staff could engage in. I had to let go of some of my best guys. [Participant 10, Male Engineering Sector]

Another participant also echoed the same sentiment around staff cut-backs. Despite the dominant theme here being cut-backs, this participant showed some flair by introducing work rotation. This assisted in guaranteeing work for everyone at a low cost. A situation better than retrenchments.

> I called all the employees together. We had to find innovative responses to the pandemic. One such means was work rotation. Yes, we were cutting back but at minimal damage. This was a better approach than retrenchments." [Participant 3, Male Engineering Sector]

Table 1.2 presents additional quotes from the participants supporting theme one of the study around cut-backs.

This leads to the second finding, the cushions against the identified challenges.

Theme two: cushions to the challenges of the pandemic

The second finding focuses on the range of cushions utilised by the small business owners to the impact of the COVID-19 pandemic. One participated emphasised the role of government-assisted programs:

Table 1.2 Cut-backs as a challenge of the COVID-19 pandemic

Cutting back within the business	*Cutting back related to human-resource-related issues*
"We had to merge certain functions. In so doing, this allowed for an assessment of what we could re-define and what we could not" **[Participant 3, Male, Engineering Sector].**	"The human resource budget was affected. This included letting go of some employees but also making sure some activities such as training and staff development were re-adjusted" **[Participant 1, Male, Construction Sector].**
"Where we could, we made some of our employees work from home at a reduced rate. This was better than losing your job. We had a few clients we consulted with online, but the nature of our work requires us to be onsite" **[Participant 10, Male, Engineering Sector].**	"A cellular phone provider offered us a package where we could have a mobile office setup For instance, this allowed our receptionist to work from home and connect to the others. Sadly, it means releasing the office cleaner and other non-essential services" **[Participant 12, Male, Construction Sector].**
"The pandemic taught us the value of cost-saving. However, it also taught us how to cut back on the unnecessary" **[Participant 17, Female, Construction].**	"Our human resources and marketing team was cut down drastically. In addition, we even had to sell some furniture and hire our office space at a cheap rate" **[Participant 22, Female, Engineering Sector].**

Source: Analysed data.

> A stimulus package by the government targeted at small business owners was beneficial for us. Though this was not enough, it helped at least keep us going. It compliments with aspects related to your registration, this allowed us room to benefit. [Participant 1, Male Construction Sector]

Concerning the human resources side, one small business owner praised the help of agencies that provide well-being support as beneficial for their enterprise:

> We approached some agencies to assist with providing well-being support for our employees. The challenge here was to cut back on our human resource activity. So getting this help at such notice helped us greatly, especially our employees." [Participant 18, Female Construction Sector]

Regrettably, the COVID-19 pandemic also affected the human resource component of the enterprise. Notably, it resulted in some of the small businesses releasing some of their staff in a bid to stay afloat.

> Having to let go of your staff members was the most difficult experience for us. Remember, the tender system was closed at the start of the pandemic due to the restrictions. So I had no work or projects from which staff could engage in. I had to let go of some of my best guys. [Participant 10, Male Engineering Sector]

The role of formal associations was praised for providing a network in which small businesses could network. This was also valuable for the cross-pollination of ideas, including strategies to respond to the COVID-19 pandemic.

> Being a member of the Black Business Forum also assisted our efforts. Here was a network of businesspeople facing the same challenge of the COVID-19 pandemic. We had more online meetings in which we could exchange ideas." [Participant 12, Male Construction Sector]

Technology was used as a significant factor to cushion the challenges of the COVID-19 pandemic.

> "We started investing in technology to assist our business. Working from home became normal. So we got licenses to online communication software to allow for communication. We also got negotiated cellular contracts to help us also communicate at a reduced cost." [Participant 20, Female Construction Sector].

Discussion

The purpose of the study was to investigate the challenges entrepreneurs face in light of the COVID-19 pandemic, especially concerning human resources for entrepreneurship development. In essence, the study identifies the challenges and the strategies being used to ameliorate the consequences of the COVID-19 pandemic.

Participating entrepreneurs reported a cutting back, especially on the activities around human resources. As shown in the study, affected by this is the idea of business configurations (Meyer et al., 1993) and the organisational architecture (Du et al., 2021). In this study, the manifestation of cut-backs was utilised as a tool to keep these two intact, albeit the challenges faced. These cut-backs ultimately limited not just enterprise but also human resource development. Interestingly, the identified cushion to the COVID-19 pandemic appears to also serve as a potential aid in promoting back enterprise and human resource development. This study thus magnifies the human resource activity for enterprise development (Bapuji et al., 2020).

Another salient finding relates to the ensuing cushions around the impact of the COVID-19 pandemic. The findings of this study argue for the need to support the small business sector in view of the challenges from the

COVID-19 pandemic (Park & Fowler, 2021). Based on this study, the clarion call from the small businesses is the necessity for more responsiveness to assist the entrepreneurial ecosystem. The identified findings can assist in providing understanding how organisations can become resilient albeit challenges faced especially from the COVID-19 pandemic. This can be a helpful feeder for enterprise development.

Implications

Theoretical implications

The study and its findings provide a useful basis in understanding theoretically aspects related to enterprise development. The idea of studying how enterprises respond to crisis especially the COVID-19 pandemic provides a basis for understanding aspects of interdependence coupled (Furnari et al., 2021). In essence, the focus is not just on the enterprise but also aspects of responsiveness to challenges posed by the COVID-19 pandemic. This affirms aspects of interaction between the human resource function and the environment (Razmdoost et al., 2020). Support is therefore shown for the human capital theory and the dynamic capabilities perspective as crucial in framing understanding of organisations.

The finding of this study answer also an important call from the literature in understanding how the resilience of small businesses can come about (Maruping et al., 2021). The role of the entrepreneurs becomes important in driving for such resilience manifest in the intentionality exercised and illustrated in this study (Ahlqvist et al., 2020; Mishra et al., 2021). Such cushions also appear to promote people management and development within the enterprise. This makes a contribution given the calls for understanding how such processes happen, albeit the challenges being faced (Handfield et al., 2020; Trautrims et al., 2020). The context of the COVID-19 pandemic period brings appreciation to the importance of these theories.

Implications for practitioners

Based on the findings of the study, some implications can be drawn. First, there is a need for the continued development of entrepreneurial ecosystems that adopt a form of resilience to the challenges posed by the COVID-19 pandemic. The role of the human resources capability becomes vital in doing so. At the core of such resilient ecosystems is the need to pay attention to the challenges employees face within such systems. The study's findings highlight the need for employee well-being interventions, especially as a response to the pandemic. This is an essential human resource development imperative that can potentially spill into a greater entrepreneurial quests. In essence, this prioritisation of the entrepreneurial system focuses on human resource development. There is room and latitude for the government to create such an ecosystem (Park & Fowler, 2021). The government is there to provide a context in which small business can operate. However, this should also extend to where needed providing financial and expert assistance to small business owners. The context of the COVID-19 pandemic places focus on the necessity for such assistance.

Another implication of the study is the need for intentional managerial strategies (Mishra et al., 2021) in response to the challenges posed by the COVID-19 pandemic. The study's findings appear to show any inclination of solutions coming from outside rather than inside. This includes looking to stakeholders such as the provincial and national governments. This research magnifies the role of managerial response to the pandemic (Ahlqvist et al., 2020). However, this alone is not enough; small business owners may need to form more collaborative efforts in response to the pandemic. This appears not to be happening especially given the more competitive spirit opted for. Collaborative efforts are being argued for in the form of push strategies towards business continuity and survival (Baur, 2020). The focus can be on people management tactics and approaches (Handfield et al., 2020; Trautrims et al., 2020).

Another potential implication concerns paying attention to an investment not only into digital technologies but digital literacies. Interface such as digital technologies and remote working have become popular in response to the new normal of working (Opute, 2022; Opute et al., 2020). Given this, there is need to make sure that small businesses including their human resource function develop competencies and capabilities that support the new normal through the requisite technologies adopted. This potentially can affect how the small business performs. Finally, there is room for networks and training opportunities to empower small business owners in response to the COVID-19 pandemic. The priority here could be alerting the small business owners to opportunities that may exist within their local context. This is a welcome move from a dependency approach that seeks to ascribe responsibility to the government.

Limitations of the study

Some limitations exist with this research. First, this study explored general challenges entrepreneurs face given the COVID-19 pandemic. The identified challenges are not generalisable to the experience of all entrepreneurs. Caution should be exercised in this regard. Two sectors were chosen for this study as a matter of convenience. The findings of this study are not meant to represent all the small business sectors not only in South Africa or in the Eastern Cape Province. Another limitation was the reliance on single respondents in the form of entrepreneurs running their businesses. Given the focus of the study being on human resources matters, the voice of employees is equally essential and warranting attention.

Future research

Future research could improve on the identified limitations. First, interviews could also be conducted with employees. This can potentially enrich understanding by incorporating the views of an essential stakeholder to the human resources activity, employees. Second, future research can solicit responses from different sectors. Notably, within the Eastern Cape Province of South Africa, the construction and agriculture space appear core areas of interest. Third, future research can narrow focus only on specific entrepreneur categories. For instance, the focus could be given only to the issues faced by women entrepreneurs concerning human resources and entrepreneur development. The thinking here is that women-owned businesses are being argued to be most affected by the COVID-19 pandemic (Manolova et al., 2020). Finally, each of the findings of the study deserves further unpacking. This can be done through a more in-depth focus. For instance, the issue around the challenges of a lack of employee well-being interventions in response to the COVID-19 pandemic warrants this further investigation.

Conclusion

Despite the impact of the COVID-19 pandemic, the chapter explored the lived experiences of entrepreneurs and how they seek to emerge from the challenge of the pandemic. The findings of this study and as presented in this chapter proffer understanding to an important area of research around the impact of the COVID-19 pandemic on the small business sector.

References

Abbady, M., Akkaya, M., & Sari, A. (2019). Big data governance, dynamic capability and decision-making effectiveness: Fuzzy sets approach. *Decision Science Letters*, 8(4), 429–440.

Agostino, D., Arnaboldi, M., & Diaz Lema, M. (2020). New development: COVID-19 as an accelerator of digital transformation in public service delivery. *Public Money & Management*, 41(1), 69–72. 10.1080/09540962.2020.1764206

Ahlqvist, V., Norrman, A., & Jahre, M. (2020). Supply chain risk governance: Towards a conceptual multi-level framework. *Operations and Supply Chain Management: An International Journal*, 13(4), 382–395.

Andrew, J., Baker, M., Guthrie, J., & Martin-Sardesai, A. (2020). Australia's COVID-19 public budgeting response: The straitjacket of neoliberalism, *Journal of Public Budgeting, Accounting & Financial Management*, 32(5), 759–770.

Atiku, S. O., Jeremiah, A., & Boateng, F. (2020). Perceptions of flexible work arrangements in selected African countries during the coronavirus pandemic. *South African Journal of Business Management*, 51(1), 1–10.

Bag, S., & Gupta, S. (2019). Examining the effect of green human capital availability in adoption of reverse logistics and remanufacturing operations performance. *International Journal of Manpower*. 10.1108/IJM-07-2019-0349

Bapuji, H., de Bakker, F., Brown, J., Higgins, C., Rehbein, K., & Spicer, A. (2020). Business and society research in the times of the corona crisis. *Business & Society*, 59(6), 1067–1078.

Barreto, L., Amaral, A., & Pereira. T. (2017). Industry 4.0 implications in logistics: An overview. *Procedia Manufacturing*, 13, 1245–1252.

Baur, P. W. (2020). An examination of the impact of COVID-19 on the financial markets and how this directs investment into the market for fine art. *Journal of Economic and Financial Sciences*, 13(1), 1–22.

Braun, V., Clarke, V., Hayfield, N., & Terry, G. (2019). *Thematic analysis*. Singapore: Springer.

Bressan, A., Alonso, A. D., & Kok, S. K. (2021). Confronting the unprecedented: Micro and small businesses in the age of COVID-19. *International Journal of Entrepreneurial Behaviour & Research*, 27(3), 799–820. 10.1108/IJEBR-09-2020-0602

Brown, R., & Cowling, M. (2021). The geographical impact of the Covid-19 crisis on precautionary savings, firm survival and jobs: Evidence from the United Kingdom's 100 largest towns and cities. *International Small Business Journal: Researching Entrepreneurship*, 39(4), 319–329.

Brown, R., Rocha, A., & Cowling, M. (2020). Financing entrepreneurship in times of crisis: Exploring the impact of COVID-19 on the market for entrepreneurial finance in the United Kingdom. *International Small Business Journal: Researching Entrepreneurship*, 38(5), 380–390.

Bryman, A., Bell, E., Hirschohn, P., Dos Santos, A., Du Toit, J. Masenge, A., Van Aardt, I., & Wagner, C., (2018). *Research methodology: Business and management context*. Cape Town: Oxford University Press.

Chinyamurindi, W. T. (2020). "Breaking through the morass": Narratives of resistance and persuasion by individuals in creative economy careers. *African Review of Economics and Finance*, 12(2), 68–83.

Chinyamurindi, W. T., Masha, A. K., & Tshabalala, N. (2021). The impact of the COVID-19 pandemic on Industrial Organisational Psychologists in South Africa: Imagining new professional roles. *South African Journal of Industrial Psychology*, 47, 1–10. 10.4102/sajip.v47i0.1876

Cho, E. (2020). Examining boundaries to understand the impact of COVID-19 on vocational behaviours. *Journal of Vocational Behaviour*, 119. http://refhub.elsevier.com/S0001-8791(20)30066-X/rf0015

Cohen, L., Manion, L., & Morrison, K. (2018). *Research methods in education*. London: Routledge.

Cortez, R. M., & Johnston, W. J. (2020). The coronavirus crisis in B2B settings: Crisis uniqueness and managerial implications based on social exchange theory. *Industrial Marketing Management*, 88, 125–135.

Cowling, M., Brown, R., & Rocha, A. (2020). Did you save some cash for a rainy COVID-19 day? The crisis and SMEs. *International Small Business Journal: Researching Entrepreneurship*, 38(7), 593–604.

Delport, C. S. L., Fouché, C. B., & Schurink, W. (2018). Theory and literature in qualitative research. In A. S. De Vos, H. Strydom, C. B. Fouché, & C. S. L. Delport (Eds.), *Research at grassroots for the social sciences and human service professionals*. Pretoria: Van Schaik.

Devlin, A. S. (2018). *The research experience. Planning, conducting and reporting research*. London: Sage.

Doern, R. (2016). Entrepreneurship and crisis management: The experience of small businesses during the London 2011 riots. *International Small Business Journal*, 34(3), 276–302.

Du, Y. Z., Li, J. X., Liu, Q. C., Zhao, S. T., & Chen, K. W. (2021). Configurational theorizing and QCA from a complex and dynamic perspective: Research progress and future directions. *Management World (in Chinese)*, 37(3), 180–197.

Evans, P. (2019). Making an HRD domain: Identity work in an online professional community. *Human Resource Development International*, 22(2), 116–139.

Ferreira, R. (2018). Writing a research proposal. In K. Maree (Ed.), *Complete your thesis or dissertation successfully: Practical guidelines*. Cape Town: Juta.

Furnari, S., Crilly, D., Misangyi, V. F., Greckhamer, T., Fiss, P.C., & Aguilera, R.V. (2021). Capturing causal complexity: Heuristics for configurational theorizing. *Academy of Management Review*, 46, 778–799.

Galindo-Martin, M. A., Castaño-Martínez, M. S., & Méndez-Picazo, M. T. (2021). Effects of the pandemic crisis on entrepreneurship and sustainable development. *Journal of Business Research*, 137, 345–353.

Glyptis, L., Hadjielias, E., Christofi, M., Kvasova, O., & Vrontis, D. (2021). Dynamic families capabilities and family business growth: A longitudinal perspective framed within management accounting. *Journal of Business Research*, 127, 346–363.

Handfield, R. B., Graham, G., & Burns, L. (2020). Coronavirus, tariffs, trade wars and supply chain evolutionary design. *International Journal of Operations & Production Management*, 40(10), 1649–1660.

Hinings, B., Gegenhuber, T., & Greenwood, R. (2018). Digital innovation and transformation: An institutional perspective. *Information and Organization*, 28(1), 52–61. 10.1016/j.infoandorg.2018.02.004

Hoffmann, E., & Rüsch, M. (2017). Industry 4.0 and the current status as well as future prospects on logistics. *Computers in Industry*, 89, 23–34.

Hossain, D. A. (2021). The impact of COVID-19 on accounting profession. 10.2139/ssrn.3923710

Hudecheck, M., Siren, C., Grichnik, D., & Wincent, J. (2020). How companies can respond to the coronavirus. *MIT Sloan Management Review*. Retrieved May 31, 2020, from https://sloanreview.mit.edu/article/how-companies-can-respondto-the-coronavirus/

Iswanto, A. H. (2021). Impact of lean six sigma at pharmacy unit on hospital profitability before and during COVID-19 pandemic. *International Journal of Lean Six Sigma*, 12(4), 718–743. 10.1108/IJLSS-10-2020-0182

Kim, P. H., Wennberg, K., & Croidieu, G. (2016). Untapped riches of meso-level applications in multi-level entrepreneurial mechanisms. *Academy of Management Perspectives*, 30(3), 273–291.

Kleinaltenkamp, M., Brodie, R. J., Frow, P., Hughes, T., Peters, L. D., & Woratschek, H. (2012). Resource integration. *Marketing Theory*, 12(2), 201–205.

Knudsen, D. R. (2020). Elusive boundaries, power relations, and knowledge production: A systematic review of the literature on digitalization in accounting. *International Journal of Accounting Information Systems*, 36, 1–22. 10.1016/j.accinf.2019.100441

Korsgaard, S., Hunt, R. A., Townsend, D. M., & Ingstrup, M. B. (2020). COVID-19 and the importance of space in entrepreneurship research and policy. *International Small Business Journal: Researching Entrepreneurship*, 38(8), 697–710.

Kuckertz, A. (2021). Standing up against crisis-induced entrepreneurial uncertainty: Fewer teams, more habitual entrepreneurs. *International Small Business Journal: Researching Entrepreneurship*, 39(3), 191–201.

Lim, D. S. K., Morse, E. A., & Yu, N. (2020). The impact of the global crisis on the growth of SMEs: A resource system perspective. *International Small Business Journal: Researching Entrepreneurship*, 38(6), 492–503.

Manolova, T. S., Brush, C. G., Edelman, L. F., & Elam, A. (2020). Pivoting to stay the course: How women entrepreneurs take advantage of opportunities created by the COVID-19 pandemic. *International Small Business Journal: Researching Entrepreneurship*, 38(6), 48–491.

Maruping, L., Rai, A., Aljafari, R., & Venkatesh, V. (2021). Overcoming cross-organizational barriers to success in offshore projects. *Industrial Management & Data Systems*, 121(12), 2365–2386.

Matsa, D. A. (2010). Capital structure as a strategic variable: Evidence from collective bargaining. *The Journal of Finance*, 65(3), 1197–1232.

Meyer, A. D., Tsui, A. S., & Hinings, C. R. (1993). Configurational approaches to organizational analysis. *Academy of Management Journal*, 36(6), 1175–1195.

Mishra, M. N., Mohan, A., & Sarkar, A. (2021). Role of lean six sigma in the Indian MSMEs during COVID-19. *International Journal of Lean Six Sigma*, 12(4), 697–717. 10.1108/IJLSS-10-2020-0176

Mitra, R. (2020). COVID-19 is killing education budgets: Are educational public-private partnerships an answer? *Journal of Professional Capital and Community*, 5(3/4), 255–264. 10.1108/JPCC-07-2020-0056

Mkhonza, V. M., & Sifolo, P. P. (2022). Investigating small, medium and micro-scale enterprises strategic planning techniques in Johannesburg central business district post-COVID-19 lockdown. *Southern African Journal of Entrepreneurship and Small Business Management*, 14(1), 1–13.

Mooi, E., Sarstedt, M., & Mooi-Reci, I. (2018). *Market research: The process, data, and methods using Stata*. Melbourne: Springer.

Morgan, B., & Sklar, R. (2018). Sampling and research paradigms. In K. Maree (Ed.), *Complete your thesis or dissertation successfully: Practical guidelines*. Cape Town: Juta

Nambisan, S., Siegel, D., & Kenney, M. (2018). On open innovation, platforms and entrepreneurship. *Strategic Entrepreneurship Journal*, 12(3), 354–368.

Nardi, P. M. (2018). *Doing survey research: A guide to quantitative methods*. London: Routledge.

Neuman, W. (2014). *Social research methods: Qualitative and quantitative approaches*. Essex: Pearson.

Newman, A., Martin, O., & Joern, B. (2022). Small businesses and entrepreneurship in times of crises: The renaissance of entrepreneur-focused micro perspectives. *International Small Business Journal: Researching Entrepreneurship*, 40(2), 119–129.

Nummela, N., Paavilainen-Mäntymäki, E., Harikkala-Laihinen, R., & Raitis, J. (2020). When all doors close: Implications of COVID-19 for cosmopolitan entrepreneurs. *International Small Business Journal: Researching Entrepreneurship*, 38(8), 711–717.

Oni, O., & Omonona, S. (2020). The effect of COVID-19 on small retail businesses in Alice Town, South Africa. *The Retail and Marketing Review*, 16(3), 48–57.

Opute, A. P. (2022). Virtual teams: The new work norm for the post Covid-19 era. In O. Adeola, J. N. Edeh, R. E. Hinson, & F. Netswera (Eds.), Digital service delivery in Africa. Palgrave studies of marketing in emerging economies. Cham: Palgrave Macmillan. 10.1007/978-3-030-83909-3_13

Opute, A. P., Iwu, C. G., Adeola, O., Mugobo, V. V., Okeke-Uzodike, O. E., Fagbola, O., & Jaiyeoba, O. (2020). The COVID-19-pandemic and implications for businesses: Innovative retail marketing viewpoint. *The Retail and Marketing Review*, 16(3), 85–100.

Pajo, B. (2018). *Introduction to research methods: A hands-on approach*. London: SAGE Publications.

Park, S., & Fowler, L. (2021). Political and administrative decentralization and responses to COVID-19: Comparison of the United States and South Korea. *International Journal of Organization Theory & Behavior*, 24(4), 289–299. 10.1108/IJOTB-02-2021-0022

Parker, L. (2020). Australian universities in a pandemic world: Transforming a broken business model? *Journal of Accounting & Organizational Change*, 16(4), 541–548.

Patten, M. L., & Newhart, M. (2018). *Understanding research: An overview of the essentials* (10th ed.). New York: Routledge.

Peterson, R. M., Malshe, A., Friend, S., & Dover, H. (2020). Sales enablement: Conceptualizing and developing a dynamic. *Journal of the Academy of Marketing Science*, 49, 542–565.

Puck, J., & Filatotchev, I. (2020). Finance and the multinational company: Building bridges between finance and global strategy research. *Global Strategy Journal*, 10(4), 655–675.

Ragmoun, W., & Alwehabie, A. (2020). Sustainable human resource management (SHRM) and corporate social responsibility (CSR): An Integrated Mediated Moderation Model of dynamic capabilities (DC) on family business industry. *Management Science Letters*, 10(10), 2259–2268.

Razmdoost, K., Alinaghian, L., & Linder, C. (2020). New venture formation: A capability configurational approach. *Journal of Business Research*, 113, 290–302.

Redda, E. H. (2021). Initial impact assessment of COVID-19 on retailing: Changing consumer behaviour and retail trade sales. *Journal of Contemporary Management*, 18(2), 1–20.

Reuben, S., & Bobat, S. (2014). Constructing racial hierarchies of skill – Experiencing affirmative action in a South African organisation: A qualitative review. *South African Journal of Industrial Psychology*, 40(1), 1–12.

Roper, S., & Turner, J. (2020). R&D and innovation after COVID-19: What can we expect? A review of prior research and data trends after the great financial crisis. *International Small Business Journal: Researching Entrepreneurship*, 38(6), 504–514.

Ruiz-Alba, J. L., Guesalaga, R., Ayestarán, R., & Morales, M. J. (2020). International coordination: The role of digitalization. *Journal of Business & Industrial Marketing*, 35 (3), 404–419. 10.1108/JBIM-03-2019-0129

Rule, P., & John, V. (2017). *Your guide to case study research*. Pretoria: Van Schaik.

Samsudin, Z. B., & Ismail, M. D. (2019). The concept of theory of dynamic capabilities in changing environment. *International Journal of Academic Research in Business and Social Sciences*, 9(6), 1071–1078.

Saunders, M., & Lewis, P. (2018). *Doing research in business and management: An essential guide to planning your project*. London: Pearson.

Schiavone, F., Rivieccio, G., Paolone, F., & Rocca, A. (2021). The macro-level determinants of user entrepreneurship in healthcare: An explorative cross-country analysis. *Management Decision*, 59(5), 1158–1178. 10.1108/MD-10-2019-1427

Scull, J., Phillips, M., Sharma, U., & Garnier, K. (2020). Innovations in teacher education at the time of COVID 19: An Australian perspective. *Journal of Education for Teaching*, 46(4), 497–506.

Semke, L. M., & Tiberius, V. (2020). Corporate foresight and dynamic capabilities: An exploratory study. *Forecasting*, 2(2), 180–193.

Shava, H., & Chinyamurindi, W. T. (2022). Barriers of growth within an informal sector business: Narratives of women subsistence entrepreneurs in South Africa. *African Journal of Economic Management Studies*. 10.1108/AJEMS-08-2021-0354

Silverman, D. (2021). *Qualitative research*. London: SAGE Publications.

Spicer, Z., Goodman, N., & Olmstead, N. (2021). The frontier of digital opportunity: Smart city implementation in small, rural and remote communities in Canada. *Urban Studies* 58(3), 535–558. 10.1177%2F0042098019863666

Teece, D. J., Pisano, G., & Shuen, A. (1997). Dynamic capabilities and strategic management. *Strategic Management Journal*, 18(7), 509–533.

Teece, J., & Pisano, G. P. (1994). The dynamic capabilities of firms: An introduction. *Industrial and Corporate Change*, 3(3), 537–556.

Telukdarie, A., Buhulaiga, E., Bag, S., Gupta, S., & Luo, Z. (2018). Industry 4.0 implementation for multinationals. *Process Safety and Environmental Protection*, 118, 316–329.

Trautrims, A., Schleper, M. C., Cakir, M. S., & Gold, S. (2020). Survival at the expense of the weakest? Managing modern slavery risks in supply chains during COVID-19. *Journal of Risk Research*, 23(7/8), 1067–1072.

Vaismoradi, M., Turunen, H., & Bondas, T. (2013). Content analysis and thematic analysis: Implications for conducting a qualitative descriptive study. *Nursing and Health Sciences*, 15(3), 398–405.

Walker, P. G. T., Whittaker, C., & Watson, O. (2020). *The global impact of COVID-19 and strategies for mitigation and suppression*. Imperial College London: United Kingdom-London.

Wang, D., Zhou, T., & Wang, M. (2021). Information and communication technology (ICT), digital divide and urbanisation: Evidence from Chinese cities. *Technology in Society*, 64, 1–11. 10.1016/j.techsoc.2020.101516

Wieland, A. (2021). Dancing the supply chain: Toward transformative supply chain management. *Journal of Supply Chain Management*, 57(1), 58–73.

Yue, W., & Cowling, M. (2021). The Covid-19 lockdown in the United Kingdom and subjective well-being: Have the self-employed suffered more due to hours and income reductions? *International Small Business Journal: Researching Entrepreneurship*, 39(2), 93–108.

2 The Concept and Evolution of Social Entrepreneurship: An International and South African Perspective

Olabanji Oni and Gebregziabher Gebreyesus Fiseha

Introduction

The social entrepreneurship (SE) has stirred as an area of concern for some decades. In the early 1970s, the SE was coined in the North America and the European regions (Ebrashi, 2013; International Labour Organisation, 2017). SE gained popularity and widely spread across the globe during the 1980s, with the creation US Ashoka Foundation, this was the debut organisation to provide backing for SE across the globe (Ebrashi, 2013). Different nomenclature has been giving to SE since its creation, some referred to SE as social economy, the third sector, the citizen sector, the independence sector and non-profit organisations. The NGOs, government agencies and private companies participate in SE activities in efforts to minimise social problems. The SE is a part of the economy which provides social services and products in any community and directly benefits the society (Mair et al., 2006). The benefits aligned with SE can be social, environmental or both (social and environmental). The SE can operate in different geographical areas, such as neighborhoods, communities, regions and international.

The advent of the free-market policy and neo-liberalism in the United States and other Western European countries led to the growth and development of SE (Sepulveda, 2015; Zahra et al., 2009). The rise in capitalism witnessed people become more linked to religious, political ideologies and creation of associations, i.e. charities, voluntary and cooperatives for the sole purpose of solving socio-economic issues and for service delivery in the society (Sepulveda, 2015). The SE was at first linked social cooperatives and the Italian socialist towards the late 1980s in response to social problems like unemployment and poverty (Sepulveda, 2015).

Individuals, groups and organisations engage in SE activities in order to find innovative solutions to socio-economic problems (Ndhlovu & Ndinda, 2017). Entrepreneurial activities are employed to bring desirable social change in different areas of the economy, like communication, banking and microfinancing, health, energy, education and communication which are not within the coverage of the commercial businesses or government. In essence,

DOI: 10.4324/9781003216469-2

social entrepreneurs are creative and exploit new frontiers, and eventually make a difference to impact the world.

Social entrepreneurs operate their social enterprises under various legal structures such as cooperatives, foundations, non-governmental organisations (NGOs), community organisations and charities (Ferreira, 2019). This is due to the lack of specific legal frameworks to guide the operation of social entrepreneurs.

Like many countries across the world, the concept of SE in Africa in general is broad and not widely known among the public (Littlewood & Holt, 2018). Its definition and role in addressing socio-economic problems in Africa remain unknown. There is limited empirical studies on SE in Africa and in the world. However, scholars (Franchi et al., 2014; Littlewood & Holt, 2018; Poon, 2011; Smith & Darko, 2014) believe that the concept of SE in Africa was introduced after the introduction of Structural Adjustment programme in the early 1990s as a response to socio-economic problems (poverty, unemployment and inequality). There is no specific policy framework for SE in South Africa like other countries in the world (Franchi et al., 2014; Littlewood & Holt, 2018; Steinman, 2010; Urban, 2008; Visser, 2011). In light of this, this chapter, therefore, aims to contribute to the SE theory in the African context. This chapter further seeks to contribute to the conceptualisation of SE and its historical development in North America, Europe, Asia and Africa. With the focus on enhancing SE theory in the African context, this chapter also aims to provide useful recommendations towards driving effective SE practices in the African context where entrepreneurship has been seemingly survivalist and relatively unproductive.

Social entrepreneurship definition

The emergence and evaluation of SE has remained a contested debate among scholars (Ferreira, 2019; Hossain, 2019; Littlewood & Holt, 2018). Studies reveal that SE was initially defined in a seminal work by Joseph Banks in 1972 titled, *The Sociology of Social Movements* (Hossain, 2019). Furthermore, the term SE was used by Joseph Banks to demonstrate management skills known as a solution to diverse social problems.

Other European scholars such as Borzaga and Defourny claimed in *The Emergence of Social Enterprises* that the notion of SE began in France with the social economy in the form of mutual assistance in cooperative associations (Hossain, 2019). Other scholars (Defourny & Nyssens, 2010; Ebrashi, 2013) have argued that the origin of SE can be traced to the 1980s, after the founding of the Bill Drayton's Ashoka Foundation, a grant organisation that is in supported social entrepreneurs to solve social problems in the United States.

Compromise on the classification and definition of SE has not yet been reached up till date (Abu-Saifan, 2012; European Union (EU), 2013; Hanley & Garland, 2016; Holmes & Sandhar, 2017; Roper & Cheney,

2005; Sepulveda, 2015; Soni et al., 2014). In Europe, SE connotes to the engagement of many non-governmental enterprise, including non-profit organisations, cooperatives and in-public service activities to tackle the socio-economic problems (Defourny & Nyssens, 2010; Kadol, 2021). By contrast, in the United States, SE describes the undertaking of commercial ventures and engagement with business co-operations across a broad spectrum of public service-related activities (Defourny & Nyssens, 2010).

SE incorporates managing a profit-oriented business and performing social services to the communities and the people therein. In some cases, social entrepreneurs operate their social enterprises as NGOs to provide social value for the communities by addressing social issues, such as education, health care, energy, housing and sanitation. In other cases, social entrepreneurs operate their social enterprises as market-based businesses, like cooperatives, where products and services for are manufactured and sold for the communities in addition to empower the vulnerable and marginalised groups economically, such as women and mostly elderly people, through income growth, employment and skills opportunities (Holmes & Sandhar, 2017).

SE is viewed in different perspectives. One perspective perceives SE as involving persons that established a not-for-profit organisation; while other perspectives view SE as involving business owners that includes social responsibility into their operation and act of philanthropy (Blount & Nunley, 2014; Noruzi et al., 2010; Rahim & Mohtar, 2015; Rykaszewski et al., 2013; Short et al., 2009). The varied perspectives make it difficult to present an exact definition of SE. Moreover, lack of uniformity in the definitions of SE suggest that there is a need for more empirical research on the concept and evolution of SE in Africa.

The historical development of social entrepreneurship in North America

SE in North American countries (the United States and Canada) is perceived as not-for-income organisation, and is greater orientated in the direction of the marketplace and growing incomes profits techniques as a reaction to lowering public subsidies and bounds of personal presents from foundations (Doeringer, 2010; Poon, 2011). Religious and community groups have practiced the social entrepreneurial activity in the United States, for instance, holding sales of homemade items to augment the voluntary donations received (Poon, 2011). Since the 1970s, SE has gained prominence in the United States. The up soar of oil prices in 1973 led to an economic downturn in the United States, which consequently led to a decline in government funding for NPOs (Poon, 2011). Such a decline led to the increase in race for funds due to the expansion of non-profit sectors and the rise in social needs (Doeringer, 2010; Poon, 2011). The reduction of funding from donors led social entrepreneurs to search for alternative incomes for their social enterprises in order to continue providing the services to the poor people. Social entrepreneurs found trading engagement as a means of substituting for government funding, and this made it easier for the social enterprise sector to play a crucial role in addressing social problems.

In the United States, the SE initiative was formed by Harvard Business School in 1993 (Defourny & Nyssens, 2010). The initiative involved many stakeholders, such as practitioners, academics and policymakers who came together to generate knowledge about the function of SE in solving socio-economic problems. The initiative created over 500 social enterprises and also contributed to social enterprise research worldwide (Defourny & Nyssens, 2010). Further, the initiative also contributed to the academic formulation and consultancy in the area of social enterprises.

Since 1993, the debate concerning SE has expanded in various institutions (Defourny & Nyssens, 2010). Many universities have developed research and training programmes for the promotion of SE. Foundations, such as Schwab, Ashoka and Skoll emerged and played a crucial role in promoting SE growth in the region (Defourny & Nyssens, 2010). Further, the SE became more prominent in the United States in the late 1970s and early 1980s reacting to the economic collapse and the reduction of government spending (Doeringer, 2010). These developments resulted in the loss of funding for many NGOs, while social needs increased due to the rise in unemployment. At this time, NGOs saw it befitting to increase revenue from other sources other than grants and donations, and this witnessed an increase in the reliance on commercial activities as a source for revenues for most NPOs (Doeringer, 2010; Poon, 2011). Over time, this type of business greatly expanded throughout the United States. As a result, there was a 20% increase in the income of the donations received from commercial between 1982 and 2002 (Doeringer, 2010).

The evolution of social entrepreneurship in Europe

SE is linked to community enterprises, churches, charities, voluntary organisations and NPOs. Collectively, these fall under the social economy or third sector, seeking to address socio-economic problems, rather than making profit or wealth accumulation (Shaw & Carter, 2007). In most countries in Europe, organisations in the third sector, such as NPOs, cooperatives and mutual societies, held an important position in the provision of social services since the beginning of 20th century (Defourny & Nyssens, 2010). However, their importance in the delivery of social services improved in the late 1950s. Most of these organisations were promoted by a Christian charitable tradition (Defourny & Nyssens, 2010). However, in the later 1960s and early 1970s, the quest for more democracy and equality led the blooming of civil society's movements in addressing the major social issues through advocacy and provision of social services (Defourny & Nyssens, 2010). The economic meltdown was the leading factor for the cause of the contemporary SE growth in Europe, particularly, the Western European countries (Doeringer, 2010; Poon, 2011; Defourny & Nyssens, 2010). The economic meltdown led to high poverty, unemployment, inequality and poor social services. Against this backdrop, civil societies developed various programmes and initiatives. For instance, community-owned organisations were initiated by NGOs throughout European region as intervention mechanisms for socio-economic problems (Hoogendoorn et al., 2010).

The SE sector received strong recognition from European governments (Doeringer, 2010; Defourny & Nyssens, 2010; Hoogendoorn et al., 2010; Poon, 2011). The governments viewed SE as a key intervention strategy for socio-economic problems and, in turn, the governments created a conducive environment for SE growth. For instance, in case of the United Kingdom, the government launched an initiative for SE development and created a unit of social enterprise in the Department of Trade and Industry (Poon, 2011).

The SE emerged in Europe a few years after it was introduced in the United States. The most common form of social enterprise in Europe was cooperatives. The notion of SE first emerged in Italy in the late 1980s and thereafter it spread widely to many other European countries in the mid-1990s (Defourny & Nyssens, 2010). It was promoted by a journal launched in the 1990s, entitled *impresa sociale* (Defourny & Nyssens, 2010). Italy was the first pioneering European country to adopt the legal form for SE. Cooperatives were a common form of social enterprise in Italy. The rise of the social cooperatives played an important role in the expansion and development of the social economy in Italy (Prakash & Tan, 2014). In 1991, the government of Italy enacted a law on social cooperatives to recognise and control cooperatives working in the social services sector.

The development of social cooperatives did not prohibit the spread of other types of SE activities in Italy (Defourny & Nyssens, 2010). Subsequently, a broader law on SE was approved in 2005. This broader law allowed for the adoption of various types of organisations for social enterprise. There were approximately 11 808 social cooperatives in Italy in 2011, which accounted for about 380 000 employees. Meanwhile, following the adoption of a policy on SE in Italy, many other European countries also passed new laws and policies for SE development (Defourny & Nyssens, 2010). For example, France, Portugal, Spain, Poland, Sweden, Greece, Dutch and Belgium adopted cooperatives as a legal framework of social enterprises. These cooperatives provided social services (education, health, clean water and sanitation and housing) as well as employment opportunities for the local communities, particularly, the socially disadvantaged families and communities, such as children, women and people with disabilities.

The global economic meltdown in the 1970s exacerbated high unemployment rates in Belgium (Doeringer, 2010). In response to this, many charity organisations were established in the late 1980s and early 1990s.

They were operated in the form of non-profit entities recognised as Associations sans but Lucratifs (ASBLs). ASBLs are identical to American non-profit co-operations that conduct limited commercial activities and receive subsidies from the government (Doeringer, 2010).

Belgium was among the first European countries to adopt a policy on SE. The Belgian government introduced a legal framework for SE in 1995, which was known as cooperative or Societe a Finalite Sociale (SFS). Indeed, European governments included SE in their development policy since the early 1990s (Doeringer, 2010; Poon, 2011; Sepulveda, 2015). Them rise of the SE policy in the United Kingdom was ultimately linked to the New Labour government. In the United Kingdom, a New Labour administration created the SE initiatives in the 1990s. The New Labour government was dedicated to promoting social entrepreneurial activities and acknowledging SE as an indispensable tool to alleviate socio-economic problems, such as poverty, inequality and social exclusion and unemployment (Li & Wong, 2007; Mawson, 2010).

In 2001, the Social Enterprise Unit (SEU) was created by the New Labour government in the Department of Trade and Industry (DTI) to promote SE (Defourny & Nyssens, 2010; Sepulveda, 2015). The SEU formed a website devoted to open regional social enterprise and centers for development. Furthermore, the SEU nominated 35 social entrepreneurs' representatives to aid the spread of information in rural communities. The UK government also provided an investment fund of £10 million in social enterprises.

Additionally, a new legal framework for SE, called "Community Interest Company" was approved in 2004 by the British parliament. In less than two years, more than 1000 social entrepreneurs registered under CIC were created. This success was credited to the creation-enabling environment provided by the government. The British government created an environment, which was conducive for the development of SE in the country. The government started a couple of programmes, like the design of legal framework, implementation of public procurement, financial support award, management support and training (Tanimoto, 2008). Since Blair's government came to power, various types of social enterprises emerged in the United Kingdom (Tanimoto, 2008). This include co-operatives, worker's collectives, voluntary trading organisations, community businesses, social firms and credit unions. These social enterprises offered employment opportunities and social services to the communities, particularly vulnerable and disadvantaged groups of people.

Social entrepreneurship in Asia

In Asia, SE was introduced in the late 1990s as a response to the socio-economic challenges in the region (Defourny & Kim, 2011). Since the mid-2000s, some Eastern Asian countries such as Singapore, Japan, Hong

Kong, Taiwan and South Korea developed strong interests in SE development (Liang, 2015). In most Asian countries, SE activities were initiated largely by civil societies. In South Korea, SE was initiated and actively promoted by the government (Liang, 2015). The top-down development model distinguished the Korean social enterprise from the European and the US SE development model. South Korea was the first Asian country to start a legal framework for SE (Prakash & Tan, 2014). The government passed the Social Enterprise Promotion Act (SEPA) in 2007. Its aim was to enhance social integration and improve quality of life through the expansion of social services and creating new jobs.

In Japan and South Korea, SE emerged in the quest to fight poverty and unemployment. Cooperatives, NPOs and community-owned enterprises were the common forms of social enterprises (Defourny & Kim, 2011). The establishment of the worker's cooperative movement as a business unit in Japan around the 1980s was the pioneer initiative in creating job opportunities for disabled people and women.

Also, in South Korea the One Top Services Centre for the Unemployed (OSCUs) was launched in 1998 to organise business units for public work at the national level, with the motive to create jobs opportunities and provide social services.

The concept in South Korea gained popularity after the Seoul social enterprise international forum in 2000 (Defourny & Kim, 2011). Subsequently, the government introduced an initiative for SE development. The Social Enterprise Development Agency was founded in 2001. The agency played a key part in spreading and promoting the concept of SE throughout the country. The unexpected South Korea huge unemployment increased as the Asian financial crisis began in the early 2000s. Since then, the government recognised the importance of self-support organisations in providing job opportunities as well as ensuring welfare benefits for the jobless people, and started promoting and supporting SE.

In the 1990s, the Welfare and Health Ministry established the "Self-Support Programme" which was designed as a social enterprise model focusing on how to cope with the socio-economic problems, like unemployment and poverty in the country (Liang, 2015). This programme was the first initiative which was provided by the government for SE growth. Later in 2003, the Social Work Place Programme was introduced to support self-sufficiency organisations for job creation. However, these programmes/initiatives failed to create sustainable jobs to the unemployed people due to the heavy dependency on government subsidies. This failure led the government to come up with new solutions to trigger SE in the country. As such, the government introduced a certified social enterprise in South Korea (Liang, 2015).

In 2007, the South Korean government enacted a law on SE. The act created conditions to flourish and grow social entrepreneurs in the country. Moreover, the act forbid other organisations from using the term of social enterprise. The Korean government set up a total budget of 1.3 trillion won in 2007 for SE. A social enterprise support committee was established for the deliberation to back social enterprises, with focus on issues concerning the standards for the accreditation of a social enterprise in the country (Park, 2009). Following the legislation, KSEPA was established in 2010 with the aim to provide financial and administrative support to social entrepreneurs in the country. Since then, the government has provided a series of support initiatives to social entrepreneurs in the country. This led to a swift development of social entrepreneurial activities in South Korea. In 2014, there were over 1100 certified social entrepreneurs in South Korea (Liang, 2015).

The welfare expenditure increased significantly in Honk Kong in the late 1990s and early 2000s due to economic collapse and financial crisis (Defourny & Kim, 2011). The government started employment aid programmes based on Western approaches of social investment and welfare. The government also recognised and advocated for the use of SE as a means to ease poverty, unemployment and inequality. The government and publicity for social enterprises initiated various funding schemes. In Hong Kong, social enterprises primarily emerged to provide employment and social services to disadvantaged and vulnerable groups of people.

Social entrepreneurship in Africa

SE can be the most effective tool in addressing the challenges of development in Africa. This is due to the fact of that SE creates innovations, employment opportunities and provides basic needs to the vulnerable and disadvantaged people (women, elderly and physically challenged).

SE is growing significantly in Africa like other countries in the world. The emergence of SE in Africa is attributed to the reduction of state expenditure in basic needs (Poon, 2011; Smith & Darko, 2014). The concept of SE in Africa emerged after the introduction of the Structural Adjustment Policy (SAP) by the World Bank and International Monetary Fund (Poon, 2011). The SAPs adopted policies of state expenditure reduction, deregulation and privatisation. The reduction of state expenditure led to the growth of public services provision by non-state actors, such as NGOs and commercial businesses. Due to the competition for donor grants funding, many NGOs adopted a business model to raise funds through the sale of goods and services (Smith & Darko, 2014).

At the same time, the introduction of privatisation and deregulation by the SAPs led to the diminishing role of the state in the economy. As a result, the socio-economic problems in Africa deteriorated. Thus, the inability of the state to address these socio-economic problems contributed to the expansion of SE growth (Poon, 2011). However, there is paucity of research on SE in Africa. Furthermore, studies on SE and its impact in addressing the development challenges in Africa are limited (Smith & Darko, 2014; Franchi et al., 2014; Littlewood & Holt, 2018; Poon, 2011). In many parts of the world, African countries did not have a specific policy and strategy that dealt with the growth and development of social enterprises for poverty reduction. Therefore, social enterprises operated as NGOs, private companies and cooperatives. The reduction of state expenditure and the introduction of SAPs in Africa led to the increase of socio-economic problems in Africa, such as poverty, unemployment, inequality and lack of social services. These socio-economic problems were the key drivers behind the emergence of social enterprises in Africa (Littlewood & Holt, 2018; Poon, 2011; Urban, 2008).

Social entrepreneurship in South Africa

SE plays a significant role in addressing the daunting socio-economic problems in South Africa such as poverty, unemployment and inequality (Dzomonda, 2020). The failure of government policies in addressing the development challenges (poverty and unemployment) in South Africa led to the emergence of SE. In South Africa, the concept of SE emerged when the US Ashoka Foundation first opened their offices in the country in 1991 (Littlewood & Holt, 2018). The World Economic Forum's Conference on SE for Africa, held in Cape Town in 2006, is credited for the rapid expansion of SE in South Africa (Urban, 2008).

Venture philanthropists, grant sponsors, policymakers, development practitioners, non-profit entrepreneurs, consultants and academicians have increased interests in the development of SE in South Africa. However, there has not been much research into SE in South Africa. Therefore, the nature and roles of these enterprises in poverty reduction is not well understood (Urban, 2008; Littlewood & Holt, 2018; Visser, 2011). As a result, social entrepreneurs struggle in accessing resources to enhance their contribution to poverty reduction in the country. South Africa like many other countries in the world does not have a specific policy framework for SE (Franchi et al., 2014; Littlewood & Holt, 2018; Urban, 2008; Steinman, 2010; Visser, 2011). Due to the policy gap, social enterprises come in various forms of organisations, such as cooperatives, NGOs, trusts, foundations and private businesses.

It is believed that SE practice has a long history in South Africa even though the term gained recognition lately in the country. The emergence of SE practices can be traced back to the colonial times, with the introduction of cooperatives. According to the Department of Economic Development and Environmental Affairs Council (DEDEA, 2009), the history of cooperative development in South Africa can be traced back to the apartheid era. The Pietermaritzburg Consumer was the first formal cooperative, established in 1892 under the Companies Act. During the apartheid period, white farming cooperatives were an important source of agricultural commercialisation, food and rural development. In the 1980s, there were 250 agricultural cooperatives, 142 000 people memberships, total assets of 12.7 billion rands, a total turnover of 22.5 billion rands and pre-tax profits of more than 500 million rands (DEDEA, 2009).

The two legislations, which are the Companies Act of 2008 and NPOs Act of 1997, was a key influence on the emergence of social enterprises in South Africa. The Companies Act of 2008, which is a major review of the company law of South Africa and partly in response to the emergence of new forms of the enterprise; and the Non-Profit Organisations Act of 1997, governs NGOs and Civil Societies Organisations (CSOs). The most appropriate policy framework for social enterprise operations in South Africa is the Non-Profit Company (NPC) Act of 1997 (Steinman, 2010). The South African law defines an NPC as a company formed for the benefits of the public or other objectives relating cultural/social activities or communal/interest groups. The members or owners are not given incomes and properties in such an entity, but used for the purpose for which it was created (Moreno & Agapitova, 2017).

The NPCs in South Africa are strictly viewed as non-profit entities because they register with the Department of Social Development (DSD) rather than the DTI, which is used by the profit entities. The non-profit sector in South Africa has shown remarkable growth over the last few years. According to DSD (2012), the number of registered NPOs in South Africa increased to 85 248 in 2012 from 76 757 in 2011. Most of the NPOs were registered under voluntary associations.

The non-profit sector plays a crucial role in the South African economy. In 2007, the non-profit sector had total assets of 12.5 billion rand. There is no need for minimum initial capital for individuals or organisations to start social ventures. Social enterprises obtain tax incentives as any other commercial businesses. Some NGOs may qualify as Public Benefit Organisations (PBOs), which gives them full tax exemption status as long as they derive their income purely from public funding and grants (Moreno & Agapitova, 2017). Social enterprises registered as non-profits are subjected to the same rights and responsibilities as any NPOs registered in South Africa. However, the laws and public practices do not prohibit NGOs from adopting hybrid income models.

In South Africa, social entrepreneurs can register their social enterprises under voluntary associations, cooperatives, close corporations, trusts and public or private companies.

In the last few years, a number of private and public organisations were established to create an enabling environment for entrepreneurship growth in South Africa (Steinman, 2010). The National Youth Development Agency (NYDA), Small Enterprise Development Agency (SEDA), Industrial Development Cooperation (IDC), National Development Agency (NDA) and Black Economic Empowerment (BEE) were among the institutions that were established to support entrepreneurs throughout the country (Steinman, 2010). NYDA as a public organisation offers small grants and business advice to entrepreneurs. It emerges from the merger of the National Youth Commission and the Umsobomvu Youth Fund (UYF).

SEDA is also a public organisation, which was established to provide financial and non-financial assistance for social and commercial entrepreneurs. The objectives of SEDA are as follows:

- Strengthen financial support for small businesses including social enterprise
- Expand marketing opportunities for both commercial and social businesses
- Provide business consultation and advice for entrepreneurs
- Expand education and training for small businesses
- Offer business infrastructure

In addition, UnLtd South Africa is an NPO which provides financial and non-financial support to social entrepreneurs (Moreno & Agapitova, 2017). South African commercial banks offer credit to business people including social entrepreneurs. The banks provide credit only to registered enterprises with financial statements that show good prospects of return on investment for the bank. However, credit conditions for small businesses are too tight because of the growing concerns in South Africa about rising debt and default rates (Steinman, 2010).

The IDC and the Development Bank of Southern Africa (DBSA) are the largest South African development finance institutions, which provide fund assistance for medium or large scale-businesses across Southern Africa (Steinman, 2010). Small businesses including social enterprises receive support and funding through the Small Enterprise Finance Agency (SEFA), which falls under the Department of Trade and Industry (DTI). Meanwhile, the African Social Enterprise Network (ASEN) established in 2008 includes more than 3800 social entrepreneurs across Africa, mostly found in South Africa. Some universities in South Africa have also established research centres for SE within their institutions. For instance, the Gordon Institute of Business Science's Network for Social entrepreneurs (NSE) at Pretoria University and the Bertha Centre for Social Innovation at Cape Town University were established (Steinman, 2010).

The Job Creation Trust was founded by the merger of the Congress of South African Trade Unions (COSATU), the National Council of Trade Unions (NCTU) and the Federation of Unions of South Africa (FEDUSA) in 2000. The South African workers contributed one day's wages (89 million rand) for the establishment of the fund in 2000. The fund contributed to the establishment of cooperatives and community-driven projects in the country. The trust created more than 38 000 job opportunities for marginalised and vulnerable groups of people and awarded approximately 25 000 people with various business skills (Steinman, 2010). The NDA is also another public entity, which mandates poverty reduction through providing funds for community projects (Steinman, 2010). Furthermore, the NDA offers various business support programmes, such as market, business skills and business infrastructure for the youth, entrepreneurs and SMEs. Despite these interventions, South Africa still has the lowest rate of entrepreneurship activities in the world. The Global Entrepreneurship Monitor (GEM) reported that, less than 2% of adults in South Africa are engaged in SE activities (Bosma et al., 2017).

COVID-19 and social entrepreneurship

COVID-19 is novel to scholars around the world (Kuckertz et al., 2020). The advent of COVID-19 created societal issues which worsened social problems (Mair, 2020; Weaver, 2020). Many scholarly articles in the past have examined the effect of the COVID-19 pandemic on SMEs (Anakpo & Mishi, 2021; Fubah & Moos, 2022; Oni & Omonona, 2020). There are limited studies that examined the effect of COVID-19 pandemic on SE activities (Jalaga, 2021; Mair 2020; Weaver, 2020). A need, therefore, exists not just to examine the effect of the COVID-19 pandemic on SMEs but to also understand the challenges and the opportunities SE experience during the COVID-19 era (Bacq et al., 2020; Mair, 2020).

Battilana et al. (2012) in Jalaga (2021) opined that the SE activities have been plagued with limited funding and start-up capital during the pandemic era. The author further added that the COVID-19 pandemic made it difficult for investors and social entrepreneurs to secure loans or funding for their businesses. Teasdale et al. (2012) in Jalaga (2021) also supported the assertion that some businesses find it difficult to obtain loans for operation and expansion. The author amplified that most lenders are scared of non-payment due to the uncertainty posed by the COVID-19 pandemic. The challenges faced by SE are psychological in nature, for example, anxiety, fear of failure, work stress and a strong dislike for risk (Jalaga, 2021).

Despite these challenges, there are opportunities that exist for SE during the COVID-19 era. In fact, the COVID-19 pandemic created opportunities for most SE businesses such as fellowships, online platforms, social networks, grants, loan providers and crowdfunding (Bacq et al., 2020; Lyons & Kickul, 2013). The idea of SE discourses a number of the limitations that civil society groups in SA experience. The pandemic created new roles for the existence of businesses, which essentially changes the manner social entrepreneurs approach their work (Bizzcommunity, 2022). We therefore advise the national government to put in place a regulatory framework and policies that will encourage skills development, create pertinent technical support and ensure accessibility of financial capital. There is also a need to promote a cultural model that support youth social entrepreneurship in South Africa.

Opportunity creation theory

Alvarez and Barney (2007) proposed the opportunity creation theory. The purpose of the theory was to understand how an entrepreneurial opportunity is formed and exploited (Alvarez & Barney, 2007; Paula, 2016). The theory argues that opportunities are not just waiting to be discovered, rather, they are created by entrepreneurs' actions or activities. The entrepreneurs build mountains and are an essential source of opportunities (Alvarez & Barney, 2007). This implies that opportunities depend on entrepreneurial actions or activities.

The opportunity creation theory avows that opportunities are not mere theoretics formed by external effects to an industry or market (Alvarez & Barney, 2007; Shinde & Shinde, 2011). The opportunities do not emerge out of previous industries or markets, rather entrepreneurs create them. In this theory, the seeds of opportunities to produce new products or services do not necessarily lie in previous existing industries or markets; instead, they are created from entrepreneurs' own actions (Alvarez & Barney, 2007; Paula, 2016). The theory assumes that opportunities are not recognised by entrepreneurs before they act, rather they act and then create them (Alvarez & Barney, 2007; Hang et al., 2013; Paula, 2016). When social entrepreneurs act, they bring changes in the societies. This theory argues that the process of enactment and entrepreneurs' actions and reactions will not only create new opportunities, but also bring about changes in the individuals and communities (Alvarez & Young, 2017).

Social entrepreneurs act to create opportunities and solve social or environmental problems (Gonzalez et al., 2017). Therefore, social entrepreneurs' activities create opportunities for the poor people. Opportunities can be the creation of employment, innovation, provision of social services and entrepreneurship skills and training. Additionally, opportunities can also be the reduction of ignorance or hunger and diseases (Murphy & Coombes, 2007).

The finding of solutions to social problems, such as education, health care, electricity, water and sanitation, unemployment, poverty and hunger can be considered as opportunity creation. Opportunity is a key characteristic of SE. In SE, opportunity means the creation of solutions for social or environmental problems (Kamran et al., 2022).

Therefore, one of the efforts of SE is to reduce the number of people living in extreme poverty through the enhancement of nutrition, health, education, employment opportunities, innovation and entrepreneurship training and skills. Furthermore, opportunities can be economic, profit, marketing, innovative and entrepreneurial opportunities. These opportunities are created because of the entrepreneur's actions or activities, which consequently create value and change the economy and the society.

The entrepreneur in the opportunity creation theory is not searching for an existing business opportunities; rather, he or she begins to create opportunities through his or her own actions or activities (Alvarez & Barney, 2007; Paula, 2016; Gonzalez et al., 2017). This theory suggests that the evolutionary enactment process might not stop until the entrepreneurs create opportunities. Thus, social entrepreneurs create opportunities that have not existed before. This means that actions will evolve until entrepreneurs create opportunities.

This paradigm assumes that opportunities do not exist without actions of the entrepreneur (Alvarez & Barney, 2007; Alvarez & Young, 2017; Gonzalez et al., 2017). Endogenous actions, enactment and reactions of entrepreneurs are resultant effect of opportunities. Social entrepreneurs can decide on what opportunities to create and use the available resources to create the opportunities for the benefit of the communities. Social entrepreneurs combine resources that produce new products or services and bring them to the market. This act of creating a new combination (new product and service) can be seen as the creation of opportunities (Alvarez & Young, 2017).

There are two assumptions in the opportunity creation theory. The first assumption is that opportunities are not created without the actions of an entrepreneur. The second view on opportunity creation assumes that opportunities are out there and need only to be discovered by an alert entrepreneur in order to exploit them (Alvarez & Barney, 2007; Oyson & Whittaker, 2012). Entrepreneurs are able to detect an opportunity which others would not. Therefore, social entrepreneurs can create or discover opportunities.

According to opportunity creation theory, opportunities are social and economic value creation as the consequence of entrepreneurial activities. In other words, opportunities are investment, employment creation, enhancement of entrepreneurship training and skills, creating new organisations or markets and bringing products and services to the market. Whether social entrepreneurs operate in non-profit, for-profit or public sectors, they create opportunities for the communities (Dushin & Dodson, 2018). Social entrepreneurs have vast potential for value creation than value capture because the benefit for society is larger than the financial benefits gained by the social entrepreneurs (Seelos & Mair, 2005). Social ventures create value by producing goods and services and employing disadvantaged populations. Other social entrepreneurs create social value by providing basic needs such as education, health care, water and sanitation as well as affording loans to the poor that do not have access to capital due to lack of collateral. Therefore, this theory is very essential in informing the identification of opportunities that were created by social entrepreneurs.

Conclusion

This chapter provided an evaluation of SE and its historical development in Europe, Asia, Africa and North America. Furthermore, the chapter discussed the definition of SE and its operationalisation in various parts of the world. The chapter also provided a theoretical underpinning to support SE. These objectives were achieved and the authors concluded from the analysis of previous studies that the concept of SE has been in existence for many years. The concept of SE was introduced to the world in the 19th century. The concept initially emerged in Western European countries as a response to the socio-economic problems like unemployment, poverty and inequality. The concept of SE widely spread across the world with the establishment of the Ashoka foundation. SE has been conceptualised in different perspectives. To date, there is no specific definition of SE. The definition of SE varies from country to country, as well as region to region. For instance, SE is viewed as innovation that uses business skills to pursue social goals instead of a traditional entrepreneurial goal of financial profit.

On the other hand, SE is viewed as the founding of establishments like charities, volunteer associations and cooperatives to combat poverty and unemployment.

The chapter also discussed the legal structure of SE. In most countries of the world especially in Africa, there is no specific policy framework that guides the operations of SE. This leaves the social entrepreneurs with the option to register their ventures under cooperatives, NGOs, trust, private businesses and other forms of businesses. Social entrepreneurs can choose any legal structure that is suitable for their business, making it difficult to understand the concept of SE.

Recommendations

Firstly, SE is a broad concept. Since its inception in 1960s, scholars have given a number of definitions to SE. Therefore, in defining SE, it is important to establish the boundaries with its definition. In developed countries, particularly in the United Kingdom, Italy, Australia, Canada and the United States, governments have established an appropriate legal and regulatory framework to guide SE. However, to date in South Africa, there is no specific legal framework for SE and no specific policies and regulations have been put in place to support SE. SE is yet to be recognised as a sector in South African legislation. Therefore, the authors recommend the development of policy frameworks to govern the operations of SE in South Africa. The authors are of the view that there should be policies and strategies for SE development in South Africa.

Secondly, like profit businesses, social entrepreneurs need advice, consultation, training and skills in order to enhance their contribution towards poverty reduction. However, the numbers of institutions that provide support services for social entrepreneurs in South Africa are very few. These support institutions are concentrated in few areas. The authors recommend an increase in the development of support institutions that provide advice and training as well as funding for social entrepreneurs in South Africa to scale up the contribution towards providing solutions to communities through poverty reduction and job creation.

Thirdly, currently, South Africa does not have a specific legal structure for SE. Social entrepreneurs in South Africa can register their social enterprises in various sectors such as trusts, NPOs, private companies, cooperatives, foundations and voluntary associations. However, social entrepreneurs have a difficult task to choose the appropriate sector for their social enterprises because each sector attracts different legal implications in relation to costs, tax liability and access to finance, market and the distribution and use of profits (Steinman, 2010). The registration process is also time consuming and tiring. Social entrepreneurs need to register their social enterprises with different governmental organisations. The authors therefore, recommend that there should be a specific legal model for SE businesses so that social entrepreneurs can easily register their social enterprises.

Lastly, despite the role of SE in poverty reduction and sustainable development, many countries in the world, particularly developing countries including South Africa do not include SE in the education systems like other fields, such as accounting, marketing, engineering and agriculture among others. South Africa does not have a social entrepreneurial development curriculum in its education system (Steinman, 2010). Most universities and colleges in South Africa do not have a SE course for their students. For this reason, SE remains unknown in the country. SE education should be taught at high school, college and university levels in order to increase awareness among the youth. Such awareness can increase the number of people involved in social entrepreneurial activities in South Africa.

Avenue for further research

SE is a recent concept, particularly in the African continent. There is no universal agreement on the definition of SE. Individuals, organisations and governments provide various definitions of SE. This causes challenges in understanding the concept of SE and its function. Therefore, the concept of SE needs further research in Africa in order for people to gain a clearer understanding. This is expected to assist the government and the responsible departments in establishing appropriate regulatory frameworks to legitimise operations.

Future studies may also benefit from the comparison of the concept of SE among African countries. This is expected to provide a rich empirical study and a better understanding of the concept of SE from the different African countries. Furthermore, future research can take advantage of studies on the boundaries, characteristics of SE and the differences between the SE in the profit model and non-profit model. Finally, future studies may investigate the role of SE in ensuring environmental sustainability and its implication on poverty reduction in Africa.

References

Abu-Saifan, S. (2012). Social entrepreneurship: Definition and boundaries. *Technology Innovation Management Review*, 2(2) 22–27.

Alvarez, S., & Barney, J. B. (2007). Discovery and creation: Alternative theories of entrepreneurial. *Strategic Entrepreneurship Journal*, 1(1-2) 11–26.

Alvarez, S., & Young, S. L. (2017, September 8). Debates in entrepreneurship: Opportunity formation and implications for the field of entrepreneurship. https://works.bepress.com/susan-young

Anakpo, G., & Mishi, S. (2021). Business response to COVID-19 impact: Effectiveness analysis in South Africa. *The Southern African Journal of Entrepreneurship and Small Business Management*, 23(1), 1–7. ISSN: (Online) 2071-3185.

Bacq, S., Geoghegan, W., Josefy, M., Stevenson, R., & Williams, T. A. (2020). The COVID-19 virtual idea blitz: Marshaling social entrepreneurship to rapidly respond to urgent grand challenges. *Business Horizons*, 63(6), 705–723.

Battilana, J., Lee, M., Walker, J., & Dorsey, C. (2012). In search of the hybrid ideal. *Stanford Social Innovation Review*, 10(3). Retrieved March 3, 2021, from: https://ssir.org/articles/entry/in_search_of_the_hybrid_ideal#

Bizzcommunity. (2022). Why social entrepreneurship in South Africa? *Marketing & Media Company News South Africa*. https://www.bizcommunity.com/Article/196/713/189610.html#

Blount, J., & Nunley, P. (2014). What is a social business and why does the answer matter. *Brooklyn Journal of Corporate, Financial and Commercial law*, 8(2), 279–316.

Bosma, N., Schott, T., Terjesen, S., & Kew, P. (2017, July 17). Global entrepreneurship monitor. Special topic report social entrepreneurship. http://www.gem-spain.com/wp-content/uploads/2015/03/gem-2015-special-report-onsocial entrepreneurship.pdf.

Defourny, J., & Kim, S. Y. (2011). Emerging models of social enterprise in Eastern Asia: A cross-country analysis. *Social Enterprise Journal*, 7(1) 86–111.

Defourny, J., & Nyssens, M. (2010). Conceptions of social enterprise and social entrepreneurship in Europe and the United States: Convergences and divergences. *Journal of Social Entrepreneurship*, 1(1) 32–53.

Defourny, J., & Nyssens, M. (2017, July 14). *The EMES approach of social enterprise in a comparative perspective*. EMES European Research Network. http://www.emes.net/site/wp-content/uploads/emes-wp_Defourny-Nyssens.pdf

Department of Economic Development and Environmental Affairs. (2009). *Cooperatives in the Eastern Cape: Struggle for survival and sustainability*. Summary report of a baseline study, Pretoria.

Doeringer, M. F. (2010). Fostering social enterprise: A historical and international analysis. *Duke Journal of Comparative and International Law*, 20(291) 291–329.

Dushin, M. D., & Odson, S. (2018, July 9). *Developing a social enterprise business plan*. http://www.hbs.edu/newventurecompetition/documents/setrackdevelopingsSE business plan 2015.

Dzomonda, O. (2020). Social entrepreneurship and sustainable development in South Africa. *Journal of Review on Global Economics*, 9(1), 274–281.

Ebrashi, R. E. (2013). Social entrepreneurship theory and sustainable social impact. *Social Responsibility Journal*, 9(2) 188–209.

European Union. (2013). *Policy brief on social entrepreneurship in Europe*. Luxembourg: European Union.

Ferreira, S. (2019). *Social enterprises and their ecosystems in Europe*. Luxembourg: European Union.

Franchi, S., Bellucci, M., & Testi, E. (2014). *Social enterprise, social innovation and social entrepreneurship in South Africa. A national report*. http://www.fp7-efeseiis.eu>national–report–south Africa. [2019, April 25].

Fubah, C. N., & Moos, M. (2022). Exploring COVID-19 challenges and coping mechanisms for SMEs in the South African entrepreneurial ecosystem. *Sustainability*, 14, 1944. 10.3390/su14041944

Gonzalez, M. F., Husted, B. W., & Aigner, D. J. (2017). Opportunity discovery and creation in social entrepreneurship: An exploratory study in Mexico. *Journal of Business Research*, 9(362), 1–9.

Hang, C. C., Garnsey, E., & Ruan, Y. (2013). *Opportunity discovery and creation in distributive innovation*. UK: University of Cambridge.

Hanley, L., & Garland, A. (2016). *Locating social entrepreneurship in the Global South*. Washington DC: Wilson Center.

Holmes, R., & Sandhar, J. (2017). *Do adolescent girls benefit from social enterprises?* London: SAGE Publications.

Hoogendoorn, B., Pennings, E., & Thurik, R. (2010). What do we know about social entrpreneurship: An analysis of empirical research. *International Review of Entrepreneurship*, 8(2) 2–42.

Hossain, S. (2019). The historical evaluation of social entrepreneurship field. https://hotcubator.com.au/social-entrepreneurship/the-historical-evolution-of-social-entrepreneurship-field/#:~:text=%20The%20Hi [2019, March 28].

International Labour Organisation. (2017). *Promoting social entrepreneurship and social capital. A practice guide to supporting social entrepreneurship and inclusiveness in rural communities*. Geneva: ILO.

Jalaga, R. C. (2021). Social entrepreneurship amid COVID-19 pandemic uncertainties. *St. Theresa Journal of Humanities and Social Sciences*, 7(2), 1–13.

Kadol, N. (2021). The practice of social entrepreneurship: The experience of the republic Belarus. *International Journal of entrepreneurship*, 25(4), 1–9.

Kamran, S. M., Khaskhely, M. K., Nassani, A. A., Haffar, M., & Qazi Abro, M. M. (2022). Social entrepreneurship opportunities via distant socialization and social value creation. *Sustainability MDPI*, 14, 3170. 10.3390/su14063170

Kuckertz, A., Leif BrÉandle, A. G., Sebastian Hinderer, C. A. M. R., Alicia Prochotta, K. M. S., & Berger, E. S. C. (2020). Startups in times of crisis – a rapid response to the COVID-19 pandemic. *Journal of Business Venturing Insights*, 13, e00169. 10.1016/j.jbvi.2020.e00169

Li, S., & Wong, T. (2007). *Social enterprise policies of the United Kingdom, Spain and Hong Kong*. Hong Kong: LCC.

Liang, S. (2015). The development of social enterprises in a developmental state. *International Journal of Social Science and Humanity*, 6, 775–778. 10.18178/ijssh.2016.V6.747

Littlewood, D., & Holt, D. (2018). Social entrepreneurship in South Africa: Exploring the influence of environment. *Business & Society*, 57(3), 525–561.

Lyons, T. S., & J. R. Kickul. (2013). The social enterprise financing landscape: The lay of the land and new research on the horizon. *Entrepreneurship Research Journal*, 3(2), 147–159. 10.1515/erj-2013-0045

Mair, J. (2020). Social entrepreneurship: Research as disciplined exploration. In W. W. Powell & P. Bromley (Eds.), *The nonprofit sector: A research handbook* (3rd ed., pp. 333–357). Palo Alto, CA: Stanford University Press.

Mair, J., Robinson, J., & Hockerts, K. (2006). *Social entrepreneurship*. New York: Palgrave Macmillan.

Mawson, J. (2010). Social enterprise, strategic networks and regional development: The west midlands experience. *International Journal of Sociology and Social Policy*, 30(1/2), 66–83.

Moreno, C. N., & Agapitova, N. (2017). *Emerging of social enterprise ecosystems in East and South African countries. A diagnosis of supporting environment and activity of social enterprises in Kenya, Malawi, Rwanda, South Africa, Tanzania, Uganda and Zambia*. Washington DC: WB.

Murphy, P. J., & Coombes, S. M. T. (2007). *A conceptual and theoretic examination of social entrepreneurial discovery*. Paper presented at the 2007 academy of management meeting, Philadelphia, PA.

Ndhlovu, P. T., & Ndinda, C. (2017). *Social entrepreneurship in sub-Saharan African: A critical analysis of diaspora social investments*. Hershey, PA: IGA Global.

Noruzi, M. R., Westover, J., & Rahimi, G. R. (2010). An exploration of social entrepreneurship in the entrepreneurship era. *Asian Social Science Journal*, 6(6), 3–10.

Oni, O., & Omonona, S. (2020). The effect of COVID-19 on small retail businesses in Alice Town, South Africa. *Journal of Retail Marketing*, 16(3), 49–57.

Oyson, M., & Whittaker, D. H. (2012). *An opportunity based approach to international entrepreneurship: Pursuing opportunities internationally through prospection*. New Zealand: University of Auckland.

Park, C. U. (2009). *The Korean model of social enterprises: A comparison with European experiences*. Paper presented at the social policy association conference: Edinburgh, England.

Paula, L. (2016). *Creation theory explaining inclusive business: Case study of a community –operated business venture development in rural Africa*. Conference paper presented at the Africa Academy management (AFAM), 2016.

Poon, D. (2011). The emergence and development of social enterprise sectors. *Social Impact Research Experience Journal*. University of Pennsylvania scholarly commons. http://repository.upenn.edu/sire/8/ [March 10, 2017].

Prakash, R., & Tan, P. (2014). *Landscape of social enterprises in Singapore Social entrepreneurship in Asia*. Working paper no. 1. Singapore: National University of Singapore.

Rahim, H. L., & Mohtar, S. (2015). Social entrepreneurship: A different perspective. *International Academic Research Journal of Business and Technology*, 1(1), 9–15.

Roper, J., & Cheney, G. (2005). Leadership, learning and human resources management: The meanings of social entrepreneurship today. *The International Journal of Business in Society*, 5(3), 95–104.

Rykaszewski, S., Ma, M., & Shen, Y. (2013). *Failure in social enterprises*. Research paper commissioned by SEE change magazine and conducted by MBA students at Rotman of Management, University of Toronto.

Seelos, C., & Mair, J. (2005). Social entrepreneurship: Creating new business models to serve the poor. *Business horizon*, 48(3), 241–246.

Sepulveda, L. (2015) Social enterprise – a new phenomenon in the field of economic and social welfare. *Social Policy and Administration*, 49(7), 842–861.

Shaw, E., & Carter, S. (2007). Social entrepreneurship: Theoretical antecedents and empirical analysis of entrepreneurial processes and outcomes. *Journal of Small Business and Enterprise Development*, 14(3), 418–434.

Shinde, J. S., & Shinde, U. S. (2011). The perennial perspective on entrepreneurship. *Journal of Strategic Innovation and Sustainability*, 7(1) 72–86.

Short, J. C., Moss, T. W., & Lumpkin, G. T. (2009). Research in social entrepreneurship: Past contributions and future opportunities. *Strategic Entrepreneurship Journal*, 3, 161–194.

Smith, W., & Darko, E. (2014). *Social enterprise: Constraints and opportunities-evidence from Vietnam and Kenya*. London: ODI.

Soni, P., Shaikh, A., & Karodia, M. (2014). Social entrepreneurship and social innovation: Reclaiming sustainable development in South Africa http://regent.ac.za/wp-content/uploads/2015/10/social-entrepreneurship-and-social innovation [March 17, 2018].

Steinman, S. (2010). *An exploratory study into factors influencing an enabling environment for social enterprises in South Africa*. Pretoria: ILO.

Tanimoto, K. (2008). A conceptual framework of social entrepreneurship and social innovation cluster: A preliminary study. *Journal of Commerce and Management*, 42(1)1–16.

Teasdale, S., Sunley, P., & Pinch, S. (2012). Financing social enterprise: Social bricolage or evolutionary entrepreneurialism? *Social Enterprise Journal*, 8(2), 108–122.

Urban, B. (2008). Social entrepreneurship in South Africa: Delineating the construct with associated skills. *International Journal of Entrepreneurial Behavior & Research*, 14(5), 346–364.

Visser, K. (2011). Social entrepreneurship in South Africa: Context, relevance and extent.

Weaver, R. L. (2020). The impact of COVID-19 on the social enterprise sector. *Journal of Social Entrepreneurship*, 1–9. 10.1080/19420676.2020.1861476

Zahra, S. A., Gedajlovic, E., Neubaum, D. O., & Shulman, J. M. (2009). A typology of social entrepreneurs: Motives, search processes and ethical challenges. *Journal of Business Venturing*, 24(5), 519–532.

3 Entrepreneurship Ecosystem: A Focus on King William's Town, South Africa

Solomon Omonona, Olabanji Oni, and Olugbenga Joseph Oluwole

Introduction

Entrepreneurship has continued to gain dominance in scholarly discussions as a vital component for emerging economies. Scholars have described entrepreneurship as the mainstay of some flourishing economies in the world (Choto et al., 2014; Kuratko & Hodgetts, 2001). According to Wennekers and Thurik (2014), entrepreneurship remains the main engine that drives growth and supersedes politics in the economy. What then is entrepreneurship? Entrepreneurship is the act of establishing a business, while at the same time, building and nurturing it to make profit. Naudé (2021, p. 7) defines entrepreneurship as "the resource, process and state of being through and in which individuals utilise positive opportunities in the market by creating and growing new business firms". Entrepreneurship is a normal phenomenon in businesses and a fragment of business life that contributes to successful business organisations (Diandra & Azmy, 2020). Barot (2015, p. 236) adds that the practice of entrepreneurship "begins with action and the creation of new organisations".

There have been vast improvements in the entrepreneurial activities in South Africa in the last eight years. However, there are still gaps in the economy that can benefit from productive entrepreneurial engagement (Naidoo, 2020). This is evident in the Eastern Cape, with reports that the province is too sluggish; revenues have not been growing significantly enough and over the past five years, the province has also witnessed the added burden of frequent protests and xenophobia (Bizcommunity, 2021). This sluggish movement and challenges have contributed to the rise in unemployment among the youth. This undoubtedly contributes to the poor ranking of South Africa as the 49th of 54 countries on GEM's National Entrepreneurship Context Index, ahead of Croatia, Puerto Rico, Paraguay, Guatemala and Iran (Bowmaker-Falconer & Herrington, 2020).

The agenda of the South African government is stirred by the inclusion of economic initiatives and the present National Development Plan directed at raising the quality of life of South Africans. It is estimated that by 2030, an estimate of about 11 million new jobs will be created and there is

DOI: 10.4324/9781003216469-3

commitment from the government to build the capacity of industry and individuals (OC & C Strategy consultants, 2018). There is a necessity to boost the entrepreneurship ecosystem literature and to examine the effects of business support and advice on the challenges affecting businesses, mostly during a pandemic (McAdam et al., 2016; McAdam et al., 2018; Opute et al., 2021; Turkina, 2018).

Therefore, this chapter provides a discussion on South Africa's entrepreneurial ecosystem. The specific objectives of this chapter are to identify the challenges affecting entrepreneurs; test the significant differences in the levels (groups) of entrepreneur businesses based on the challenges affecting the business and examine the effects of business support and advice on the challenges affecting the business especially during the COVID-19 pandemic. The chapter outlines the conceptual and theoretical framework used in guiding the South African entrepreneurial ecosystem. The chapter further provides a discussion on the methodology, results and conclusions as well as the recommendations and avenues for future research.

South Africa's entrepreneurial ecosystem

The entrepreneurial ecosystem as a school of thought was first conceived by Moore (1993, p. 77) in Flores and Kovacs (2018), who defined the entrepreneurial ecosystem as "a space of interconnection and mutual dependence between economic agents whose collective health is essential for the success and survival of organisations". His concept includes features like relationships between participants, structures, diversity of functions and forms of connection (Flores & Kovacs, 2018). The entrepreneurial ecosystem represents the complex network and systematic nature of entrepreneurship. It describes the dynamics that are involved in creating, aiding, enabling and hindering entrepreneurship activities (Isenberg, 2011; Majaja, 2019).

The entrepreneurial ecosystem in South Africa is growing. However, there are certain aspects which restrain it from achieving its full potential. A nation's business ecosystem is concerned with its infrastructure, technological readiness, macro-economic stability, efficiency of labour market, education and market size (NSBC, 2021). Mason and Brown (2014) resolved that entrepreneurial ecosystem consists of entrepreneurs, business angels and businesses, universities, venture capitalists, banks and public sector agencies. It also includes the entrepreneurial processes of the ecosystem and the entrepreneurial ambition. South Africa holds an exceptional position in sub-Saharan Africa, with better supporting establishments than most African countries, consequently giving it a strong entrepreneurial ecosystem foundation.

Challenges affecting business in South Africa

The SMEs in South Africa are a very important aspect of the state. This sector contributes greatly to the development of the economy by increasing the

Gross Domestic Product (GDP) in South Africa and plummet the level of unemployment and poverty levels as well as promoting entrepreneurship activity (Sitharam & Hoque, 2016). Small-, medium- and micro-sized enterprises (SMMEs) in South Africa account for about 36% of the total GDP in the South African economy. Despite this huge contribution, the rate at which SMEs fail in South Africa is worrisome and is reported to range between 70% and 80% over all subdivisions of the economy (Moos & Sambo, 2018). As a result, it is evident that there are different challenges confronting businesses in South Africa. Cant and Wiid (2013, p. 707), opine that "inflation and interest rates, crime and unemployment, low demand for products, the wrong pricing strategies implemented and the location of the business are the major problems experienced by SMEs". Moos and Sambo (2018) identify barriers in six categories, namely access to funding, skills challenges, compliance problems, insufficient services for the development of businesses, infrastructure and modern suitable technology (Table 3.1).

The above summarises the challenges that entrepreneurs face when running a business in South Africa. Based on the above, this study hypothesises that

Table 3.1 Barriers to SMME development

Inadequate managerial prowse	Kambwale et al. (2015, p. 99), Lekhanya (2015, p. 414)
Unavailability of new technology	Thomas (2014, p. 2)
Dominance of illiteracy among the populace	Chiloane-Tsoka (2013, p. 184)
leadership and management blunders	Kalane (2015, p. 45)
Lack of financial management knowledge	Jindrichovska (2013, p. 82)
No business education training	Seeletse (2012, p. 11000), Cant (2017, p. 110), Ramukumba (2014, p. 24)
Lack of business skills	Ntshona (2012, p. 1), Skae (2017, p. 1)
Poor financial records keeping system in the business	Mungal and Garbharran (2014, p. 81)
Funding	Mazanai and Fatoki (2012, p. 58), Fatoki (2014, p. 48), Rector et al. (2016, p. 68), Quartey et al. (2017, p. 18)
Unavailability of basic amenities, space and land	Cant (2017, p. 110), Nkwinika and Munzhedzii (2016, p. 77), Mcgaffin et al. (2015, p. 17)
About 90% fail from a lack of experience and competence	Agwu and Emeti (2014, p. 104), Mamman et al. (2018, p. 7)
Poor entrepreneurial skills	Phelan and Sharpley (2012, p. 1)
Hostile regulatory environment	Ladzani et al. (2011, p. 1466), Agwa-Ejon and Mbohwa (2015, p. 523)
lack of access to business care schemes	Van Aardt et al. (2011, p. 104)

Source: Adapted from Moos and Sambo (2018).

There is no significant difference in the levels (groups) of entrepreneur businesses based on the challenges affecting the business.

Entrepreneurship development

Entrepreneurial development is regarded by many successive governments as a programme of events to improve the skills, knowledge, behaviours and attitudes of groups and to take on the roles of entrepreneurs (Osemeke, 2012). Earlier in the chapter, the author referred to entrepreneurship as entrepreneurial enhancing knowledge and skills through systematic institution-building and training programmes. However, entrepreneurship has been identified with the economies of countries (Cavallo et al., 2019; Davidsson et al., 2006; Mason & Brown, 2014; Wong et al. 2005). Researchers across the globe view entrepreneurship differently through the nature of businesses, and their role in economic growth and development. Table 3.2 is an adapted comprehensive table of entrepreneurship types and their influence on economic development (Opute et al., 2021).

Resource-based entrepreneurship theories

The entrepreneurship resource-based theory is one of the most cited theories in the history of management theorising. It argues that, it is imperative for founders to have access to resources as a determinant of opportunity-based entrepreneurship and new venture growth (Alvarez & Busenitz, 2001, cited in Simpeh, 2011). Entrepreneurship researchers have developed an understanding from this theory to better diffuse the elements of entrepreneurial performance (Alvarez & Busenitz, 2001; Chandler & Hanks, 1994; Chrisman et al., 1998; Walter et al., 2016; Wiklund & Shepherd, 2003, cited in Kellermanns, 2016). The theory emphasises the significance of human, social and financial resources (Aldrich, 1999). Thus, availability of resources improves an individual's skill to sense and act on new openings (Davidson & Honing, 2003). Financial, human and social capital signify three clusters of elements in the resource-based entrepreneurship theories.

Research methodology

This research employed a quantitative approach with a cross-section survey design. The population comprised of the micro, small and medium enterprises situated in King William's Town, Eastern Cape Province. Samples were collected using purposive random sampling techniques from 210 respondents. Questionnaires were used as a data collection instrument, from either the business owners or managers of the businesses approached, which cut across businesses under different categories. Approximately 62.4% of the respondents were female and 37.6% were male, while the mean age of the

Table 3.2 Entrepreneurship types and economic development influence

Nature of business	*Role in economic growth and development*	*Source*
Small and medium enterprises (SMEs)	Insight from Germany suggests that entrepreneurship is an an important contributor to the creation of knowledge and technological innovations. SMEs and entrepreneurship occupy a key role in the creation of jobs, employment and social integration across the EU countries. SMEs were mostly noticeable in Cyprus, Malta, Estonia, Greece, Lithuania, Latvia and Italy with SMEs giving more than two-thirds of the total value added in each of their non-financial business economies. Across many other EU countries, SMEs provide a stock of tangible and intangible knowledge assets that enable the diffusion of key ICT tools to build enough internal capacity technology-intensive activities.	Fuerlinger et al. (2015), Bowmaker-Falconer and Herrington (2020), Hayton and Cacciotti (2013), The Organisation for Economic Cooperation and Development (OECD) (2019)
	Activities	
	In the United States, SMEs are tremendously vital for economic growth, innovation, creating jobs, encouraging start-up innovations, for example, SMEs are at the forefront of technological innovation across many developed countries, for ex-ample, in the United States, they are widely successful entrepreneurial start-ups, for example, Apple, Yahoo, Google and Facebook that have advanced growth and development. SMEs remain an important source of economic activities, employment, innovation and savings in the US economy. In Germany, SMEs contribute to expanding research and enabling market expansion promotes social change. Across Finland and the United Kingdom, entrepreneurs serve as an engine to local and	Haltiwanger et al. (2009), Bernard et al. (2009), Haltiwanger et al. (2013), Acs et al. (2018), Audretsch et al. (2018), Rhodes (2019), Social Enterprise UK, OECD (2017)

(*Continued*)

Table 3.2 (Continued)

Nature of business	*Role in economic growth and development*	*Source*
	national economic growth, foster a more sustainable society and act as an agent of social change. In the United Kingdom and Finland, SMEs account for 90% and 70% respectively of all clean technology businesses with improved greener supply change in the local cleantech market and provides the opportunity for skill and technological advancement.	
Family business	Generate job, income and wealth for family members and the economy. Contribute to economic growth through technological development and expansion into foreign markets. Provides income that supports family well-being and contributes to poverty alleviation. Provide intergenerational wealth and investment for the family.	Ramadani and Hoy (2015), Opute (2020), Morck and Yeung (2003), Herrington and Coduras (2019)
Women business	Women businesses serve as a vehicle for social development and create economic independence, income, self-reliant and empowerment. Women businesses contribute a lot to balancing family needs, reducing child poverty and disadvantage associated with individual differences.	Brush et al. (2010), Minniti et al. (2005), Hechavarria et al. (2019), Welsh et al. (2014), Brush et al. (2010)

Source: Adopted from entrepreneurial ecosystem approach by Opute et al. (2021).

respondents was 30 years (Sd. = 1.12). Around 51.4% of the respondents had a bachelor's degree, 26.2% had a matric qualification and 22.4% had an honours degree. The data collected was analysed using SPSS software, and one-way ANOVA was used to differentiate the levels of business and challenges affecting business. Regression analysis was also utilised to determine the effects of business support and advice on challenges affecting business.

Presentation of results

Table 3.3 shows the frequency distribution of challenges affecting entrepreneurs in the Eastern Cape Province. The results in the table show that the majority of the items listed yielded very high mean scores which ranged from 2.30 to 4.14. This shows that the majority of the entrepreneurs agreed on the stated items as challenges affecting their businesses. The outcomes show that 75.2% of the respondents approve that one of the challenges affecting their business is competition, while 44.7% reported that lack of skills was one of the challenges affecting their business, 23.8% were indifferent and 31.4% disagreed. The table further shows that 80.9% identified inadequate resources as one of the challenges affecting entrepreneurs, 70% indicated lack of opportunity, 53.8% pointed on time and 44.2% agreed while 41% disagreed and 14.8% were indifferent. On the other hand, 52.4% disagreed that high tax was one of the challenges affecting their businesses, 51.9% disagreed that multi-taxing system was a challenge, 54.3% disagreed that legal issues and office space (52.8%) was a challenge affecting their businesses. Almost 43.8% disagreed that workforce recruitment/retention affects their business, and 25.7% were indifferent. The results show that lack of teamwork among staff members, difficulties with business registration and difficulties in accessing loans and tax compliance are not critical factors affecting entrepreneur businesses. These results imply that the entrepreneurs do not consider steps to formalise their businesses and regulations compliance as critical factors affecting their businesses. Instead, factors that pertain to growing the business seem to be more challenging factors affecting businesses.

Hypothesis one: There is no significant difference in the levels (groups) of entrepreneur businesses based on the challenges affecting the business. It was tested using a one-way analysis of variance as shown below.

The results in Table 3.4 indicate that the levels of entrepreneur business differ significantly ($F(4,205) = 2.80$, $p < 0.05$) from one another. This implies that there is a significant difference in the levels of entrepreneur business and the challenges affecting the business. The null hypothesis one, which states that there is no significant difference in the levels (groups) of entrepreneur business based on the challenges affecting business, stands rejected. Further, the specific significant differences among the five grouping levels of entrepreneur business were examined using the least significance difference (LSD) post hoc test presented in Table 3.5.

Table 3.3 The frequency of the challenges encountered by an entrepreneur in Eastern Cape Province

	Strongly disagree	*Disagree*	*Indifferent*	*Agree*	*Strongly agree*	*X*	*SD*
Competitions	45 (21.4%)	0	7 (3.3%)	3 (1.4%)	155 (73.8%)	4.06	1.65
Lack of skills	42 (20%)	24 (11.4%)	50 (23.8%)	54 (25.7%)	40 (19%)	3.12	1.39
Inadequate resources	25 (11.9%)	0	15 (7.1%)	50 (23.8%)	120 (57.1%)	4.14	1.31
Lack of opportunities	27 (12.9%)	7 (3.3%)	29 (13.8%)	30 (14.3%)	117 (55.7%)	3.97	1.41
Strict/cumbersome regulations	77 (36.7%)	9 (4.3%)	31 (14.8%)	53 (25.2%)	40 (19%)	2.86	1.59
Time	31 (14.8%)	14 (6.7%)	52 (24.8%)	14 (6.7%)	99 (47.1%)	3.65	1.48
High tax	97 (46.2%)	13 (6.2%)	39 (18.6%)	0	61 (29%)	2.59	1.71
Multi-taxing system	96 (45.7%)	13 (6.2%)	56 (26.7%)	0	45 (21.4%)	2.45	1.57
Legal issues	108 (51.4%)	6 (2.9%)	50 (23.8%)	17 (8.1%)	29 (13.8%)	2.30	1.49
Office space	96 (45.7%)	15 (7.1%)	35 (16.7%)	7 (3.3%)	57 (27.1%)	2.59	1.69
Workforce recruitment/retention	75 (35.7%)	17 (8.1%)	54 (25.7%)	22 (10.5%)	42 (20%)	2.71	1.53
Lack of time	27 (12.9%)	19 (9%)	70 (33.3%)	7 (3.3%)	87 (41.4%)	3.51	1.43
Lack/inadequate qualified staff	30 (14.3%)	26 (12.4%)	64 (30.5%)	23 (11%)	67 (31.9%)	3.34	1.41
Lack of team work among staff members	30 (14.3%)	22 (10.5%)	80 (38.1%)	26 (12.4%)	52 (24.8%)	3.23	1.32
Difficulties on business registration	55 (26.2%)	11 (5.2%)	69 (32.9%)	7 (3.3%)	68 (32.4%)	3.11	1.56
Difficulties in accessing loan	62 (29.5%)	19 (9%)	53 (25.2%)	19 (9%)	57 (27.1%)	2.95	1.57
Tax compliance	56 (26.7%)	11 (5.2%)	69 (32.9%)	32 (15.2%)	42 (20%)	2.97	1.44
Other (please specify)	8 (3.8%)	2 (1%)	160 (76.2%)	0	40 (19%)	3.29	0.92
	Weight average mean					**3.16**	**1.47**

Source: Research Fieldwork (2021).

Table 3.4 One-way ANOVA of difference in levels of business and challenges affecting business

	Sum of squares	*Df*	*Mean square*	*F*	*Sig.*
Between groups	885.451	4	221.363	2.800	.027
Within groups	16205.673	205	79.052		
Total	17091.124	209			

Source: Research Fieldwork (2021).

Table 3.5 LSD test for different levels of entrepreneur business and challenges affecting business

Group I	*Group J*	*Mean difference (I-J)*	*Sig.*
Start-up stage	Pre-profit profitable and growing stage	−4.19	.09
	Established and growing	−5.96*	.02
	Established and stable	−.34	.88
	Established but stressed	−1.95	.37
Pre-profit profitable and growing stage	Start-up stage	4.19	.09
	Established and growing	−1.77	.43
	Established and stable	3.85	.07
	Established but stressed	2.24	.25
Established and growing	Start-up stage	5.96*	.02
	Pre-profit profitable and growing stage	1.77	.43
	Established and stable	5.62*	.01
	Established but stressed	4.00*	.03
Established and stable	Start-up stage	.337	.88
	Pre-profit profitable and growing stage	−3.85	.07
	Established and growing	−5.62*	.01
	Established but stressed	−1.62	.32
Established but stressed	Start-up stage	1.95	.37
	Pre-profit profitable and growing stage	−2.24	.25
	Established and growing	−4.00*	.03
	Established and stable	1.62	.32

Source: Research Fieldwork (2021).

Note
* The mean difference is significant at the 0.05 level.

The results of the post hoc test in Table 3.5 show that the levels of entrepreneur businesses exhibit a direct and significant difference with the challenges affecting business. The results indicate that the challenges affecting businesses that are established and growing differs significantly from the challenges affecting businesses in the start-up stage (=5.96, $p < 0.5$), businesses that are established and stable (=5.62, $p < 0.5$) and also, businesses that are established but stressed (=4.00, $p < 0.5$). However, no significant difference was found in businesses at the pre-profit, profitable and growing stage (=1.77, ns). A graphical representation comparing the levels of differences of the five groupings of entrepreneur businesses is presented in Figure 3.1. The results, based on the mean values and the graphical representation, show that the overall difference in challenges affecting business among categories of the five entrepreneur businesses descriptions, is significantly higher among businesses that are growing and established.

Hypothesis two: There is a significant positive effect of business support and advice on challenges affecting business.

Table 3.6 shows the effects of business support and advice on the challenges affecting business. The results of the regression analysis (R^2 = .02, F (2,207) = 1.67, ns) show that there is no significant effect of business support and advice on challenges affecting entrepreneur businesses in the

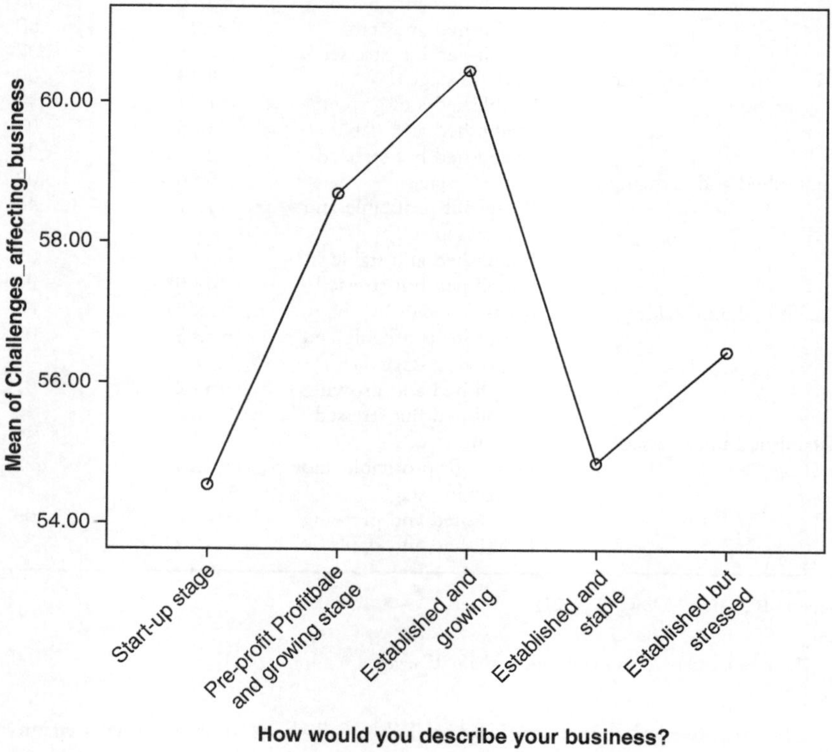

Figure 3.1 Comparison of challenges affecting the business of different levels of entrepreneur businesses.

Source: Research Fieldwork (2021).

Table 3.6 Regression analysis of the effect of business support and advice on challenges affecting business

	Slightly easy	*Difficult*	*Very difficult*	*Don't know/ not relevant*	*X*	*Sd.*	*ANOVA*
In your experience, how easy is it to find business support and advice in Eastern Cape, South Africa?	20 (9.5%)	76 (36.2%)	72 (34.3%)	42 (20%)	3.65	.91	$r = .89$
In your experience, how helpful have you found business support and advice on the government?	6 (2.9%)	77 (36.7%)	78 (37.1%)	49 (23.3%)	3.81	.83	$r = .09$*
			(R^2 = .02, F 2,207) = 1.67, ns)				

Source: Research Fieldwork (2021).

Note
* significance level at a = 0.05

study area. That is, the business support and advice have no significant reduction effects on challenges affecting micro, small and medium businesses in the study area. Also, the results show that the ease of finding business support and advice does not affect the business, while there is a relation between those that found business support and advice helpful and challenges affecting their business. The descriptive analysis, however, shows that the majority of the respondents (70.5%) find it difficult to get business support and advice. In addition, 73.1% found it difficult to get help from the government. These results imply that the respondents found it difficult to get business support and advice from the government.

Discussion

The dearth of information about the dynamism of the challenges affecting entrepreneurs is one of the factors facing policymakers. This section attempts to explore the ecosystem of an entrepreneur by looking into the challenges affecting their businesses, while focusing on different stages used to describe the business. Findings on challenges affecting business show that competition, lack of skills, inadequate resources, lack of opportunity and time are expressed as some of the major factors affecting entrepreneur business. However high taxes, multi-taxing system, legal issues and office space were not indicated as major factors affecting business in the study area. Furthermore, the findings show that workforce recruitment/retention, lack of teamwork among staff members, difficulties with business registration, and difficulties in accessing loans and tax compliance are not major critical factors affecting entrepreneur businesses. These findings indicate that in the study area, the entrepreneur does not see steps to formalise their businesses and regulations compliance as critical factors affecting their businesses, rather, external factors that pertain to growing business seem to be more challenging factors affecting the business. In addition, it was established from previous literature that COVID-19 pandemic significantly affects entrepreneur business activities because of the lockdown instituted by the government. Table 3.7 presents different authors' views on the influence of COVID-19 on entrepreneurs' business activities and SMEs. Most of the authors assert that COVID-19 significantly affected the running of businesses because of the lockdown restrictions instituted by the government in mid-March 2020. The response plan was sectioned into three stages by the president, the first stage commenced in March 2020 when the COVID-19 pandemic was declared a national calamity. This fused wide-ranging opportunities to ease the prominent unpleasant impact of the pandemic on organisations, people and communities (The Presidency RSA, 2020).

The results of this study align with some outcomes of a study done by Visser et al. (2019) on small business constraints in South Africa. The authors reported a lack of business information sources and intensive competition besides other high-rated constraints that comprise financial support

Table 3.7 Impact of COVID-19 on the entrepreneur business

S/N	*Authors*	*Topics*	*Results*
1.	Oni and Omonona (2020)	"The Effect of COVID-19 on Small Retail Businesses in Alice Town, South Africa"	The findings disclosed that SMEs were adversely affected by COVID-19.
2.	Anakpo and Mishi (2021)	"Business Response to COVID-19 Impact: Effectiveness Analysis in South Africa"	Small businesses and pure export were significantly affected and possess less capacity to recover quickly.
3.	Fubah and Moos (2022)	"Exploring COVID-19 Challenges and Coping Mechanisms for SMEs in the South African Entrepreneurial Ecosystem"	The study opined that SMEs were bedevilled with the challenges of customer loss, limited government support, lockdown restrictions and shortage of raw materials.
4.	Chetty et al. (2022)	"The Impact of COVID-19 on Youth Entrepreneurship in South Africa"	The study revealed that the closures of businesses and the stay at home protection of the elderly, significantly affect their businesses. This affected the youth negatively during the lockdown.
5.	Omonona et al. (2021)	"COVID-19 Pandemic and the South African Township Economy: A Focus on King Williams Town, Eastern Cape, South Africa"	SMEs in the township area were negatively impacted by the effects of COVID-19.
6.	Mkhonza and Sifolo (2020)	"COVID-19 Effect on Business Performance: SMMEs Perspectives in a South African Context"	It was discovered in the study that COVID-19 has disastrous effects on SMMEs in South Africa.
7.	Naidoo (2021)	"SME Sustainability in South Africa Post COVID-19"	SMEs were badly hit by the effects of COVID 19 lockdown level 5 instituted by the South African government. SMEs experienced high financial losses due to COVID-19 lockdown.

Source: Author's compilation (2022).

and high transport costs faced by small businesses in the study area. Similar findings consistent with the present findings were also reported by Sitharam and Hoque (2016) on aspects of SMEs performance in KwaZulu-Natal, South Africa. The authors found that competition was reported by a majority of the respondents as a key challenge affecting business performance. Raj (2016), in a study on problems faced by entrepreneurs in some cities in India, reported similar findings to the present study. Raj (2016) found that micro, small and medium enterprises face issues relating to finances, location and competition. The author also noted that entrepreneurs found the regulatory framework cumbersome based on the multiple window policy of the government with references to taxes. Though high tax, multi-taxing system, legal issues and office space are not seen as major challenging factors affecting businesses in the study area, it does not confute it to be a challenging factor. Although there are many other factors affecting entrepreneur businesses' growth which are not captured in the present study, weak competitive position, lack of skills, inadequate resources and lack of opportunity are critical areas in which small businesses struggle to grow.

Findings also revealed that the levels of entrepreneur businesses' description differ significantly from one another. The findings revealed that there is a significant difference among the five groupings of entrepreneurs' business descriptions as regards the challenges affecting their businesses. The post hoc findings revealed that the challenges affecting businesses that are established and growing differ significantly from challenges affecting businesses that are in the start-up stage, businesses that are established and stable as well as businesses that are established but stressed. Although, no significant differences were reported in businesses at the pre-profit, profitable and growing stage. The findings revealed that the overall difference regarding challenges affecting businesses among each category of the five-entrepreneur business description is significantly higher among businesses that are established and growing. This reveals an understanding of Willemse's (2010) report which stated that in the first five years, the number of small and medium enterprises (SMEs) failures ranges between 50% and 95%. Similarly, the findings may give an inclusive reason for the position of Yeboah (2015) on why 75% of SMEs do not become established businesses. This shows that there may be varied challenges affecting businesses at different levels and descriptions which policymakers need to observe to reduce the rate of SMEs failure in South Africa.

In addition, the findings revealed no significant effects of business support and advice on challenges affecting entrepreneur businesses in the study area. This implies that the business support and advice have no significant reduction effects on challenges affecting micro, small and medium business in the study area. The findings further revealed that the ease of finding business support and advice does not affect the business while there is a significant relationship between those that found business support and advice helpful and challenges affecting their business. However, further analysis shows that most of the participants found it difficult to get business support and advice as well as help from the government.

Lastly, the findings from empirical literature reveal significant relations between COVID-19, entrepreneurs and SMEs performance in South Africa. This is in line with the work of Fubah and Moos (2022) who discovered that the SMEs' COVID-19 challenges included lockdown restrictions, lack of government support, customer loss and scarcity of raw materials. Similarly, Omonona et al. (2021) studied the effects of COVID-19 pandemic and the South African township economy. The outcome of their investigation bared negative effects of COVID-19 on SMEs in the township area. Hence, there exists a negative relationship between COVID-19 and business entrepreneur activities.

Conclusion

The chapter explored the ecosystem of entrepreneurs and examined the challenges affecting micro, small and medium enterprises. The findings revealed competition, lack of skills, inadequate resources, lack of opportunities and time as some of the major factors affecting entrepreneur businesses. Meanwhile, high taxes, multi-taxing system, legal issues, office space, workforce recruitment/retention, lack of teamwork among staff members, difficulties in business registration, difficulties in accessing loans and tax compliance are not the major factors affecting entrepreneur businesses. The findings also showed differences among the five groupings of entrepreneurs' business descriptions regarding the challenges affecting their businesses. The challenges affecting established and growing businesses differ significantly from challenges affecting businesses in the start-up stage, established and stable businesses, as well as businesses that are established but stressed. The findings showed no significant effects of business support and advice on challenges affecting entrepreneur businesses. Lastly, the findings from empirical literature revealed significant relations between COVID-19, entrepreneurs and SMEs performance in South Africa.

Recommendations

Given the very high incidence rate of SMEs failures in South Africa, the government needs to put forth more effort and develop genuine solutions like organising training and workshop programmes with financial assistance packages for SME operators across the country, rather than theoretical solutions to the alarming rate of SME failures and dissolutions.

Collaborations among SMEs may be a good way for SMEs to compete. Government entities at the provincial and district levels can carry out entrepreneurial efforts such as speaking about successful entrepreneurs, their success stories, the challenges they face and how courageous they are in overcoming them. SME collaborations can help small- and medium-sized businesses to compete.

Avenues for further research

Despite the versatility of this chapter, there is a need for future research to focus on the following areas: framework for effective solutions in re-vitalising the SMEs in South Africa, the nature of the South African Entrepreneurship ecosystem among other research areas. Lastly, future studies should endeavour to diagnose the entrepreneurship ecosystem using a different methodological approach.

References

Acs, Z. J., Estrin, S., Mickiewicz, T., & Szerb, L. (2018). Entrepreneurship, institutional economics, and economic growth: An ecosystem perspective. *Small Business Economics*, 51(2), 501–514.

Agwa-Ejon, J., & Mbohwa, C. (2015). Financial challenges faced by SMMES in Gauteng South Africa. International Association for Management of Technology: IAMOT 2015 Conference Proceedings.

Agwu, M. O. & , Emeti, C. I. (2014). Issues, challenges and prospects of small and medium scale enterprises (SMEs) in Port-Harcourt City, Nigeria. *European Journal of Sustainable Development*, 3(1), 101–114.

Alvarez, S., & Busenitz, L. (2001). The entrepreneurship of resource-based theory. *Journal of Management*, 27, 755–775.

Aldrich, H.E. (1999). *Organisations evolving*. Sage Publications.

Anakpo, G., & Mishi, S. (2021). Business response to COVID-19 impact: Effectiveness analysis in South Africa. *The Southern African Journal of Entrepreneurship and Small Business Management*. ISSN: (Online) 2071-3185

Audretsch, D. B., Belitski, M., & Desai, S. (2018). National business regulations and city entrepreneurship in Europe: A multilevel nested analysis. *Entrepreneurship Theory and Practice*, 4(6), 1148–1165.

Barot, H. (2015). Entrepreneurship: A key to success. *The International Journal of Business and Management*, 3(1), 163–165.

Bernard, A. B., Bradford, J., & Schott, P. K. (2009). Importers, exporters and multinationals: A portrait of firms in the U.S. that trade goods. In T. Dunne, J., & M. J. Roberts (Eds.), *Producer dynamics: New evidence from microdata* (pp. 513–556). United States: National Bureau of Economic Research.

Bizcommunity. (2021). *What is the state of entrepreneurship in South Africa?* https://www.bizcommunity.com/Article/196/846/199161.html

Bowmaker-Falconer, A., & Herrington, M. (2020). South Africa's global entrepreneurship monitor (GEM) report. *USB Management Review*. https://www.usb.ac.za/usb_reports/south-africas-gem-report/

Brush, C., de Bruin, A., Welter, F., & Allen, E. (2010). Gender embeddedness of women entrepreneurs: An empirical test of the 5 "M" Framework. *Frontiers of Entrepreneurship Research*, Wellesley, MA: Babson College, 30(8), 8–24.

Cant, M., & Wiid, J. A. (2013). Establishing the challenges affecting South African SMEs. *International Business & Economics Research Journal*, 12(6), 707–716.

Cant, M. C. (2017). The availability of infrastructure in townships: Is there hope for township businesses? *International Review of Management and Marketing*, 7(4), 108–115.

Cavallo, A., Ghezzi, A., & Balocco, R. (2019). Entrepreneurial ecosystem research: Present debates and future directions. *International Entrepreneurship and Management Journal*, 15, 1291–1321.

Chetty, R., Ramraj, A. R., & Gurayah, J. R. (2022). The impacts of Covid-19 on youth entrepreneurship in South Africa. *African Journal of Development Studies (formerly AFFRIKA Journal of Politics, Economics and Society)*. https://hdl.handle.net/10520/ejc-aa_affrika1_v2022_nsi1_a13

Chiloane-Tsoka, G. E. (2013). An investigation into the financial barriers facing women entrepreneurs operating in SMMEs in Tshwane, South Africa. *Journal of Economic and Financial Sciences*, 6(2), 347–358.

Choto, P., Tengeh, R. K., & Iwu, C. G. (2014). Daring to survive or to grow? The growth aspirations and challenges of survivalist entrepreneurs in South Africa. *Environmental Economics*, 5(4), 93–101.

Davidsson, P., Delmar, F., & Wiklund, J. (2006). *Entrepreneurship and the growth of firms*. Edward Elgar Publishing.

Davidson, P., & Honing, B. (2003). The role of social and human capital among nascent entrepreneurs. *Journal of Business Venturing*, 20, 121.

Diandra, D., & Azmy, A. (2020). Understanding definition of entrepreneurship. *International Journal of Management, Accounting and Economics*, 7(5), 235–241.

Fatoki, O. (2014). The financing options for new small and medium enterprises in South Africa. *Mediterranean Journal of Social Sciences*, 5(20), 748.

Flores, G. K. M., & Kovacs, J. K. (2018). Defining the entrepreneurship ecosystem. *SEA – Practical Application of Science*, 6(18), 299–306.

Fubah, C. N., & Moos, M. (2022). Exploring COVID-19 challenges and coping mechanisms for SMEs in the South African entrepreneurial ecosystem. *Sustainability*, 14, 1944. 10.3390/su14041944

Fuerlinger, G., Fandl, U., & Funke, T. (2015). The role of the state in the entrepreneurship ecosystem. *Insights from Germany Triple Helix*, 3, 20–35.

Global Entrepreneurship Monitor (GEM). (2017). Global report 2016/17.

Haltiwanger, J., Jarmin, R. S., & Javier, M. (2009). Jobs created from business start-ups in the United States. *Ewing Marion Kauffman Foundation*, 303–372.

Haltiwanger, J., Jarmin, R. S., & Miranda, J. (2013). Who creates jobs? Small versus large versus young. *Review of Economics and Statistics*, 95(2), 347–361.

Hayton, J. C., & Cacciotti, G. (2013). Is there an entrepreneurial culture? A review of empirical research. *Entrepreneurship & Regional Development*, 25(9–10), 708–731.

Hechavarria, D., Bullough, A., Brush, C., & Edelman, L. (2019). High-growth women's entrepreneurship: Fuelling social and economic development. *Journal of Small Business Management*, 57(1), 5–13. 10.1111/jsbm.12503

Herrington, M., & Coduras, A. (2019). The national entrepreneurship framework conditions in sub-Saharan Africa: A comparative study of GEM data/National expert surveys for South Africa, Angola, Mozambique and Madagascar. *Journal of Global Entrepreneurship Research*, 9(1), 1–24.

Isenberg, D. (2011). *The entrepreneurship ecosystem strategy as a new paradigm for economic policy: Principles for cultivating entrepreneurship* (1st ed.). Washington: Babson Global.

Jindrichovska, I. (2013). Financial management in SMEs. *European Research Studies*, 16, 79–96.

Kalane, L. (2015). *Reasons for failure of SMEs in the Free State*. Free State: South Africa. University of Free State (Master of Business Administration thesis).

Kambwale, J. N., Chisoro, C., & Karodia, A. M. (2015). Investigation into the causes of small and medium enterprise failures in Windhoek, Namibia. *Arabian Journal of Business and Management Review (OMAN Chapter)*, 4(7), 80–109.

Kellermanns, F., Walter, J., Crook, T. R., Kemmerer, B., & Narayanan, V. (2016). The resource-based view in entrepreneurship: A content-analytical comparison of researchers' and entrepreneurs' views. *Journal of Small Business Management*, 54(1), 26–48.

Kuratko, D.F., & Hodgetts, R.M. (2001). *Entrepreneurship – A contemporary approach*. Orlando: Harcourt Brace College Publishers.

Ladzani, M. W., Nieuwenhuizen, C., & Nhlapo, S. (2011). Government support and factors hindering small business survival in the Kroonstad area. *Journal of Public Administration*, 46(4), 1459–1478.

Lekhanya, L. M. (2015). Public outlook on small and medium enterprises as a strategic tool for economic growth and job creation in South Africa. *Journal of Governance and Regulation*, 4(4), 412–418.

Majaja, B. (2019). The needs and challenges of SMEs in the City of Johannesburg: A focus on the entrepreneurship ecosystem. *A research report submitted to the Faculty of Commerce, Law and Management, University of the Witwatersrand, in partial fulfilment of the requirements for the degree of Master of Management in Entrepreneurship and New Venture Creation.*

Mamman, A., Bawole, J., Agbebi, M., & Alhassan, A. R. (2018). SME policy formulation and implementation in Africa: Unpacking assumptions as opportunity for research direction. *Journal of Business Research*. (Unpublished article)

Mason, P. C., & Brown, D. R. (2014). *Entrepreneurial ecosystems and growth oriented entrepreneurship*. The Hague, Netherlands: OECD LEED Programme and the Dutch Ministry of Economic Affairs.

Mazanai, M., & Fatoki, O. (2012). Access to finance in the SME sector: A South African perspective. *Asian Journal of Business Management*, 4(1), 58–67.

McAdam, M., McAdam, R., Dunn, A., & McCall, C. (2016). Regional horizontal networks within the SME agri-food sector: An innovation and social network perspective. *Regional Studies*, 50(8), 1316–1329.

McAdam, M., Harrison, R. T., & Leitch, C. M. (2018). Stories from the field: Women's networking as gender capital in entrepreneurial ecosystems. *Small Business Economics*, 53, 459–474. 10.1007/S11187-018-9995-6

Mcgaffin, R., Napier, M., & Karuri-Sebina, G. (2015). South African township economies and commercial property markets: A conceptualisation and overview. http://www.urbanlandmark.org.za/downloads/SACN_ULM_township_economies.pdf; downloaded on January 24, 2016.

Minniti, M., Arenius, P., & Langowitz, N. (2005). GEM 2004 report on women and entrepreneurship. In M. Hay (Ed.), *Global entrepreneurship monitor*. Massachusetts, United States: Babson College and London Business School.

Mkhonza, V. M., & Sifolo, P. P. S. (2020). Covid-19 effect on business performance: SMMEs perspectives in a South African context. *International Journal of Entrepreneurship and Business Development*, 4(5), 727–743.

Moore, J. F. (1993). Predators and prey: A new ecology of competition. *Harvard Business Review*, 71(3), 75–83.

Moos, M., & Sambo, W. (2018). An exploratory study of challenges faced by small automotive businesses in townships: The case of Garankuwa, South Africa. *Journal of Contemporary Management*, 15, 1–28.

Morck, R., & Yeung, B. (2003). Agency problems in large family business groups. *Entrepreneurship Theory and Practice*, 27(4), 367–382.

Mungal, A., & Garbharran, H.L. (2014). The perceptions of small businesses in the implementation of cash management techniques. *Journal of Economics and Behavioural Studies*, 6(1), 75–83.

Naidoo, N. (2020). The state of entrepreneurship in South Africa. The EOY Entrepreneur of the Year. https://www.eoy.co.za/the-state-of-entrepreneurship-in-south-africa/

Naidoo, V. (2021). SME sustainability in South Africa post-COVID-19. *A handbook of research on sustaining SMEs and entrepreneurial innovation in the post-COVID-19 era*. Hershey, Pennsylvania: IGI Global Publisher of Timely Knowledge.

Naudé, W. (2021). Entrepreneurship and economic development: Theory, evidence and policy. *SSRN Electronic Journal*, no. 7507. 10.2139/ssrn.2314802

Nkwinika, M. K. K., & Munzhedzii, P. H. (2016). The role of small medium enterprises in the implementation of local economic development South Africa. SAAPAM Limpopo Chapter. (5th Annual Conference Proceedings 2016.)

NSBC. (2021). The start-up ecosystem in South Africa. *The small business site*. https://www.thesmallbusinesssite.co.za/2017/06/13/start-ecosystem-south-africa/

Ntshona, S. (2012). States that lack of business acumen hampers small and medium enterprise development. *Business Day*, October 1. http://www.bdlive.co.za/africa/africanbusiness/2013/06/05/companies-usingsmes-can-drive-growth-in-africa (downloaded on January 19, 2015).

OC & C Strategy Consultants. (2018). Tech entrepreneurship ecosystem in South Africa. https://www.occstrategy.com/media/1295/tech-entrepreneurship-ecosystem-in-south-africa.pdf

OECD. (2017). Key issues for digital transformation in the G20 [Report prepared for a joint G20 German residency/OECD conference].

OECD. (2019) Annual report on the European SMEs 2018/19, research and development and innovation by SMEs, Luxemburg, Europe.

Omonona, S., Oni, O., & Oluwole, O. J. (2021). COVID-19 pandemic and the South African township economy: A focus on King Williams Town, Eastern Cape, South Africa. *Harvard Deusto Business Research*, X(2), 370–381. 10.48132/hdbr.356

Oni, O., & Omonona, S. (2020). The effect of COVID-19 on small retail businesses in Alice Town, South Africa. *Journal of Retail Marketing*, 16(3), 49–57.

Opute, A. P. (2020). Small and medium enterprises marketing: Innovation and sustainable economic growth perspective. In S. Nwankwo, & A. Gbadamosi (Eds.), *Entrepreneurship marketing: Principles and practice of SME Marketing*. London: Routledge Publishers.

Opute, A. P., Kalu, K. I., Adeola, O., & Iwu, C. G. (2021). Steering sustainable economic growth: Entrepreneurial ecosystem approach Abdullah promise. *Journal of Entrepreneurship and Innovation in Emerging Economies*, 7(2), 216–245.

Osemeke, M. (2012). Entrepreneurial development and interventionist agencies in Nigeria. *International Journal of Business and Social Science*, 3(8), 255–265.

Phelan, C., & Sharpley, R. (2012). Exploring entrepreneurial skills and competencies in farm tourism. *Journal of Local Economy*, 27(2), 103–118.

Quartey, P., Turkson, E., Abor, J. Y., & Iddrisu, A. M. (2017). Financing the growth of SMEs in Africa: What are the constraints to SME financing within ECOWAS? *Review of Development Finance*, 7(1), 18–28

Raj, S. J. (2016). Problems faced by entrepreneurs: A special reference to micro and small entrepreneurs in Mumbai and Pune. *International Journal of Business Management & Research (IJBMR)*, 6(3), 57–62

Ramadani, V., & Hoy, F. (2015). Context and uniqueness of family businesses. In *Family businesses in transition economies* (pp. 9–37). Cham: Springer.

Ramukumba, T. (2014). Overcoming SMEs challenges through critical success factors: A case of SMEs in the Western Cape Province, South Africa. *Economic and Business Review for Central and South-Eastern Europe*, 16(1), 19.

Rector, M., Fatoki, O., & Oni, O. (2016). Access to debt finance by young entrepreneurs in Polokwane, South Africa . *Journal of Social Sciences*, 49(1–2), 67–69.

Rhodes, C. (2019). Business statistics, House of Commons [Briefing Paper No. 06152]. House of Commons Library, London.

Seeletse, S. M. (2012). Common causes of small businesses failure in the townships of West Rand district municipality in the Gauteng Province of South Africa. *African Journal of Business Management*, 6(44), 10994–11002.

Simpeh, K. N. (2011). Entrepreneurship theories and empirical research: A summary review of the literature. *European Journal of Business and Management*, 3(6), ISSN 2222-1905 (Paper) ISSN 2222-2839 (Online).

Sitharam, S., & Hoque, M. (2016). Factors affecting the performance of small and medium enterprises in KwaZulu-Natal, South Africa. *Problems and Perspectives in Management*, 14(2-2), 277–288. 10.21511/ppm.14(2-2).2016.03

Skae, O. (2017). Critical thought: SA's entrepreneur ecosystem needs sweeping overhaul. http://criticalthought.co.za/sas-entrepreneur-ecosystem-needs-sweeping-overhaul/ (downloaded on February 1, 2018).

The Presidency RSA. (2020). The presidency republic of South Africa. http://www.thepresidency.gov.za/speeches/address-president-cyril-ramaphosa-south-africa%E2%80%99s-response-coronavirus-pandemic%2C-union-buildings%2C-tshwane-4

Thomas, W. C. (2014). Khayelitsha small business project: Needs and challenges of small businesses in Khayelitsha. Small Business Academy, University of Stellenbosch Business School, Cape Town, South Africa.

Turkina, E. (2018). The importance of networking to entrepreneurship: Montrealas artificial intelligence cluster and its born-global firm element AI. *Journal of Small Business and Entrepreneurship*, 30(1, 1–8.

Van Aardt, I., Hewitt, M., Bendeman, H., Bezuidenhout, S., Janse Van Rensburg Naidoo, L. P., Van Aardt, C., Van Der Bank, J., & Visser, T. (2011). *Entrepreneurship and new venture management* (4th ed.). Cape Town: Oxford University Press.

Visser, T., Chodokufa, K., Amadi-Echendu, A., & Phillips, M. (2019). Small business constraints: The influence of time. *Academy of Entrepreneurship Journal*, 25(4).

Welsh, D. H., Memili, E., Kaciak, E., & Ochi, M. (2014). Japanese women entrepreneurs: Implications for family firms. *Journal of Small Business Management*, 52(2), 286–305.

Wennekers, S., & Thurik, R. (2014). Linking entrepreneurship and economic growth. *Small Business Economics*, 13(1), 27–55.

Willemse, J. (2010). *The forum SA: SME failure statistics*. Retrieved September 1, 2016, from: http://www.theforumsa.co.za/forums/showthread.php?t=7808

Wong, P. K., Ho, Y. P., & Autio, E. (2005). Entrepreneurship, innovation and economic growth: Evidence from GEM data. *Small Business Economics*, 24(3), 335–350.

Yeboah, M. A. (2015). Determinants of SME growth: An empirical perspective of SMEs in the Cape Coast Metropolis, Ghana. *The Journal of Business in Developing Nations*, 14(1), 2–31.

4 To What Extent Is Entrepreneurship a Sustainable Career Choice for the Youth? A Post-COVID-19 Descriptive Analysis

Tendai Makwara, Lucky Sibanda, and Chux Gervase Iwu

Introduction and background

One of the many challenges confronting the global socioeconomic order is creating avenues for youths to participate in economic development. Globally, many youths struggle to find employment or engage in meaningful economic activities to better their lives. According to the International Labor Organization (ILO) (2020, p. 33), the global youth unemployment rate was 13.8%, with North Africa at 29.6 % and 8.7% in sub-Saharan Africa. As of the second quarter of 2021, the youth unemployment rate in South Africa was 64.4% (South Africa Youth Unemployment Rate – 2021, n.d.; Statistics SA, 2021). Future figures may be higher with the continued decline in global economic activity (O'Higgins & Verick, 2021) and can be projected to be even higher post-COVID-19 pandemic. Thus, the problem of youth unemployment and its accompanying social and economic burdens are causes for concern globally (De Jongh & Meyer, 2017; Fergusson & Yeates, 2021).

Consequently, as a strategic response to address unemployment, youth entrepreneurship has been pushed to the fore (De Jongh & Meyer, 2017; Gough & Langevang, 2016; Rambe & Mosweunyane, 2017) globally but more apparent in developing countries. Arguably the popularity of youth entrepreneurship has foregrounded its possibilities as a career option and as a means of economic liberation. Remarkably, leveraging entrepreneurship to solve youth problems is not a new phenomenon. For over 50 years, entrepreneurship has been debated at local, national, and international levels with divergent views, including claims that it has no substantive empirical evidence of perceived capabilities to ameliorate youth-related challenges (Organisation for Economic Co-operation and Development (OECD), 2013) and that it is a crucial mechanism of economic development encouraging youth participation in the economy (see Chigunta, 2002; Chigunta et al., 2005; Diraditsile & Maphula, 2018). While advocacy for

DOI: 10.4324/9781003216469-4

youth entrepreneurship is warranted, critics of its contested effectiveness rarely argue that entrepreneurship has contributed insignificantly towards addressing critical social and economic questions confronting the youth and barely stimulated some level of economic participation among the youths. These critics claim that unsuccessful entrepreneurship programmes have created few jobs, often with low pay and limited sustainability (Barford & Coombe 2019, p. 35). Those new small firm jobs are more volatile, less productive, and less well-paid have fewer benefits and have higher rates of accidents (Nightingale & Coad, 2014). Others posit that the number of youths becoming entrepreneurs remains marginal (see Minola et al., 2014, p. 234), undermining its assumed synergy with youth aspirations. Pompa (2013) claims that nobody knows what works and does not about youth entrepreneurship and how to make it successful. Arguably these views pose a complex puzzle in trying to validate and disprove the propriety of youth entrepreneurship as an effective alternative to resolving youth economic problems.

Nonetheless, the field of youth entrepreneurship has inspired numerous research efforts. Some have examined young people's career ambitions (e.g., Iwu et al., 2020), others the number of youth entrepreneurs in the economy and the effectiveness of institutional support by government and youth support agencies (Gwija et al., 2014). This chapter focuses on youth economic behaviours, career aspirations, and entrepreneurial intents. It is vital to understand the nexus between these variables, particularly given research and policy claims that entrepreneurship is a default career choice for youths if they fail to find work. For example, Chigunta (2002) states that youths in developing countries tend to go into business out of economic necessity. Namatovu et al. (2016) assert that the pressing need to survive and failure to find jobs inspire youths to become entrepreneurial. This view is supported by Diraditsile and Maphula (2018) in Botswana, who found that poverty and unemployment compel youths to become entrepreneurs. Regarding its attractiveness as a career option, a study conducted in Sri Lanka by Thrikawala (2011) revealed that entrepreneurship is the second or last choice of employability among youths. A cross-cultural comparative study of Indian and Chinese youth attitudes towards entrepreneurship also concurred and concluded that starting a business ranked third by the Chinese and fourth by Indians (Goel et al., 2007, p. 24). These studies fly in the face of conventional wisdom that popularise youth entrepreneurship as a flagship approach to deal with youth concerns globally, more so in developing countries. Such contrasting views unavoidably raise two questions which this chapter aims to answer.

1. Can entrepreneurship be relied upon to solve youth unemployment?
2. Does sufficient empirical evidence exist to define youth entrepreneurship as a career?

Method

This chapter aims to synthesise the literature to reveal any possible interpretable patterns (Guzzo et al., 1987; Harb & Abu-Shanab, 2000) on the potency of youth entrepreneurship as an alternative to job creation. Thus, non-empirical research based on a thorough descriptive literature review was adopted. From a broad range of literature consulted, publicly available articles and working papers relevant to the research question were identified. With the aim to present a nuanced view, we also considered local and global literature that shed light on job creation and youth entrepreneurship.

Literature review

Definition of youth entrepreneurship

Across entrepreneurship studies and the global economy, the definition of youth varies depending on the specific socio-cultural, institutional, economic, and political factors (Hassani & Khouni, 2013). Definitions on youth vary from being young persons between ages 15 and 29 across nations and regions, according to the global Solutions for Youth Employment (S4YE) Coalition (Goldin et al., 2015) to those between ages 15 and 24 in developing and emerging economies (Alam, 2019). The United Nations Youth (n.d.) defines youths as young persons aged 15–35 and indicates that the African Youth Charter (AYC) classifies youths as persons aged between 15 and 35 years old. In South Africa, the youth are persons between 15 to 34 years (Dawson & Fouksman, 2020). The lack of a commonly agreed definition of youths invites distortions into youth entrepreneurship discourse. For example, Ellis and Williams (2011) argue that an age cohort with 35 years as the upper age bracket will include a reasonably high proportion of all entrepreneurs (from age cohorts with 24 years as the upper limit). Nonetheless, despite having no universally agreed international definition of the youth age group, youth entrepreneurship is generally understood to mean, as Chigunta (2002) stated, the practical application of enterprising qualities, such as initiative, innovation, creativity, and risk-taking by youths into the work environment (either in self-employment or employment in small startup firms), using the appropriate skills necessary for success in that environment and culture.

The role of youth entrepreneurship

The primary role of youth entrepreneurship is creating corridors of participation in the economy. However, youth entrepreneurship is also lauded for its social impact, particularly curtailing youth social and political discontent. For example, in Nigeria, Awogbenle and Iwuamadi (2010) reckoned entrepreneurship is simply a short-term intervention to deal with youth unemployment issues, ultimately leading to social instability. Relatedly it serves to mop out the out-of-school youths and the ever-increasing number of jobless graduates from the streets. Chigunta et al. (2005) noted that entrepreneurship helped deal with unemployed youths viewed as pausing additional threats to national security if they, in other countries, end up joining rebel armies. The authors also add that unemployed youths are prone to drug abuse, criminality, engaging in organised violence, violent protests and spreading human immunodeficiency virus/acquired immunodeficiency syndrome (HIV/AIDS) through risky sexual behaviours. Likewise, Gazi and Akter (2014) underscored the role of entrepreneurship in addressing some of the socio-psychological problems and delinquency arising from joblessness. Goldin et al. (2015) referred to uprisings experienced in Egypt and Tunisia as examples of how youth unemployment manifested social and political instability. Collectively these scholars positioned entrepreneurship as a buffer to keep youths from destabilising societies.

In the main, the above perspectives complement a broader mainstream argument encouraging youth entrepreneurship as a provider of solutions to youth's economic aspirations (Sharma & Madan, 2014) and mitigating societal and political dangers associated with a dormant youth population. Moreover, entrepreneurship stimulates economic activities in poor communities and may be the only realistic opportunity for youths to kick-start their careers amidst high levels of unemployment. Additionally, youths who create sustainable entrepreneurial operations gain dignity, respect, and recognition (Dzomonda & Fatoki, 2019) in these communities. Other evidence suggests that most youths likely to start small ventures tend to be lowly educated and driven by necessity (see Goldin et al., 2015; Llisterri et al., 2006, p. 5; Namatovu et al., 2016, p. 24). In that sense, entrepreneurship provides opportunities to lowly skilled individuals to participate in the economy and dignify their life experiences. However, a counter perspective to this assertion is that such levels of self-employment rarely take people out of poverty (Rambe & Mosweunyane, 2017, p. 11), although Dzomonda and Fatoki (2019) insist that it is a misconception to associate entrepreneurship with income instability. In our view, Dzomonda and Fatoki do not make a strong case considering that financial issues largely explain why many entrepreneurial ventures fail and why some individuals do not find it as an attractive career path.

Many youth business ventures fail, which undermines entrepreneurship clout as an effective strategy for youth empowerment. Youth ventures fail due to reasons almost identical to those related to the high death rate of small businesses. For example, some youth's projects die because youths lack the entrepreneurial flair such as dedication and enthusiasm to endure the challenges of starting a new business. Others lack essential skillsets to manage the business (Gough & Langevang, 2016). Some youth ventures fail to successfully deal with operational challenges such as lack of access to credit, regulatory bottlenecks, limited access to finance, crime and corruption (Brixiova et al., 2014). These challenges are underpinned by low youth entrepreneurial uptake (Bux & Van Vuuren, 2019; Motts, 2000; Olugbola, 2017; Sibanda & Iwu, 2021), thus raising questions of synergy between youth behaviours and entrepreneurship as a career option. In South Africa, the probability of youths starting their own business has even declined over the past decade (De Jongh & Meyer, 2017, p. 72), with Turton and Herrington (2013) also have found that only 15% of South African youths harbored intentions to start a business. Although these reasons underpinning high failure rates of entrepreneurial ventures and low levels of youth entrepreneurship in South Africa are well known, the development of corresponding solutions to curtail these challenges has not been forthcoming. The above is evident in the presence of persistently low Total Entrepreneurial Activity (TEA) score, reported in the literature over many years (Bosma & Kelley, 2019). As a result, while the academic prospects of entrepreneurship can be advanced, its realisation in practice as an alternative to formal employment is hardly evident.

The youth entrepreneurship rationale

Burchell and Coutts (2019, p. 3) claim that youth entrepreneurship rationale rides an untested assumption that self-employment programmes work and can be as attractive as creating formal jobs. It may be added that the other assumption is that youths can be persuaded to see it this way and consider entrepreneurship a realistic career path. Additionally, the youth entrepreneurship narrative seems to categorise youth unemployment as an "economic and social problem" that needs to be solved by reminding youths that they need to self-employ and not wait for the governments to create jobs. In line with this thinking, the United Nations, Department of Economic and Social Affairs (UNDESA) (2018) stated that youth entrepreneurship is necessary because there are no more guarantees of lifelong employment within firms (UNDESA, 2018, p. 36). Moreover, traditional career paths and opportunities are disappearing rapidly (Gazi & Akter, 2014, p. 198). Awogbenle and Iwuamadi (2010) observed that the capabilities of governments and big businesses to create jobs are shrinking, thus leaving self-empowerment as the primary entry point towards active participation in the economy. Iwu et al. (2020) emphasise that youths need support towards establishing sustainable ventures. Therefore, it seemingly appears that the lack of jobs rather than entrepreneurship's proven capabilities to solve youth problems has put entrepreneurship in the spotlight.

As earlier stated, for over 50 years, entrepreneurship has not produced clear evidence that it is a sustainable method to solve youth-centred problems such as reduced unemployment, poverty, and social restlessness in general society (OECD, 2013). Experiences in Botswana suggest that youth entrepreneurship in its current format will barely solve the youth unemployment problem, hence it is just an idealism (Diraditsile & Maphula, 2018). To this end, some scholars have charged that encouraging more people to become entrepreneurs is bad public policy (see Acs et al., 2016; Arshed et al., 2014; Shane, 2009) as it encourages individuals to start marginal businesses that are likely to fail, have a little economic impact and generate little employment (Shane, 2009). Considering that many youths in developing countries resort to necessity entrepreneurial activities requiring little or no capital injection (such as vending) and due to lack of an ideal environment for business to survive, the fuss about youth entrepreneurship has fallen foul of what White and Kenyon (2001) feared most-becoming token activities to keep them busy and nothing more.

Moreover, claims that entrepreneurship can address youth problems are often framed and justified in developing countries and poverty-stricken contexts like rural areas. In such situations marked by high levels of unemployment, low educational levels, fewer job opportunities, social instability and general economic decay (see Llisterri et al., 2006; Namatovu et al., 2016, p. 24), any activity different from economic inactivity is appealing. However, such discourse ignores how youth self-employment opportunities fail to either guarantee economic success or a decent lifestyle comparable to formal jobs. Burchell and Coutts (2019, p. 3) observed that existing positive discourse about youth entrepreneurship masks a theory that self-employment provides the same financial and non-pecuniary rewards as fully employed persons, which is often practically untrue. Studies by Ajani and Oyekola (2019) in Nigeria and Barsoum (2018) in Egypt revealed that lack of job security and financial benefits discouraged youths from pursuing self-employment opportunities favouring government jobs instead. A study investigating youth aspiration and the future of work covering Eastern Europe, Latin America and the Caribbean, Asia, and Africa by Gardiner et al. (2021) made similar observations. They found that 57% of students in the countries surveyed overwhelmingly aspired to work in the public sector. In the same vein, Dzomonda and Fatoki (2019) asserted that South African youths prefer finding employment in large firms and the government regardless of the difficulty of being absorbed into the system. Even in ordinary society, evidence of successful youth enterprises is few and far, raising questions about the cogency of youth entrepreneurship as an absolute alternative to formal employment.

Developed nations appear cognisant that entrepreneurship cannot solve all youth economic and social problems. As a result, commitment towards creating formal jobs remains paramount. For example, in Europe, countries have placed the European Youth Employment package to prevent youths from beginning their working careers with a joblessness experience. Under this package, all youths up to 25 years can receive a quality job offer, continue with education, or access some apprenticeship or a traineeship within four months of leaving formal education or becoming unemployed (Dietrich & Moller, 2016, p. 20). In the same vein, Tubadji et al. (2021) posited that job creation and placement will most likely be a more successful solution to youth unemployment than expectations for a boost in youth entrepreneurship during the high youth unemployment period akin to what is happening in many developing countries. Equally so, in the United States of America, Jacobs (2014) excluded entrepreneurship from a list of 12 ways to fix the youth unemployment crisis in the country, recommending alternative strategies such as apprenticeship programmes instead, paid internships and reducing school dropout rates. Consistent with this pattern, a global review of youth employment programmes aimed at improving labour market outcomes by Kluve et al. (2016) suggests that developed nations do not invest so much into entrepreneurship as a critical intervention strategy to address youth problems compared to developing nations. In that study, only low-income (e.g., Uganda and Liberia) and upper-middle-income economies (Peru, Colombia, Tunisia, Bosnia, and Herzegovina) mentioned entrepreneurship as a critical economic intervention strategy to address youth concerns (see Kluve et al., 2016, p. 19). The researchers explicitly noted minimal focus towards entrepreneurship promotion in the data set surveyed, of which 58% of data were from high-income countries. Instead, these countries prioritised training and skills development, employment services, and subsidised employment interventions to support youth integration into the economy through employment-related initiatives. These observations support Ferreira et al. (2017), who posited that the importance of entrepreneurship depends on a country's stage of economic development.

Youth entrepreneurial intentions and behaviours

According to a 54-county global survey of students' entrepreneurial career choices, intentions, and underlying motivations, the norm for many youths is being "first employee, then entrepreneur" later (Sieger et al., 2018, p. 3). Likewise, Motts (2000), in a study of South African youths, asserted that their first livelihood experience is to find employment. Later, De Jongh and Meyer (2017, p. 72) cited literature studies in the country supporting a view that graduates prefer waged work rather than undertaking the risk of creating their business ventures. This view is also confirmed in a study that focused on multinational countries by Sieger et al. (2016). Sieger et al. (2016) found that 80.3% of students target formal employment after their studies, with a paltry 8.8% intending to work in their own business directly after studies. Thus collectively, these studies concur with the Prince's Trust (2019) and the assertion of Bosma and Levie (2010) and Kapitsa (2002, p. 4) that only a tiny proportion of youths with entrepreneurial intention are progressing into entrepreneurial action. In the study of Bosma and Levie (2010), of the 25.3% of the global youths (aged between 18 and 29 years) who reported a desire to start their venture, only 7.2% followed through to set up ventures, 6.1% self-managed businesses younger than 48 months, with only 3.0% owning businesses older than 48 months. In this context, there is clear evidence of the lack of a nexus between entrepreneurial intentions and becoming entrepreneurs in practice among the youths (see also Sieger et al., 2016; Sieger et al., 2018).

However, some seminal studies (Matthews & Moser, 1996; Scott & Twomey, 1988) posit that transition to active youth entrepreneurship is augmented by first acquiring job experience. They claim that work experience influences interest in an entrepreneurial career and competencies, while Fox and Gandhi (2021) add that many researchers concur that most successful entrepreneurs first work for someone else, learning business skills. Various southern African studies have also supported this view. For example, in South Africa, Fatoki (2014) looked at the entrepreneurial intentions of undergraduate students and the impact of previous work experience and found that individuals with prior experience possessed higher entrepreneurial intent than those with no prior experience. Relatedly, in Zimbabwe, Chimucheka (2012, p. 10392) found "youths [who] believed that they could not also establish their businesses without experience in any industry", thus underlining the importance of job experiences in stimulating and sustaining youth entrepreneurial potential. These observations concur with Brixiova et al. (2014) in Swaziland, who concluded that youths rely on work experience to promote entrepreneurial success. Similarly, in Malaysia, Othman et al. (2006) conducted a study among university students, which found that students with working experience had a higher entrepreneurial probability than those without work experience. In the same vein, Green (2013) and Kautonen et al. (2010) pointed out that youth who lack social capital from work relations may struggle to build "legitimacy" amongst critical stakeholders such as financiers, customers, and suppliers who help make their business ventures survive. Therefore, job experience as a precursor to successful entrepreneurship is well-grounded.

Therefore, the correlation between past work experience and entrepreneurial action is compelling despite some findings from related studies reporting nil and negative effect of past working experience on entrepreneurship choices. For example, Miralles et al. (2016) and Kautonen et al. (2010) find that the link between one's work experience and propensity to follow an entrepreneurial career is not strong. These findings are like those of Sharma and Madan (2014), who found a weak relationship between work experiences of less than three years and becoming entrepreneurial. While these studies cast doubts on the importance of work experience in propping up youth entrepreneurial capabilities, they do not challenge the skills youths gain from the workplace. Thus, youths can exploit the skills gained if they become entrepreneurs. Overall, therefore, this chapter argues that (1) formal job opportunities provide a valuable internship opportunity for youths to learn the trade and create sustainable ventures and (2) for youth entrepreneurship to be sustainable, youths must be exposed to the intricates of challenges and skills required to run a business.

Moreover, besides the need for workplace experience, several research studies (Bux & Van Vuuren, 2019; Dzomonda & Fatoki, 2019; Lackeus, 2015; Mahlaole & Malebana, 2021; Sibanda & Iwu, 2021) advocate entrepreneurial education to prop up youth entrepreneurial interest and capabilities. However, there are contradictory findings regarding the impact of education on entrepreneurship in literature. For example, Bux and Van Vuuren (2019) found a positive correlation between entrepreneurship education and the self-efficacy skills required to start a business venture among high school South African youth aged 15–18 years. However, a comparable study by Mahlaole and Malebana (2021) in the same country found that while entrepreneurship education had a statistically significant effect on perceived behavioural control, subjective norms and attitude towards behaviour, it nevertheless had an insignificant direct effect on entrepreneurial intentions. At the same time, while arriving at similar conclusions, Purwati et al. (2020) also cited literature with mixed results. Likewise, Alam (2019) claimed that it is not clear from existing studies if entrepreneurship education translates into entrepreneurial activity or income in the long run. In fact, the common fault line between these contrasting views about the impact of entrepreneurial education is that most of the affirmative quantitative evidence that has been put forward is methodologically flawed due to inherent challenges in the field (Lackeus, 2015, p. 20). The flaws mentioned above may suggest that the impact assessment framework in entrepreneurship lacks strong credibility to produce unchallengeable results. Therefore, this chapter argues that there is an apparent lack of understanding of youth entrepreneurial intentions and behaviours by academics, practitioners, and government, resulting in entrepreneurship initiatives that fail.

Post-COVID-19 perspectives on youth entrepreneurship

Undoubtedly, the coronavirus pandemic largely disrupted the economy and society in almost every country. The disruption – "economic costs, social crises, and long-term effects of Covid-19 will fall disproportionately on young adults" (Townsend, 2021) and may alter youth perceptions towards entrepreneurship in several ways. El-Chaarani (2021) posited that the pandemic affected the economic potential of nearly every group in society but none more so than youths. Pinet et al. (2021) also opined that the pandemic had disproportionately affected youth. For youths, the pandemic invited the implementation of COVID-19 related containment measures such as national lockdowns, which deprived them of opportunities to learn as higher institutions suspended classes and left limited opportunities for employment as firms ceased operations. Moreover, with firm closures, many older and experienced employees joined the unemployment pool, increasing competition among job seekers, many of whom are inexperienced youths. These developments stirred by the pandemic merged with a pre-COVID-19 era already marked by massive youth unemployment and declining youth entrepreneurial intentions (Herrington & Kew, 2018; OECD/European Union, 2019; The Kauffman Index, 2017) in a context defined by ineffective youth entrepreneurship policies and support infrastructure. Consequently, these developments forestalled a post-COVID-19 era defined by a different approach and discourse if developing countries and the global community are to revive opportunities for youth economic participation meaningfully.

Concurrent evidence suggests that COVID-19 left firms and governments with strained capacities to create formal jobs. In South Africa, the pandemic has fostered a stagnant economy and dwindling job opportunities (Masenya, 2021), with the economic recovery path likely to be long. It, therefore, appeals to reason that entrepreneurship could provide an immediate practicable solution for inclusive post-pandemic economic participation among the youth. The World Bank (2021) preview of "building back better from Covid-19, with a special focus on jobs" also claimed that young entrepreneurs are one of South Africa's best hopes for solving the jobs crisis entrenched by the epidemic. The World Bank further notes that many youth-led businesses are more likely to use digital solutions, thus, suggesting that the future of post-COVID-19 youth entrepreneurship relies on digital technology. According to Masenya (2021), digital entrepreneurship means business activity primarily takes place online or on a digital medium and often enables companies or individuals to expand their target market and reach more people than is possible with a face-to-face business contact. As a result, possible patterns of the post-COVID-19 era will see extensive use of the internet social media platforms like Facebook, Twitter, and WhatsApp by youths to operate their businesses. However, Pinet et al. (2021) hint that access to and skills required to navigate the digital world can hinder meaningful exploitation of technology resources, thus can undermine the success of entrepreneurship ventures. Therefore, it is argued that, besides mobilising young people to become entrepreneurial, digital skills and resource investments are also necessary to ensure that their businesses can survive.

The success of youth entrepreneurship is a more pressing issue in the post-COVID-19 era. Duval et al. (2021) observed that COVID-19 had further strained South Africa's defective labour market, which already fails to absorb young people. Likewise, The World Bank (2021) argued that acute unemployment is supported by the government's lack of action on strangulating labour market regulations. Furthermore, the World Bank (2021) further mentions that COVID-19 has worsened South Africa's youth unemployment rate because many youths lost jobs, thus supporting the notion of self-employment as a way out. However, as argued elsewhere in this chapter, leveraging entrepreneurship as a "silver bullet" to address youth unemployment challenges is simplistic, as it ignores many critical considerations that may enable self-employment to be effectual. Among these are exposure to formal jobs (Chimucheka, 2012; Fatoki, 2014), a positive business climate and entrepreneurship ecosystem, and easy access to finance (Brixiova et al., 2014). Arguably, with developing nations' governments struggling to sustain the economy, which has been further battered by COVID-19, access to financing and jobs necessary for stimulating youth entrepreneurial interest will become serious challenges youths will face. Therefore, driving the youth entrepreneurship agenda while these issues and resources for the transition to digital entrepreneurship are still lacking, effectively sets up young people for failure.

Moreover, given the high level of youth unemployment in the country, it may be argued that there is an oversupply of potential candidates for youth entrepreneurship, which affects the aspects of policy planning and establishment of a sustainable youth entrepreneurship support system in the country. The oversupply problem arises when one considers, among other things, that not every unemployed youth wants to be an entrepreneur, that the likelihood of youths becoming entrepreneurs is declining over time (De Jongh & Meyer, 2017), and that only 15% of South African youths intended to start a business (Turton & Herrington, 2013). Thus, if post-COVID-19 initiatives are to make a meaningful contribution towards youth entrepreneurship, they need to be based on the realities about youth behaviours towards entrepreneurship as a career undertaking and the resources available to support those who want to become entrepreneurial.

Findings and discussion

Policy assumptions of the necessity for youth entrepreneurship

This chapter first sought to examine whether entrepreneurship can be relied upon to solve youth unemployment and secondly if sufficient empirical evidence of youth entrepreneurship as a viable career alternative to formal employment exists. These questions are pertinent considering that there seems to be a mismatch between the rhetoric about entrepreneurship as a panacea to youth unemployment and its deliverables. Scholars agree on many issues that hold back youth entrepreneurship, which at the same time appear to have minimal practicable solutions. For example, despite years of alluding to the need for an effective entrepreneurship policy, easy access to finance, trust from the financing sector, skills development, friendly regulatory frameworks to nurture the entrepreneurship sector, there is hardly any tangible progress in achieving the above. In South Africa, these problems are still relevant in recent years (Gough & Langevang, 2016) as they were in the formative years post-1994 (Brink et al., 2003). Thus, for lack of solutions to problems entrepreneurs face, youth entrepreneurship provides fewer prospects of solving the youth unemployment crisis.

The inadequacy of the business environment to support youth entrepreneurship

Furthermore, youths may seem an unlikely population for successful entrepreneurial undertakings because of their inexperience and lack of finances and business management skills (OECD, 2013). Overall, they lack the most basic requirements to make the business successful (Motts, 2000, p. 7), and those in developing countries are content with fragile business climates with weak business support systems that undermine business sustainability. Hence Motts (2000) argued that it is improper to push youths (as is happening with the youths' entrepreneurship agenda globally) to start businesses but instead allow them to choose the career they like. This perspective otherwise suggests that governments must approach youth employment issues, recognising that they cannot avoid a reality that many youths prefer and are predisposed to looking for jobs rather than becoming entrepreneurs. As a result, job creation should be a central strategy to integrate youths into the economy. In line with this perspective, "entrepreneurship is a path suitable for some youths but must be viewed in the context of a broader youth employment strategy and not seen as the main approach to youth employment" (UNDESA, 2018, p. 61).

The above narrative calls for a balanced approach to pursuing job creation and youth entrepreneurship to resolve youth economic challenges. Thus, overemphasising the importance of youth entrepreneurship, while it has not proved to be practically effective in eliminating youth economic goals, is misplaced and contradicts emerging empirical data revealing declines in youth participation levels in entrepreneurship projects globally. This decline is evident in Europe, where self-employed youths fell from 2.7 million in 2009 to 2.5 million in 2018 (OECD/European Union, 2019). This trend is comparable with experiences in South Africa, where entrepreneurial activity in the age group 25–34 years has reversed. The downward trend has increased from the low 2016 levels of 6.3–14.5% in 2017 (Herrington & Kew, 2018, p. 8). Similarly, in the United States of America, the number of younger entrepreneurs (ages 20–34) has declined from 34.3% of all new entrepreneurs in 1996 to 24.4 per cent in 2016 (The Kauffman Index, 2017, p. 5). Considering these trends are emerging in a period of massive youth unemployment, it is puzzling why youths are shunning self-employment opportunities and remaining unemployed. Furthermore, this is puzzling considering the overwhelming political and media publicity targeted at youths and government and youth support agencies' efforts to convince youths to become entrepreneurial.

Job and education-related interventions as higher-order strategies to complement the failures of entrepreneurship

Therefore, it is not surprising that, as previously stated, European nations are shifting focus to job and education-related interventions as higher-order strategies to complement the failures of entrepreneurship to absorb youths into the economy. This strategy can be problematic for developing nations given the inherent lack of capacity to develop functional economies that can create jobs to the levels required, hence the ready-made approach to encourage youths to take up entrepreneurship as a default career choice. This approach is supported by claims that self-employment projects significantly impact developing countries more than developed countries (Stam et al., 2011), mainly because they stimulate economic life in struggling economies. However, considering that many of these ventures are nascent and do not survive long enough to impact society positively, continued focus on youth entrepreneurship with limited support mechanisms will barely help developing countries significantly reduce unemployment levels. Therefore, this study argues that there should be a stronger emphasis on job creation and employment skills development to align with the behavioural interests of many youths. As Jeffrey and Dyson (2013) cautioned, there is also the risk that an excessive focus on entrepreneurship becomes a way to blame youths themselves for their misfortunes and provides an excuse for states not to deliver welfare services and ensure decent jobs. Unfortunately, this seems to have become the case in many countries.

Post-COVID-19 entrepreneurship possibilities

There is little doubt that the immediate future career of young people in the post-COVID-19 era lies in self-employment and leveraging technology to gain access to and exploit economic opportunities. However, despite prospects arising from digital entrepreneurship (Modgil et al., 2022), more needs to be done to ensure that youth self-employment initiatives survive. While young people could benefit from digital entrepreneurship, innovation is a key skill to navigate crises such as COVID-19. In countries with high levels of corruption, as in South Africa, such resources may not even reach the intended beneficiaries (Mmakwena & Moses, 2022). Thus, the future of youth entrepreneurship also depends on good corporate behaviours in institutions supporting entrepreneurship. Moreover, it can be argued that the many common challenges that hamper the success of youth business ventures will still need attention in the post-COVID-19 era due to the poor development of youth (Chetty et al., 2022).

While the youth expect substantial support from the government, it is noteworthy to highlight the scarcity of resources that may not always be available to support youths' initiatives. At times, governments may consider channelling resources towards the most pressing issues. The COVID-19 pandemic pushed most governments to support businesses (Modgil et al., 2022), subsidising tests and vaccinations (Mmakwena & Moses, 2022). In addition, the South African government is currently putting most of its resources towards temporary employment creation in various government departments through the Presidential Employment Stimulus (PES) (Philip, 2021). While sustainable employment is critical, the government addresses the most pressing issue at hand. Therefore, the youth should not wait for government support. With COVID-19 forcing all agents of commerce from entrepreneurs, customers, and suppliers to adopt behaviours and towards digital business conduct, youths' transition post-COVID-19 can be centred on embracing entrepreneurship skills such as innovation (Mmakwena & Moses, 2022), self-reliance and resourcefulness (Rajak & Dolan, 2021).

Implications, limitations, and suggestions for future research

Implications for theory and policy

The chapter brings together discussions around thinking on the acclaimed usefulness of youth entrepreneurial uptake. The chapter further challenges some of the general assumptions about the effectiveness of entrepreneurship to address youth economic challenges and fulfil their aspirations. It also underscores the importance of youth entrepreneurship in the post-COVID-19 era and the need for more support for youths to make their ventures successful. We make these claims against the backdrop of the conundrum between entrepreneurship uptake as a panacea to youth unemployment and the obvious lack of solutions to problems entrepreneurs face. A call, therefore, goes out to academics and practitioners to begin to highlight the necessity for a supportive entrepreneurial ecosystem that offers the requisite support to youth entrepreneurs. A policy ramification follows in this direction and that is to note the many issues that hold back youth entrepreneurship, which at the same time appear to be unsolvable. The insolvability relates to the need for an effective entrepreneurship policy, easy access to finance, trust from the financing sector, skills development, and friendly regulatory frameworks to nurture entrepreneurship. Therefore, in the presence of these challenges, youth entrepreneurship provides fewer prospects of solving the youth unemployment crisis. Essentially, this chapter offers a reference point for policy directions considering the increasing concern on youth unemployment.

There is no doubt that future careers are dependent upon a sound knowledge of information technology. A core policy implication for South Africa, therefore, is to provide the youth with meaningful access to technology to exploit economic opportunities post-COVID-19. Furthering the access to technology discourse could mean militarily conscripting the youth following Netswera's (2021) admonition that "most advanced engineering, Information and Technology (IT), and medical innovations come from well-oiled military establishments" and that "the South African military needs to give rise to innovations that spawn construction, engineering and IT industries, among other things".

Limitations and suggestions for future research

This chapter relied on a descriptive literature review and, thus, is limited to desk research. Thus, future studies that use rigorous literature review methods are suggested to eliminate the risk of bias possible on descriptive literature review (Grant & Booth, 2009). Also, this chapter took a descriptive approach to the literature review, which may have impacted the research questions' detailed analysis. Thus, we recommend that future research be undertaken to adopt empirical studies such as meta-analysis to refute or hold the conclusions in this chapter.

Conclusion

We set out to answer two questions: (1) Can entrepreneurship be relied upon to solve youth unemployment? and (2) Does sufficient empirical evidence exist to define youth entrepreneurship as a career? Through a literature review and adopting a search criterion that involved the use of keywords and databases, what we found suggests that although entrepreneurship has come to the fore in recent years, its potency to solve youth problems appears overstated. This leaves us to argue that there is little evidence of the positive impact of entrepreneurship on creating sustainable solutions to pressing issues of youth economic participation and youth unemployment compared to formal jobs. Therefore, our view is that formal job creation remains a sustainable approach to solving youth problems. This view is reinforced by our understanding that for the youth to be persuaded to become entrepreneurial, there is the need to create a business climate/entrepreneurial ecosystem supporting this call. At present, it seems these are lacking.

References

Acs, Z., Astebro, T., Audretsch, D., & Robinson, D. T. (2016). Public policy to promote entrepreneurship, a call to arms. *Small Business Economics*, 47(1), 35–51.

Ajani, O. A., & Oyekola, I. A. (2019). Reasons for public sector jobs preference in Nigeria. *African Research Review*, 13(1), 114–130.

Alam, A. (2019). https://www.unicef.org/globalinsight/media/821/file/UNICEF-Global-Insight-youth-entrepreneurship-issue-brief-2019.pdf (Accessed February 22, 2022) Youth entrepreneurship, concepts and evidence, UNICEF Office of Global Insight and Policy

Arshed, N., Carter, S., & Mason, C. (2014). The ineffectiveness of entrepreneurship policy, is policy formulation to blame? *Small Business Economics*, 43(3), 639–659.

Awogbenle, A. C., & Iwuamadi, K. C. (2010). Youth unemployment, entrepreneurship development programme as an intervention mechanism. *African Journal of Business Management*, 4(6), 831–835.

Barford, A., & Coombe, R. (2019). Getting by, young people's working lives. 10.17863/CAM.39460

Barsoum, G. (2018). Youth-focused active labour market programmes in a constraining welfare regime: A qualitative reading of programmes in Egypt. *International Journal of Social Welfare*, 26(2), 168–176.

Bosma, N., & Kelley, D. (2019). Global entrepreneurship monitor 2018/2019 global report. https://www.gemconsortium.org/file/open?fileId=50213 (accessed February 18, 2022).

Bosma, N., & Levie, J. (2010). Global entrepreneurship monitor 2009 executive report. Babson College. http://dev.houdini.se/entreprenorskapsforum/wp-content/uploads/2010/02/GEM-Global-2009-Report.pdf (accessed March 1, 2022).

Brink, A., Cant, M., & Ligthelm, A. (2003, September). Problems experienced by small businesses in South Africa. In *16th Annual Conference of Small Enterprise Association of Australia and New Zealand*, 28, 1–20.

Brixiova, Z., Ncube, M., & Bicab, Z. (2014). Skills and youth entrepreneurship in Africa. Working Paper, No. 204, African Development Bank Group, Tunisia. 10.1016/j.worlddev.2014.09.027

Burchell, B. J., & Coutts, A. P. (2019). The experience of self-employment among young people, an exploratory analysis of 28 low- to middle-income countries. *American Behavioural Scientist*, 63(2), 147–165.

Bux, S., & Van Vuuren, J. (2019). The effect of entrepreneurship education programmes on the development of self-efficacy, entrepreneurial intention and predictions for entrepreneurial activity, *Acta Commercii*, 19(2), 1–13. 10.4102/ac.v19i2.615

Chetty, R., Beharry-Ramraj, A., & Gurayah, J. R. (2022). The impacts of COVID-19 on youth entrepreneurship in South Africa. *African Journal of Development Studies (formerly AFFRIKA Journal of Politics, Economics and Society)*, 2022(si1), 223–242.

Chigunta, F., Schnurr, J., James-Wilson, D., Torres, V., & Creation, J. (2005). Being "real" about youth entrepreneurship in eastern and southern Africa. *SEED Working Paper*, 72, 1–105.

Chigunta, F. J. (2002). *Youth entrepreneurship: Meeting the key policy challenges*. England: Oxford University.

Chimucheka, T. (2012). Impediments to youth entrepreneurship in rural areas of Zimbabwe. *African Journal of Business Management*, 6(38), 10389–10395.

Dawson, H. J., & Fouksman, E. (2020). Labour, laziness and distribution, work imaginaries among the South African unemployed. *Africa, the Journal of the International African Institute*, 90(2), 229–251.

De Jongh, J., & Meyer, N. (2017). An investigation into the factors affecting young people's entrepreneurial inclination: The case of selected areas in South Africa. *International Journal of Business and Management Studies*, 9(2), 69–86.

Dietrich, H., & Moller, J. (2016). Youth unemployment in Europe–business cycle and institutional effects. *International Economics and Economic Policy*, 13(1), 5–25.

Diraditsile, K., & Maphula, P. (2018). Entrepreneurship as a mechanism for addressing youth unemployment in botswana: A reality or idealism. *International Journal of Development and Sustainability*, 7(3), 836–847.

Duval, R. A., Ji, Y., & Shibata, I. (2021). Labor market reform options to boost employment in South Africa. IMF Working Paper No. 2021/165. https://www.imf.org/en/Publications/WP/Issues/2021/06/11/Labor-Market-Reform-Options-to-Boost-Employment-in-South-Africa-460735 (accessed February 27, 2022).

Dzomonda, O., & Fatoki, O. (2019). The role of institutions of higher learning towards youth entrepreneurship development in South Africa. *Academy of Entrepreneurship Journal*, 25(1), 1–11.

El-Chaarani, H. (2021). Covid-19, problems, challenges and business opportunities. *Journal of Contemporary Research in Business Administration and Economic Sciences*, 1(1), 1–4.

Ellis, K., & Williams, C. (2011). Maximising impact of youth entrepreneurship support in different contexts. London: Overseas Development Institute. https://cdn.odi.org/media/documents/7728.pdf (accessed February 5, 2022).

Fatoki, O. (2014). The entrepreneurial intention of undergraduate students in South Africa: The influences of entrepreneurship education and previous work experience. *Mediterranean Journal of Social Sciences*, 5(7), 294–299.

Fergusson, R., & Yeates, N. (2021). *Global youth unemployment, history, governance and policy*. Cheltenham: Edward Elgar Publishing.

Ferreira, J. J., Fayolle, A., Fernandes, C., & Raposo, M. (2017). Effects of Schumpeterian and kirznerian entrepreneurship on economic growth: Panel data evidence. *Entrepreneurship & Regional Development*, 29(1-2), 27–50.

Fox, L., & Gandhi, D. (2021). Youth employment in sub-Saharan Africa, progress and prospects. Brookings Africa Growth Initiative. https://media.africaportal.org/documents/21.03.24-IWOSS-Intro-paper_FINAL.pdf (accessed March 12, 2022].

Gardiner, D., Goedhuys, M., & Amador, M. G. (2021). Youth aspirations and the future of work. In J. Chacaltana & S. Dasgupta (eds), *Is the future ready for youths?* (pp. 213–229). Geneva: International Labour Organisation.

Gazi, M., & Akter, N. (2014). Youth entrepreneurship as a road show of reducing youth unemployment and sustainable economic growth: Challenges, issues and policy support in Bangladesh. *Indian Journal of Development Research and Social Action*, 10(1-2), 195–214.

Goel, A., Vohra, N., Zhang, L., & Arora, B. (2007). *Attitudes of the youth towards entrepreneurs and entrepreneurship: A cross-cultural comparison of India and China*. Ahmedabad: Indian Institute of Management, Working Papers WP2007-01-06.

Goldin, N., Hobson, M., Glick, P., Lundberg, M., & Puerto, S. (2015). *Toward solutions for youth employment: A 2015 baseline report*. Washington, DC: Solutions for Youth Employment.

Gough, K. V., & Langevang, T. (2016). *Young entrepreneurs in sub-Saharan Africa*. London: Routledge.

Grant, M. J., & Booth, A. (2009). A typology of reviews, an analysis of 14 review types and associated methodologies. *Health Information & Libraries Journal*, 26(2), 91–108.

Green, F. (2013). *Youth entrepreneurship* (background paper for the OECD centre for entrepreneurship, SMEs and local development. Paris, organisation for economic co-operation and development.

Guzzo, R. A., Jackson, S. E., & Katzell, R. A. (1987). Meta-analysis analysis. *Research in Organizational Behavior*, 9(1), 407–442.

Gwija, S. A., Eke, C. E., & Iwu, C. G. (2014). Challenges and prospects of youth entrepreneurship development in a designated community in the Western Cape, South Africa. *Journal of Economics and Behavioural Studies*, 6(1), 10–20.

Harb, Y., & Abu-Shanab, E. (2000). A descriptive framework for the field of knowledge management. *Knowledge and Information Systems*, 62(12), 4481–4508.

Hassani, R. & Khouni, R. (2013). The importance of entrepreneurship education and training

Hassani, R., & Khouni, R. (2013). The importance of entrepreneurship education and training programsin the promotion and the success of youth entrepreneurship. *Revue des Sciences Humaines*, 30, 15–121.

Herrington, M., & Kew, P. (2018). Is there a change in attitude towards the small and medium business sector in South Africa? *Global Entrepreneurship Monitor*. 1–84.

International Labor Organization. (2020). *Global employment trends for youth 2020: Technology and the future of jobs*. Geneva: International Labor Office.

Iwu, C. G., Muresherwa, G., Nchu, R., & Eresia-Eke, C. E. (2020). University students' perception of entrepreneurship as a career option. *Academia*, (20-21), 177–201.

Jacobs, E. (2014). Twelve ways to fix the youth unemployment crisis. *Massachusetts, the Brookings Institute*. https://www.brookings.edu/wp-content/uploads/2016/06/brookings_jacobsunemployment_to-print.pdf (accessed February 7, 2022).

Jeffrey, C., & Dyson, J. (2013). Zigzag capitalism, youth entrepreneurship in the contemporary global South. *Geoforum*, (49), R1–R3. https://gsdrc.org/wp-content/uploads/2016/03/JeffreyDyson_Zigzagcapitalism.pdf (accessed February 2, 2022).

Kapitsa, L. (2002). Youth entrepreneurship policies and programmes in the UNECE member states. Paper for the Youth Employment Summit Alexandria, Egypt, 7–11.

Kautonen, T., Luoto, S., & Tornikoski, E. T. (2010). Influence of work history on entrepreneurial intentions in 'prime age 'and 'third age': A preliminary study. *International Small Business Journal*, 28(6), 583–601.

Kluve, J., Puerto, S., Robalino, D., Romero, J. M., Rother, F., Stoterau, J., Weidenkaff, F. Witte, M. (2016). Do youth employment programs improve labor market outcomes? A systematic review, ruhr economic papers, RWI – leibniz-institut für wirtschaftsforschung, essen. 10.4419/86788754

Lackeus, M. (2015). Entrepreneurship in education: What, why, when how. *Entrepreneurship 360 Background Paper*. http://www.schooleducationgateway.eu/downloads/entrepreneurship/40.1%20 OECD%20(2014)_BGP_Entrepreneurship%20in%20Education.pdf

Llisterri, J. J., Kantis, H., Angelelli, P., & Tejerina, L. (2006). *Is youth entrepreneurship a necessity or an opportunity? A first exploration of household and new enterprise surveys in Latin America*. Inter-American Development Bank.

Mahlaole, S. T., & Malebana, M. J. (2021). The effects of entrepreneurship education on students entrepreneurial intentions at a South African University of Technology. *Journal of Entrepreneurship Education*, 24, 1–16.

Masenya, T. M. (2021). Promotion of digital entrepreneurship for youth employability in the post Covid-19 era. In N. Baporikar (Ed.), *Handbook of research on sustaining SMEs and entrepreneurial innovation in the post-COVID-19 era* (pp. 122–142). IGI Global. 10.4018/978-1-7998-6632-9.ch007

Matthews, C. H., & Moser, S. B. (1996). A longitudinal investigation of the impact of family background. *Journal of Small Business Management*, 34(2), 29–43.

Minola, T., Criaco, G., & Cassia, L. (2014). Are youth really different? New beliefs for old practices in entrepreneurship. *International Journal Entrepreneurship and Innovation Management*, 18(2-3), 233–259.

Miralles, F., Giones, F., & Riverola, C. (2016). Evaluating the impact of prior experience in entrepreneurial intention. *International Entrepreneurship and Management Journal*, 12(3), 791–813.

Mmakwena, M., & Moses, M. (2022). The nexus between corruption and opportunistic crimes during Covid-19 in South Africa. *Technium Social Sciences Journal*, 27, 980–994.

Modgil, S., Dwivedi, Y. K., Rana, N. P., Gupta, S., & Kamble, S. (2022). Has Covid-19 accelerated opportunities for digital entrepreneurship? *An Indian perspective. Technological Forecasting and Social Change*, 175, 121415.

Motts, N. (2000). Current youth entrepreneurship practice in Africa, does it work? An interview with Sharda Naidoo, director of the Alliance for Micro Enterprise Development Practitioners. Paper to IRDC, Canada. https://idl-bnc-idrc.dspacedirect.org/bitstream/handle/10625/32150/118503.pdf (accessed January 5, 2022).

Namatovu, R., Langevang, T., Dawa, S., & Kyejjusa, S. (2016). Youth entrepreneurship trends and policies in Uganda. In K. V. Gough & T. Langevang (Eds.), *Young entrepreneurs in sub-Saharan Africa* (pp. 18–31). London: Routledge.

Netswera, F. (2021, April). Introducing military conscription could save South Africa and its youth. https://www.news24.com/news24/columnists/guestcolumn/opinion-introducing-military-conscription-could-save-south-africa-and-its-youth-20210415 (accessed March 14, 2022).

Nightingale, P., & Coad, A. (2014). Muppets and gazelles, political and methodological biases in entrepreneurship research. *Industrial and Corporate Change*, 23(1), 113–143.

O'Higgins, N., & Verick, S. (2021). *ILO brief – an update on the youth labour market impact of the Covid-19 crisis.* https://www.ilo.org/wcmsp5/groups/public/---ed_emp/documents/briefingnote/wcms_795479.pdf (accessed February 17, 2022).

OECD. (2013). *Implications of global value chains for trade, investment, development and jobs.* Prepared for the G-20 Leaders Summit, Saint Petersburg (Russian Federation) September 2013. OECD.

OECD/European Union. (2019). Youth self-employment and entrepreneurship activities. In *The missing entrepreneurs 2019, policies for inclusive entrepreneurship.* Paris: OECD Publishing. https://www.oecd-ilibrary.org/docserver/3ec10f3b-en.pdf?expires=1645240950&id=id&accname=guest&checksum=5E4AF73FD436C091FD142E0055009263 (accessed February 15, 2022).

Olugbola, S. A. (2017). Exploring entrepreneurial readiness of youth and startup success components, entrepreneurship training as a moderator. *Journal of Innovation & Knowledge*, 2(3), 155–171.

Othman, M. N., Ghazali, E., & Sung, Y. S. (2006). Graduate versus non-graduate entrepreneurs in urban Malaysia, some insights into entrepreneurial personality, company and family background differences. *Journal for International Business and Entrepreneurship Development*, 3(1-2), 57–76.

Philip, K. (2021). OP-ED, the presidential employment stimulus, commitment a crucial and catalytic part of the wider economic recovery. Daily Maverick. https://www.dailymaverick.co.za/article/2021-02-09-the-presidential-employment-stimulus-commitment-a-crucial-and-catalytic-part-of-the-wider-economic-recovery (accessed February 20, 2022).

Pinet, M., Sanyu, P., & Youn, A. (2021). Advancing youth-centred digital ecosystems in Africa in a post-Covid-19 world. London: Overseas Development Institute. https://cdn.odi.org/media/documents/digisoc-yf_youth-centred_digital_ecosystems_170321_FINAL.pdf (accessed March 10, 2022).

Pompa, C. (2013). How to tailor youth entrepreneurship programmes for success? [online] *The Guardian.* https://www.theguardian.com/global-development-professionals-network/2013/aug/16/context-measuring-youth-enterprise-entrepreneurship (accessed January 24, 2022).

Purwati, A. A., Hamzah, M. L., & Suhermin, S. (2020). Entrepreneurship education and its impact on student's intention to entrepreneurship. *Revista Espacios*, 41(9), 4. https://www.revistaespacios.com/a20v41n09/a20v41n09p04.pdf (accessed February 1, 2022).

Rajak, D., & Dolan, C. (2021). Aspiring minds, a generation of entrepreneurs in the making. *Sociological Research Online*, 1–20. 10.1177/13607804211042905

Rambe, P., & Mosweunyane, L. (2017). A poverty-reduction oriented perspective to small business development in South Africa: A human capabilities approach. *African Journal of Science, Technology, Innovation and Development*, 9(3), 289–302.

Scott, M. G., & Twomey, D. F. (1988). The long-term supply of entrepreneurs, students' career aspirations in relation to entrepreneurship. *Journal of Small Business Management*, 26(4), 5–13.

Shane, S. (2009). Why encouraging more people to become entrepreneurs is bad public policy? *Small Business Economics*, 33(2), 141–149.

Sharma, L., & Madan, P. (2014). Effect of individual factors on youth entrepreneurship – a study of Uttarakhand State, India. *Journal of Global Entrepreneurship Research*, 2(3), 1–17.

Sibanda, L., & Iwu, C. G. (2021). The academic journey of entrepreneurship students in higher education institutions – the systems theory approach. *Education, Modern Discourses*, (4), 135–145. 10.37472/2617-3107-2021-4-13

Sieger, P., Fueglistaller, U., & Zellweger, T. (2016). Student entrepreneurship 2016, insights from 50 countries. https://boris.unibe.ch/89857/1/GUESSS_2016_INT_Report_final.pdf (accessed February 12, 2022).

Sieger, P., Fueglistaller, U., Zellweger, T., & Braun, I. (2018). Global student entrepreneurship 2018, insights from 54 countries. *St. Gallen/Bern, KMU-HSG/IMU.* Retrieved from www.guesssurvey.org/resources/PDF_InterReports/GUESSS_Global_2018.pdf

Statistics SA. (2021). Quarterly labour force survey (QLFS), quarter 1, media release. Pretoria, Stats SA.

Stam, E., Hartog, C., Stel, A., & Thurik, R. (2011). Ambitious entrepreneurship, high-growth firms and macroeconomic growth. *The dynamics of entrepreneurship: Evidence from global entrepreneurship monitor data*, pp. 231–250. 10.1093/acprof:oso/9780199580866.003.0011

The Kauffman Index. (2017). Startup activity, national trends. www.KauffmanIndex.org

The Prince's Trust. (2019). The young entrepreneurship review, a report from the prince's trust 2019–2021.

Thrikawala, S. (2011). The determinants of entrepreneurial intention among academics in Sri Lanka. *International Proceedings of Economics Development & Research*, 4, 454–468.

Townsend, M. (2021). Effects of Covid-19 on youth entrepreneurs. https://www.cipe.org/blog/2021/07/22/effects-of-covid-19-on-youth-entrepreneurs/ (accessed February 11, 2022).

Tradingeconomics.com. n.d. South Africa Youth Unemployment Rate. (2021). https://tradingeconomics.com/south-africa/youth-unemployment-rate#,~,text=Youth%20Unemployment%20Rate%20in%20South%20Africa%20averaged%2054.21%20percent%20from,the%20fourth%20quarter%20of%202014 (accessed February 17, 2022).

Tubadji, A., Dietrich, H., Angelis, V., Haas, A., & Schels, B. (2021). Fear-of-failure and cultural persistence in youth entrepreneurship, comparative analysis, Greece versus Germany. *Journal of Small Business and Entrepreneurship*, 33(5), 513–538.

Turton, N., & Herrington, M. (2013). Global entrepreneurship monitor South African 2012 report. Cape Town, Development Unit for New Enterprise, University of Cape Town.

United Nations Youth. (n.d.). Definition of youth. https://www.un.org/esa/socdev/documents/youth/fact-sheets/youth-definition.pdf (accessed February 4, 2022).

United Nations, Department of Economic and Social Affairs. (2018). *World youth report, Youth and the 2030 agenda for sustainable development*. United Nations Publications. https://www.un.org/development/desa/youth/wp-content/uploads/sites/21/2018/12/WorldYouthReport-2030Agenda.pdf (accessed February 20, 2022).

White, S., & Kenyon, P. (2001). *Enterprise-based youth employment policies, strategies and programmes initiatives for the development of enterprise action and strategies*. Working paper, in focus programme on skills, knowledge and employability. Geneva: ILO.

World Bank. (2021). *South Africa economic update, edition 13, building back better from Covid-19 with a special focus on jobs*. World Bank.

5 Smart Township Digital Framework: Growing the Township Economy Post-COVID-19 Pandemic

Motshedisi Mathibe, Tonderai Muchenje, and Moshe T. Masonta

Introduction

Township economy plays a vital role in eradicating poverty, reducing unemployment, and contributing to the country's gross domestic product (GDP) (Charman, 2017; Udimal & Biyase, 2021). Despite being dominated by the informal sector, the townships are considered to contribute about 30% of the GDP in South Africa (Rogerson, 2016). The township economy referred to the formal and informal small, micro, and medium enterprises (small businesses) and markets based in the townships (Rogerson, 2019). For the purposes of this chapter, a township is defined as a densely populated settlement, dominated by black people, located in the outskirts of the city centres and far from commercial and industrial activities (Rogerson, 2018; Siyakhana, 2020). The townships are characterised by poverty, high unemployment rate, and poor or lack of reliable basic infrastructure, making them the top priority for inclusive growth and development (Başbay et al., 2018; Volschenk et al., 2021).

The emergence of the coronavirus (COVID-19) pandemic during the first quarter of 2020 had devastating impact on the townships (Omonona et al., 2021). While some small businesses, both formal and informal, may no longer return to any form of operation, the advent of the COVID-19 pandemic has fast-tracked the need to pivot and transform businesses faster than expected. In most cases, pivoting would require the small business to transform to digitally serve its new market post COVID-19 pandemic. The availability and accessibility of information and communication technology (ICT), telecommunication and digital infrastructure in the townships are crucial to support, enable and fast-track the digital transformation within the townships (Rashid, 2020). Furthermore, digital transformation requires small businesses to become actively involved in the digital economy, introducing a paradigm shift from the traditional analogous model (e.g. cash-based business) to a digital business model (e.g. e-commerce).

The chapter starts off by providing a background on the township economy, its challenges and the types of businesses operating in this

DOI: 10.4324/9781003216469-5

economy. This is followed by a brief introduction of the smart township and the outline of key elements of digitisation when developing a smart township. A systematic literature review method is applied to help critique to the township's current situation, followed by an assessment of the context. Next, the proposed smart digital township framework is discussed before concluding the chapter with recommendations to the policymakers and the township economy ecosystem. This chapter builds on our initial paper titled "assessing the effectiveness of 4IR strategy on South African Township Economy: smart township perspective", and was presented during the virtual international conference on Management, Business, Administration and Legal Initiatives (MBALI) in 2021 (Mathibe et al., 2021).

Literature review

The township economy and the effect of the coronavirus pandemic

Development of the township economy remains one of the key focus areas for the South African government (Udimal & Biyase, 2021). However, there are still inequalities when it comes to economic opportunities, especially the small businesses in the townships which are often excluded from growth benefits and constrained in their ability to contribute to the development. Despite the government's efforts in setting out strategies to channel resources and create opportunities for township businesses (Charman, 2017), an economic gap remains. Meanwhile, the informal sector is the main contributor to the South African township economy (Charman et al., 2020), and makes up 30% of the township economy (Statistics South Africa, 2017). Between the 2016 and 2017 financial years, the South African informal sector employed at least 2 689 000 people, contributing between 60% and 70% of jobs in the country (Statistics South Africa, 2017). Furthermore, the South African National Development Plan (NDP) sees the informal sector creating between 1.2 and 2 million new jobs by 2030 (Statistics South Africa, 2017; United Nations Development Programme, 2021). Therefore, the informal sector is viewed as one of the primary drivers of a country's economy (Mintah & Darkwah, 2018).

It was observed that most of those who operate in the informal sector are necessity entrepreneurs often relegated from the formal sector into the informal sector (Alrawadieh & Alrawadieh, 2018; Rogerson, 2018). Furthermore, a study by Simanis (2013) found that the cost of remaining informal is relatively higher for some businesses. Despite all these, several scholars argue that there is a growing need for well-designed policies to enable and support the township economy (Bozhikin et al., 2019; Rogerson, 2018).

The COVID-19 pandemic affected the small businesses in three significant ways: (1) by directly changing production and demand (Narula, 2020), (2) by creating supply chain and market disruption, and (3) by its financial impact and financial markets, leading to limitations in cash reserves and other vital resources (Spicer, 2020). As a result, many small businesses had to close or operate with a reduced workforce (Asad & Kashif, 2021). Reduced staff and businesses closing led to a 40% decline in active employment (Jain et al., 2020), which created a financial problem and brought into question issues of sustainability for both the small business owners and the 1.6 billion employees within the sector (International Labour Organization, 2020; ILO Monitor: COVID-19 and the world of work, 2020). This background shows the need for identifying ways that can help sustain township economy post the pandemic (Msomi et al., 2021).

Digitisation, digitalisation, and digital transformation

Digitisation and digitalisation play a vital role in digitally transforming businesses that want to take advantage of the fourth industrial revolution (4IR) benefits (Averina et al., 2021; Zhao et al., 2020). As depicted in Figure 5.1, digitisation is the first stage in the digital transformation as it aims at converting the analogue and paper-based documents into electronic formats that will be usable in a computer system (Mathibe et al., 2021). Digitalisation is the second stage of digital transformation. It focuses on transforming the non-digital traditional operations and processes by using digital technologies such as smartphones, e-commerce, and social media, and many more digital technologies. The final stage for digital business is to digital transformation, where a firm optimises its business operations and processes, thereby becoming competitive and constantly adapting new innovative ways to stay relevant to the needs of its customers.

The development of digital technologies continues to change how the society, businesses, and technology interact (Van Veldhoven & Vanthienen, 2021). Such changes vary from customer relationships, connectivity, offerings, communication, marketing, support, payment, to name just a few, as described in van Veldhoven and Vanthienen (2021).

Figure 5.1 The process of digital transformation, starting with digitisation followed by digitalisation.

Source: Authors' compilation.

Digital technologies can be described as a range of electronic tools, systems, devices, and resources that generate, store, or process data using various types of hardware and software (Tulinayo et al., 2018). Gharbi et al. (2021) outlined digital technologies to consist of all electronic devices, automatic systems, and technological resources that generate, process, or store information such as smartphones, websites, blockchain technology, drones and missiles, cryptocurrency, 5G mobile networks, artificial intelligence, cloud computing, voice interfaces or chatbots, robotics, gadgets, e-books, and video streaming.

The impact of these various digital technologies has changed businesses and societies. These digital technologies challenge the entrepreneurs to start asking these questions: what product the business sells, how businesses sell their products, and what competency the business needs to sell its products effectively (Opute, 2020; Ritter & Pedersen, 2020). Therefore, this chapter aims to influence the township entrepreneur's mindset to adopt new concepts to their business to stay relevant and survive in the ever-changing a digital economy characterised by disruptive technologies and possible future pandemics (Zhao et al., 2020).

The smart township

The concept of the smart township can be achieved through the digitalisation of township residential dwellings (Mathibe et al., 2021). These residential dwellings can be turned into smart homes that are connected via various ICTs such as Wi-Fi or fibre-to-home connectivity, Geographical Positioning System (GPS), closed-circuit television (CCTV), Internet of Things (IoT), and radio frequency identification (RFID) (Khatoun & Zeadally, 2016; Nallathiga et al., 2021). These smart homes are the primary components that could give rise to the smart township. Within the smart townships and smart cities, this is deployment of smart grids, smart transport systems, communication networks, and connectivity to better the living conditions of its citizens.

According to Zhao et al. (2020), the smart grids are aimed at improving smart townships with various benefits, such as the following:

- Smart education using remote online learning with smart classrooms.
- Safety and security using 24/7 surveillance using CCTV cameras.
- Smart environment and smart transportation, which includes intelligent traffic management systems to reduce traffic congestions, smart lighting systems to manage public energy usage, and advanced air pollution monitoring systems.
- Smart energy using smart grids that manage renewable and non-renewable energy.

In South Africa, the smart townships proposition is to redress the various social ills of the past, such as the social and economic inclusion, digital divide, and better-equipped small businesses to achieve sustainable competitive advantage post-COVID-19 pandemic (Ahmed & Gillwald, 2020).

Khatoun and Zeadally (2016) further outline that smart township become the base through which smart cities will be built. In principle, the smart township consists of interconnected smart homes, while the smart cities interconnect smart townships. Based on the discussion above, smart townships demand digital entrepreneurs where their businesses are digitally transformed to supply goods and services.

Digitisation and the smart township

The realisation of digitalisation for smart townships depends on the availability and accessibility of the ICT and digital infrastructure. Unfortunately, the South African township setup does not only disable the economic participation of township communities, but it continues to exclude these townships from gaining adequate access to ICT services such as high-speed broadband. For instance, providing fibre-to-the-home (FTTH) in townships remains a challenge in South Africa (Ntsandeni, 2018). It is partially for these reasons (among others) that the digital infrastructure in most South African townships remain in dire condition and require a substantial investment to be optimal to support the digital economy and the realisation of the South African fourth industrial revolution (4IR), as recommended in the Presidential Commission on 4IR report (Presidential Commission on 4IR, 2020). Such digital infrastructure investments will ensure ubiquitous and inclusive broadband connectivity to the townships and underserved rural areas.

On the other hand, deployment of the fifth generation (5G) mobile networks to the townships remain one of the most feasible options given the proximity of townships to the city centres, dense population and the speed of deploying wireless networks compared to fibre (where trenches are to be dug). In his opinion piece, Masonta (2021) argued that South Africa was ready for 5G deployment, which is crucial in narrowing the digital divide.

To support the township economy, the South African government, more specifically at the provincial level should partner with the business and communities to focus on the three fundamental pillars identified within the Presidential Commission on 4IR, namely, (1) digital infrastructure, (2) human capital, and (3) coordination, engagement, and monitoring. These three pillars are believed to be the primary enablers to building a South African smart township economy successfully. This view was also echoed by Maisiri and van Dyk (2019), who noted that government and business partnership, skilling, and infrastructure resources are lacking in South Africa, yet they are essential for the realisation of the 4IR readiness. Hence, the government needs to partner with big corporates and small businesses in building digital infrastructure, upskilling small businesses with digital skills and eventually digitising the townships to become a smart township.

It is evident from the literature that the township economy was significantly impacted negatively by the emergence of COVID-19 (Singh et al., 2021; Zizzamia et al., 2020). Majority of small businesses from the township relied on a conventional method such as (1) brick-and-mortar and (2) the exchange of hard cash. In addition, these businesses were found unprepared for the pandemic. Hence, they were the most affected. Many of these businesses closed down and could not cope with the government regulations to curb the spread of coronavirus. As a result of these findings, the articles reviewed led to digitisation and digitalisation as a solution to help the small businesses to navigate during and post-COVID-19 pandemic (Averina et al., 2021; van Veldhoven & Vanthienen, 2021).

Research methodology

Methodologically, a qualitative research approach was used. A two-phase approach to the investigation of the phenomenon was conducted. Firstly, a systematic literature review (SLR) of the role of digital transformation within the township economy forms the basis for further investigations. Second, the findings of the SLR were used to assess possible digitisation frameworks suitable for building the smart township.

The literature review for the research focused on township economy and township businesses within Gauteng, South Africa. Therefore, the best way to understand the concept of the smart township from the perspective of digitisation and entrepreneurship is to undertake a systematic literature review based on methodological precedence (Kitchenham et al., 2009; Xiao & Watson, 2019). Kitchenham et al. (2009) defined the three distinct steps for conducting a SLR as planning the review, conducting the review, and reporting on the review.

This SLR first defined the smart township problem regarding digitisation and entrepreneurship. The journals used in the system literature review search were sourced from major journal repositories such as Ebscohost, Science Direct, Emerald, Google Scholar, Scopus (Xiao & Watson, 2019).

The specific journal included for synthesis were *South African Journal on Industrial Engineering*, *Theoretical and Empirical Research in Urban Management*, *Management*, *Association for Computing Machinery*, *South African Journal of Information Management*, *Asian Journal Social Sciences and Legal Studies*, *International Journal of Educational Technology in Higher Education*, *Information and Software Technology*, *Journal of Cleaner Production*, *Economic Systems*, *Springer*, *Tourism Management Perspectives*, *South African Journal of Economic and Management Sciences*, and *Journal of Planning Education and Research*. The search limitation on journal articles was based on their extensive peer-review mechanisms contributing to the body of knowledge. Various combinations of words were used to form a search criterion while narrowing the body of work in conducting the SLR similar to the approach used in (Mathibe et al., 2021). The search criteria used are outlined as follows; "digitise", "digitisation", "digitalisation", "digital", "digitisation and/or digitalisation" were used to gather literature on the difference between digitisation and digitalisation. Given that this research focused on entrepreneurship and digitisation in the smart township economy, further search criteria were used to collect information on the correlation between digitisation and entrepreneurship (Mathibe et al., 2021).

The search criteria adopted in this chapter included the phrases such as "impact of digitisation on entrepreneurship", "digital entrepreneurship", and "digitisations AND/OR entrepreneurship". The search also added phrases such as "coronavirus", "COVID-19", "township small businesses", "formal businesses", "informal business", "township", "township economy", AND/OR "informal economy", and "formal economy". The literature search was on the word concept of the smart township. As a result, the search criteria employed included "smart township", AND/OR "entrepreneurs", "smart township" or "digital entrepreneurs", "digital economy", digital entrepreneurs AND/OR "smart township", AND "digital economy", AND/OR "businesses".

The search was conducted from October 18, 2021 to January 12, 2022. The search period on the literature was limited to between 2006 and 2022. Therefore, research articles published before 2006 were omitted. Moreover, the search only included articles written in the English language. Finally, the full-text articles were extracted and then further synthesised, analysed, and reported in the recommendation for future research opportunities.

The processes used in the literature search and evaluation for inclusion in our study are well defined by Xiao and Watson (2019). The articles initially searched based on the search criteria were 265 articles. Then, the total articles excluded for duplication were 105 articles and 96 articles with only titles and abstracts. After that, 37 articles were excluded for eligibility, and, finally, only 27 articles were used for synthesis and final reporting.

The proposed solution: smart township digital framework

Given the current challenges presented by the COVID-19 pandemic, the government may need to acknowledge the growth of the informal sector of the township economy and identify strategies to support this sector. The smart township should not be a copy-and-paste form of the smart suburb; it must be digitised in its original form without being diluted. Core to the realisation of the smart township is the digital transformation. When digitally transformed, businesses in the township can become digitally competitive and participate in the digital economy. The ICT and related digital technological innovation continue to evolve. This innovation can support the realisation of a digital economy for all. As witnessed during the COVID-19 pandemic, digitally transformed businesses benefited from the endless opportunities that disrupted the traditional (non-digital) businesses while intensifying their competition and increasing customer expectations (Komninos & Mora, 2018).

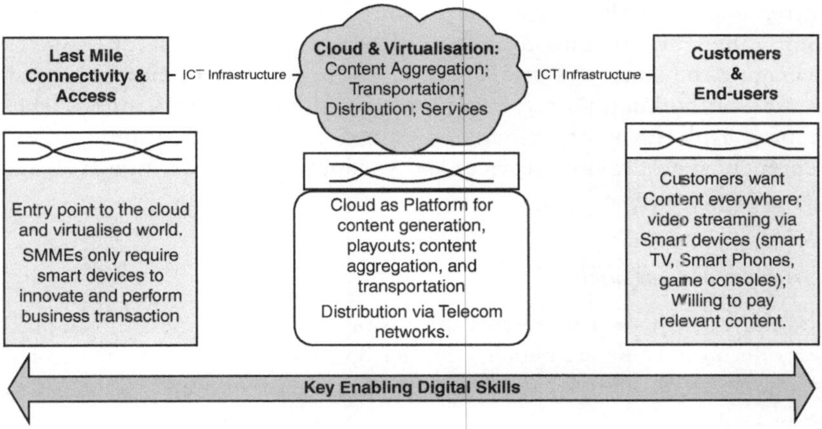

Figure 5.2 The smart township digital framework.

Source: Authors' compilation.

This chapter proposes a smart digital township framework to support the digital transformation of the township economy. The proposed framework is developed to better prepare the township small businesses with a creative and innovative way to survive future pandemics and be equipped to participate in the digital economy. As shown in Figure 5.2, the framework is built on four components: (1) last-mile connectivity, (2) cloud and virtualisation, (3) customers and end-users, and (4) key enabling digital skills. The next sub-sections present each component of the proposed framework.

Last-mile connectivity

The first component represents the entry point for digital entrepreneurs. It represents a last-mile connectivity or access network to connect the small businesses to the cloud and the rest of the world. This could take the form of the fifth generation (5G) mobile network, Wi-Fi network, fibre optic network or even satellite. Therefore, anyone with access to telecommunications or ICT infrastructure and having a bankable business model can become an entrepreneur in the digital economy. Without access to such infrastructure, it becomes difficult for small businesses to participate in the digital economy.

Cloud and virtualisation

The middle component of the diagram represents the cloud and virtualisation provided to the entrepreneurs as a service. This means that the township entrepreneurs do not have to worry about the infrastructure.

This will depend on the type of business such entrepreneurs are running. Entrepreneurs with innovative business models can use the high-computing infrastructure to create, develop, and sell their offerings by leveraging the cloud and virtualisation. For instance, if an entrepreneur is focused on building an access network or an end-to-end network, they become a player on the cloud. For simplicity, we shall assume an entrepreneur who provides services and products over an existing ICT and digital infrastructure.

Customers and end-users

The third component represents the customers and end-users to the business offerings. These are people or other businesses who are willing to pay for the services offered by the entrepreneurs. For example, an end-user could be a household in the township who uses a smartphone to stream a live YouTube video of a concert hosted within the same or neighbouring township and produced by a local entrepreneur. The proliferation of smart devices means that many end-users are digitally ready to participate in the township digital economy. Affordability of broadband data, combined with the attractiveness of the local content, will drive the willingness to pay by most customers.

Key enabling digital skills

Cutting across these three components are key enabling digital skills to be acquired by small businesses and other key stakeholders. Digital and ICT capabilities and skills are needed to implement the value chain (Magwentshu et al., 2019). To remain competitive and relevant, township entrepreneurs should quickly embrace the digital economy, which requires developing new digitalisation skills. The framework identifies digital skills training and upskilling township small businesses to reposition and align themselves within the smart township ecosystems (Mathibe et al., 2021).

Benefits of implementing the proposed framework to the township businesses

Enhanced online shopping experience

The COVID-19 pandemic fast-tracked the infiltration of online shopping due to the strict regulations prohibiting movement by people. However, to most townships, online shopping remains a challenge due to some factors, including security for the courier vehicles, lack of accurate street addresses and poor access or unaffordability to the internet. The smart township digitisation framework could assist in addressing these challenges using drone delivery technologies. Drone delivery would encourage township communities to enjoy online shopping like their counterparts in the suburbs. Nevertheless, if the community adopts technology as a solution that works for them, it is far less likely to happen. In addition, other options could be considered to address the safety issues. For example, delivery points could be centralised within walking distance per section of the township near the reach of the community members.

A digitally transformed company that thrived during the pandemic: the Drip Footwear (Zwane et al., 2022)

Mr. Lekau Sehoana, launched his online business, Drip Footwear, just before the pandemic hit the world. Sehoana sold his first 600 pairs of footwear (sneakers) from his car's trunk within six weeks. Within the next four months, he manufactured and sold 1 200 pairs of footwear, based on the high demand of locally made sneakers. After realising that his sneakers were in a high demand, he started the process of formally establishing and launching his footwear business. It was during that same time that the COVID-19 pandemic was detected in South Africa, and the business world was faced with great uncertainty. Sehoana had to reconsider his business approach and how he was going to launch the business, grow the brand's visibility, and decide on the mode of operation.

In March 2020, South Africa was placed under alert level 5 lockdown (Government Gazette, 2020), which restricted most businesses from operating inclusive of Sehoana's business. He resorted to online, where he used social media platform to market his business and for his consumers to place orders. He would then deliver the products to customer in person or corriere, depending on the location of the customer. Despite the extremely severe lockdown regulations in place at the time, in May 2021, Sehoana had already managed to open 11 stores in reputable malls and sold multiple thousands of his sneakers.

Discussions and recommendations

The proposed smart township digital framework calls for collaboration among crucial role players in the township economy: entrepreneurs (business), government (local, provincial, and national level), and end-users (communities). This section discusses key recommendations for a successful implementation of the proposed framework.

An enabling environment

The South African government levels (local, provincial, and national) need to create enabling business-friendly environment for the township small businesses to thrive. A business-friendly environment would mean that the government prioritises building the business parks in the townships. These business parks would be entirely digitally transformed and connected to enable the effectiveness of small businesses operations. Creating these spaces in partnership with the communities fosters a sense of ownership and community stewardship. This would assist with infrastructure security and create a safer environment for the townships to thrive. The benefit of the business parks in the provision of *connectivity hubs*, which are set up with high-speed broadband access and datacentres with powerful computing capabilities to support cloud services.

A connectivity hub would offer training facilities and courses to upskill the entrepreneurs and the township communities related digital skills. Such will require a partnership between local government, small businesses, and large corporates who want to run such initiatives as part of their enterprise development and socioeconomic investment programmes. These centres could offer training on everything from business skills to software coding and intellectual property at various levels. Through these connectivity hubs, township innovators will have easy access to the local cloud and virtualisation capabilities provided to the small businesses as a service. Thus, the business parks could create bridges between township entrepreneurs and corporates based away from the townships.

Access to ICT and digital infrastructure

The availability of the ICT and digital infrastructure in the townships is essential to effectively support a digital transformed business and economy. There is a need for the government to ensure that there are clear policies and regulation which will enable businesses (big and small) to deploy ICT infrastructure to the township to enable a digital economy. For example, through infrastructure, businesses could create Wi-Fi hotspots to provide connectivity in the townships and allow township entrepreneurs to build networks with communities. Moreover, the availability of ICT infrastructure makes it even easy for entrepreneurs to compete at national and international platforms without the need for capital investment into infrastructure. In this chapter, telecommunications infrastructure, digital infrastructure, and ICT infrastructure are used interchangeably as they refer to the same infrastructure.

Financing

More attention is needed in financing the township small businesses (Madichie et al., 2020). For example, rather than directly funding entrepreneurs, the government could upskill the entrepreneur towards the digital economy and train and educate them on protecting their intellectual property. In doing so, entrepreneurs would be able to finance and grow their businesses, and contribute to the future development of the smart township and digital economy.

Conclusion

The current economic structure of South Africa has not changed from the pre-democracy setting, where black dwellings (commonly known as townships) are located far away, at the outskirts of the big towns and cities of economic hubs. This chapter argues for the need to support township small businesses to become digitally transformed so they can bounce back post COVID-19 pandemic, and to be resilient against future pandemics. The chapter proposes a smart township digital framework which is built on four components: (1) last-mile connectivity, (2) cloud and virtualisation, (3) customers and end-users, and (4) key enabling digital skills.

As witnessed during the COVID-19 pandemic, digitally transformed businesses benefited from the endless opportunities that disrupted the traditional (non-digital) businesses while intensifying their competition and increasing customer expectations. The chapter used South Africa as a starting point to create smart townships. The proposed model can be tested in the townships of Gauteng Province (the densely populated South Africa the province with many townships), and if successful, can be replicated in other African countries and beyond. Therefore, the proposed smart township digital framework would enable any township entrepreneur, with access to the digital infrastructure and having a bankable business model, to contribute to the growth of informal and formal small businesses and be part of the growing digital economy.

Further work includes promoting the framework to key stakeholders in order to get support for testing or implementing the framework within the Gauteng Province, South Africa. There is a need to identify the factors causing a slow adoption of digital transformation from the township entrepreneurs' point of view. Gathering of more information and experiences from township entrepreneurs, with the aim of refining the proposed model, will also form part of our future work. Further studies should be conducted to find the most suitable, sustainable, and appealing funding models to support the small businesses in the townships. More specifically, the immediate steps are to enhance the framework by piloting in one area with selected SMMEs with the aim of scaling it within and beyond South Affrica. This will be followed by influencing policy direction through engaging government at different levels.

References

Ahmed, S., & Gillwald, A. (2020). Smart townships will build smarter cities (policy brief 2020, no. 3). Research ICT Africa. https://researchictafrica.net/publication/smart-townships-will-build-smarter-cities/

Alrawadieh, Z., & Alrawadieh, Z. (2018). Exploring entrepreneurship in the sharing accommodation sector: Empirical evidence from a developing country. *Tourism Management Perspectives*, 28, 179–188.

Asad, M., & Kashif, M. (2021). Unveiling success factors for small and medium enterprises during COVID-19 pandemic. *Arab Journal of Basic and Applied Sciences*, 28(1), 187–194. 10.1080/25765299.2020.1830514

Averina, T., Barkalov, S., Fedorova, I., & Poryadina, V. (2021). Impact of digital technologies on the company's business model. *E3S Web Conference*, 244, 1–10. 10.1051/e3sconf/202124410002.

Başbay, M. M., Elgin, C., & Torul, O. (2018). Socio-demographics, political attitudes, and informal sector employment: A cross-country analysis. *Economic Systems*, 42(4), 556–568. 10.1016/j.ecosys.2018.03.003

Bozhikin, I., Macke, J., & da Costa, L. F. (2019). The role of government and key non-state actors in social entrepreneurship: A systematic literature review. *Journal of Cleaner Production*, 226, 730–747. 10.1016/j.jclepro.2019.04.076

Charman, A. (2017). Micro-enterprise predicament in township economic development: Evidence from ivory park and Tembisa. *South African Journal of Economic and Management Sciences*, 20(1), a1617. https://hdl.handle.net/10520/EJC-8b88af6a3

Charman, A., Petersen, L., & Govender, T. (2020). *Township economy: People, spaces and practices*. South Africa: HSRC Press.

Gharbi, I., Daoud, Y., & Kammoun, A. (2021). The digitalization in the COVID-19 era: A review, synthesis, and challenges – mitigating the impact of COVID-19 via digitalization, handbook of research on interdisciplinary perspectives on the threats and impacts of pandemics, Pages: 21. 10.4018/978-1-7998-8674-7.ch015

Government Gazette (2020). Department of Co-operative Governance and Traditional Affairs no 43258/3, Disaster Management Act 2002: Regulations Issued in terms of Section 27(2) of the Disaster Management Act 2002. chrome-extension://efaidnbmnnnibpcajpcglclefindmkaj/https://www.gov.za/sites/default/files/gcis_document/202004/43258rg11098gon480s.pdf

International Labour Organization (2020). ILO Standards and COVID-19 (coronavirus) https://respect.international/ilo-standards-and-covid-19-coronavirus/ (retrieved October, 10, 2022).

ILO Monitor: COVID-19 and the world of work (2020). Fourth Edition: Updated Estimates and Analysis, International Labour Organization, 2020. https://respect.international/%E2%80%8Ailo-monitor-covid-19-and-the-world-of-work-fourth-edition-updated-estimates-and-analysis/

Jain, R., Budlender, J., Zizzamia, R., & Bassier, I. (2020). The labor market and poverty impacts of COVID-19 in South Africa. Working Paper. http://hdl.handle.net/11090/980

Khatoun, R., & Zeadally, S. (2016). Smart cities: Concepts, architectures, research opportunities. *Communications of the ACM*, 59(8), 46–57. 10.1145/2858789

Kitchenham, B., Brereton, O. P., Budgen, D., Turner, M., Bailey, J., & Linkman, S. (2009). Systematic literature reviews in software engineering: A systematic literature review. *Information and Software Technology*, 51(1), 7–15, ISSN 0950-5849, 10.1016/j.infsof.2008.09.009

Komninos, N., & Mora, L. (2018). Exploring the big picture of smart city research. *Scienze Regionali*, 17(1), 15–38. 10.14650/88815

Madichie, N. O., Nkamnebe, A. D., & Ekanem, I. U. (2020). Marketing in the informal economy: An entrepreneurial perspective and research agenda. *Entrepreneurship Marketing*, 412–428.

Magwentshu, N., Rajagopaul, A., Chui, M., & Singh, A. (2019). *The future of work in South Africa: Digitisation, productivity and job creation*. Johannesburg: Mckinsey & Company.

Maisiri, W., & van Dyk, L. (2019). Industry 4.0 readiness assessment for South African industries. *South African Journal on Industrial Engineering*, 30(3), Pretoria Nov. 2019, 10.7166/30-3-2231

Masonta, M. T. (2021, March 4). Yes, SA is ready for 5G, Cape Argus. https://bit.ly/3mQVcxh

Mathibe, M., Mochenje, T., & Masonta, M. T. (2021). Assessing the effectiveness of 4IR strategy on South African township economy: Smart township perspective. In Mbali Conference 2021 Proceedings (pp. 103–120).

Mintah, S., & Darkwah, S. (2018). Drivers of informal sector participation of small and medium enterprises in Ghana. *Scientia Agriculturae Bohemica*, 49(1), 60–67. 10.2478/sab-2018-0010

Msomi, T.S., Olarewaju, O.M., & Ngcobo, X. (2021). Sustaining South African small and medium-sized enterprises through monetary access and literacy in the COVID-19 ERA. *Folia Oeconomica Stetinensia*, 21(2), 57–75. 10.2478/foli-2021-0016

Nallathiga, R., Tewari, K., Saboo, A., & Varghese, S. (2021). From ROM satellite townships to smart townships: Evolution of township development in Pune, India. *Theoretical and Empirical Research in Urban Management*, 16(1), 86–106. https://www.proquest.com/scholarly-journals/satellite-townships-smart-evolution-township/docview/2491618282/se-2

Narula, R. (2020). Policy opportunities and challenges from the COVID-19 pandemic for economies with large informal sectors. *Journal of International Business Policy*, 3(3), 302–310. https://doi.org/10.1057/s42214-020-00059-5

Ntsandeni, A. (2018). Innovation-based competitive differentiation amongst South African fibre to the home (FTTH) operators (Doctoral dissertation). University of the Witwatersrand. Johannesburg. South Africa.

Omonona, S., Oni, O., & Oluwole, O. J. (2021). COVID-19 pandemic and the South African township economy: A focus on King William's Town, Eastern Cape, South Africa. *Harvard Deusto Business, Research* , X(2), 370–381. 10.48132/hdbr.356

Opute, A. P. (2020). Small and medium enterprises marketing: Innovation and sustainable economic growth perspective (chapter 2). In *Entrepreneurship marketing: Principles and practice of SME marketing*. Routledge Publishers.

Presidential Commission on 4IR. (2020). Report of the Presidential Commission on the 4th industrial revolution. South Africa, Gazette No. 43834. https://www.gov.za/documents/report-presidential-commission-4th-industrial-revolution-23-oct-2020-0000

Rashid, M. H. (2020). Prospects of digital financial services in Bangladesh in the context of fourth industrial revolution. *Asian Journal Social Sciences and Legal Studies*, 2(5), 88–95.

Ritter, T., & Pedersen, C. L. (2020). Digitization capability and the digitalization of business models in business-to-business firms: Past, present, and future. *Industrial Marketing Management*, 86, 180–190.

Rogerson, C. M. (2016). South Africa's informal economy: Reframing debates in national policy. *Local Economy*, 31(1-2), 172–186.

Rogerson, C. M. (2018). Informal sector city tourism: Cross-border shoppers in Johannesburg. *Journal of Tourism and Geosites*, 22(2), 381–392.

Rogerson, C. M. (2019). The economic development of South Africa's townships. In J. Knight, & C. Rogerson (Eds.), *The geography of South Africa. World regional geography book series*. Cham: Springer. 10.1007/978-3-319-94974-1_20

Simanis, E. (2013). Bringing bottom of the pyramid into business focus. A planet for life: Reducing inequalities–a sustainable development challenge, 217–228.

Siyakhana. (2020). Assessment of the viability and potential of township economies for a municipality, lgseta, creating greater impact. Accessed February 14, 2022, https://cdn.lgseta.co.za/resources/research_and_reports/2019%20%E2%80%93%202020%20RESEARCH%20PROJECTS/RESEARCH%20REPORT%20-%20TOWNSHIP%20ECONOMY.pdf

Spicer, A. (2020). Organizational culture and COVID-19. *Journal of Management Studies*, 57: 1737–1740. https://doi.org/10.1111/joms.12625

Statistics South Africa. (2017). National development plan 2030-our future-make-make it work. *The Idea & Craft Collective Print & binding: Sherino Printers.*

Tulinayo, F., Ssentume, P., & Najjuma, R. (2018). Digital technologies in resource-constrained higher institutions of learning: A study on students' acceptance and usability. *International Journal of Educational Technology in Higher Education*, 15(36). 10.1186/s41239-018-0117-y

Udimal, T. B., & Biyase, M. (2021). Identifying the binding constraints of the township economy of South Africa. *The Journal of Developing Areas*, 55(4), 455–464.

United Nations Development Programme. (2021). The impact of COVID-19 on micro and informal businesses: South Africa. Accessed February 14, 2022, from http://www.dsbd.gov.za/sites/default/files/publications/Impact-of-covid19-on-businesses.pdf

van Veldhoven, Z., & Vanthienen, J. (2021). Digital transformation as an interaction-driven perspective between business, society, and technology. *Electronic Markets*. 10.1007/s12525-021-00464-5

Volschenk, L., Viljoen, K., & Schenck, C. (2021). Socio-economic factors affecting household participation in curb-side recycling programmes: Evidence from Drakenstein municipality, South Africa. *African Journal of Business & Economic Research*, 16(1). https://hdl.handle.net/10520/ejc-aa_ajber_v16_n1_a6

Xiao, Y., & Watson, M. (2019). Guidance on conducting a systematic literature review. *Journal of Planning Education and Research*, 39(1), 93–112. 10.1177/0739456X17723971

Zhao, Z., Zhang, M., Xu, G., Zhang, D., & Huang, G. Q. (2020). Logistics sustainability practices: An IoT-enabled smart indoor parking system for industrial hazardous chemical vehicles. *International Journal of Production Research*, 58(24), 7490–7506. 10.1080/00207543.2020.1720928

Zwane, S., Mathibe, M. S., & Mamabolo, A. (2022). The Drip Sneaker brand: Managing a successful start-up launch and rapid expansion during COVID-19 pandemic: Emerald Emerging markets case studies.

6 Entrepreneurship and COVID-19: A Socio-Psychological Perspective

Ogechi Adeola, Abdullah Promise Opute, Blessing Chukwuka, Isaiah Adisa, and Ibrahim Orekoya

Introduction

Entrepreneurship drives social and economic growth (Dean & McMullen, 2007; Schumpeter, 1934). Given that plausibility, there is increasing attention on how to foster entrepreneurship and boost its economic growth (e.g. Ferreira et al., 2017; Opute, 2020; Opute et al., 2021) and social growth (e.g. Ferreira et al., 2017) impacts. While the critical importance of entrepreneurship in steering economic growth and indeed achieving a snowballing economic growth impact, as captioned by Opute et al. (2021), has been severally documented in academic discourse in the Western context (e.g. Acs et al., 2018; Audretsch et al., 2018; Rhodes, 2019), entrepreneurship discourse documents a contrast in the African setting (e.g. Iwu & Opute, 2019; Iwu et al., 2020a). With the growing research attention on entrepreneurship in the African setting, it would seem legitimate to suggest that there is increasing recognition that entrepreneurship would drive economic growth. For example, in the recent past, entrepreneurship insights on Africa have sensitised women entrepreneurship (e.g. Lipoko et al., 2021; Adeola et al., 2021; Ribeiro et al., 2021; Irene et al., 2022), SMEs (e.g. Opute, 2020; Adeola, 2020; Iwu & Opute, 2019), entrepreneurship education (e.g. Iwu et al., 2020b; Iwu et al., 2020c; Madichie et al., 2020), *inter alia*.

Despite this encouraging development, recent literature has also lamented the survivalist nature of entrepreneurship (e.g. Iwu & Opute, 2019; Iwu et al., 2020a) and, therefore, the unproductiveness of entrepreneurship in the African setting. According to domain literature, critical contributing factors to the low economic growth impact of entrepreneurship on the African context includes, amongst others, poor entrepreneurial training (e.g. Iwu & Opute, 2021; Iwu et al., 2020b), financial handicap (e.g. Iwu & Opute, 2019; Iwu et al., 2020a), and the failure of the government to play its facilitating role (e.g. Iwu & Opute, 2019; Opute et al., 2021a). These enormous challenges that entrepreneurs face in the African setting have

DOI: 10.4324/9781003216469-6

been compounded by the ongoing Covid-19 pandemic. While the global impact of the pandemic has been undoubtedly immense, the recovery challenge for the African counterparts would no doubt be more significant owing to the fact that most countries in the African setting lack the necessary economic and infrastructural processes for managing critical shock dynamics induced by the Covid-19 pandemic. The Covid-19 pandemic has significantly affected SMEs and aggravated existing African socio-economic problems (Adeola et al., 2021).

Socio-economic problems such as unemployment, acute poverty, bad governance, and poor infrastructure are significant hurdles in Africa, and Covid-19 has further worsened the situation (Naude, 2021). According to a recent UN Economic Commission for Africa (2021) report, an estimated 514 million Africans will fall below the extreme poverty level by the end of 2021 if the Covid-19 impact is not effectively contained.[1] There is a critical need to illuminate the response strategies that organisations are embracing to effectively overcome the pandemic's economic implications (e.g. Opute et al., 2020a; Howe & Watson, 2021). Recognising that need, this chapter takes a socio-psychological approach to contribute to entrepreneurship knowledge and the impact of the Covid-19 pandemic in the African setting. Unfortunately, unlike the economic impact, the socio-psychological effects of the pandemic among entrepreneurs have not been given due attention (Spoorthy et al., 2020). The pandemic has exacerbated feelings of uncertainty, anxiety, depression, stress, and other mental health challenges, which need to be addressed in African society, hence the conceptual framing of this chapter.

While premised in the theoretical domain of entrepreneurship, the conceptual framing of this chapter is inspired by the ongoing Covid-19 pandemic that has significantly threatened entrepreneurship activity in the African setting that is not only characterised by survivalist entrepreneurship form (e.g. Iwu & Opute, 2019; Iwu et al., 2020a) but also lack of adequate facilitating support from the government (e.g. Iwu, 2021; Iwu & Opute, 2019). To achieve the conceptual premise of this chapter and, in that regard, contribute to knowledge development and also inform entrepreneurial practice in the African setting, this chapter is further organised thus: First, the entrepreneurship conceptualisation for this chapter is explained. Thereafter, entrepreneurship and Covid-19 in Africa are summarised. In line with the central premise of this chapter, entrepreneurship, Covid-19, and the socio-psychological implications follow next. In the concluding part of this chapter, recommendations are offered underlining critical entrepreneurs-based as well as government-based initiatives. In the final concluding part of this chapter, critical research directions for developing domain knowledge are flagged.

Entrepreneurship conceptualisation

Entrepreneurship has been defined diversely in the literature. Professor Howard Stevenson viewed as the godfather of entrepreneurship studies at the Harvard Business School, defined entrepreneurship as "the pursuit of opportunity beyond the resources you currently control" (see Eisenmann, 2013). Expatiating Stevenson's working definition, Eisenmann (2013) explains three core terms, viewing "*pursuit*" as "a singular, relentless focus", "*opportunity*" as a novel offering, and "*beyond resources controlled*" as resources constraints. According to Eisenmann (2013), an opportunity could take one of four forms: (1) pioneering a truly innovative product; (2) Creating a new business model; (3) creating an improved or more cost-effective version of an existing product; or (4) penetrating a new market segment with an existing product/service. In conclusion, Eisenman notes that the working definition by Stevenson offers a guidepost for entrepreneurial action and draws attention to typical risks associated with entrepreneurial activity, how to manage them, and also how to mobilise scarce resources.

In another effort to define entrepreneurship, Kuratko and Hodgetts (2003) forward a perspective that emphasises innovation as a core feature of entrepreneurship. They define entrepreneurship as "a dynamic process of vision, change, and creation, which requires an application of energy and passion". This conceptual viewpoint portrays entrepreneurship as a generator of novel ideas that would add value to an organisation and society, a theoretical viewpoint that has been reinforced in further literature (e.g. Opute, 2020). Furthering that perspective, Linan et al. (2010) conceptualised entrepreneurship as a process of discovering, evaluating, and exploiting an opportunity.

Analysed in tandem, the above entrepreneurship perspectives resonate closely with Schumpeter's use of creative activity to describe entrepreneurship. According to Schumpeter (1934), entrepreneurship is a proactive and creative activity that recognises opportunities and creates something new and is driven by value creation as the essence of economic development. While supporting the importance of value creation importance, the scope of entrepreneurship should not focus only on wealth creation in formal settings (Klapper et al., 2010) but also on not-for-profit organisations that provide creative ideas that would impact society (Kuratko, 2004). Thus, entrepreneurship encompasses the informal and formal sectors (Valerio et al., 2014).

From the above, an entrepreneur is innovative, creative, recognises opportunities in the market space, and converts these ideas into substantive value while also being risk-open. In doing these, critical attributes for value creation entrepreneurship include a proactive mindset and entrepreneurship marketing orientation (e.g. Opute, 2020; Opute et al., 2021a). Recent entrepreneurship insights also draw attention to the need for entrepreneurs to be dynamic and innovative in crisis situations (Ratten, 2020; Opute et al., 2020a).

Effectively navigating crises would require specific skills, such as proactiveness, ability to identify opportunities, innovativeness, risk management, and resilience (Branicki et al., 2018; Portuguez Castro & Gmez Zermeo, 2021). Recent literature relating specifically to the ongoing Covid-19 crisis underscores the criticality of proactiveness and digital innovation (e.g. Naude, 2021; Opute et al., 2020a). Focusing on entrepreneurship, but considering the ongoing Covid-19 crisis, this chapter takes a perspective that views entrepreneurship as a process that involves a proactive and innovative effort towards creating value that contributes to economic development.

Entrepreneurship and Covid-19 in Africa

The novel coronavirus (COVID-19) was announced as a global pandemic by the World Health Organization in March 2020 (WHO, 2020). This was followed by the shutdown of various economic and social activities in different parts of the world, straining and crippling many socio-economic sectors (Kuckertz et al., 2020). Several preventive measures were put in place to contain the spread of the deadly virus, such as the mandatory habit of wearing a face mask, frequent handwashing, isolation, and social distancing were paramount. The pandemic brought substantial change to the world and created a world of uncertainty with long-term effects on businesses and entrepreneurs, with new businesses experiencing the impact even more (Brown & Rocha, 2020). It has been documented that the Covid-19 pandemic is a "great crisis" that has disrupted the existing patterns in social, economic, political, and health systems that need to be addressed urgently (Bacq et al., 2020).

As a result of the pandemic, borders were closed to limit the spread of the virus, and this invariably resulted in the loss of jobs and business failures among entrepreneurs whose daily livelihood depends on day-to-day sales and who also have limited capital to revive the business (OECD, 2020). In a study conducted by Apedo-Amah et al. (2020), Covid-19 influenced the operations of many businesses and impacted sales and employment rates across several countries. The outbreak of Covid-19 disease in African countries was primarily felt in major business cities such as Lagos, Accra, and Johannesburg; these cities are globally recognised for international businesses as well as travel, thus significantly altering economic activities. For instance, a study conducted in South Africa documents the challenges resulting from Covid-19, which affected entrepreneurs, included lockdown restrictions, customer loss, lack of government support, and scarcity of raw materials., (Fubah et al., 2022). Many retail entrepreneurial businesses operating in market areas were shut down as well; this had grave implications on the financial resources available to entrepreneurs during the lockdown (Fubah et al., 2022). Many families found it challenging to feed during the lockdown, and government palliatives were not sufficient to go around citizens and sustain large family members.

Covid-19 has been described as a crisis with no end date in the near future (He & Harris, 2020), which further poses a challenge in planning, strategising, and implementation. To Booth (1993), a situation is defined as a crisis if it is faced by an individual, group or organisation whereby they do not have the capability to cope with the normal routine processes and also cannot control the range of events following suit. Booth further classified crises to include gradual threats, periodic threats, and sudden threats (Booth, 1993), and Covid-19 fell under the category of a sudden threat. While this pandemic is a source of concern for the world, some scholars believe that this pandemic could present itself as a valuable opportunity for some entrepreneurs, whereas for others, it could be a disastrous experience for most businesses, all depending on the response strategies of the entrepreneurs (Alon et al., 2020).

Currently, the virus has not entirely been eradicated; although the number of cases and deaths has reduced drastically with the help of the Covid vaccination, there are, however, still cases of infections and deaths. While the global implications of Covid-19 persist, international borders are gradually opening and also re-closing with more critical measures in place to curtail the virus further. It is argued that Covid-19 will slow down entrepreneur progress in different dimensions – especially among women and youth, who are also the most affected and somewhat vulnerable (Naude, 2021). Entrepreneurship has been promoted as the activity that will drive Africa to her next phase of development (Obonyo, 2016; Fubah et al., 2022); the restrictions and limitations to a business activity that affected entrepreneurship in Africa have raised questions over the existence and threatened the growth expectation of entrepreneurship in Africa (Prah & Sibiri, 2021). Women and youth entrepreneurs have suffered most during the pandemic, the former because of the nature of informality associated with their business ecosystem and the latter due to their limitation in the availability of a digital ecosystem which appeals more to the youth. In addition, Covid-19 has affected formal entrepreneurship, SMEs, and large-scale entrepreneurship in various ways. For instance, Odeku (2021) highlighted that many SMEs were not eligible for Covid-19 relief funds and government support schemes, which crippled their ability to maintain business activities – these aspects must be considered in government post-pandemic recovery plans in Africa. Bizoza and Sibomana (2020) examined the indication of the socio-economic impact of the pandemic and found that external merchandise trade and SMEs will experience more negative effects than those in the agricultural sector. The authors further emphasised that the implication of the pandemic on entrepreneurs will be varying, hence, government intervention and policy must be diversified to respond to the needs of varying entrepreneur dimensions. The pandemic had a disparaging impact on dominant SMEs sectors such as tourism and trade and is likely to increase the financial gap among SMEs (Amoussou et al., 2021). A one size fits all approach cannot be considered in ameliorating the impact of the pandemic on SMEs in Africa; government must explore different levels of entrepreneurial impact to drive the recovery process fully.

Entrepreneurship, Covid-19, and socio-psychological implications (case study of Nigerian entrepreneurs)

The coronavirus pandemic has caused global pandemonium as nations scramble to contain the outbreak. While much effort has been directed at the safety and health issues, it is also important to give due attention to the social-psychological implications of this outbreak on entrepreneurs. Many entrepreneurs and business owners have lost fortunes that will definitely take years to rebuild (Mathew et al., 2020). All of these problems and more arise from entrepreneurs' financial instability, household conflicts, mob violence, mental depression, and nationalistic attitude (Lonescu-Somers & Tarnawa, 2020; Oyafunke-Omoniyi et al., 2021). The emphasis on Nigeria as a case study for examining the linkage between entrepreneurship, Covid-19 and the psychological implications resulted from the existing gap in the literature. While there is considerable research on entrepreneurship development in Nigeria, the socio-psychological aspect has not recorded much attention. In view of this, the most fundamental issues related to this pandemic are more concerning in terms of social and psychological effects that may have long-term ramifications. Since a global pandemic is a significant, serious issue, it is to be expected that a range of intense negative emotions will exacerbate. This includes feelings of fear, anxiety, stress, distress, anger, and confusion (Brooks et al., 2020). There are many stressors in a person's life that can cause inner distress. Mental health problems, further magnified by a host of factors such as social isolation and perceived helplessness, can particularly affect vulnerable segments of the population such as women, girl-child, the elderly, and people with special needs.

The conditions surrounding the Covid-19 pandemic resulted in social and psychological challenges that must not be ignored (Saladino et al., 2020). Especially to the most vulnerable (women, the girl-child and entrepreneurs), the discussion on the social and psychological implications of the pandemic has attracted less attention. Entrepreneurs are severely affected by the pandemic with economic, social, and psychological impacts – especially women entrepreneurs (OECD, 2020). From a global perspective, Xu and Jia (2022) found that Covid-19 reduced the psychological well-being of entrepreneurs in China. Similarly, Torrès et al. (2022) emphasised that the risk of burnout increased among French entrepreneurs during the pandemic and also increased the chances of bankruptcy. The strands of literature across the globe on the impact of the pandemic on entrepreneurs point out that mental health issues increased while the sustainable growth of businesses was cut short. In Nigeria, the impact on women entrepreneurs has been much documented with limited literature on other forms of entrepreneurship.

For entrepreneurs with formality, they have had to initiate the working from a home policy which resulted in issues of isolation, loneliness, anxiety, and pressure to hustle for 24 hrs – 7 days which ultimately resulted in stress (Lonescu-Somers & Tarnawa, 2020). In Nigeria, the pandemic caused operational disruptions for entrepreneurs; across the country two-thirds of the entrepreneurship businesses in Nigeria were closed down (UNDP, 2021). According to Holmes et al. (2020), Covid-19 has a recognisable impact on people's social and psychological states, which can further hamper their mental health during and post-pandemic. This impact on mental health could be huge and long-lasting if not adequately addressed. Due to social isolation, the pandemic recorded a series of Covid-19-induced socio-psychological effects such as acute stress disorders, anxiety, irritability, poor concentration and indecisiveness, deteriorating work performance, post-traumatic stress disorders, high psychological distress, depressive symptoms, and insomnia (Brooks et al., 2020).

A study carried out by the United Nations emphasised that due to the isolation and social distancing, coupled with financial loss faced by the population, individuals' mental health was affected as the levels of stress indicated thus; anxiety, depression, increased suicide rate, and fracture of the family institution (UNDP, 2021). The social implications of the Covid-19 pandemic on Nigerian entrepreneurs have been viewed in many lights. For instance, in Nigeria, preventive measures such as social distancing have affected Nigerians in their social dealings, and feelings of isolation and loneliness were visible due to the limited social interactions. The psychological implications of the pandemic were experienced at the nick of the event, and this buttressed the point that many Nigerian entrepreneurs experienced retrogression in their business development trajectory (UNDP, 2021). The pandemic resulted in financial hardship as most economic activities were halted for a long time to curtail the virus. This financial loss contributed to the stress and anxiety experienced by entrepreneurs. Similarly, a lack of social interaction further aggravated this situation (Brooks et al., 2020). Individuals were apprehensive and worried about the rise of business activities and how life after the pandemic would be. More specifically, the pandemic has affected the employment sector, leaving many unemployed. During the virus outbreak, most entrepreneurs experienced a salary pay cut for staff and those who could not afford the extra costs laid off staff (UNDP, 2021). Similarly, many entrepreneurs lost their businesses and have not been able to recover (UNDP, 2021). These aspects of job insecurity and financial insecurity have affected many Nigerian entrepreneurs in an unprecedented manner.

Entrepreneurship in Africa is at the forefront of the continent's economic growth, with six of the fastest-growing economies in the world housed in Africa (Costa, 2020). One of the challenges of the entrepreneurship market in Africa is the lack of a formal structure which makes it vulnerable to uncertainties such as the Covid-19 pandemic. Though creating new paths of recovery and confronting the pandemic (Fröhlich, 2021), African entrepreneurs have tremendously been affected by the uncertainties associated with the pandemic (IFC, 2020). For example, 80% of the Nigerian working population is in the informal sector and earns daily wages based on their daily business activities. Restrictions in movement and the need for lockdown meant that so many entrepreneurs lost their source of livelihood without any hope of monthly allowance or government support. Restrictions in physical-social activities had social and psychological implications for many entrepreneurs.

Socially, the pandemic has affected entrepreneurs who depend on their daily earnings to survive and meet various family needs. Families have had to cut down on consumption patterns to manage whatever little resources they have left. Women are the most represented in the entrepreneurial landscape in Africa, and the pandemic has negatively affected the quest for equality in family roles and responsibilities. Female entrepreneurs had to abandon their entrepreneurial businesses to focus on domestic duties, such as taking care of their children and attending to domestic family needs. With the closure of schools, women's attention is shifted from their entrepreneurial endeavours to household responsibilities.[2] Furthermore, social gatherings for women's networking activities were hindered due to restrictions in movement. However, technology afforded its continuity; many women still had limitations in accessing digital platforms. Due to the consumption of resources that would have been invested in their businesses, the gender gap is set to increase (Toku-Appiah, 2021). In Uganda and Ethiopia, the gender gap in employment has widened by 14%, and in South Africa, it is projected that two-thirds of women will lose their jobs due to the pandemic (Toku-Appiah, 2021). The pandemic has restored the gendered roles of women as their economic empowerment has been severely affected. With fewer financial opportunities for women and more cultural expectations to stay at home and take care of the children as the continent gradually recovers from the pandemic, women are at a social disadvantage once again.

Psychologically, women entrepreneurs have also been affected by an increasing trend of domestic violence during the pandemic. The stay-at-home orders meant that many women spent more time with their abusive spouses. The longer the Covid-19 restrictions took, the more anxiety and tension increased, leading to violence. Olaseni et al. (2020), in their study on the psychological distress experienced by Nigerians during the Covid-19, revealed that Nigerians experienced psychological distress such as insomnia, depression, post-traumatic stress symptoms (PTSS), and anxiety during the Covid-19 pandemic. Similarly, Foleu et al. (2021), in their study on the impact of Covid-19 on entrepreneurs' mental health in Africa, revealed that several entrepreneurs experienced severe symptoms of psychological distress because of the effect of the pandemic on their businesses. The authors identified contrasting realities of psychological distress among entrepreneurs in Africa with personal characteristics (age and experience) and enterprise characteristics contributing to this difference. Though African entrepreneurs are confronting the pandemic through technological innovations (Fröhlich, 2021), the government must provide an enabling environment for their recovery.

Socio-psychological perspective on entrepreneurship and Covid-19 pandemic

The socio-psychological perspective is suitable for understanding entrepreneurship because entrepreneurship begins with identifying an opportunity and interactions with individuals, which results in a new venture that symbolises the firm's culture as obtained from the pioneers (Turkina & Thai, 2015). The determination to establish a business is swayed by the way the outside world is portrayed in the mind of the entrepreneur (Shaver & Scott, 1991).

Turkina and Thai (2015) argued that socio-psychological theories could be divided into the following categories: the theory of planned behaviour, the model of entrepreneurial event, the theory of social legitimation, and individual-level theories of self-efficacy. The theory of planned behaviour and the model of the entrepreneurial event suggests that the resolve to embark on a new venture is hinged on not only the recognition of its viability but also on the recognition of its appeal (Ajzen, 1996; Ajzen, 1991; Turkina & Thai, 2015). Turkina and Thai (2015) assert that the absence of the viability of entrepreneurship would neutralise any entrepreneurial ambition despite the viability of the new venture. These theories imply that the motivation for entrepreneurship is influenced by the benefits of entrepreneurship and the confidence of the people in their capacity to be in control of their entrepreneurial behaviour and accomplish their goals in the society. The desire to embark on a new venture depends on how firm the intention is, which may or may not lead to the establishment of the enterprise. Nevertheless, the practicability of entrepreneurship depends on the individual. Turkina and Thai (2015) argue that "entrepreneurship takes place only when it is both desirable and feasible for people in their socio-psychological context." (p. 216).

Moreover, the theory of self-efficacy describes how people act on what they believe they can do and the plausible effects of their actions. Previous studies have shown that self-efficacy predicts intentions of start-ups, new venture growth, and individual achievement (Drnovšek et al., 2010; Markman et al., 2002). According to Drnovšek et al. (2010), prior to deciding and fulfilling objectives, an individual "invokes personal cognitive capabilities to weigh, evaluate, and integrate information about personal skills relative to specific challenges and to form beliefs about probabilities of attaining success. The strength of these beliefs and certainty with which they are held are personal self-efficacy beliefs relative to that set of challenges" (p. 334). Thus, self-efficacy as a motivational construct has been identified to affect the choice of individuals' engagements, degree of objectives, tenacity, and execution of tasks in a diverse context (Zhao et al., 2005). Also, social legitimation theory suggests that the recognition of an entrepreneurial opportunity and the viability of a new venture is dependent on the social norms, culture, and cognitive structures that superintend, limit, and emancipate entrepreneurial activities in a community (Turkina & Thai, 2015). With this background, we assert that socio-psychological aspects prepare the structure for economic activities by determining the possible method of working available to the people, including stating the uncertainties and rewards for diverse pursuits and describing the climate that empowers entrepreneurs with social and economic legitimacy (Turkina & Thai, 2015).

Enterprises are constantly facing uncertainty regarding economic, national, or societal issues in today's business environment. These challenges threaten the survival and viability of enterprises to respond and adapt while managing their personnel (Carnevale & Hatak, 2020). The outbreak of Covid-19 has brought about immense challenges that have altered the enterprise's labour force to adjust to remote work environments (Opute, 2022). It has been noted that the Covid-19 challenge will aggravate socio-psychological outcomes of new work arrangements such as remote working, which has increased loneliness and lack of interaction with colleagues, thus bringing about mental health and productivity issues in organisations. While it has been noted that the pandemic has serious socio-psychological indications in adjusting the work environment, it would also lead to new techniques to combat the challenges enterprise employees face in their day-to-day duties and the current nature of work uncertainty.

Therefore, entrepreneurship activities are dependent on the social realities in the entrepreneur's environment. These realities have psychological implications for entrepreneurs (Kothari, 2013). The socio-psychological perspective argues that events in the society affect the social and psychological state of the individual and determines the individual's mood, actions, and inactions. In the context of our narrative in this chapter, we argue that the Covid-19 pandemic emanated out of social interactions in society, which has affected entrepreneurial engagements with a resultant psychological effect. Psychological effects include anxiety, depression, PTSS, insomnia, and mental health-related issues (Olaseni et al., 2020; Foleu et al., 2021). Entrepreneurs and their activities depend on society's social framework for existence and sustenance. Covid-19, a health-centred pandemic, threatened the continuity of society and, ultimately, the fabrics that promote entrepreneurial success in Africa. In other words, the direct influence of Covid-19 on society also affects the survival of the entrepreneurial business. Hence, Covid-19 has a social implication with a resultant psychological effect on entrepreneurs.

We further illustrate our argument in Figure 6.1.

From the theoretical lens of socio-psychological theory, it is evident that a pandemic such as Covid-19 has psychological implications for entrepreneurs (Mathew et al., 2020). Both men and women entrepreneurs are affected by the pandemic; however, women, youth, and informal entrepreneurs have suffered the most in Africa. Informal entrepreneurs are more affected because of the unavailability of policies and crisis resistance

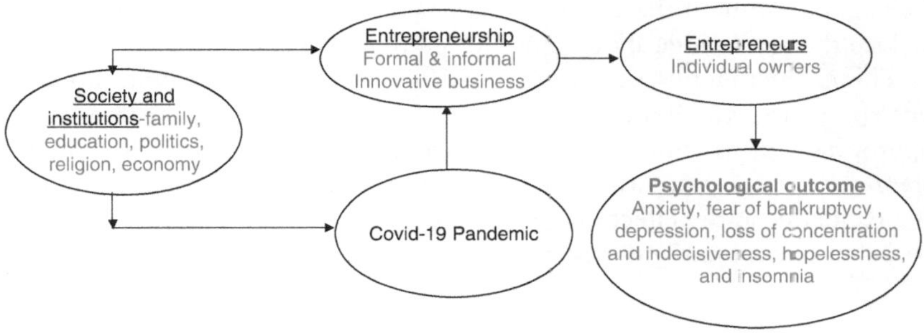

Figure 6.1 The socio-psychological implication of Covid-19 on entrepreneurs.
Source: Authors.

frameworks to protect them in challenging times, such as Covid-19 (UNDP, 2021). The socio-psychological theory suggests an intricate interaction between individuals and society (Foleu et al., 2021). Figure 6.1 shows that the society is made up of institutions such as the family, politics, education, religion, and the economic system (Olaseni et al., 2020; Foleu et al., 2021). People make up this system, and they create society. Social issues such as Covid-19 emanate through the interactions between all institutions, which is usually quick to affect economic institutions (e.g. formal and informal entrepreneurs). Prolonged restrictions and limitations as a result of the pandemic affect the means of livelihood (the business) and the business owner, which if not managed could lead to social and psychological manifestations such as anxiety, fear of bankruptcy, depression, loss of concentration and indecisiveness, hopelessness, and insomnia (Olaseni et al., 2020; Foleu et al., 2021; Mathew, et al., 2020)

The relationship between individuals and society is interdependent. Social institutions such as the family, school, economy, religion, and political structures of the society have been severely affected by unexpected disruptions to the social activities that make these institutions normal (UNDP, 2021). Disruption as a result of social interactions in the society has unintended economic consequences on social actors. Entrepreneurship is an economic institution affected by social outcomes such as Covid-19. The disruptions to entrepreneurship activities have a more telling effect on social actors – entrepreneurs, one of which is psychological in nature. For instance, Mathew et al. (2020) found that hopelessness to revive business psychological trauma and difficulty in keeping children indoors were challenges women entrepreneurs faced in Zambia during the pandemic. The compulsory lockdown resulted in working from home among formal entrepreneurs, which increased isolation and loneliness. Due to economic loss experienced by entrepreneurs and the unavailability of stimulus packages to help mitigate the effect of the pandemic, many entrepreneurs experienced psychological states of depression, insomnia, and hopelessness. The availability of structural packages to cushion the effect of disasters such as a pandemic would likely reduce the psychological outcomes for entrepreneurs.

This chapter emphasises that Covid-19 has psychological implications for entrepreneurs, which must be prevented in future crises. At the same time, appropriate plans must be put in place to restore the activities of entrepreneurs in Africa. Crucial steps are needed to respond to the scourge of the pandemic as the effect on entrepreneurs has a lasting implication on the social and economic growth of African countries.

Recommendations

Entrepreneurship discourse has documented multiple problems that plausibly explain why entrepreneurship remains relatively unproductive in the African context (e.g. Iwu & Opute, 2019; Iwu et al., 2020a). Reinforcing the severity of these problems, Iwu (2021) notes that while SMEs are widely acknowledged as core economic growth drivers, their continued existence in the African setting remains threatened. The Corona pandemic has compounded the problems undermining entrepreneurship productivity in the African setting. Iwu (2021) did not only flag dilapidated infrastructure and poor governance as critical antecedents of poor entrepreneurship outcomes in the African setting but also commented that the pandemic effect is unimaginable. Thriving in these turbulent periods requires an entrepreneurship focus that recognises the pertinence of a goal-oriented change approach. Typical reinforcing entrepreneurship processes should be embraced and enforced towards coping effectively in challenging crisis situations. In this chapter, we offer entrepreneurs-related and government-related (facilitating) recommendations.

Entrepreneurs-related recommendations

Entrepreneurs in the African setting are encouraged to embrace innovative- and entrepreneurship marketing strategies towards achieving productive entrepreneurship. In doing that, entrepreneurs should strive to acquire modern entrepreneurship marketing strategies, including digital technology technology-based skills, to effectively adapt to the paradigm shift from traditional marketing to digital technology-based marketing (Opute et al., 2020a). Acquiring modern digital skills is critical not only for staying entrepreneurially active in the current challenging situations caused by Covid-19-induced physical mobility restriction but also for a long-term perspective that would require entrepreneurs to stay proactive, innovative and strategic marketing focused on surviving in the ever-competitive market landscape (Opute, 2020; Opute et al., 2020a).

Entrepreneurial networking – leveraging entrepreneurial ecosystem (e.g. Opute et al., 2021a) and social-embeddedness (e.g. Opute et al., 2020b) foundations, this chapter recommends that entrepreneurs in the African setting should intensify their efforts to leverage the goodwill in their entrepreneurial networks to expand their outreach and exploit new market segments and also offset marketing costs (Opute et al., 2020b). Such networks can also be leveraged for social, human, and financial capital benefits (Opute et al., 2021b; Opute et al., 2020b). The Covid-19 pandemic has, in addition to economic implications, exerted immense psychological damages in the form of anxiety, depression, and mental health challenges on entrepreneurs and individuals in general. Entrepreneurs in the African setting should explore the option of pooling resources and joining forces with closely situated entrepreneurs to cope with overwork and burnout stress-related factors. Doing that will enable them to share their experiences and leverage functional strategies utilised by entrepreneurs to respond better to the challenges they encounter.

Active governmental support in facilitating entrepreneurship

The government in the sub-Saharan African setting, in general, must intensify its effort to facilitate active entrepreneurship that would boost economic growth and reduce unemployment and poverty levels in the region. Coping with the ongoing Covid-19 pandemic situation has been very challenging. Most entrepreneurs have been seriously stifled and their businesses are on on the verge of collapse while some have actually collapsed. In its facilitating capacity, the government can enforce relevant hands-on-deck mechanisms for steering productive entrepreneurship (e.g. Iwu & Opute, 2019; Opute et al., 2021a). One of such involves the government providing a funding package that offers tax relief to entrepreneurs to enable them to cope in challenging stages of their entrepreneurship cycle and in crisis periods like the Covid-19 pandemic.

Further, on the point of financial support, the government in Africa should make a committed effort towards facilitating productive entrepreneurship by providing adequate funding. Especially in these challenging times of the Covid-19 pandemic, where job losses, enterprise failure, and huge debts were and still remain a huge threat, the governments in the African setting should embrace the facilitating strategies enforced in Western societies of offering Corona packages to firms and individuals to enable them to offset the economic setbacks associated with the pandemic. For entrepreneurs with loan repayment obligations, the government should consider the relaxation of loan repayment deadlines as a way of motivating the resurgence of entrepreneurial activities and protecting businesses and start-up enterprises affected by the Covid-19 pandemic.

If governments in Africa effectively fulfil their facilitating role, entrepreneurship activity in that setting would be massively boosted (e.g. Iwu & Opute, 2021; Opute et al., 2021a). This boosting impact is long overdue in the African setting, where scholars (e.g. Iwu & Opute, 2019; Iwu et al., 2020a) have argued that entrepreneurship remains largely survivalist in nature. A further critical step in achieving that facilitating function relates to enacting suitable policies that enable entrepreneurial creativity, innovation, and digitisation processes. The Covid-19 pandemic has precipitated enormous challenges for entrepreneurs. Unprecedented challenges of nature have exposed entrepreneurs in the African setting to immense life-threatening outcomes for their entrepreneurial activities as well as individuals and income earners for their families. These unprecedented developments have seriously exposed the fragility of the African setting and the lack of existing frameworks for responding to emergency situations, a predicament that is attributable to the failure of the government to play its facilitating role. The mental and economic strains experienced (and also currently experienced) by entrepreneurs as a consequence of the ongoing pandemic could have been relatively mitigated if the government ensured appropriate facilitating mechanisms. The continued dilapidation of infrastructure in sub-Saharan Africa will remain a major setback in promoting economic growth (Makhathini, Mlambo, & Mpanza, 2020). Insufficient investment in infrastructure will continue to debilitate the progress SMEs are likely to make in terms of reducing poverty and improving socio-economic development (Asitik et al., 2016). Unfortunately, many SMEs in Africa leverage new technologies in their entrepreneurial activities (e.g. Muriithi, 2017; Opute, 2020). The government could invest in information and communication technologies and digitisation processes that aid innovative and value-creation-driven entrepreneurship.

Further steps that the government can take in that regard relate to ensuring relevant policies that augment the infrastructure investment. The governments in Africa should ensure appropriate policies that stimulate and enable entrepreneurs to embrace creative-, innovative-, and digitised processes in their entrepreneurial activities. The governments should also initiate strategic policies that promote a mentorship plan for supporting incubator firms and entrepreneurship in their infancy.

In the Covid-19 pandemic era, entrepreneurs are not only embracing home-office working. Still, they are. However, they are also faced with the challenge of effectively overseeing and also teaching the children at home, which is playing an active role in the homeschooling of the children. This development has work-life implications, amongst other stress-related implications. The African governments can play substantial roles in enabling entrepreneurs to effectively negotiate these stress-related challenges. The government can invest in facilities and resources (structural and human) to aid entrepreneurs in navigating the overwork and stress-related and extended psychological implications.

Future research directions

The Covid-19 pandemic has exerted devastating effects on a global scale (e.g. Opute et al., 2020a; Li et al., 2021). On the one hand, individuals and organisations (including entrepreneurs) are still struggling to identify and implement appropriate strategies for effectively navigating the pandemic-induced challenges, as has been documented in recent literature (e.g. Opute et al., 2020a; Opute, 2022) recognising that the Covid-19-pandemic-induced operational practices have become the new norm. As underlined by Opute (2022), the Covid-19 pandemic has reinvigorated a digitised operational modus that previously was driven by (1) digital technology evolution, and (2) trade internalisation and global networks.

Critical challenges that individuals and entrepreneurs are facing as a consequence of the Covid-19 pandemic are of socio-psychological nature. In the drive to steer entrepreneurship in the African setting towards a productive level that contributes meaningfully to achieving sustainable economic development goals of curtailing increasing unemployment and poverty levels in that setting, the significance of leveraging the impacting role of research must be recognised. More research is required on entrepreneurship, especially in this Covid-19 era (Li et al., 2021; Iwu, 2021). Critical in that regard is research that enhances understanding of socio-psychological implications of critical crisis episodes like the Covid-19 pandemic where movement restriction remains an unavoidable response option. This is an obvious response strategy that individuals and organisations are adopting to thrive in the Covid-19 era. However, it is not to say that coping with the new operational modus offers only challenges without opportunities. A commensurate response is also required from the point of research in documenting the response strategies of entrepreneurs and success (and or) failure episodes in that regard.

More critically, from the socio-psychological viewpoint, research is required from the point of understanding the work-life implications of working in the Covid-19 pandemic-induced operational modus. Compelled by Covid-19-induced movement restrictions, home-office working has become a rational strategy for entrepreneurs to survive in challenging circumstances. Critical processes in that working modus require IT and digital skills. Future research should aim to illuminate how entrepreneurs are negotiating the transition to digitised working processes and how they are navigating the inherent challenges. Core questions in that regard could relate to: what forms of training did they require to make the upgrade? what forms of support did they get in overcoming the challenges?

Additional to coping with the IT and digital challenges of the digital technology-based home-office working modus, entrepreneurs also have the responsibility of assisting with the homeschooling responsibilities of their children. This creates additional stress factors for entrepreneurs, which could lead to workloads that may trigger work overload and burnout. Future research should explore the nature of such stress factors and what coping strategies entrepreneurs are embracing. To leverage an entrepreneurial ecosystem foundation that reinforces the significant role of the government and institutions in facilitating productive entrepreneurship (e.g. Opute et al., 2021a; Iwu et al., 2020a), future research should also seek to illuminate whether the government is actively playing its facilitating role in that coping regard.

Notes

1 https://reliefweb.int/report/world/if-covid19-impact-not-contained-2021-514-million-africans-may-fall-below-extreme
2 https://www.intracen.org/layouts/2coltemplate.aspx?pageid=47244640256&id=47244679884

References

Acs, Z. J., Estrin, S., Mickiewicz, T., & Szerb, L. (2018). Entrepreneurship, institutional economics, and economic growth: An ecosystem perspective. *Small Business Economics*, 51(2), 501–514.

Adeola, O. (2020). Introduction: Empowering African women–towards achieving the UN's 2030 sustainable development goals. *In Empowering African Women for Sustainable Development* (pp. 1–10). Cham: Palgrave Macmillan.

Adeola, O., Gyimah, P., Appiah, K. O., & Lussier, R. N. (2021). Can critical success factors of small businesses in emerging markets advance UN sustainable development goals? *World Journal of Entrepreneurship, Management and Sustainable Development*, 17(1), 85–105.

Adeola, O., Igwe, P. A., & Evans, O. (2021). Women economic empowerment and post-pandemic recovery in Africa: Normalising the "Un-Normal" Outcome of Covid-19. In *Gendered Perspectives on Covid-19 Recovery in Africa* (pp. 305–327). Cham: Palgrave Macmillan.

Ajzen, I. (1991). The theory of planned behavior. *Organisational Behavior and Human Decision Processes*, 50(2), 179–211.

Ajzen, I. (1996). The social psychology of decision making. In E. T. Higgins & A. W. Kruglanski (Eds.), *Social psychology: Handbook of basic principles* (pp. 297–325). New York: Guilford.

Alon, I., Farrell, M., & Li, S.. (2020). Regime type and COVID-19 response. FIIB Business Review 1–9. doi:10.1177/2319714520928884.

Amoussou, O., Karagueuzian, C., & Bah, M. (2021). African SMEs through Covid-19 challenges, policy responses and recommendations. *African Development Bank Group*, 12(5), 1–7

Apedo-Amah, M. C., Avdiu, B., Cirera, X., Cruz, M., Davies, E., Grover, A. G., Iacovone, L., Kılınç, U., Medvedev, D., Maduko, F. O., Poupakis, S., Torres, J., & Tran, T. T. (2020). Unmasking the impact of COVID-19 on businesses: Firm level evidence from across the world.

Asitik, A.J., Sharpley, R., & Phelan, C. (2016). Establishing the link between entrepreneurship, built capital and poverty reduction in rural northern Ghana. *International Journal of Arts & Sciences*, 9, 495–508.

Audretsch, D. B., Belitski, M., & Desai, S. (2018). National business regulations and city entrepreneurship in Europe: a multilevel nested analysis. *Entrepreneurship Theory and Practice*, 4, 6

Bacq, S., Geoghegan, W., Josefy, M., Stevenson, R., & Williams, T. A. (2020). The COVID-19 virtual idea blitz: marshaling social entrepreneurship to rapidly respond to urgent grand challenges. *Business Horizons*, 1–19, doi: 10.1016/j.bushor.2020.05.002.

Barot, H. (2015). Entrepreneurship - a key to success. *The International Journal of Business and Management*, 3(1), January 2015, 163–165.

Beyene, A. (2002). Enhancing the competitiveness and productivity of small and medium scale enterprises (SMEs) in Africa: An analysis of differential roles of national governments through improved support services. *Africa Development*, XXVII(3 & 4), 130–156.

Bizoza, A., & Sibomana, S. (2020). Indicative socio-economic impacts of the novel coronavirus (Covid-19) outbreak in Eastern Africa: Case of Rwanda. *Available at SSRN 3586622*.

Booth, S. A. (1993). *Crisis Management Strategy: Competition and change in modern enterprises*. London and New York: Routledge

Branicki, L. J., Sullivan-Taylor, B., & Livschitz, S. R. (2018). How entrepreneurial resilience generates resilient SMEs. *International Journal of Entrepreneurial Behavior & Research*, 24(7), 1244–1263. doi: 10.1108/ijebr-11-2016-0396

Brooks, S. K., Webster, R. K., Smith, L. E., Woodland, L., Wessely, S., Greenberg, N., & Rubin, G. J. (2020). The psychological impact of quarantine and how to reduce it: Rapid review of the evidence. *Lancet*, 395, 912–920

Brown, R., & Rocha, A. (2020). Entrepreneurial uncertainty during the covid-19 crisis: nmapping the temporal dynamics of entrepreneurial finance. *Journal of Business Venturing Insights*, 14, 1–10, available at: 10.1016/j.jbvi.2020.e00174.

Carnevale, J. B., & Hatak, I. (2020). Employee adjustment and well-being in the era of COVID-19: Implications for human resource management. Journal of Business Research, 116, 183–187.

Da Costa, J. (2020). How Jack Ma sees a thriving future of entrepreneurship in Africa. https://www.weforum.org/agenda/2020/03/jack-ma-alibaba-digital-entrepreneurship-africa/

Dean, T. J., & McMullen, J. S. (2007). Toward a theory of sustainable entrepreneurship: Reducing environmental degradation through entrepreneurial action. *Journal of Business Venturing*, 22(1), 50–76.

Drnovšek, M., Wincent, J., & Cardon, M. S. (2010). Entrepreneurial self-efficacy and business start-up: Developing a multi-dimensional definition. *International Journal of Entrepreneurial Behavior& Research*, 16(4), 329–348.

Eisenmann, T. (2013). What is entrepreneurship? Harvard Business Review, 3 January, 2013. https://hbr.org/2013/01/what-is-entrepreneurship.

Ferreira, J. J. M., Fernandes, C. I., & Ratten, V. (2017). The influence of entrepreneurship education on entrepreneurial intentions. 10.1007/978-3-319-4794 9-1_2. book chapter.

Foleu, C. L., Enagogo, C. A., Menguele, J. P. D., & Obam, G. E. (2021). Covid-19 impacts on entrepreneurs' mental health in Africa. *Revue InternationalePme*, 34(2), 36–61.

Fröhlich, S. (2021). Start-ups in Africa confront the pandemic. https://www.dw.com/en/startups-in-africa-confront-the-pandemic/a-56573005

Fubah, C. N., & Moos, M. (2022). Exploring COVID-19 challenges and coping mechanisms for SMEs in the South African entrepreneurial ecosystem. *Sustainability*, 14(4), 1944. 10.3390/su14041944

Gorman, G., Hanlon, D., & King, W. (1997). Some research perspectives on entrepreneurship education, enterprise education and education for small business management: A ten year literature review. *International Small Business Journal*, 15(3), 56–77. 10.1177/0266242697153004

He, H., & Harris, L. (2020). The impact of Covid-19 pandemic on corporate social responsibility and marketing philosophy. *Journal of Business Research*, 116, 176–182.

Holmes, E. A., O'Connor, R. C., Perry, V. H., Tracey, I., Wessely, S., Arseneault, L., Ballard, C., Christensen, H., Cohen Silver, R., Everall, I.; et al. (2020). Multidisciplinary research priorities for the COVID-19 pandemic: A call for action for mental health science. *Lancet Psychiatry*, 7, 547–560.

Howe, R. E., & Watson, G. C. (2021). Finding our way through a pandemic: Teaching in alternate modes of delivery. *Frontier in Education*, 6. doi: 10.3389/feduc.2021.661513.

IFC (2020). Uncertainty, fear, and coronavirus: The new reality for Africa's entrepreneurs. https://www.ifc.org/wps/wcm/connect/news_ext_content/ifc_external_corporate_site/news+and+events/news/impact-stories/smes-africa-covid19

Irene, B. N. O., Opute, A. P., & Murithi, W. (2022). An empirical insight into the factors affecting the oscillation of women between self and paid employment in South Africa. In *The Palgrave Handbook of African Entrepreneurship*. Palgrave Macmillan.

Iwu, C. G. (2021). COVID-19 lessons for mitigation and future SME prospects. In *Handbook of Research on Strategies and Interventions to Mitigate COVID-19 Impact on SMEs* (pp. 74–100). IGI Global.

Iwu, C. G., Opute, A. P., Nchu, R., Babatunde, A. A., Iwu, C. H., & Eze, I. F. (2020c). The antecedents of university students' entrepreneurship intention. The theory of planned behaviour viewpoint. *Harvard Deusto Business Research*, IX(2), 221–240.

Iwu, C. G., Opute, A. P., Nchu, R., Eresia-Eke, C., Tengeh, R. K., Jaiyeoba, O., & Aliyu, O. A. (2020b). Entrepreneurship education, curriculum and lecturer - competency as antecedents of student entrepreneurial intention. *International Journal of Management Education*. 10.1016/j.ijme.2019.03.007

Iwu, C. G., & Opute, A. P. (2019). Eradicating poverty and unemployment: Narratives of survivalist entrepreneurs. *Journal of Reviews on Global Economics*, 1438–1451. DOI:10.6000/1929-7092.2019.08.127.

Iwu, C. G., & Opute, A. P. (2021) Steering productive entrepreneurship activities in emerging markets: The role of the University, Chapter 14 In *Universities, Entrepreneurial Ecosystems and Sustainability* (edited by C. Fernandes, M. Ramírez-Pasillas, J. J. Ferreira). De Gruyter Studies in Knowledge Management and Entrepreneurial Ecosystems. Walter De Gruyter GmbH, Berlin/Boston. ISBN 9783110670165. Berlin, Germany: De Gruyter.

Iwu, C. G., Eze, I., Opute, A. P., Dongo, G., & Dongo, O. W. (2020a). Scavenging for survival and its health implications. The nexus between unemployment and ill-health. *WSEAS Transactions on Environment and Development*, 17(1), 1–18.

Klapper, L., Amit, R., & Guillén, M. F. (2010). Entrepreneurship and firm formation across countries'. In J. Lerner and A. Scoar (eds), *International Differences in Entrepreneurship* (pp. 129–158). University of Chicago Press. 10.7208/chicago/9780226473109.003.0005

Kothari, H. C. (2013). Socio-psychological factors of entrepreneurship: A survey. *Research journali's Journal of Entrepreneurship*, 1(1), 1–11.

Kuckertz, A., Brändle, L., Gaudig, A., Hinderer, S., Morales Reyes, C. A., Prochotta, A., Steinbrink, K. M., & Berger, E. S.C. (2020). Startups in times of crisis – A rapid response to the COVID-19 pandemic. *Journal of Business Venturing Insights*, 13, e00169.

Kuratko, D. (2004). Entrepreneurship education in the 21st century: From legitimisation to leadership, A Coleman foundation white paper, USASBE National Conference, January 16, 2004. https://pdfs.semanticscholar.org/d89d/3a2a96b5c645ab42b0e28f6d73be7f961fe6.pdf

Kuratko, D., & Hodgetts. R. (2003). *Entrepreneurship: Theory, Process, and Practice*. South Cincinnati OH (USA): Western College Publisher.

Li, P., Li, B., & Liu, Z. (2021). The Impact of entrepreneurship perceptions on entrepreneurial intention during the COVID-19 pandemic. *Frontiers in Education*, 6, 770710. doi: 10.3389/feduc.2021.770710

Linan, F., Rodrigues-Cohard, J., & Rueda-Cantuche, J. (2010). Factors affecting entrepreneurial level: A role for education. *International Entrepreneurship Management Journal*, 7, 195–218.

Lipoko, D. U. D., Iwu, C. G., & Opute, A. P. (2021). Gender discrepancy in economic participation: The case of young women in the Democratic Republic of Congo. *EUREKA: Social and Humanities, Number 6*. DOI: 10.21303/2504-5571.2021.002121.

Lonescu-Somers, A., & Tarnawa, A. (2020). Diagnosing COVID-19 impacts on entrepreneurship. *Global entrepreneurship monitor*. https://www.gemconsortium.org/file/open?fileId=50521

Madichie, N. O., Ibrahim, M., Adam, D. R., & Ustarz, Y. (2020). Entrepreneurial intentions amongst African students: A case study of the University of Education, Winneba, Ghana. In Entrepreneurial Universities (pp. 169–190). Cham: Palgrave Macmillan.

Makhathini, M.S.M., Mlambo, V. H., & Mpanza, S. (2020). Infrastructure provision as a catalyst for local economic development in South Africa. *Strategic Review for Southern Africa*, 42(1), 99–122.

Markman, G. D., Balkin, D. B., & Baron, R. A. (2002). Inventors and new venture formation: The effects of general self–efficacy and regretful thinking. *Entrepreneurship Theory and Practice*, 27(2), 149–165.

Mathew, N., Deborah, I., Karonga, T., & Rumbidzai, C. (2020). The impact of COVID-19 lockdown in a developing country: Narratives of self-employed women in Ndola, Zambia. *Health Care for Women International*, 41(11-12), 1370–1383.

Muriithi, S.M. (2017). African small and medium enterprises contributions, challenges and solutions. *European Journal of Research and Reflection in Management Sciences*, 5(1), ISSN 2056-5992.

Naude, W. (2021). How COVID-19 is likely to slow down a decade of youth development in Africa. Retrieved from: https://theconversation.com/how-covid-19-is-likely-to-slow-down-a-decade-of-youth-development-in-africa-159288

Nwankwo, S. (2020). Contemporary issues in entrepreneurship marketing sustainability, ethics and social responsibility. In S. Nwankwo, and A. Gbadamosi (Eds.), *Entrepreneurship marketing: Principles and practice of SME Marketing*. Routledge Publishers.

Obiakpor, T. (2020). COVID 19 and the informal sector in Nigeria: The socio-economic cost implications. https://cseaafrica.org/covid-19-and-the-informal-sector-in-nigeria-the-socio-economic-cost-implications/

Obonyo, R. (2016). Africa looks to its entrepreneurs. *Africa Renewal*, Volume *30*(1), pp. 16–17.

Odeku, K. O. (2021). The impact of the Covid-19 pandemic on black-owned small and micro-businesses in South Africa. *Acad. Entrep. J.*, 27, 1–5.

OECD (2020). A systemic resilience approach to dealing with covid-19 and future shocks, available at: www.oecd.org/coronavirus/policy-responses/a-systemic-resilienceapproach-to-dealingwith-covid-19-and-future-shocks-36a5bdfb/

OECD (May, 2020). Start-ups in the time of COVID-19: Facing the challenges, seizing the opportunities. https://www.oecd.org/coronavirus/policy-responses/start-ups-in-the-time-of-covid-19-facing-the-challenges-seizing-the-opportunities-87219267/

Olaseni, A. O., Akinsola, O. S., Agberotimi, S. F., & Oguntayo, R. (2020). Psychological distress experiences of Nigerians during Covid-19 pandemic; the gender difference. *Social Sciences & Humanities Open*, 2(1), 100052.

Opute, A. P. (2020). Small and medium enterprises marketing: Innovation and sustainable economic growth perspective. In S. Nwankwo, and A. Gbadamosi (Eds.), *Entrepreneurship marketing: Principles and practice of SME Marketing*. Routledge Publishers.

Opute, A. P. (2022). Virtual teams: The new work norm for the post Covid-19 Era, (Chapter 13) In *Digital Service Delivery in Africa*. DOI: 10.1007/978-3-030-83909-3.

Opute, A. P., Iwu, C. G., Adeola, O., Mugobo, V., Okeke-Uzodike, O. E., Fagbola, S., & Jaiyeoba, O. (2020a). The Covid-19-pandemic and implications for businesses: Innovative retail marketing viewpoint. *Retail Marketing Review*, 16(3), 85–100.

Opute, A. P., Iwu, C. G., Khosa, R. M., Eresia-Eke, C., Hagos, S. B., & Irene, B. N. O. (2021b). African Immigrant entrepreneurship in the UK: The hidden hand of family influence on entrepreneurial orientation. *Harvard Deusto Business Research*, X (1), 53–79.

Opute, A. P., Kalu, K. I., Adeola, O., & Iwu, C. G. (2021a). Steering sustainable economic growth: Entrepreneurial ecosystem approach. *Journal of Entrepreneurship and Innovation in Emerging Economies*, 7(2), 1–30.

Opute, A. P., Madichie, N. O., Hagos, S. B., & Ojra, J. (2020b). Entrepreneurship behaviour of African minorities in the UK: 'Demystifying cultural influence'. *International Journal of Entrepreneurship and Small Business*, 44(3), 298–322.

Oyafunke-Omoniyi, C. O., Adisa, I., & Obileye, A. A. (2021). Gender-based violence and Covid-19: The shadow pandemic in Africa. In O. Adeola (eds) *Gendered Perspectives on Covid-19 Recovery in Africa*. Cham: Palgrave Macmillan. 10.1007/978-3-030-88152-8_4

Portuguez Castro, M., & Gmez Zermeo, M. G. (2021). Being an entrepreneur post-COVID-19 – resilience in times of crisis: A systematic literature review. *Journal of Entrepreneurship in Emerging Economies*, 13(4), 721–746. 10.1108/jeee-07-2020-0246

Prah, D. and Sibiri, H. (2021). The resilience of African migrant entrepreneurs in China under COVID-19. *Journal of Entrepreneurship in Emerging Economies*, 13(5), 1119–1133. 10.1108/JEEE-05-2020-0111

Ratten, V. (2020). Coronavirus (covid-19) and entrepreneurship: Changing life and work landscape. *Journal of Small Business & Entrepreneurship*, 32(5), 503–516, DOI:10.1080/08276331.2020.1790167.

Rhodes, C. (2019). *Business statistics, house of commons* [Briefing Paper No. 06152]. London: House of Commons Library.

Ribeiro, M. A., Adam, I., Kimbu, A. N., Afenyo-Agbe, E., Adeola, O., Figueroa-Domecq, C., & de Jong, A. (2021). Women entrepreneurship orientation, networks and firm performance in the tourism industry in resource-scarce contexts. *Tourism Management*, 86, 104343.

Saladino, V., Algeri, D., & Auriemma, V. (2020). The psychological and social impact of Covid-19: New perspectives of well-being. *Frontiers in Psychology*, 11, 2550.

Schumpeter, J. (1934). *The theory of economic development*. Cambridge, MA: Harvard University Press.

Sergi, B. S., Popkova, E. G., Bogoviz, A. V., & Ragulina, J. V. (2019). Entrepreneurship and economic growth: The experience of developed and developing countries. In *Entrepreneurship and Development in the 21st Century*. Emerald publishing limited.

Shaver, K. G., & Scott, L. R. (1991). Person, process, choice: The psychology of new venture creation. *Entrepreneurship: Theory and Practice*, 16(2), 23–45.

Spoorthy, M. S., Pratapa, S. K., & Mahant, S. (2020). Mental health problems faced by healthcare workers due to the COVID-19 pandemic: A review. *Asian Journal of Psychiatry*, 51, 102119. 10.1016/j.ajp.2020.10211

Toku-Appiah, R. (2021). How Covid-19 disproportionately affected women-led businesses. https://www.theafricareport.com/102008/how-covid-19-disproportionately-affected-women-led-businesses/

Torrès, O., Benzari, A , Fisch, C., Mukerjee, J., Swalhi, A., & Thurik, R. (2022). Risk of burnout in French entrepreneurs during the COVID-19 crisis. *Small Business Economics*, 58(2), 717–739.

Turkina, E., & Thai, M. T. T. (2015). Socio-psychological determinants of opportunity entrepreneurship. *International Entrepreneurship and Management Journal*, 11(1), 213–238.

UNDP (2021). The impact of Covid-19 on business enterprises in Nigeria. https://www.ng.undp.org/content/nigeria/en/home/library/mdg/the-impact-of-covid-19-on-business-enterprises-in-nigeria.html

Valerio, A., Parton, B., and Robb, A. (2014). *Entrepreneurship Education and Training Programs around the World*. Washington D.C: The World Bank. https://openknowledge.worldbank.org/bitstream/handle/10986/18031/9781464802027.pf World Bank

World Health Organisation. (2020). WHO, coronavirus disease (COVID-19) outbreak. https://www.who.int/emergencies/diseases/novel-coronavirus-2019

Xu, Z., & Jia, H. (2022). The Influence of COVID-19 on entrepreneur's psychological well-being. *Frontiers in psychology*, 12, 823542. 10.3389/fpsyg.2021.823542

Zeidy, I. A. (2020). Economic impact of covid-19 on micro, small and medium enterprises (MSMEs) in Africa and policy options for mitigation. Common Mark. East. South. Africa. Nairobi.

Zhao, H., Seibert, S. E., & Hills, G. E. (2005). The mediating role of self-efficacy in the development of entrepreneurial intentions. *Journal of Applied Psychology*, 90(6), 1265–1272.

7 Entrepreneurship Financial Stability and Implications

Leonard U. Agwuna

Background

Croitori began researching the relationship between entrepreneurship and finance as early as 1911, beginning with Joseph Schumpeter's early work, published in 1911 and translated into English in 1934. Temporary monopoly profits, according to Schumpeter, spur innovation, and financial institutions play a vital role in the analysis and financing of new ideas. In two ways, the financial system influences investment decisions in productivity-enhancing businesses. First, the financial system evaluates potential entrepreneurs and then provides loans to the most promising firms. As a result of entrepreneurial selection, the cost of productivity-enhancing investments is reduced, which contributes to growth. Secondly, the resulting instability in the financial system limits the ability of financial institutions to support innovative ventures in the economy and can disrupt the pace of economic growth.

The term "systemic financial instability" refers to a change in the initial state of the financial system that can lead to financial instability in a variety of forms. Financial instability can hinder creative activity and limit the economic success of citizens. By limiting capital inflows into productive assets, unstable financial markets shift pressure from their primary institutions to firms and households, leading to systemic risk. Systemic risk can lead to the failure of many firms. A stable financial system, conversely, indicates that the financial system can absorb shocks and variations induced by the internal and external environment while continuing to function. The easy availability of credit and payment systems and the ease with which households and firms can move financial assets through a stable financial system contribute to economic growth and entrepreneurial development (Babajide & Olokoyo, 2017).

The stability of the financial system allows firms and households to store value and transfer financial assets without fear of loss. This contributes to the growth and development of societies. One of the Sustainable Development Goals (SDGs) set in 2015 is to reduce all forms of poverty in the world. According to the most recent data available as of the end of 2018, extreme poverty has hit a new low, but it is now focused in one

DOI: 10.4324/9781003216469-7

region of the world: Sub-Saharan Africa (SSA) according to the World Bank. In 1990, 36% of the global population lived in poverty; by 2015, this figure has reduced to 10%. While poverty rates in other areas of the globe are dropping, the number of poor people in SSA grew by 67% from 278 million in 1990 to 413 million in 2015. SSA is home to 27 of the world's 28 nations with poverty rates exceeding 30%. SSA has a poverty rate of 41%, whereas the rest of the world has a rate of less than 12%.

By establishing a worldwide fund, world leaders have expressed their support for entrepreneurship and inclusive growth. The G7 recognised female entrepreneurship as a significant engine of economic growth, innovation, and job creation in 2015, and established a fund to help women gain access to financing, develop their skills, and expand their leadership chances and networks. President Trump introduced the $1 billion Women Entrepreneurs Finance Initiative (We-Fi) in 2017 with a $325 million initial commitment and cooperation from international G20 "leaders" to encourage women to start businesses. G7 leaders authorised $251 million in funding for the African Development Bank's (ADB) Affirmative Finance Action for African Women (AFAWA) program to assist African women entrepreneurs in August of this year. According to a recent survey, SSA boasts the world's largest proportion of female entrepreneurs, with 25.9% of adult women operating as entrepreneurs. In comparison to males, entrepreneurs who are females invest most of their earnings into consumption, education, and the health of their relatives and societies (Global Entrepreneurship Monitor [GEM 2016/2017]).

Several theoretical and empirical contributions demonstrate that entrepreneurship is a key driver of economic growth because it encourages innovation and competition, which leads to increased efficiency and output (Acs et al., 2009; Agarwal et al., 2010; Aghion et al., 2009; Carree & Thurik, 2003; Fritsch & Changoluisa, 2017; Kirzner, 1997; Metcalfe, 2004; Quadrini, 2009; Schumpeter, 1934; Schwienbacher, 2009; Van Stel et al., 2005; Wennekers & Thurik, 1999). Given that entrepreneurship is important in terms of driving growth and development in economies around the world, understanding the factors that support or discourage entrepreneurship is crucial. This type of analysis can be done on an individual, corporate, or national level (Wennekers & Thurik, 1999). The choice of being an entrepreneur can be impacted by individual characteristics which may include risk management, education, experience in line with age, and different employment possibilities. When it comes to the business or industry segment, competitiveness, the size of the market, size of the firm, and corporate values can all be critical (Wennekers & Thurik, 1999).

Furthermore, entrepreneurial activity may differ and can be attributed to the variances found in different economic development strategies, macroeconomic factors, and institutional frameworks (Bjornksov & Foss, 2008; Freytag & Thurik, 2007). According to Schumpeter (1934), some countries are specific in recognising the importance of entrepreneurial variables, the author acknowledges that there is stimulating effect of the financial sector on entrepreneurship that is significant. The banker, Schumpeter wrote, "is not so much the mediator of the 'purchasing power' of a commodity as the creator of it" (1934: 174). They act as a buffer among those who seek to develop new ideas (entrepreneurs) and those who own the means of production. It is the creation of people for the good of society that makes possible the creation of new combinations. It is the "Maxim (supervisor) of the commercial economy."

Lack of funds has been shown to limit individual entrepreneurial activities (Evans & Jovanovic, 1989; Kan & Tsai, 2006). According to empirical research (Beck & Demirgüc-Kunt, 2006; Beck et al., 2008, 2015), access to funds, equipment, assets, and financial support promotes entrepreneurship and market involvement at the sectoral level. Finally, national entrepreneurship according to prior research get more financial support (Fan & Zhang, 2017; Klapper & Love, 2011; Klapper et al., 2015; Leon, 2019; Munemo, 2018; Omri & Ayadi-Frikha, 2014).

Across the USA, small business and entrepreneurship development is an important driver and source of employment, economic independence and a place in the lives of young people of all races and genders. At the same time, economic reforms aimed at fostering entrepreneurship and strengthening its legal and regulatory framework are one of the most pressing issues in the trend towards economic liberalisation. It is no exaggeration to say that it has become a modern imperative to run a business that does not require large investments, modernises quickly and adapts well to changing market requirements. SMEs are one of the most important sectors that supply the market with essential goods and services and determine the structural basis of the economy. The experience of developed countries shows that entrepreneurship plays a very important role in the modernisation and diversification of the national economy, ensuring its sustainable development, technological innovation, development of new products, and supply of goods and services for the domestic market.

Regulators also routinely assess and submit financial sustainability indicators to the World Bank on a quarterly basis. Their aim is to give an unbiased assessment of the financial system using a supervisory procedure that evaluates the financial sector's soundness and stability using important macroeconomic indicators. In SSA, there are only enough data. The quality of assets, capital sustainability, profitability, and funding of significant institutions are the four fundamental components of stability measurement.

Despite high unemployment and poverty rates, SSA has been one of the fastest growing economies in the world. The countries in this region have seen a rise in entrepreneurial activities in the 21st century compared to other regions globally. With the correct support and a favourable economic and business climate, the region should be able to reduce unemployment and alleviate poverty. Residents in the region, according to Herrington and Kelly (2012) have a good attitude towards entrepreneurship, and fear of failure does not appear to be a disincentive to entrepreneurship. Demand, on the other hand, appears to be the driving force for regional entrepreneurship. Prior to the current epidemic of infectious illnesses, many people relied on subsistence occupations, even though many individuals created enterprises.

As a result of the COVID-19 pandemic, businesses throughout the world endured enormous disruption. As individuals have reduced face-to-face contact and grown more active in virtual contacts, businesses have faced considerable changes in regulation, organisational procedures, and consumer expectations. These pandemic experiences are likely to have a long-term influence on the capacity of firms. As a result, many observers predict significant and long-term changes in business models, international value chains (Gereffi, 2020; Shih, 2020), and individuals' work and career patterns, particularly in emerging economies (Caligiuri et al., 2020; Coté et al., 2020).

The COVID-19 epidemic has generally been tackled in Sub-Saharan African nations by less effective institutional structures and less generous financial allocations (Gao et al., 2017; Meyer & Grosse, 2019). Many developing economies, on the other hand, have well-developed corporate communities with expertise harnessing traditional resources. The capacity to integrate shared resources to develop new competitive advantages (Luo & Child, 2015; Zhou et al., 2020) is particularly useful in an environment where many customers are both cost-conscious and exceedingly flexible (Krishnan & Prashantham, 2019; Luo & Child, 2015). Although finance appears to be an issue in most situations, these strategies have lately evolved beyond the usual focus on resource scarcity to incorporate strong innovation strategies that alter sectors through business model innovation (Park et al., 2013; Williamson & Wan, 2019; Yip & McKern, 2016).

Despite high unemployment and poverty levels, SSA remains one of the world's fastest growing regions. In comparison to most other regions of the world, there is a high degree of entrepreneurial activity in the region. With a sufficient support system and a favourable economic climate, the area should be able to decrease the growth in unemployment and reduce poverty. Residents in the region, according to Herrington and Kelly (2012), have a favourable attitude towards entrepreneurship; fear of failure does not discourage them from following their entrepreneurial goals. However, it appears that necessity is driving entrepreneurial activity in the region. Even though many people start enterprises, most of them stay poor. The support and funding structure, as well as the chances afforded by the region to foster business growth and innovation, must be considered.

Moreover, when it comes to financing new enterprises, venture capital has always had a good reputation. Not only have venture capitalists been recognised as an inevitable cornerstone in the formation of new businesses, but they have also been regarded as critical market turbulence elements, since they sit between the demand and supply of money (Cumming & Zhang, 2016; Samila & Sorenson, 2011). For three key reasons, venture capital may be outstripped by the expanding amount of relevant entrepreneurial funding through bank debt (Aparicio et al., 2016; Cole et al., 2016; Cumming & Zhang, 2016). First, entrepreneurs may turn down venture financing because they want to keep control of their company's management. Secondly, entrepreneurs may be unable to obtain venture capital financing. Thirdly, since transportation and communication have become less of a financial burden with the help of technology, entrepreneurs in emerging markets within the Sub-Saharan African region, in recent years, have seen a reduction in terms of acquiring finance from the government or other institutions. As a result, debt financing may be a viable choice for minor loans. Nonetheless, during the recent global financial crisis, banks provided significantly less credit to small and medium-sized enterprises (SMEs), notably in developed countries (Block et al., 2018). Early-stage companies, in fact, may be more affected by credit crunches caused by financial instability due to their limited collateral base and young age. As a result, young business may be affected more by financial constraints due to their interbank dependence, new firms are more vulnerable to foreign financial shocks than established ones, especially in well-integrated economies (Ferrando et al., 2013).

Financial intermediation is the most important historical variable in this formulation, and this chapter presents case studies illustrating the various impacts of financial intermediation on business opportunities. The expansion of credit markets and financial products, the increased exchange of information between lenders and related innovations such as "shadow banking" and "non-bank lending" before and after the recent COVID-19 pandemic, and the automation of lending decisions, may increase transaction costs and prevent entrepreneurs from taking advantage of product market innovations.. There is a risk of this. This provides a dynamic context for explaining the relationship between entrepreneurship as a historical economic variable and entrepreneurship and economic performance in SSA.

This chapter contributes to the conceptualisation of the historical perspective of entrepreneurship in the following ways. First, by analysing the interaction between financial intermediation and entrepreneurship, it helps to explain the dilemmas posed by different historical combinations of entrepreneurial opportunities. Secondly, by examining these combinations in contrasting time periods and analysing general financial institutional norms, it shows how the historical perspective contributes to a broader understanding of entrepreneurial opportunities. In this way, a theoretical overview can be provided that is suitable for analysing the entrepreneurial landscape and the interaction between different types of entrepreneurial opportunities and business creation in SSA.

Development and financial intermediation for entrepreneurship

Levine (1997) identifies five primary financial services provided by financial intermediaries (such as banks): (1) risk management, (2) production and processing of information about potential investments, (3) manager monitoring and corporate control, (4) mobilising savings and pooling them, and (5) provision of an infrastructure for facilitating the exchange of goods. Entrepreneurs and investors can take advantage of these financial services to start a business.

Starting and managing a firm, especially for (potential) entrepreneurs, frequently implies hefty start-up and operating expenditures. To put it another way, entrepreneurs often require enough external credit at affordable pricing to establish and operate their businesses. For two reasons, financial intermediation can meet the credit demand of entrepreneurs. First, financial intermediaries can deploy savings at a low cost. A focus on saving collection, for example, can allow them to cut costs associated with mobilising savings (Levine, 1997). Secondly, financial intermediaries may give access to huge quantities of credit, lowering the risk of inefficient scaling and increasing the incentive for entrepreneurs to pursue capital-intensive business models. Furthermore, by using financial intermediaries (e.g., credit card payments, wire transfers), entrepreneurs may run their businesses with minimal operational expenses, incentivising activities that would otherwise fail owing to excessively high operating costs.

Financial intermediation, on the other hand, provides (potential) benefits to creditors, allowing them to participate in entrepreneurial activity. Risk and information management are two areas where these creditors are particularly concerned. To begin, every investing decision involves some degree of idiosyncratic risk. Risk should be especially high when starting a new business because market conditions, innovative activity outcomes, steep learning curves, and unknown business networks are all factors to consider. Investing in entrepreneurial operations may become less tempting because of this risk. Individual investors, on the other hand, can use financial intermediation to control and diversify their investment risk (for example, through portfolio diversification) and thereby limit their exposure to the risk of certain investment initiatives (Levine, 1997). Secondly, creditors pay significant information costs when analysing individual investment projects (examples may include that they must study them) and contemplating broad investment initiatives (example may include they must review them), as well as after making a successful investment decision.

Entrepreneurs (who prefer information) are induced by information exchange between lenders and investors (e.g., corporate profits) to misrepresent themselves (Kirzner, 1997). Considering these costs, lenders may turn to financial intermediaries for the collection and processing of information about potential investments and may outsource monitoring of investment projects, thereby lowering monitoring costs (Levine, 1997).

In summary, the demand for financial services is driven by entrepreneurs' desire for accessible, low-cost, and broad-based loans, and by investors' desire for efficient, cost-effective risk and information management. Financial development at the national level is defined as a significant improvement in the quality of the five core financial functions outlined above (risk management, information management and resource allocation, corporate governance, mobilisation and pooling of savings, and facilitation of financial transactions through financial infrastructure).

Cihak et al. (2012) further identified four aspects of country-level financial development that are related to entrepreneurship and financial intermediation. First, financial system depth refers to the size of the financial system in relation to the real economy, and so reflects the credit and financial services offered by the entire financial system. Greater financial depth, for example, should encourage entrepreneurship by providing appropriate external finance.

As a second dimension, financial inclusion refers to the ability of the broader society to have access to financial services. For example, greater financial inclusion may help entrepreneurs by reducing their reliance on social ties and extending the pool of potential entrepreneurs. The financial system would also become more accessible to a broader range of potential lenders. Thirdly, financial efficiency refers to credit availability and cost. The benefits of greater financial efficiency include fewer resources remaining in the financial system (e.g., fees), while lenders send more resources to entrepreneurs. Financial efficiency, for example, allows firms to raise adequate capital at the right price because it allows them to raise sufficient funds. The fourth aspect of financial stability is system stability. Entrepreneurship is conducive to financial stability, for example, because it gives lenders confidence in the long-term safety of their investments.

Further, countries with a more advanced financial development are more likely to have a deep financial system, higher access to the financial system, and greater financial efficiency. All these factors will support entrepreneurship. By increasing financial inclusion, entrepreneurs are more likely to be able to obtain credit based on their ability rather than their social status, increasing the pool of potential entrepreneurs and thus increasing economic growth. Building on the seminal findings of Schumpeter (1934), we assume that financial development has a positive effect on entrepreneurship (1993a).

In general, evidence suggests that the institutional environment influences financial development's impact on economic growth (Ahlin & Pang, 2008). Several empirical studies have discovered that when the financial system is entrenched in a solid institutional framework, it supports entrepreneurship, which leads to economic growth. According to Law et al. (2013), financial development only promotes entrepreneurship and economic growth when institutional quality is adequate. Financial progress has little impact on economic performance when institutional quality is poor. Inadequate democratic controls, for example, may permit money (collected and mobilised by the financial system) to be channelled to specific entrepreneurial companies based on political insider deals rather than the most productive ideas (i.e., growth-inducing).

Financial growth and systematisation of social entrepreneurship

In the 1970s, social entrepreneurship began to emerge as a form of economic activity, particularly in the USA and Western Europe. A review of the literature on the subject identified four main strands of research that shed light on the nature of this phenomenon: the social innovation school, the social entrepreneurship school (Crimmings & Kiel, 1983), EMES, the British school of social entrepreneurship (Dees & Anderson, 2006; Popov et al., 2019). In the American approach, to which the first two schools belong, social entrepreneurship is largely considered as an economic market activity that serves social purposes, regardless of the field of activity and organisational and legal structure. The European method, including the third and fourth schools, is based on the development of a third economic sector to replace public services in areas where they do not exist.

In Western Europe, this has led to the emergence of new social enterprises by civil society actors, while in the USA, social activities have been carried out by existing organisations (Popov et al., 2019). Social enterprises have emerged in many European and are seen as an example of inclusive long-term development that can help the public sector to address social challenges. As a result, to date, there is no unified understanding of the term "social entrepreneurship", which greatly complicates the discussion of the goals and future direction of this type of activity (Popov et al., 2019).

Russian experience in the development of social entrepreneurship combines both American and European traditions. Examples of social enterprises in this context are small and micro enterprises and socially oriented non-profit organisations. As a result of this phenomenon, the terms social enterprise, social entrepreneur, socially oriented enterprise, social start-up (the life cycle of organisations in the Russian Federation in this area often does not exceed 3–5 years), social entrepreneurship, social project, initiative, etc. are used as synonyms for the issues and forms of social entrepreneurship.

Entrepreneurship, economic development, and financial stability

Economic development in SSA requires sustained economic growth. In this sense, economic growth can be defined in terms of economic indicators such as the creation of additional jobs and improved living conditions for citizens. In modern economics, economic development refers to the transformation of economic fundamentals into a more technologically advanced economy which is based on real productivity and innovation (Naudé, 2010a). It is the long-term development of a society measured in terms of productivity and employment, GDP per capita, human capital indicators, child and maternal mortality, education, social justice, GDP growth, and poverty reduction (Naudé, 2010b). It includes the development of programmes and policies to improve the business environment, such as improving access to finance, promoting products, creating a favourable business environment, developing, maintaining firms, expanding ownership, and transferring technology (OECD, 2008).

International organisations, government officials, and policymakers have all been drawn to the significance of entrepreneurship in aiding economic growth. Since the turn of the millennium, economic development has emphasised the creation of small businesses and entrepreneurship above large-scale employment creation. Some leaders are beginning to understand that entrepreneurship is not simply an answer to unemployment, but also a drive for better economic development that leads to a better GDP per capita and more inclusive growth. Entrepreneurship can help speed the accomplishment of the SDG if given the attention it deserves (UNCTAD, 2017). Entrepreneurial success needs access to capital and markets, and public policy plays a critical role in facilitating this (Kressel & Lento, 2012).

According to Schumpeter, entrepreneurship presents itself in five contexts: new markets, new items, new raw material sources, new manufacturing processes, and new institutions. Entrepreneurship entails the capacity to offer new processes, goods, services, organisational structures, or marketing, as well as recreate or rethink previous ones (Olokundun, 2018). According to the Small Business Administration (1998), the continuous establishment of new small enterprises in various sectors of an economy is an indication of social welfare and economic independence. In recently, job creation, economic growth and national success in both developed and developing countries have been greatly influenced by entrepreneurship. Entrepreneurship, when effectively utilised, has the potential to accelerate progress towards the SDG in emerging economies. Access to financing for new businesses is thus one of the variables that relates economic growth to entrepreneurship (Tomaa et al., 2014). The current research on growth and finance suggests that the credit constraint has impeded private sector-led development in the context of financial stability (CarbóValverde et al., 2016; IMF-GFSR, 2018).

Credit tightening is common during periods of financial instability, limiting enterprises' operating capital and eventually leading to lower future investment expenditure on production and company bankruptcies (IMF-GFSR, 2018). Financial insecurity is a negative shock to the credit supply, resulting in a lack of productive capacity in the economy. To preserve financial stability regardless of market conditions, emerging economies' financial systems must be resilient, flexible, and efficient. They must maintain their effectiveness in a fast-changing economic environment while adhering to core economic concepts and resource allocation procedures. Financial systems must also be robust enough to enable timely payment and transaction settlement without relying on other economic considerations.

Schinasi (2004) states that financial stability is the strength of the financial system that allows for the transfer of wealth between individuals and countries and the allocation of resources that leads to economic prosperity. Financial stability is a state in which the financial system effectively manages financial risk through appropriate valuation and pricing and can perform as it should against external shocks and instability. When exposed to external shocks, the financial system should be able to rebalance through internal stabilisers; a stable financial system, according to Isărescu (2009), enhances the business climate and fosters genuine economic growth through intermediation processes. The financial system maintains a steady supply of capital and absorbs shocks while allowing economic expansion to continue. While Davis (2001) emphasises that the actual economy expands through access to credit and payment systems, financial instability exacerbates information asymmetries and impedes the process of financial intermediation in the economy. He contends that systemic risk arises from the failure of market liquidity and insufficient infrastructure.

Ferguson (2003) argued that financial instability will emerge as a result of large changes in national or worldwide credit markets occur, resulting in a credit crisis. Financial instability can also emerge when financial asset prices diverge significantly from expectations or when the economy's output falls short of the population's consumption potential. Financial instability, according to Chan (2003), is "the threat posed by financial markets to economic growth and performance as a result of financial system malfunction". Mishkin (1999) contends that the separation between macroeconomic and financial instability is strong. Financial instability is generated by shocks in aggregate demand and supply, whereas macroeconomic instability is caused by shocks in aggregate demand and supply. Financial markets are characterised by continuous pricing and market condition volatility; as a result, financial volatility should be addressed in terms of its potential impact on the actual economy.

Klapper and Love (2011) investigated the impact of the 2008 financial crisis on the establishment of new firms (entrepreneurship). They observed that the crisis had a stronger influence on the formation of new enterprises in countries with higher levels of financial growth. During the crisis, new business development fell dramatically in almost all the nations analysed. This implies that the more bank capital a country has, the more probable new business entrance will be hampered by the 2008 financial crises. In a study of ten countries in SSA, Herrington and Kelly (2012) discovered that access to financing and corruption were the two most common causes of entrepreneurship. Households confront two major challenges, according to the researchers: a lack of a strong sense of ownership and a lack of a strong sense of responsibility. For entrepreneurs to have a substantial influence on the region, the economic climate must significantly improve; Fayissa and Nsiah (2013) discovered a positive significant relationship between economic growth and governance quality.

Good governance favours advanced economies, but it has little effect on low-income economies and areas. Human capital development is important in business, according to Kolstad and Wiig (2015). Both believe that increasing educational attainment encourages entrepreneurship and hence economic growth. The effect of financial instability on entrepreneurial growth must be investigated in order to assess the financial system's potential to encourage entrepreneurship in SSA, since the strength of the financial system is critical to achieving the SDGs through entrepreneurship.

Bank financing and entrepreneurship

Several scholars have developed models that point towards the role of financial intermediaries as a means of leveraging innovation. These include, among others, who showed that these intermediaries foster technological innovation and boost productivity growth through their role in supporting entrepreneurs with the most suitable features to succeed in the development of innovative projects. However, significant disparities across countries and economies exist regarding how these financing structures can identify the start-ups that are most likely to succeed. Ultimately, this may result in different levels not only of entrepreneurship but productivity as well (Levine, 1997).

In addition, the academic literature emphasises that access to finance plays a crucial role in entrepreneurship. New businesses are more likely to be created when financing needs are met (Van Gelderen et al., 2005). Aparicio et al. (2016) suggest that easier access to banking credit positively impacts entrepreneurship by guaranteeing a start-up's viability. The authors also point out that entrepreneurs are more likely to broaden their business activity, perhaps internationally, if access to credit is facilitated. Moreover, two major factors favouring entrepreneurship appear to include higher capitalisation and reduced risk perception (Van Gelderen et al., 2005).

This is supported by Kibler (2013), who argues that a business environment is perceived as conducive in terms of financing when there is greater availability of funding sources such as bank financing, to increase the capitalisation of firms. From a broader perspective, certain financial regulations negatively influence entrepreneurship. If potential entrepreneurs perceive regulations regarding financing as a barrier to the implementation of their projects, this ultimately will result in the interruption of business activity (Alvarez & Urbano, 2011; Gnyawali & Fogel, 1994).

Venture capital and entrepreneurship

When it comes to venture financing, and following Winton and Yerramilli (2008), entrepreneurs favour it over bank financing, especially among uncertainty and risk. When the entrepreneur is faced with the reluctance of traditional banks to assume the risk of financing a new company, particularly in the field of new technologies, venture capital can take over. This is also supported by De Bettignies and Brander (2007), who point out that entrepreneurs tend to turn to bank financing when capital costs are reduced (this often can remain constrained by the difficulty of funding access). For venture capital investors, their principal motivation is return on investment, with the primary goal of growing a business to the point where they can benefit by selling its shares as part of an Initial Public Offering (IPO) or to other private investors. In addition, the literature agrees that when investors are confident, venture capital supplies increase, achieving a positive symbiosis with entrepreneurship.

Overall, according to Kortum and Lerner (2000), venture capital is seen as an effective way of financing new innovation-driven businesses. For example, Samila and Sorenson (2011) highlighted that the increased availability of venture capital in U.S. metropolitan areas augments the numbers of firms, employment, and income growth. This positive venture capital effect is also confirmed by Cole et al. (2016). With reference to Cumming and Zhang (2016), venture capital can be a powerful incentive for innovation, actively contributing to the development of entrepreneurs' projects.

According to Gu et al. (2018), there are two types of venture capital that influence entrepreneurship. To begin with, venture capital provides financial assistance to SMEs, which are the primary source of technical innovation. Traditional financing techniques, such as bank loans, are usually ineffective in such situations because SMEs have significant risk and little collateral. Because high-risk industries can yield significant profits, venture capital firms choose to invest in them. By limiting the amount of finance and giving money in stages, venture capital can provide a firm budget constraint, avoiding the complications that standard financing techniques might cause. As a result, venture capital can be more effectively invested in creative companies, broadening the financing channels for SMEs. Secondly, venture capital provides management assistance. Because of the high risk of investment, large cash flow, and other features, the management must have excellent insight and risk control capabilities. Meanwhile, professionals with great management abilities and deep investment knowledge may be able to help creative enterprises improve their management and increase their chances of success. They help new enterprises create teams, extend their market share, and so on, all of which will have a huge influence on their creativity and learning. After receiving venture capital, businesses can reduce costs, expand their market, and promote full development. However, due to the industry's poor rules and regulations, China's young capital market may make management less successful.

The emergence of venture capital investing offers a chance to entrepreneurs but are short of money. Because of the huge number of VC institutions, it is easier for innovators to obtain venture capital funding, and more innovators are participating in technological innovation activities. As a result, the growth of venture capital can create a social environment in which innovators are encouraged to innovate, and the success of the creative firm encourages further entrepreneurship in innovation activities. This phenomenon happens in China, numerous other emerging markets, and established nations due to varied fevered policies for Venture Capital Institutions and the rise of many high-tech start-ups in recent years. According to Gu et al. (2018) and Samila and Sorenson (2011), venture capital firms can stimulate entrepreneurial activity by demonstrating their impacts or encouraging future company founders.

More start-ups and employment should arise if venture capital is actually advantageous to entrepreneurship and the formation of new businesses. The majority of relevant research examines the link between venture capital and employment and finds that it has a favourable and significant impact. Bertoni and Tykvovább1 (2015) studied 865 biotech pharmaceutical start-ups in seven European nations, and the empirical findings revealed that the output of venture capital-backed enterprises grows much quicker than that of non-venture capital-backed firms. The literature on venture capital funding has demonstrated that it is critical to establish a trust connection between venture capital and the entrepreneur because of the numerous benefits that it provides, even though it is costly and time-consuming to develop. This is a crucial factor for venture capitalists to consider when deciding whether to partner with a contractor (Bengtsson, 2013). Indeed, rather than taking the risk of investing in a new enterprise with an unknown entrepreneur (however potential), investors will frequently choose to work with a contractor with whom they have previously done business. The fundamental reason for this is that they see the entrepreneur's relationship as a source of "insider" information that the market does not have (Morandin et al., 2006). Furthermore, there is evidence that businesses obtain different sorts of finance depending on their stage of development. Even though venture capital is designed to support budding entrepreneurship at the start-up stage, it appears to meddle at later stages of growth (Aernoudt, 2005a; Wong et al., 2009). Furthermore, the notion of rapid and essential growth might sway investors' opinions, causing them to overlook bright young entrepreneurs who are motivated by other factors (Franke et al., 2006). Many venture capital investors have a strong need for high growth, even if this corporate growth and performance culture might stifle the formation of new enterprises and entrepreneurship (Klotz et al., 2014).

Financial constraints and entrepreneurship

Furthermore, scholars may argue that because their new businesses tend to have extremely low capital requirements, meeting financing needs is not particularly problematic for nascent entrepreneurs (Hurst & Lusardi, 2004; Mitter & Kraus, 2011). On top of this, advantages exist in not drawing on external sources of financing. These are the results of reduced pressure exerted by financial structures, allowing entrepreneurs to be freer in their management decisions. Indeed, if personal capital lasts and additional cash flow can be generated, the benefits of personal financing remain, and the risks of external financing are reduced (Markova & Petkovska-Mircevska,

2009). In addition, it appears that most of a nascent entrepreneur's equity capital comes from individual savings, which might also involve funds obtained from the family (Mitter & Kraus, 2011). It is also more likely that individuals save money (financial deposits) rather than self-financing by investing in physical Capital only when the return offered by a financial intermediary on deposits exceeds what would be expected from an investment in physical capital (something which is the case with developed financial systems; Deidda & Fattouh, 2002). It therefore appears that financial development in terms of bank financing does not necessarily imply a high level of entrepreneurial investment. From this perspective, we can assume that: Banking financing will not favour nascent entrepreneurship.

Regarding venture capital financing, the literature has revealed that it is important to establish a trust relationship between venture capital and the entrepreneur because of the many benefits that result from it, even though it is expensive and takes time to develop. This is therefore an important reason for venture capitalists in their decision whether to enter into a business relationship with a contractor (Bengtsson, 2013). Indeed, instead of running the risk of investing in a new venture with an entrepreneur they do not know (as promising as it may be), investors will often decide to join a contractor with whom they have already done business. The main reason for this is that they perceive the relationship with the entrepreneur as a kind of "insider" information that the market does not have access to (Morandin et al., 2006). In addition, there is evidence supporting the idea that businesses receive different types of financing according to their developmental stage.

Although venture capital is supposed to fund particularly nascent entrepreneurship in the start-up stage, it appears to rather intervene at companies' subsequent stages of growth (Aernoudt, 2005a; Wong et al., 2009). Furthermore, the perception of rapid and necessary growth can skew the judgement of investors who consequently will tend to exclude talented young entrepreneurs who are driven by other motivations (Franke et al., 2006). The desire for strong growth is prevalent among many venture capital investors, even though this culture of corporate growth and performance can hinder the emergence of new businesses (Klotz et al., 2014). On the other hand, as far as the behaviour of future entrepreneurs is concerned, venture capital can be considered risky compared to other sources of finance, discouraging new firms from adopting it as a result. According to De Bettignies and Brander (2007), one of the main differences between venture capital and bank financing is control. In fact, by choosing bank financing entrepreneurs remain in charge of all decisions related to their business, while being encouraged to remain entrepreneurial/risk-taking. Venture capital, on the other hand, is a two-way street involving not only the contribution in terms of management but also the transfer of part of an individual's property, which in turn reduces the incentive to make an actual business effort. In addition, the role of business angels (Elitzur 2003), crowdfunding, and business incubators (Block et al., 2018; Vismara, 2016) in the early stages of a company should not be neglected, especially compared to venture capitalists and their relationship with the entrepreneur. Although both provide added value, venture capitalists do not put in as much effort as business angels, as the latter will eventually have to convince other investors to finance the venture (Fairchild, 2011; Schwienbacher, 2009). In this sense, business angels present less risk to the entrepreneur in terms of managing the business, even if the refinancing is at greater risk (Schwienbacher, 2007). For this reason, and also because they assume the relationship with the angel to be more intimate and trusting, entrepreneurs tend to choose business angels as sources of financing. Moreover, Bigus (2002) shows that there is another risk for the entrepreneur when bringing a venture capitalist on board. Indeed, venture capitalists could expropriate or threaten to expropriate the entrepreneur, for instance, by imposing the renegotiation of equity allocation (for an extensive literature review on expropriation risk, see Bigus, 2002). According to Landier (2001), the risk of a conflicting relationship can even be bidirectional, with not only the venture capitalist refusing funding but also with the entrepreneur withdrawing from the business. It as a result seems that venture capital does not always effectively play its role as a catalyst for nascent entrepreneurship because it is not sufficiently sought after as a source of finance by future entrepreneurs, which is also reflected in the figures of several previous studies. For example, Davis (2001) highlights that nine-tenths of new businesses are not financed by venture capital, and even more small businesses use other sources to finance their enterprise. Amit et al. (1990) distinguish between better entrepreneurs and best-quality entrepreneurs. According to the authors, better entrepreneurs may prefer no financing at all to venture capital when information asymmetries exist, while best-quality entrepreneurs do not necessarily choose venture capital as an external financing source, even in the absence of information asymmetries.

Unlike Fairlie (2013), Dawson and Henley (2012a) claim that when people are unemployed, they are more likely to establish their own firms. Economic crises, according to Amit and Muller (1995), are powerful and effective push factors for entrepreneurship. Technology industries appear to favourably influence economic growth expectations in times of recession, according to Peris-Ortiz et al. (2014), albeit this nexus is difficult to document. This, according to the authors, is explained by the fact that in times of crisis, the sense of opportunities and innovation appears to be significantly more relevant than in times of economic development.

Financial instability and entrepreneurship

The academic literature does not provide consistent results on how financial turbulence impacts nascent entrepreneurship (Devece et al., 2016). Looking closely at research dealing with entrepreneurship during crisis periods, we find mixed results. The stability of the economic and financial macro context is likely to affect an entrepreneur's perception of business opportunities, which, according to Gaglio and Katz (2001), marks the beginning of all entrepreneurial activity. The perception of opportunities for entrepreneurship is the result of a combination of various factors, such as technological and market know-how, vigilance, or looking for opportunities (Baron, 2006). A poor financial macro context can complicate access to these factors, the consequences of which are not only reduced possibilities of starting a business but also (from the perspective of the entrepreneur) restrained capacities for seizing them. In this sense, cowling et al. (2012) show that it becomes more complicated to obtain access to external funding in times of macro financial turbulences.

In addition, Devece et al. (2016) stipulate that during recessions, entrepreneurship, which is essentially motivated by necessity, is inefficient. Fairlie (2013) confirms how creating new entrepreneurial ventures is less frequent during periods of crisis. According to these studies, it appears that financial instability will not favour nascent entrepreneurship. However, unlike Fairlie (2013), Dawson and Henley (2012a) argue that people tend to start their own businesses when they face a lack of employment opportunities. This kind of argument led Amit and Muller (1995) to qualify economic crises as strong and effective push factors for entrepreneurship.

According to Peris-Ortiz et al. (2014), technology sectors appear to positively influence economic growth expectations in times of recession, although this nexus is a phenomenon that is difficult to capture. The authors add that this is explained by the fact that the perception of opportunities and innovation appears to be far more important in times of crisis than during economic growth. The following hypothesis emerges from the aforementioned research: financial instability will stimulate nascent entrepreneurship.

Entrepreneurship in emerging markets

Because of fluctuating political, regulatory, and economic settings, Sub-Saharan African countries are frequently marked by high levels of uncertainty. Simultaneously, specialist resources are scarce, and consumer markets are frequently enormous, yet price sensitive, with low entry barriers and considerable volatility (Meyer & Peng, 2016). In many emerging nations, strong business communities have formed despite, or possibly because of, these contextual challenges.

Traditionally, developing market innovation has focused on localising imports and generating "good enough" (Chang & Park, 2012) or unique (Hossain et al., 2021). Entrepreneurship has gained popularity in recent years. Among the main researchers are George Yip (Greeven et al., 2019; Yip & McKern, 2016; Yip & Prashantham, 2019), Sam Park (Park et al., 2013), Ari Levin (Lewin et al., 2017), and Peter Williamson (Williamson et al., 2018). Faced with fierce competition, Chinese entrepreneurs have increased their emphasis on innovation, which necessitates enterprises constantly upgrading their knowledge base, goods, and business tactics (Luo & Bu, 2018; Yip & McKern, 2016; Yip & Prashantham, 2019). As stated in recent essays in this journal, many of the most dramatic transformations in developing markets are breakthrough business innovations (Ma & Hu, 2021; Mehotra & Velamuri, 2021).

This modernisation has been supported by catch-up education, technology diffusion throughout global value chains, relatively low-cost access to engineers and scientific professionals, and increasingly cultured local demand, such as from the developing middle class and government efforts (Yip & Prashantham, 2019). Even as local entrepreneurs increasingly compete with foreign rivals in their market niches, they face financial challenges in competing successfully on the global stage (Greeven et al., 2019; Williamson & Wan, 2019), and their attitude is still shaped by their roots in highly volatile and competitive home markets.

COVID-19 and financial stability

Many banks throughout the world were affected by the COVID-19 crisis, which had a mixed influence on equities markets. The Sanderpump 500, Dow Jones, Russell 2000, Nasdaq Composite, FTSE 100, and Nikkei 225 indexes, for example, were all roughly 30–40% lower by the end of March than they were in January (New York Times, 2020). Financial institutions in international and national economies are susceptible to shocks (Fu et al., 2014; Montgomery et al., 2014; Safiullah & Shamsuddin, 2019; Wang et al., 2018). (Kwabi et al., 2020). As a result, business owners and entrepreneurs are more vulnerable to COVID-19.

Numerous banks in many countries are unable to provide liquidity insurance as a result of the COVID-19 changes and upgrades. As many businesses fail or go out of business during and after the outbreak, and demand for products and services diminishes, banks throughout the world may face increased credit and default risk due to liquidity management and insolvency concerns. If private sector investment and consumption continue to deteriorate, bank funding is unlikely to recover during or after a pandemic. According to Beck (2020), three elements will decide the impact of COVID-19: the severity of the pandemic's impact on the global economy, fiscal and monetary policy responses to the shock, and regulators' responses to the financial system's potential susceptibility.

Furthermore, Cecchetti and Schoenholtz (2020) demonstrate that banks' business models are extremely vulnerable to economic shocks, and that their failure during the pandemic might result in massive economic upheaval. According to the resource dependence hypothesis, companies require external resources to expand since they cannot rely only on their own operating capabilities, and resources are required to generate value for the organisation.

During this outbreak, however, access to external market resources is limited. Despite the fact that many central banks and authorities actively responded to the crisis and attempted to strengthen the banking sector's resilience (by lowering benchmark interest rates to increase liquidity and mitigate the crisis's effects, for example), the blockade measures and the crisis's effects raised concerns about bank stability. Because healthcare remains a key problem in many nations, they were health-related priority measures that left little opportunity for other solutions. These extraordinary government actions resulted in the temporary or permanent closure of numerous enterprises, the turmoil of financial markets, the loss of public trust in the economy, and heightened insecurity (Tan & Floros, 2013).

Despite the fact that regulators attempted to bail out banks and corporations, we believe their stability was harmed during the epidemic because they took many risks and fared poorly financially. Several prior studies have found that "bail-in expectations" boost risk-taking (Feng et al., 2019; Gropp et al., 2011) and cause moral hazard at both the bank and system level (Mailath & Mester, 1994). Bailed-out banks, according to Duchin and Sosyura (2014), take excessive risks because their managers are protected in the event of failure.

It is impossible to evaluate the precise impact of these policies on entrepreneurship and financial stability in a quickly changing environment, but they predict a substantial drop in financial performance and business risk. Given the foregoing, we expect the COVID-19 shocks to have a negative impact on financial performance and a reduction in entrepreneurial activity in emerging economies such as South Africa.

Mitigation strategies and concluding remarks

The COVID-19 crisis has already shown that different institutions can use different policy instruments in parallel to stabilise the economy and the financial system. However, this episode also illustrates the difficulty of making a clear distinction between measures aimed at preventing deflationary risks (and general economic instability) and those aimed at financing firms and the real economy.

Based on the division of responsibilities between financial, macroprudential, and microprudential authorities, different policy instruments affect different social objectives, which poses a challenge for the smooth functioning of enterprises and SMEs. In times of crisis, authorities can of course agree on the need to take exceptional measures. On the other hand, the problem of a coherent policy response may be compounded when authorities decide on the pace of standardisation based on their own authority but use measures that may also affect other objectives of other institutions.

The overall message of our analysis of the situation is that a viral pandemic presents the risk of a financial pandemic, a type of systemic risk. Moreover, a financial pandemic could even become a global phenomenon. This could provide the basis for the creation of a common mutual insurance scheme that compensates companies for cash flow shortfalls caused by the crisis, but not for "inherited" bad performance, thus limiting (or preventing) spill over effects in the production, consumption and banking sectors.

Some countries, especially at the European level, have been quick to emphasise the sense of the COVID-19 pandemic. The diagnosis of collective action is easy, but its implementation is extremely complex. If it fails, this episode can be seen as a harbinger of the next financial crisis in Europe. However, if handled well, it could pave the way for a European Hamilton. This joint action can make the European financial union sustainable and define a form of risk sharing that shows solidarity, without undermining the typical framework of moral hazard and transfer associations.

Based on the above analysis and the literature review, we suggest joint action around public finance and a more limited role for monetary policy in SSA countries. Given the reasons for the impending failure of the corporate sector, reducing interest rates, and increasing asset purchases are unlikely to be the way to resolve liquidity shortages at the individual firm level, mainly because banks are constrained by capital requirements in addition to liquidity buffers. Indeed, there is a need to provide liquidity quickly and in a targeted manner to firms and companies facing production and supply chain disruptions, to firms with new business ideas, and to those experiencing a significant decline in demand in Sub-Saharan African countries.

Following the above analysis we made two suggestions: first, to find tools for timely assessment of crown-caused cash flow shortfalls at the firm level; and, second, to find ways to effectively channel funds to affected individuals, firms, and entrepreneurs during the COVID-19 pandemic.

The above suggestions show that there is a strong case for delegating the financial stabilisation function to the central bank. It also argues that the financial stabilisation function should include both macroprudential and microprudential responsibilities. Ideally, these two tasks should be integrated into a single policy framework with tools that allow authorities to address all the different aspects of financial stability objectives (targeted and systemic). In addition, of course, political economy considerations can be equally relevant within an appropriate institutional framework. As independent institutions such as central banks accumulate responsibilities, questions of democratic legitimacy and accountability arise. For the chosen formula to be socially acceptable and thus sustainable, these issues must be properly addressed.

We also discovered that higher per capita income is linked to more entrepreneurship. For example, this could imply that economic progress encourages entrepreneurship by aligning with greater market sizes. Secondly, we discovered that the size of the government has little bearing on entrepreneurship. Thirdly, there is evidence that more trade openness is associated with increased entrepreneurship. Trade openness, i.e., allowing enterprises to access into global markets, for example, may enhance market size while simultaneously simplifying the transfer of technology and ideas that may arouse entrepreneurial activity. This may be shown in the instance of the COVID-19 pandemic, when increasing local and worldwide demand strengthened the market for online delivery of products, services, and fast food, as well as face masks and sanitisers.

The chapter finds that SMEs, like other businesses, are having a difficult time due to significant effects on national economies. Entrepreneurs who are impacted by the COVID-19 pandemic have the potential to contribute significantly to economic growth in SSA. Even though the globe is experiencing a pandemic that is unique in its character, and still recovering from the global credit crunch of 2008 which started in the USA and spreading throughout the world, the solutions are neither impossible to implement nor too late. Governments are doing everything possible to keep their banking institutions afloat and defend their economies. Other stakeholders, such as financial market participants and significant multinational corporations, can complement the government's efforts.

In summary, the study finds that financial difficulties and stability in SSA have inhibited entrepreneurial development, which would have enhanced economic growth and promoted SSA's SDG. To fully achieve the region's potential and remove the region's high poverty and unemployment rates, governments in Sub-Saharan African nations still have a lot of work to do in terms of good government policies and stability, development of infrastructure and human capital development. Early school enrolment should be put into effect and made mandatory in the region by the various government bodies. These leaders should take their peer review process more seriously and sanction corrupt leaders to promote good governance across the region and the continent (What does the African union organisation account for if governance across regions are not accountable). The rest of SSA should learn from other emerging and developed economies throughout the world about what they're doing differently to boost entrepreneurial growth and development, so they can apply it in their own countries.

Limitations

This chapter contains limitations, which leaves room for more investigation. The first is the focus on the recent COVID-19 period. Additional research could investigate whether the nature of these linkages varies over time to determine the analytical boundary conditions (e.g., comparing the effect the credit crunch of 2008 and the COVID-19 pandemic on entrepreneurship financial stability). Secondly, this research focused on entrepreneurship and financial stability in Sub-Saharan African countries following the COVID-19 pandemic. The research is limited to theoretical literature and does not include practical research with a tangible dataset. In the case of financial stability and entrepreneurship, the utilisation of primary and secondary databases for future research can be considered.

Finally, another drawback of this research is that attempt was not made to explain why certain types of firms receive preferential funding, how company ideas evolve organically, or how these businesses perform.

References

Acs, Z. J., Braunerhjelm, P., Audretsch, D. B., & Carlsson, B. (2009). The knowledge spillover theory of entrepreneurship. *Small Business Economics*, 32, 15–30.

Aernoudt, R. (2005a). Executive forum: Seven ways to stimulate business angels' investments. *Venture Capital*, 7(4), 359–371.

Aernoudt, R. (2005b). Business angels: The smartest money for starters? Plea for a renewed policy focus on business angels. *International Journal of Business*, 10(3).

Agarwal, R., Audretsch, D., & Sarkar, M. B. (2010). Knowledge spillovers and strategic entrepreneurship. *Strategic Entrepreneurship Journal*, 4, 271–283.

Aghion, P., Blundell, R., Griffith, R., Howitt, P., & Prantl, S. (2009). The effects of entry on incumbent innovation and productivity. *The Review of Economics and Statistics*, 91, 20–32.

Ahlin, C., & Pang, J. (2008). Are financial development and corruption control substitutes in promoting growth? *Journal of Development Economics*, 86(2), 414–433.

Amit, R., Glosten, L., & Muller, E. (1990). Entrepreneurial ability, venture investments, and risk sharing. *Management Science*, 36(10), 1232–1245.

Amit, R., & Muller, E. (1995). "Push" and "pull" entrepreneurship. *Journal of Small Business and Entrepreneurship*, 12(4), 64–80.

Aparicio, S., Urbano, D., & Audretsch, D. (2016). Institutional factors, opportunity entrepreneurship and economic growth: Panel data evidence. *Technological Forecasting and Social Change*, 102, 45–61.

Babajide, A. A., & Olokoyo, F. O. (2017). Assessment of financial stability in emerging economies: Evidence from Nigeria. In *Global financial crisis and its ramifications on capital markets* (pp. 191–207). Cham: Springer.

Baron, R. A. (2006). Opportunity recognition as pattern recognition: How entrepreneurs 1135 "connect the dots" to identify new business opportunities. *Academy of Management Perspectives*, 20(1), 104–119.

Beck, T., & Demirgüc-Kunt, A. (2006). Small and medium-size enterprises: Access to finance as a growth constraint. *Journal of Banking & Finance*, 30, 2931–2943.

Beck, T., Demirgüc-Kunt, A., Laeven, L., & Levine, R. (2008). Finance, firm size, and growth. *Journal of Money, Credit, and Banking*, 40, 1379–1405.

Beck, T., Lu, L., & Yang, R. (2015). Finance and growth for microenterprises: Evidence from rural China. *World Development*, 67, 38–56.

Bengtsson, O. (2013). Relational venture capital financing of serial founders. *Journal of Financial Intermediation*, 22(3), 308–334.

Bengtsson, O., & Hand, J. R. (2013). Employee compensation in entrepreneurial companies. *Journal of Economics & Management Strategy*, 22(2), 312–340.

Bigus, J. (2002). Staging of venture financing, investor opportunism, and patent law. Working Paper. University of Hamburg.

Bjornksov, C., & Foss, N. J. (2008). Economic freedom and entrepreneurial activity: Some cross-country evidence. *Public Choice*, 134, 307–328.

Block, J. H., Colombo, M. G., Cumming, D. J., & Vismara, S. (2018). New players in entrepreneurial finance and why they are there. *Small Business Economics*, 50(2), 239–250.

Caligiuri, P., De Cieri, H., Minbaeva, D., Verbeke, A., & Zimmermann, A. (2020). International HRM insights for navigating the COVID-19 pandemic: Implications for future research and practice. *Journal of International Business Studies*, 51, 697–713.

CarbóValverde, F., RodríguezFernández, F., & Udel, G. F. (2016). Trade credit, the financial crisis, and SME access to finance. *Journal of Money, Credit, and Banking*, 48(1), 113–143.

Carree, M., & Thurik, R. (2003). The impact of entrepreneurship on economic growth. In Z. J. Acs & D. B. Audretsch (Eds.), *Handbook of entrepreneurship research* (pp. 437–471). Boston: Kluwer Academic Publishers.

Cecchetti, S. G., & Schoenholtz, K. L. (2020). Contagion: Bank runs and COVID-19. In R. Baldwin & B. W. di Mauro (Eds.), *Economics in the time of COVID-19*. London: Centre for Economic Policy Research.

Chang, S. J., & Park, S. H. (2012). Winning strategies in China: competitive dynamics between MNCs and local firms. *Long Range Planning*, 45(1), 1–15.

Čihák, M., Demirgüç-Kunt, A., Feyen, E., & Levine, R. (2012). Benchmarking financial systems around the world. *World Bank Policy Research Working Paper* (6175).

Cirera, X., Cruz, M., Davies, E., Grover, A., Lacovone, L., Lopez Cordova, J. E., Medvedev, D., Okechukwu Maduko, F., Nayyar, G., Reyes Ortega, S., & Torres, J. (2021). Policies to support businesses through the COVID-19 shock: A firm level perspective. *World Bank Research Observer*, 36(1): 41–66.

Cole, R., Cumming, D. J., & Li, D. (2016). Do banks or VCs spur small firm growth? *Journal of International Financial Markets Institutions and Money*, 41, 60–72.

Coté, C., Estrin, S., Meyer, K. E., & Shapiro, D. (2020). COVID-19 and the dynamics of distance in international business. *Academy of International Business Insights*, 20(3). p. 3.

Cowling, M., Liu, W., & Ledger, A. (2012). Small business financing in the UK before and during the current financial crisis. *International Small Business Journal*, 30(7), 778–800.

Crimmings J., & Kiel M. (1983). *Enterprise in the nonprofit sector*. Washington, DC: Partners for Livable Places.

Cumming, D. J., & Zhang, Y. (2016). Alternative investments in emerging markets: A review and new trends. *Emerging Markets Review*, 29, 1–23. doi:10.1016/j.ememar.2016.08.022.

Davis, E. (2001). A typology of financial instability, Oesterreichische National Bank (Central Bank of Austria), Financial Stability Report No. 2, 92110.

Dawson, C., & Henley, A. (2012a). Something will turn up? Financial over-optimism and mortgage arrears. *Economics Letters*, 117(1), 49–52.

Dawson, C., & Henley, A. (2012b). "Push" versus "pull" entrepreneurship: An ambiguous distinction? *International Journal of Entrepreneurial Behaviour and Research*, 18(6), 697–719.

De Bettignies, J. E., & Brander, J. A. (2007). Financing entrepreneurship: Bank finance versus venture capital. *Journal of Business Venturing*, 22(6), 808–832.

Dees J., & Anderson B. (2006). Framing a theory of entrepreneurship: Building on two schools of practice and thought. *ARNOVA Occasional Paper Series: Research on Social Entrepreneurship: Understanding and Contributing to an Emerging Field*, 1(3), 39–66.

Deidda, L., & Fattouh, B. (2002). Non-linearity between finance and growth. *Economics Letters*, 74(3), 339–345.

Devece, C., Peris-Ortiz,M., & Rueda-Armengot, C. (2016). Entrepreneurship during economic crisis: Success factors and paths to failure. *Journal of Business Research*, 69(11), 5366–5370.

Duchin, R., & Sosyura, D. (2014). Safer ratios, riskier portfolios: Banks ' response to government aid. *Journal of Financial Economics*, 113(1), 1–28.

Elitzur, R., & Gavious, A. (2003). Contracting, signalling, and moral hazard: A model of entrepreneurs, 'angels', and venture capitalists. *Journal of Business Venturing*, 18(6), 709–725.

Evans, D. S., & Jovanovic, B. (1989). An estimated model of entrepreneurial choice under liquidity constraints. *Journal of Political Economy*, 97, 808–827.

Fairchild, R. (2011). An entrepreneur's choice of venture capitalist or angel-financing: A behavioral game-theoretic approach. *Journal of Business Venturing*, 26(3), 359–374.

Fairlie, R. W. (2013). Entrepreneurship, economic conditions, and the great recession. *Journal of Economics and Management Strategy*, 22(2), 207–231.

Fan, Z., & Zhang, R. (2017). Financial Inclusion, entry barriers, and entrepreneurship: Evidence from China. *Sustainability*, 9, 203.

Fayissa, B., & Nsiah, C. (2013). The impact of governance on economic growth in Africa. *Journal Of Developing Areas*, 47(1), 91–108.

Feng, L., Fu, T., & Kutan, A. M. (2019). Can government intervention be both a curse and a blessing? Evidence from China's finance sector. *International Review of Financial Analysis*, 61, 71–81.

Ferguson, R. (2003, September). Should financial stability be an explicit Central Bank Objective? In Monetary Stability, Financial Stability and the Business Cycle: Five Views, BIS Paper No. 18, 715.

Ferrando, A., Griesshaber, N., Köhler-Ulbrich, P., Pérez-Duarte, S., & Schmitt, N. (2013). Measuring the opinion of firms on the supply and demand of external financing in the euro area. Bank for International Settlements, Proceedings of the Sixth IFC Conference on "Statistical issues and activities in a changing environment. Basel.

Franke, N., Gruber, M., Harhoff, D., & Henkel, J. (2006). What you are is what you like similarity biases in venture capitalists' evaluations of start-up teams. *Journal of Business Venturing*, 21(6), 802–826.

Freytag, A., & Thurik, R. (2007). Entrepreneurship and its determinants in a cross-country setting. *Journal of Evolutionary Economics*, 17, 117–131.

Fritsch, M., & Changoluisa, J. (2017). New business formation and the productivity of manufacturing incumbents: Effects and mechanisms. *Journal of Business Venturing*, 31, 237–259.

Fu, X., Lin, Y., & Molyneux, P. (2014). Bank competition and financial stability in Asia Pacific. *Journal of Banking and Finance*, 38, 64–77.

Gaglio, C. M., & Katz, J. (2001). The psychological basis of opportunity identification: Entrepreneurial alertness. *Small Business Economics*, 16(2), 95–111.

Gao, C., Zuzul, T., Jones G., & Khanna, T. (2017). Overcoming institutional voids: A reputation-based view of long-run survival. *Strategic Management Journal*, 38(11), 2147–2167.

Gereffi, G. (2020). What does the COVID-19 pandemic teach us about global value chains? The case of medical supplies. *Journal of International Business Policy*, 3(2), 287–301.

Grandori, A. (2020). Black swans and generative resilience. *Management and Organization Review*, 16(3), 495–501.

Greeven, M. J., Yip, G. S., & Wei, W. (2019). *Pioneers, hidden champions, change makers and underdogs: Lessons from China's innovators*. Cambridge: MIT Press.

Gropp, R., Hakenes, H., & Schnabel, I. (2011). Competition, risk-shifting, and public bail-out policies. *Review of Financial Studies*, 24, 2084–2120.

Gu, W., Qian, X. and Lu, J. (2018). Venture capital and entrepreneurship: A conceptual model and research suggestions. *International Entrepreneurship and Management Journal*, 14(1), 35–50.

Herrington, A., Schrape, J., Flintoff, K., Kelly, J., Singh, K., & Taylor, D. (2012, June). PD for ML in HE: Embedding mobile learning in a university context. In *EdMedia+ Innovate Learning* (pp. 2573–2578). Association for the Advancement of Computing in Education (AACE).

Herrington, M., & Kelly, D. (2012). African entrepreneurship: Sub-Saharan African regional report. Retrieved March 12, 2020. https://scholar.google.com/scholar?hl=en&as_sdt=0%2C5&q=Herrington%2C+M.%2C+Kelly%2C+D.%2C+2012

Hossain, M., Levänen, J., & Wierenga, M. (2021). Pursuing frugal innovation for sustainability at the grassroots level. *Management and Organization Review*, 17(2), 374–381.

Hurst, E., & Lusardi, A. (2004). Liquidity constraints, household wealth and entrepreneurship. *Journal of Political Economy*, 112(2), 319–347.

IMF-GFSR (2018) A decade after global financial crisis, are we safer? Retrieved March 17, 2020, from https://www.imf.org/en/Publications/GFSR/Issues/2018/09/25/Global-Financial-StabilityReport-October-2018.

Isărescu, M. (2009). Contribuții teoretice şi practice în domeniul politicilor monetare şi bancare. *Editura Academiei Romane*. uploads/2010/12/laudatio-dhc-mugur-isarescu.

Kan, K., & Tsai, W.-D. (2006). Entrepreneurship and risk aversion. *Small Business Economics*, 26, 465–474.

Karlan, D., & Valdivia, M. (2011, May). Teaching entrepreneurship: Impact of business training on microfinance clients and institutions. *The Review of Economics and Statistics*, 93(2), 510–527.

Kirzner, I. M. (1997). Entrepreneurial discovery and the competitive market process: An Austrian approach. *Journal of Economic Literature*, 35, 60–85.

Klapper, L., El-Zoghbi, M., & Hess, J. (2017). Achieving the sustainable development goals the role of financial inclusion. CGAP. Retrieved March 23, 2020, from. achieving sustainable-development-goals-role financial - inclusion. African+Entrepreneurship%3A+Sub-Saharan+AfricanRegional+Report.+Global+Entrepreneurship+Monitor&btnG=

Klapper, L., & Love, I. (2011). The impact of the financial crisis on new firm registration. *Economics Letters*, 113, 1–4.

Klapper, L., Love, I., & Randall, D. (2015). New firm registration and the business cycle. *The International Entrepreneurship and Management Journal*, 11, 287–306.

Klotz, A. C., Hmieleski, K. M., Bradley, B. H., & Busenitz, L. W. (2014). New venture teams a review of the literature and roadmap for future research. *Journal of Management*, 40(1), 226–255.

Kolstad, I., & Wiig, A. (2015). Education and entrepreneurial success. *Small Business Economics*, 44(4), 783–796.

Kortum, S., & Lerner, J. (2000). Assessing the contribution of venture capital to innovation. *The RAND Journal of Economics*, 31(4), 674–692.

Kressel, H., & Lento, T. V. (2012). *Entrepreneurship in the global economy: Engine for economic growth*. Cambridge University Press.

Krishnan, R. T., & Prashantham, S. (2019). Innovation in and from India: The who, where, what, and when. *Global Strategy Journal*, 9(3), 357–377.

Kwabi, F., Boateng, A., & Du, M. (2020). Impact of central bank independence and transparency on international equity portfolio allocation: A cross-country analysis. *International Review of Financial Analysis*, 69, p. 101464.

Landier, A. (2001). *Start-up financing: Banks versus venture capital*. Working Paper. MIT.

La Porta, R., Lopez-de-Silanes, F., Shleifer, A., & Vishny, R. W. (1997). Legal determinants of external finance. *The Journal of Finance*, 52(3), 1131–1150.

Leon, F. (2019). Long-term finance and entrepreneurship. *Economic Systems*, 43, 100690.

Levine, R. (1997). Financial development and economic growth: Views and agenda. *Journal of Economic Literature*, 35(2), 688–726.

Lewin, A. Y., Välikangas, L., & Chen, J. (2017). Enabling open innovation: Lessons from Haier. *International Journal of Innovation Studies*, 1(1), 5–19.

Luo, Y., & Bu, J. (2018). Contextualizing international strategy by emerging market firms: A composition-based approach. *Journal of World Business*, 53(3), 337–355.

Luo, Y., & Child, J. (2015). A composition-based view of firm growth. *Management and Organization Review*, 11(3), 379–411.

Ma, Y. L., & Hu, Y. (2021). Business model innovation and experimentation in transforming economies: ByteDance and TikTok. *Management and Organization Review*, 17(2), 382–388.

Mailath, G. J., Mester, L. J. (1994). A positive analysis of bank closure. *Journal of Financial Intermediation*, 3(3), 272–299.

Mair J., & Martí I. (2006). Social entrepreneurship research: A source of explanation, prediction, and delight. *Journal of World Business*, 41(1), 36–44.

Markova, S., & Petkovska-Mircevska, T. (2009). Financial options for entrepreneurial ventures. *Economic Interferences*, 11(26), 597–604.

Mehotra, S., & Velamuri, S. R. (2021). Secondary business model innovation in emerging economies. *Management and Organization Review*, 17(2), 344–373.

Mei, C. (2020). Policy style, consistency and the effectiveness of the policy mix in China's fight against COVID-19. *Policy and Society*, 39(3), 309–325.

Metcalfe, J. S. (2004). The entrepreneur and the style of modern economics. *Journal of Evolutionary Economics*, 14, 157–175.

Meyer, K. E., & Grosse, R. (2019). Introduction to management in emerging markets. In R. Grosse & K. E. Meyer (Eds.), *Oxford handbook to management in emerging markets*. Oxford: Oxford University Press.

Meyer, K. E., & Peng, M. W. (2016). Theoretical foundations of emerging economy research. *Journal of International Business Studies*, 47(1), 3–22.

Mishkin, F. (1999). Global financial instability: Framework, events, issues. *Journal of Economic Perspectives*, 13(4), 320. doi:10.1257/jep.13.4.3.

Mitter, C., & Kraus, S. (2011). Entrepreneurial finance – Issues and evidence, revisited. *International Journal of Entrepreneurship and Innovation Management*, 14(2/3), 132–150.

Montgomery, H., Harimaya, K., & Takahashi, Y. (2014). Too big to succeed? Banking sector consolidation and efficiency. *Journal of International Financial Markets, Institutions & Money*, 32, 86–106.

Morandin, G., Bergami, M., & Bagozzi, R. P. (2006). The hierarchical cognitive structure of entrepreneur motivation toward private equity financing. *Venture Capital*, 8(3), 253–271.

Munemo, J. (2018). Entrepreneurial success in Africa: How relevant are foreign direct investment and financial development? *African Development Review*, 30, 372–385.

Naudé, W. A. A. (2010a). *Entrepreneurship and economic development*. Palgrave Macmillan.

Naudé, W. A. A. (2010b). Entrepreneurship is not a binding constraint on growth and development in the poorest 'countries. *World Development*, 39(1), 33–44.

OECD. (2008). Measuring entrepreneurship: A digest of indicators. Retrieved January 24, 2020, from www.oecd.org

Olokundun, M. O. (2018). The role of social entrepreneurship and the state in propelling national development in Nigeria: A conceptual approach. *International Journal of Entrepreneurship*, 22(1), 1–5.

Omri, A., & Ayadi-Frikha, M. (2014). Constructing a mediational model of small business growth. *The International Entrepreneurship and Management Journal*, 10, 319–342.

Park, S. H., Zhou, N., & Ungson, G. R. (2013). *Rough diamonds*. San Francisco: Jossey-Bass.

Prashantham, S., & Floyd, S. W. (2019). Navigating liminality in new venture internationalization. *Journal of Business Venturing*, 34(3), 513–527.

Peris-Ortiz, M., Fuster-Estruch, V., & Devece-Carananana, C. (2014). Entrepreneurship and innovation in a context of crisis. In K. Rüdiger, M. Peris-Ortiz, & A. Blanco González (Eds.), *Entrepreneurship, innovation and economic crisis* (pp. 1–10). Springer.

Pfeffer, J. (1972). Size and composition of corporate boards of directors: The organization and its environment. *Administrative Science Quarterly*, 17(2), 218–228.

Pfeffer, J., & Salancik, G. (1978). *The external control of organizations: A resource dependence perspective*. New York: Harper and Row.

Popov, E. V., Veretennikova, A. Yu, & Kozinskaya, K. M. (2019). World scientific schools of social entrepreneurship research. Vestnik Tyumenskogo gosudarstvennogo universitet. Sotsial'no-ekonomicheskie i pravovye issledovaniya=Tyumen State University Herald. *Social, Economic, and Law Research*, 5(1), 157–177 (In Russian).

Quadrini, V. (2009). Entrepreneurship in macroeconomics. *Annals of Finance*, 5, 295–311.

Redding, G. (2020). Societal resilience: China and Japan. *Management and Organization Review*, 16(3), 485–493.

Safiullah, M., & Shamsuddin, A. (2019). Risk-adjusted efficiency and corporate governance: Evidence from Islamic and conventional banks. *Journal of Corporate Finance*, 55, 105–140.

Samila, S., & Sorenson, O. (2011). Venture capital, entrepreneurship, and economic growth. *The Review of Economics and Statistics*, 93(1), 338–349.

Schinasi, G. (2004). Defining financial stability. IMF Working Paper 04/187. International Monetary Fund.

Schumpeter, J. A. (1934). *Theorie der wirtschaftlichen enwicklung* [The theory of economic development]. Cambridge, MA; Leipzig: Duncker and Humblot. Translated by Redvers Opie.

Schwienbacher, A. (2007). A theoretical analysis of optimal financing strategies for different 1390 types of capital-constrained entrepreneurs. *Journal of Business Venturing*, 22(6), 753–781.

Schwienbacher, A. (2009). Financing commitments and investors incentives in entrepreneurial firms. Working Paper No. 071/2009. London School of Economics and Political Science.

Shih, W. C. (2020, September). *Global supply chains in a post-pandemic world*. Harvard Business Review.

Spear R., Defourny J., Favreau L., & Laville J.-L. (2001), Tackling social exclusion in europe. *The contribution of the social economy*. Aldershot: Ashgate.

Tan, Y., & Floros, C. (2013). Risk, capital and efficiency in Chinese banking. *Journal of International Financial Markets, Institutions & Money*, 26, 378–393.

The New York Times Company. 2020. The New York Times Company Reports 2019 Fourth-Quarter and Full-Year Results and Announces Dividend Increase. https://s1.q4cdn.com/156149269/files/doc_financials/2019/q4/Press-Release-12.29.2019-Final-for-posting.pdf.The New York Times Company. 2020. "The New York Times Company Reports 2019 Fourth-Quarter and Full-Year Results and Announces Dividend Increase." https://s1.q4cdn.com/156149269/files/doc_financials/2019/q4/Press-Release-12.29.2019-Final-for-posting.pdf

Tomaa, S.-G., Grigorea, A.-M., & Marinescu, P. (2014). Economic development and entrepreneurship. *Procedia Economics and Finance*, 8(2014), 436–443.

UNCTAD (2017). Promoting entrepreneurship for sustainable development: A selection of business cases from the empretec network. Retrieved March 15, 2020.

Välikangas, L., & Lewin, A. (2020). The lingering new normal. *Management and Organization Review*, 16(3), 467–472.

Van Gelderen, M., Van de Sluis, L., & Jansen, P. (2005). Learning opportunities and learning behaviours of small business starters: relations with goal achievement, skill development and satisfaction. *Small Business Economics*, 25(1), 97–108.

Van Stel, A., Carree, M., & Thurik, R. (2005). The effect of entrepreneurial activity on national economic growth. *Small Business Economics*, 24, 311–321.

Vismara, S. (2016). Equity retention and social network theory in equity crowdfunding. *Small Business Economics*, 46(4), 579–590.

Wang, G. J., Xie, C., Zhao, L., & Jiang, Z. Q. (2018). Volatility connectedness in the Chinese banking system: Do state-owned commercial banks contribute more? *Journal of International Financial Markets, Institutions & Money*, 57, 205–230.

Wennekers, A. R. M., & Thurik, R. (1999). Linking entrepreneurship and economic growth. *Small Business Economics*, 13, 27–55.

Williamson, S., Ardoin, E., Clow, K.E., & Cole, H.S. (2018). An exploratory study of the relationships of small business owners' ethical orientation and customer orientation. *Journal of Ethics & Entrepreneurship*, 8(2), 80.

Williamson, P. J., & Wan, F. (2019). How real are opportunities for multinationals in China. In R. Grosse & K. E. Meyer (Eds.), *Oxford handbook of management in emerging markets* (pp. 745–762). Oxford: Oxford University Press.

Winton, A., & Yerramilli, V. (2008). Entrepreneurial finance: Banks versus venture capital. *Journal of Financial Economics*, 88(1), 51–79.

Wong, A., Bhatia, M., & Freeman, Z. (2009). Angel finance: The other venture capital. *Strategic Change: Briefings in Entrepreneurial Finance*, 18(7–8), 221–230.

Wong, A. K. D., Wong, F. K., & Nadeem, A. (2009, October). Comparative roles of major stakeholders for the implementation of BIM in various countries. In *Proceedings of the International Conference on Changing Roles: New Roles, New Challenges, Noordwijk Aan Zee, The Netherlands* (Vol. 5). Delft: TU Delft, Faculty of Architecture, Real Estate and Housing.

World Business(2006). No. 41 (1), pp. 36–44. doi:10.1016/j.jwb.2005.09.002

Yip, G., & McKern, B. (2016). *China's next strategic advantage: From imitation to innovation*. Cambridge, MA: MIT Press.

Yip, G., & Prashantham, S. (2019). Innovation in emerging markets. In R. Grosse & K. E. Meyer (Eds.), *Oxford handbook of management in emerging markets* (pp. 351–372). Oxford: Oxford University Press.

Zhou, S., Li, P., Zhou, A., & Prashantham, S. (2020). The cultural roots of compositional capability in China: Balanced moderation. *Asia Pacific Journal of Management*, 37(3), 1217–1237.

8 Entrepreneurial Corporate Social Responsibility in the Post-COVID-19 Pandemic Era: Perspectives in Sub-Saharan Africa

Ndivhuho Tshikovhi and Fulufhelo Netswera

Introduction

The COVID-19 pandemic has greatly impacted entrepreneurship and corporate social responsibility (CSR) globally (Mahmud et al., 2021). As would be expected, developing nations, and sub-Saharan Africa in particular, are probably the most negatively affected. As COVID-19 continues to ravage societies, entrepreneurial investment priorities are bound to shift to major investment nations and away from developing countries, with crippling effects on economic growth, employment opportunities and CSR programmes among other aspects (Popkova et al., 2021). Debates on CSR have taken different shapes and forms over many decades. For instance, the most recent conversations about CSR suggest that it is a prescriptive, multifaceted concept whose posture depends on numerous viewpoints and affiliations between institutions, which also change in response to societal tendencies. While the former perceptions of CSR assumed a regionalised, person-centred humanitarian concentration, contemporary notions of CSR have taken a different form, and are more inclusive and diverse (Silberhorn & Warren, 2007). Furthermore, Silberhorn and Warren (2007) acknowledge that CSR is a familiar example that historically adopted a compilation of distinctive but interrelated terminologies like corporate humanity, corporate obligation, corporate nationality, social responsible investments, corporate accountability, corporate social performance, business ethics, stake-holding, community involvement or engagement, as well as sustainability and triple-bottom-line concerns. Studies conducted earlier in the United States of America in the 1970s (Fleming et al., 2015) that define CSR have mainly focused on topical issues related to CSR approaches (Bowman & Haire, 1975, Holmes, 1976).

It is acknowledged that COVID-19 deprives corporates reasons to repurpose their CSR initiatives, specifically the management of COVID-19 and its implications on economies. CSR has come to be recognised as an important budget item that companies must factor in, record and report on. CSR is crucial for bolstering relationships with stakeholders such as

DOI: 10.4324/9781003216469-8

workers, host societies, consumers and governments. Subsequently, failure to understand, to a "reasonable level", the tenets of CSR could negatively affect a firm's profit margins and strain relations among stakeholders. Notwithstanding, it is still difficult to generate a singular widely acceptable CSR definition. This concept is fluid in the sense that what is conceived as CSR by stakeholders in one community, region or country may vary slightly or even considerably, depending on stakeholders' opinions about firms' activities or their oversights within the jurisdiction of CSR. The fundamental issue in relation to the general multiplicity of the analyses of CSR is established and premised on the narrow perception that entrepreneurs must be concerned about and responsive to problems outside their constricted commercial, practical and legitimate obligations (Ako, 2012). Thus, CSR is continuously reconceptualised and revisited, based on the context of industrialised nations, and generally accommodates "corporates" to the exclusion of small- and medium-sized enterprises (SMEs). These "corporates" comprise the bulk of the economies of developing nations, and are largely responsible for "social responsibility" work. This anomaly yields a deceptive about what CSR stands for, and has fuelled misunderstandings among international businesses operating in emerging nations and their host societies (Ako, 2012).

Governmental, commercial and socio-cultural disparities between industrialised and emerging nations should be flagged when analysing CSR. These disparities are a source of dissonance and reduce the prospects of the host nations as well as delivery by foreign investment corporations. The appreciation of these "anomalies", prevalent in developing countries, should drive CSR to positively negotiate responsible and impactful work within recipient target societies, as opposed to strictly relying on framed "foreign" norms. Therefore, CSR intentions for industrialised nations such as customer security, reasonable exchange, organic promotion, environment transformation concerns and socially accountable funds are not probably appreciated in the developing economies. For developing economies, the fundamental survival concerns for poverty alleviation and the provision of basic services like water, healthcare and schooling are appropriate (Visser, 2010). The significance of an unqualified interpretation of CSR between investors and the investment recipient communities is crucial for a mutual outcome. The novel circumstance that has risen since the outbreak of the COVID-19 pandemic objectifies the necessity for new and alternative means of endorsing CSR in sub-Saharan Africa.

From a South African viewpoint, which may resonate strongly with the viewpoints held in the African continent and the rest of the developing world, wherein investments are referred to mainly in terms of mineral resource extraction, and where society is historically and currently marginalised and underdeveloped, CSR may serve to replace a weak state by providing services ordinarily associated with municipal basic services delivery like water, electricity, sanitation and road paving. According to

Ramlall (2012), prior to 1994 (during apartheid) CSR in South Africa was primarily governed through ad hoc humanitarian kind aids that reflected the firm's concentration. In the post-1994 era, however, regulations and legislation were enacted to guide "acceptable" CSR practices.

CSR is relevant and an ever-significant area for entrepreneurship. Modern-day entrepreneurs must participate in CSR as a fragment of their entrepreneurship approach or risk becoming less economical. Business success differs based on the local environmental circumstances that include suitable foundation, proper and excellent schools that would produce potential workers and ensure collaboration with local traders, among other aspects. In these business economical contexts, entrepreneurs' community plans can influence local people in numerous ways in terms of environmental improvement (İyigün, 2015). CSR fosters intimacy between firms and the community and in the process, inspire communities to lookout for the best interests of the companies thereby ensuring its stability (Eltoum et al., 2021). A pertinent question worth asking is: *Has the current COVID-19 crisis spawned sympathetic waves towards corporates by communities as they face viability and sustainability challenges?* So far little has been written if at all on the post-COVID-19 implications on CSR.

In any case, firms, countries and societies worldwide have embraced CSR – therefore CSR is no longer regarded as an option but an integral part of the corporate mandate. It is also apparent that in times of crisis, such as the COVID-19 crisis, CSR prioritises and its level of investment changes. In this chapter, we review the literature to trace, among other things, the origin of CSR, its implications on taxation and capital flight behaviour, as well as the resource curse's effect on African CSR. Central to this analysis is how corporates behave in crisis times such as during the COVID-19 pandemic in relation to their CSR? The specific emphasis is placed on the lessons learned and the challenges confronting CSR in the sub-Saharan context. The key objectives of this chapter are as follows:

- To elaborate on how international corporations working in sub-Saharan Africa have been avoiding tax though CSR
- To demonstrate the implications of CSR in entrepreneurship post the COVID-19 era
- To make CSR management recommendations for entrepreneurs and policymakers involved in the sub-Saharan Africa

The origin of corporate social responsibility

The concept "corporate social responsibility" is believed to have been conceived in the United States of America, but has, in recent times, attracted considerable interest from policymakers in industrialised and emerging nations – from worldwide corporations, the overall community and academics alike (Arli & Lasmono, 2010). The literature suggests that the industrial revolution of the mid-1800s sparked growing concerns on the well-being and welfare of employees. The livelihoods of families of deceased employees, as well as employee productivity in firms, among other things, came under the spotlight. As a result, the captains of industries such as Carnegie and Rockefeller responded by starting philanthropic ventures to address some of these challenges. Nevertheless, modern CSR emerged in the 1950s, and the terminology itself was invented in 1953 by an American economic expert, Hoard Bowen, and is documented in the journal *Social Responsibilities of the Businessman* (Thomasnet, 2019).

In the 1990s, CSR gained popular repute and approval as a responsible and acceptable behaviour by the corporate world. During this period, two important publications emerged. The first one, entitled *Corporate Social Performance Revisited,* was published by Professor Donna Wood and outlines frameworks for assessing the impact of CSR programmes (Wood, 1991). The second one, *The Pyramid of Corporate Social Responsibility,* was published by Professor Georgia Archie and outlines important CSR considerations for implementation by any organisation (Carroll, 1991). The pyramid argues that for CSR to be embraced, it should address four important constituencies: namely economic, legal, ethical and philanthropic aspirations. While this chapter does not necessarily dwell focus on describing these four layers of the pyramid, reference is made indirectly to them from time to time.

There is particular semblance of agreement, suggesting that CSR has remained triggered by the growing need from people to switch the rising control and occasionally negligent conduct of companies whose operations have devastated the environment or posed a significant danger to societal and commercial growth, as well as threaten state independence (Nyuur et al., 2014). In addition, the potential risk of bad marketing has similarly stimulated the assimilation of CSR into corporations' intentional initiatives. Planning for CSR is viewed as an important corporate decision that jostles corporates to yield accountability for their effect on people and to also work towards resolving societal, commercial and ecological complications exclusive of the forced drive of authorities, human rights organisations, as well as the affected communities (Muthuri & Gilbert, 2011).

Strategic posture towards entrepreneurship and CSR

In the aftermath of the COVID-19 pandemic, corporations from various sectors across the world reacted with their means, tools and aids to help people and authorities that were grappling with these extraordinary circumstances. Disinfectants and respective sanitation products, which are necessary in controlling the extent of the COVID-19 virus, have remained in great need and were donated by large corporations as their CSR programme. These corporations also took advantage of booming business opportunities. However, pharmaceutical corporates are considered the biggest winners in the COVID-19 era, while vulnerable societies in the third world were left without the necessary protection due to costs. To respond to this soaring demand for COVID-19 supplies, corporates with the limited capability to make disinfectants started using their current means to produce, dispense and trade disinfectants, and some did so as part of their CSR amid huge profits. These corporations, including distilleries, perfumeries and pharmacological businesses directly "volunteered" and used their means towards preparing hand disinfectants to help in the fight against COVID-19 (Ahmed et al., 2021).

It has become increasingly difficult for corporate policymakers to adopt a suitable stance for what may be termed commercial and societal accountability. Amongst the things that make this challenging are twofold widespread myths. The first myth is that CSR activities are in necessary battle with the stakeholder interest, and that means CSR originated totally out of the shareholder's compact. The second myth is that the incentive for CSR actions is found merely in the desire for nobleness than obligation on the part of the firm formulating the strategy (Bowman & Haire, 1975). The relationship between CSR and business profitability is highly complex and should be determined empirically.

Worldwide, the standard for CSR implementation is set in response to the United Nation's Sustainable Development Goals (SDGs). It assumes that the SDGs require not only countries but companies to foster organisational competences based on their CSR plans (Vizcaíno et al., 2021). In an archetype, characterised by exceptional levels of accountability and reflectivity, the adoption of sustainable entrepreneurship practices has gained considerable power. Among others, the adoption of the SDGs at firm levels has advanced to a point, where SDGs are deemed a firm's primary responsibility (ElAlfy et al., 2020). As CSR develops, it is important to appreciate, among other things, how SDGs and sustainability affect corporate CSR strategy, programmes, recording performances, disclosures, shareholder anticipations and governing obligations. By positioning the determination and standards of CSR with market drivers and shareholder expectations, CSR practices have converted to norms for safeguarding the company's authorisation to work, evading reputational impairments, constructing constancy and upholding reasonable standing (Tiba & Frikha, 2019).

The case for entrepreneurship in the post-COVID-19 era

Entrepreneurship is a crucial aspect that engenders creativeness, create employment and stimulate economic activity. To ensure that entrepreneurship thrives, important ingredients should be invested. Among these are an enabling policy environment, expertise, skilling and capital investment. The destabilisation of the financial markets due to the outbreak of COVID-19 pandemic worldwide stimulated entrepreneurship in other areas. For instance, online service providers like online shopping boomed due to the closure of retail outlets during the first wave of COVID-19.

Entrepreneurship is opportunistic and thrives on appropriates gaps in the markets. Therefore, entrepreneurs post the COVID-19 era are likely to continue providing essential goods and services that are most pertinent for such an era (Sadiq et al., 2021). Corporates must engage in numerous creativities to the benefit of their workers, consumers and societies throughout the disaster period through their expanded CSR plans as they did previously (Mahmud et al., 2021). Questions that beg answers are: *Will the online entrepreneurship boom continue unabated in the post COVID-19 era?* or *Will society revert to the old normal way of procuring services?* and *What implications will this have on CSR?*

Is taxation CSR in disguise?

In many countries across the world CSR has become a legitimate corporate function which has solicited much debate around two aspects. First, lucrative tax deductions are often offered to corporates for CSR investments. Second, there are arguments that suggest that taxes are by themselves, a form of CSR because governments use these earnings to provide the necessary social responsibility investments. Other important questions from the shareholder's viewpoint are: *Does CSR maximise corporate returns or shareholder profits?* If not, then *How else can managers convince shareholders to invest their earnings into CSR over and above their tax obligations?* Another fundamental question is: *Where should the CSR spend go between the state in form of taxes and or directly into community programmes* (Avi-Yonah, 2008)?

In the United States, profits from the business revenue tax amounted to almost a fourth of all national tax profits in 1965. These days, however, this corporate tax accounts for fewer than 10% of national revenue, and this percentage continues to dwindle (Yin, 2001). A lateral pertinent question to ask is: *Are CSR programmes on the rise, and are they enough to link the opening concerning what the government has earned in 1965 and the current 10% accounted for?* The regression in business tax profits might even be above the percentage pronounced at a worldwide scale; particularly among emerging nations that have conventionally relied on business tax for a greater percentage of their profits. There are two prospective motives for this general regression. The first is in relation to high prevalence of aggressive tax avoidance behaviour among companies, particularly where emerging nations wants suppliers to enforce tax compliance. The outcome is a tax rebate battle between nations to entice commercial funds (Avi-Yonah, 2008).

There have been minimal attempts to adopt the fundamental and strategy elements of underdevelopment (Idemudia, 2011). Jenkins (2005), for example, states that notwithstanding the fact that tax evasion in Africa is rife, with a huge gap between tax gathered and expected amounting to more than 40%, the bulk of these "saved" tax revenues are repatriated by multinational corporations (MNCs) at the outlay of local societies. Tax evasion and avoidance has become one of the biggest anti-CSR practices and it is covertly essential to the MNCs' CSR programmes in Africa (Idemudia, 2011). Subsequently, the conventional CSR programme is not accustomed with the main concern and experiences in sub-Saharan Africa and is not entirely relevant to the local context.

Even where MNCs invest in local agendas, important national priorities are often sacrificed. For instance, the priorities of oil MNCs in Nigeria to invest in societal arrangement such as streets, clinics and communal centres (micro-level CSR) frequently means that the actual developmental complications such as ecological dilapidation, dishonesty and lack of responsibility (macro-CSR) are, in turn, perpetuated by the same MNC. Unfortunately, these macro-CSR are essential, not only for the local community's development like Niger Delta but a national challenge. Furthermore, oil MNCs in Nigeria are efficiently passing on the price of mopping up ecological degradation to the Nigerian authority, which unfortunately, faces even bigger service delivery challenges (Ako, 2012). The issue here is the interrogation of imbalanced power relations when an MNC deals directly with local communities who are considered stakeholders (Abdelfattah & Aboud, 2020). The failure to contemplate authority relations in conventional CSR suggests a "one-size-fits-all model" that appears to reinforce conventional CSR programme, which yields unfortunate prospects and outcomes in sub-Sharan Africa.

The CSR dilemma for multinational entrepreneurs operating in LDC

Initiatives taken by multinational companies during COVID-19 included the provision of disinfectants, supplies to shops and online stores, as well as making available produces that can considerably reduce the risk of exposure to COVID-19. While the entrepreneurship society worldwide has been struck by numerous outward disasters in the previous years – from terrorism, quakes, worldwide commercial disasters, SARS and Ebola, COVID-19 has conveyed an unparalleled level of doubt in recent times. By June 2020, COVID-19 has spread to all regions of the globe, posing unprecedented organisational challenges (Ahmed et al., 2021). Throughout the initial phase of the COVID-19 pandemic, organisations, including but not limited to Coca-Cola, PepsiCo, distilleries, perfumeries and great international food dispensation companies put numerous interventions in place to support societies.

There has been an increasing need for multinational enterprises (MNEs) to put in place people improvement plans in workplaces, particularly in less developed countries (LDCs). In other words, it is imperative for corporations to meet profitability objectives while addressing locally defined social and economic interests at the same time. This demand is sparked by the fact that social infrastructure is mostly lacking in the developing countries and states alone are generally not strong enough to meet these expectations

(Eweje, 2006). Widespread community demands for relevant, direct benefits, as well as sustainable ways of resource (like oil or other minerals) use in their community are a relatively recent phenomenon to local communities and corporates. Thus, normally, neither authority organisations, corporates nor societies themselves have remained adequately prepared to react to these welfares.

In sub-Saharan Africa, for instance, MNEs are said to offer particular societal services and well-being plans to supplement their standard for-profit actions. Significant care has been devoted to society growth plans. For instance, MNEs build, offer bursaries and constructed streets in Nigeria; constructed hospitals and offered drugs for AIDS/HIV patients in South Africa; and also delivered vaccines for malaria in Zambia. By definition, these are state functions, but in LDCs, the provision of these services is poor, or states do not offer these services. Companies are regularly under pressure to remain operational, and are often liable for a broad range of programmes they implement in societal and ecological spheres. In turn, MNEs allege a twofold criteria: namely the decline in economic and social development in host societies because of negligence, as well as a lack of growth plans from host authorities. This has stimulated a global deliberation about what true CSR ought to be about (Görg et al., 2017).

The implications in this regard are that the activities of MNE and its societal accountability should be broadened in LDCs and intermediate economies, where free marketplace regulation instruments are neither completely shaped nor operative. In these conditions, MNEs have, at the same time, distinctive contest and a unique prospect to address societal accountability concerns, particularly where potential host nations lack the legitimate context, social structure, or recognised customs and knowledge of a marketplace economy (Eweje, 2006). Additionally, a company's societal accountability obligation means that resources may be used to challenge numerous concerns, plus contamination difficulties, poverty, ethnic perception, consumerism and other societal difficulties.

Resource curse and the entrepreneurship CSR dilemma

The severe effects of the COVID-19 pandemic, which have deepened poverty and inequalities among nations have necessitated unique consideration, specifically in reasonably exposed communities (Raimo et al., 2021). It happens that most of the LDCs that are endowed in environmental reserves like oil, gas and minerals are some among the poorest in the world. There are many theories in relation to why this is the case, but the "resource curse" theory, also known as the "paradox of plenty", formulated and fully explored by Auty (1993), offers the appropriate explanation for the current state in these nations (Auty, 1997). The resource curse is a political-economic experience and espouses the reduction of organisational responsibility. The lack of accountability and state failure underlay numerous of the difficulties usually encountered by nations that are heavily reliant on extractive activities. The challenge is that the insufficient security of individual human rights and devastation of the ecosystem, among many other things, continues (Sachs & Warner, 2001). Extractive firms working alongside the background of resource curse dynamics are regularly trapped in the medium as they explore techniques to evade being blamed for the national failures and moderate the same.

It is in resource-rich countries where CSR is most relevant because while the programme is essential for commercial growth, standard social justices in these nations are reliant on the behaviour of the extractive industry. The states' failure to raise enough taxes for the provision of basic services like water and healthcare dictates that alternative strategies to primary tax collection be implemented. First, the ability to attract investors, which might include reducing corporate taxes and, second, forging partnerships towards to ensure basic service delivery, which may reduce state bureaucracies, should be considered.

The "resource curse" see the breakdown in government accountability as some of the most critical characteristics of undue dependence on the environmental reserve rent (Genasci & Pray, 2008). In modern times, extractive companies have recorded unprecedented revenue earnings despite and in contrast to the failure of resource-rich nations where these companies operate. A country like Equatorial Guinea; for instance, is positioned second worldwide in relations of GDP per capita, by virtue of revenues derived from its oil reserves. Nevertheless, 60% of people in Equatorial Guinea are living on less than one dollar a day. There are supplementary practical examples beyond Equatorial Guinea, like Venezuela and the Democratic Republic of Congo (DRC) (Genasci & Pray, 2008).

Di John (2011) believes that it is now an established fact that the economies of resource-rich nations consistently grow slower than non-resource-rich. Importantly, while it is evident that specific sectors of resource-rich communities have benefited significantly from the resources, the high level of inequity points to the fact that many has not reaped the benefits. Importantly, corruption also takes centre stage in resource cursed countries and becomes a fundamental piece of the governmental economy. While corruption is rife in practically all political economies, it tends to be rooted and malicious in resource rich nations. Corruption happens in instances where there is enormous wealth that needs to be distributed by a comparatively insignificant number of people in a setting characterised by extraordinary levels of privacy (Ocheje, 2006).

Resource curses theory insinuates that CSR experts in natural resource-rich countries cannot discuss the weaknesses identified, as well as fundamental governmental issues as mere conditionalities. Alongside a better consideration of the governmental economy of resource-rich nations, the shortage of safe drinking water, for example, can be perceived, not only as a direct consequence of the pollution activities of the local extractive firm, but as an unintended consequence of failures of the authorities to accurately legalise conservational performance (Genasci & Pray, 2008). Overall, the resource curse disputes is premised entirely on the assumption that wealth generated through natural resource sale often reduce their potential commercial value – that is there is an absence of beneficiation value, proneness to high levels of fraud, corruption and countless political violence (Di John, 2011).

The crux of the discussion is that, by description, resource curse is an "internalist" attitude to the growth predicament in sub-Saharan Africa. It consumes on the heart of governmental and commercial foundations of the difficulty and how these foundations negatively influence the macro-economic organisation of resource-rich nations and their wealth thereof. In spite of its "internalist" and historical optic, discussions around the curse theory do not adequately explore the historic and international issues of resource utilisation, and how they have previously made emerging nations reliant on the exportation of commodities, and how they have produced a territory of extractive region in the state that contributes minimally to its GDP (Ayelazuno, 2014). Nevertheless, the persuasiveness of resource curse has given it a dominant theoretical framework that explains the failure of growth in resource-rich nations. Converging primarily on central politico-economic issues justifies why this wealth has not catalysed commercial development and enhanced the welfare of people (Abdelfattah & Aboud, 2020). This is because resource-rich nations tend to be exposed to the "Dutch disease" of relying heavily on the exportation of natural resource than paying attention to domestic industries and beneficiation.

Capital flight out of sub-Saharan Africa

Two of the biggest economic challenges that sub-Saharan Africa is faced with today are illicit financial flows and capital flight. The estimates on the wealth that is pilfered or lost to tax fraud annually ranges between $88.6 billion or 3.7% of Africa's GDP and $483 billion by multinationals and wealthy individuals (Ndikumana et al., 2014; UNCTAD, 2020). What compounds this challenge is that the debt problems that emerging nations contend with, combined with a severe regression in global lending to LDCs, evokes great interest on private capital outflows, or "capital flight" (Khan & Haque, 1987).

Considerations of capital flight and the inability to reverse these outflows may become a factor in the new lending framework towards countries that need external financial support. However, overestimated exchange rates, high national increase tariffs, administration budget discrepancies, the national versus global interest rate discrepancies, as well as wealth generation are thought to be responsible for capital flight. Consequently, these variables highlight commercial features that contradicts the national investment atmosphere (Lensink et al., 2000). Capital flight is a somewhat slick theory, which is usually associated or linked with the reality of high ambiguity and possibility, particularly to revenues on nationally held resources. As a result, citizens take their capital and run to evade exceptionally excessive costs on their assets.

In general, capital flight is associated with short-term expenses for projected determinations or expenditures resulting from commercial or governmental ambiguities in the home state. In other words, it is capital that is flying from the nation rather than outward investment shown by long-term financial considerations. Some of the triggers of flight could be ascribed to CSR avoidance by firms that use this approach to develop their home countries than the society in which they operate. Thus, a variety of often related factors lead to capital flight. Some can be attributed to government policies in the countries losing the capital, while other factors may be outside of official control. Developed countries often have systems that encourage capital inflows from developing countries as well (Ndikumana et al., 2014).

What policy options are available to governments to prevent or at least stem capital flight, and what actions can be taken to generate a possible reflow? Offering a steady economic and macroeconomic atmosphere would go a long way towards lessening national insecurity and arresting capital flight. Adopting a sound macroeconomic policy with the appropriate exchange rate and interest rates seem to be a key element in reducing resource transfers abroad and the attendant problems. It might also be helpful for sub-Sharan African countries to provide competitive securities and create a more comprehensive menu of domestic financial assets for local investors. Governments could also use tax holidays to achieve foreign-currency-denominated assets.

The past decades have seen an increasing interest in academia and policymaker groups in the capital flight from the overall emerging nations, specifically African nations (Ndikumana et al., 2014). Although the African region gets a considerable sum of capital inflows in official growth support, outward lending and foreign direct investments, it also experiences a hefty economic haemorrhage across capital flight. In sub-Saharan Africa, capital flight indicates fewer expenditure in relation to community assistances such as schooling and well-being, which also weakens the human development index. On the importation edge, companies may over charge their importation bills to raise foreign currency from financial institutions, again hiding the difference in secretive oversea accounts – a comparable instrument to capital flight. Importations may be under charged or not documented at all to avoid taxes obligations, phenomena known as "technical smuggling" and "pure smuggling" correspondingly (Ndikumana & Boyce, 2003).

Capital flight from Africa is an indicator of an underlying setback, which is the severe deliberation of capital in the hands of very insufficient entities. Actually, capital flight adds to the deteriorating burden of inequity, as it enables rich people to conceal appropriated possessions, avoid tariffs and evade the adversarial effects of currency devaluation. Additionally, globalisation and the attendant spontaneous movement of money, coupled with a deficiency of openness in the worldwide economic structure could encourage and enable capital flight from sub-Saharan African nations and other emerging nations. Poor national authority intensifies these outward consequences. Thus, capital flight is essentially a global experience that contains activities by national performers as well as outward performers.

Assuming that money flees Africa to distant locations, circumstances in those locations assist as pull factors for capital flight (Ndikumana et al., 2014). The international economic structure makes it somewhat easy to transport cash within the borders and hide it out of the official's view. The ethos and tradition of banking privacy in Western fiscal epicentres support business movement and holding of finances overseas, whether they are lawfully or unlawfully acquired.

In sub-Saharan Africa capital flight seems to be a habitual drawback, which has exploded because of the turn of time in a historical phase, evidenced by resource explosion and the resurrection of development in the region. Conversely, there are considerable variations among nations. Oil-rich nations top the slope, and are led by Nigeria, Algeria and Angola. Among numerous nations capital flight is enormous in comparison with the scope of the economy; yet the relations concerning capital flight and its prospective drivers are prone to vary from nation to nation. This suggests that regulations intended to regulate capital flight must tackle certain issues that make nations vulnerable to capital flight, and that these regulations must be custom-made to the circumstances of nations.

As sub-Saharan African nations try to organise supplementary means to achieve growth, they need to pay considerable attention to capital flight for various purposes. First, by challenging domestic assets, capital flight broadens the resource indifference that resource-rich nations contend with such as their continued reliance on outward relief. Furthermore, by thickening the resource indifference, capital flight reduces capital growth and long-term development. Second, capital flight interrupts African nations' determination to consolidate resource management plans. Capital flight corrodes the tax base, stimulates tax avoidance behaviour by people and corporations with adverse effects on government income. Third, by draining government returns, capital flight delays development and stifles poverty reduction programmes. Projections are that if the capital that leaves Africa illegally was financing continental development, Africa would meet its SDGs by halving poverty by 2030. Fourth, capital flight is an indicator and a result of governance failure in resource rich nations. It is a consequence of corruption, dysfunctional and weak laws. Fifth, capital flight degenerates revenue inequity which, in turn, has substantial implications for social justice. As far as perpetrators of capital flight are concerned, tax avoidance and evading are characteristic of corporate and governmental elites. Finally, capital flight enables dictatorships and offers resources to prop up dictatorial governments, as evidenced by the case of Mobutu Sese Seko of Zaïre and the various Nigerian, Gabonese and Equatorial Guinea military dictatorships (Boyce & Ndikumana, 2012).

Entrepreneurship development and CSR in Africa

To understand the nature of SMEs sector CSR, especially in emerging nations, one needs to remember that SMEs are largely operated by founders and owners. Consequently, decision-making concerning CSR is in the hands of a specific person or family (Amaeshi et al., 2016). Most SMEs are involved in CSR because they are part of a supply chain that requires them to be involved to fulfil their bigger customers' commercial interests. Most SMEs are likely to have no CSR departments, officials and strategies. Undeniably, SME owner-managers are singlehandedly in charge of multiple tasks.

The discrepancies in the development of CRS programmes in Africa manifest on three principal levels: conceptually, practically and in the nature of the discourse. Conceptually, African entrepreneurship can contribute to SDGs through CSR, and further through two notions, which are stakeholder theory and the social license to operate (SLO). Critics, nevertheless, dispute the ideas that informs these two concepts on the basis that these are borrowed paradigms and have little to do with sub-Saharan Africa. In contrast, African realism is somehow compelled to fit into Western ideas (Idemudia, 2014). At practical levels, supporters of CSR as an instrument for Africa's development point to corporate social investments in schooling, well-being, societal structures, micro credits systems and work opportunities, which encourage commercial development and, thus, help alleviate poverty.

There are some developmental issues with implications for imminent research, legislation and practice alike. Africa's socio-economic and socio-cultural realities dictate that for CSR in sub-Saharan Africa to be relevant, it must engage with continental developmental objectives. The lack of systematic empirical evidence implies that there is poor recording of achievement or divergence of CSR programmes from Africa's CSR agenda (Cheruiyot & Onsando, 2016). In addition, it also, relatively, defends CSR and why it continues to embrace appealing potentials for growth in Africa despite solid misgivings about its aptitude to provide for the poor and marginalised.

Thus, broadly speaking, there is a need to move beyond current controversies that question if CSR in Africa is good or bad for the growth of the continent. Instead, a more nuanced perception of the CSR-development nexus in Africa and its contradictions is warranted (Idemudia, 2014). Therefore, this discussion should extend to focus on whether there is a connection between CSR and development, and how such a connection might be positively enhanced. A critical step in this regard would be to analyse CSR from the perspective of Africans, whose interests and views are often ignored in most developmental programmes, including corporate CSR discourse. This requires rich empirical data construction to gauge how local citizens experience CSR. A further analysis needs to be conducted of how socio-cultural setups shape local society's perceptions of CSR. Equally, a comparative examination of distinctive CSR dealings and their associated consequences in different regions is necessary. At stake here is the necessity to appreciate better the conditions and systems under which CSR is most likely to contribute to progress in Africa (Muthuri, 2013).

A massive and developing body of literature is required to examine the purpose of CSR and how corporations implement it. The principle is that the roles and effects of corporate actors go

> beyond providing revenue and work and increasing revenues and hence maximising shareholder's value, that they have power and impact (actual and potential) beyond their official setting within legitimate and governmental structures, particularly those of emerging nations and that they should be recognised as conscious and significant participants in activities with an extensive range of significances. (Campbell, 2012)

The significance of the liberalisation of the African mining sector has revolved around the historic public functions of the state, which are gradually being assigned to private operators. With basic public service being central to CSR operations, rule-setting becomes critical to guarantee minimal defaulting in provisioning. The result has been an upsurge of state-like accountability by international mining corporations at the inconspicuous directive of fragile state.

Another response to the weakened governmental capabilities of many mineral-rich nations in sub-Saharan Africa has been attributed to, in part, to multidimensional companies. Consequently, some Western authorities advocate that this is in fact, extremely entrenched fundamentally and traditionally, and should be treated as "weak governance". In their opinions this can be remedied by introducing the right set of rational governmental and bureaucratic procedures with related "governance indicators" (Idemudia, 2014). Nevertheless, this by itself, is inadequate. On the one hand, the growing digitisation of decision-making processes runs the risk of side-lining and depoliticalising a fundamental question, that of resource distribution. The result is that the outcomes of the exercise would be treated as a technical issue when in fact, it is a political one (Nyuur et al., 2014). On the other hand, a framework with overriding emphasis on technical and organisational characteristics of "governance", which indorse "capacity building for resource governance" in emerging nations have missed the critical point – opening up the extractive businesses in a manner that deteriorates local authorities' governmental and official competence.

Conclusion and recommendations

During the critical period of the COVID-19 pandemic, distressed and doubtful people worldwide were devoted to working with each other and to support each other in ways imaginable. As such, the comradery was not exclusive to the business sector. Companies implemented several programmes to benefit their workers, consumers and societies throughout this predicament by diversifying CSR plans. For example, historically CSR has been remarkable in assisting vulnerable people survive natural disasters around the world. However, with COVID-19 vulnerable societies faced even more physical and economic uncertainty in relation to their health, income, shelter and well-being. Teams across various companies actively helped each other and their customers, communities, and nation state during and in the post-COVID-19 pandemic era. In this regard, COVID-19-related CSR is no longer limited to individual corporations but has galvanises corporations across various sectors in their collaboration.

CSR delivers companies with an intentional reaction to the probabilities presented by societal scepticism of firms and equally grow the possibility of obtaining a "social licence to operate". This is part of a decent business plan from this perception. Whereas the "social licence" is an important point of departure, nevertheless, CSR focuses primarily on the application of longer-term, sustainable growth plans by authorities and corporates (Hamann & Kapelus, 2004). The inability of mining corporations to determine the legitimacy of CSR in particular implies that deeper structural problems need to be addressed. The advancement of investment approaches, for example, should essentially accord with the advancement of local growth purposes at all times.

The chapter has evaluated conventional CSR discussions in relation to the sub-Saharan African CSR programme. It explored the direction CSR is likely to take in the post-COVID-19 era. In reaction to this condemnation, a critical perspective to CSR has ensued, and has been influential to the development of conventional CSR programme, which contests the often taken-for-granted conventions about CSR discussions. It is contended that the rise of a sub-Saharan African CSR programme has contributed to making the conventional CSR programme more accustomed to the realities and significances of emerging nations. Hence, it is proposed that future research in sub-Saharan Africa adopts a consolidative research focus, a multifactorial framework of reference and a bottom-up analytical methodology. The implications of adopting this approach is that the investigation must focus on what entrepreneurship has completed or unsuccessfully done in relation to the desirable developmental outcomes of nations, especially in the post-COVID-19 era.

The assumption of the distinctive characteristics of the research approaches proposed requires development academics with the vision to reclaim the programme in the CSR progress nexus discussion, identify and appreciate the conditions under which the progressive effects of CSR are most likely to transpire, and be better able to look at how such circumstances might practicably be sustained and developed in sub-Saharan Africa. Therefore, contemplating the increasing pressure from ordinary people, entrepreneurs in sub-Saharan Africa are in fact, called to display socially responsible behaviour and multiply their CSR programmes to adapt them to a new, more vigorous pandemic framework.

It appears like business principles are now dictating that commercial enterprises in sub-Saharan Africa operate according to positive ethical standards. They now must engage in activities that ordinary people are not expected to engage in – that is activities that go beyond the observation of elementary and orthodox guidelines, respect for property, agreement and traditionally customary justices. They are not merely expected to be engage in any transgression, but must act ethically for public good. The basis for such an obligation is the prerogative that their existence depends exclusively on a grant from the government. It would appear that they would be indebted somewhat to people in exchange for this and supply the required customer goods and create work opportunities. It is obvious from the above that CSR in sub-Saharan Africa is underway, with considerable scale of international companies, particularly those working in the extractive industry leading the path. The perception of CSR in Africa has become identical with that of the mining industry. There seem to be more environmental and human rights interests, with more interest groups advocating for ethical, societal and conservational accountability from corporations working in the area. Noticeably absent in the CSR programme of companies are concerns of the internal characteristic of the perception, which speaks to such problems as occupational health and safety, and the quality of life of the workers.

Thus, it is recommended that entrepreneurs and policymakers work together in a bottom-up approach whereby entrepreneurs would inform policymakers of the potential strategies that could be adopted in the post-COVID-19 era. The significance of keeping societal securities, health insurance and the intensification of the unemployment allowance for entrepreneurs – post the COVID-19 pandemic should be considered. In addition, multinational CSR must assist low-income earning countries from tax evaders.

References

Abdelfattah, T., & Aboud, A. (2020). Tax avoidance, corporate governance, and corporate social responsibility: The case of the Egyptian capital market. *Journal of International Accounting, Auditing and Taxation*, 38, 100304.

Ahmed, J. U., Islam, Q. T., Ahmed, A., Faroque, A. R., & Uddin, M. J. (2021). Corporate social responsibility in the wake of COVID-19: Multiple cases of social responsibility as an organizational value. *Society and Business Review*, 16(4), 496–516.

Ako, R. T. (2012). Re-defining corporate social responsibility (CSR) in Nigeria's post-amnesty oil industry. *African Journal of Economic and Management Studies*, 3(1), 9–22.

Amaeshi, K., Adegbite, E., Ogbechie, C., Idemudia, U., Kan, K. A. S., Issa, M., & Anakwue, O. I. J. (2016). Corporate social responsibility in SMEs: A shift from philanthropy to institutional works? *Journal of Business Ethics*, 138(2), 385–400.

Arli, D. I., & Lasmono, H. K. (2010). Consumers' perception of corporate social responsibility in a developing country. *International Journal of Consumer Studies*, 34(1), 46–51.

Auty, R. (1993). *Sustaining development in mineral economies: The resource curse thesis* (1st ed.). London: Routledge. 10.4324/9780203422595

Auty, R. M. (1997). Natural resource endowment, the state and development strategy. *Journal of International Development*, 9, 651–663. 10.1002/(SICI)1099-1328(199706)9:4<651::AID-JID474>3.0.CO;2-4

Avi-Yonah, R. S. (2008). Corporate social responsibility and strategic tax behavior – comment on the paper by Reuven S. Avi-Yonah. In W. Schön (Ed.), *Tax and corporate governance. MPI studies on intellectual property, competition and tax law* (vol. 3). Berlin, Heidelberg: Springer. 10.1007/978-3-540-77276-7_14

Ayelazuno, J. (2014). Oil wealth and the well-being of the subaltern classes in sub-Saharan Africa: A critical analysis of the resource curse in Ghana. *Resources Policy*, 40, 66–73.

Bowman, E. H., & Haire, M. (1975). A strategic posture toward corporate social responsibility. *California Management Review*, 18(2) 49–58.

Boyce, J. K., & Ndikumana, L. (2012). Capital flight from sub-Saharan African countries: Updated estimates, 1970–2010. *Political Economy Research Institute Research Report.*

Campbell, B. (2012). Corporate social responsibility and development in Africa: Redefining the roles and responsibilities of public and private actors in the mining sector. *Resources Policy*, 37(2), 138–143.

Carroll, A. B. (1991). The pyramid of corporate social responsibility: Toward the moral management of organizational stakeholders. *Business Horizons*, 34(4), 39–48. 10.1016/0007-6813(91)90005-G

Cheruiyot, T. K., & Onsando, P. (Eds.). (2016). Corporate social responsibility in Africa: Context, paradoxes, stakeholder orientations, contestations and reflections. A. StachowiczStanusch (Ed.), *Corporate social performance in the age of irresponsibility-cross national perspective.* Charlotte, NC, United States of America: Information Age Publishing.

Di John, J. (2011). Is there really a resource curse – a critical survey of theory and evidence. *Global Governance*, 17, 167.

ElAlfy, A., Palaschuk, N., El-Bassiouny, D., Wilson, J., & Weber, O. (2020). Scoping the evolution of corporate social responsibility (CSR) research in the sustainable development goals (SDGs) era. *Sustainability*, 12 (14), 5544.

Eltoum, A. M., Yatiban, A., Omar, R., & Islam, R. (2021). Corporate social responsibility practices of business firms in Dubai during the COVID-19 pandemic. *Problems and Perspectives in Management*, 19(1), 231–243.

Eweje, G. (2006). The role of MNEs in community development initiatives in developing countries: Corporate social responsibility at work in Nigeria and South Africa. *Business and Society*, 45(2), 93–129.

Fleming, D. A., Measham, T. G., & Paredes, D. (2015). Understanding the resource curse (or blessing) across national and regional scales: Theory, empirical challenges and an application. *Australian Journal of Agricultural and Resource Economics*, 59(4), 624–639.

Genasci, M., & Pray, S. (2008). Extracting accountability: The implications of the resource curse for CSR theory and practice. *Yale Human Rights and Development Law Journal*, 11, 37.

Görg, H., Hanley, A., Hoffmann, S., & Seric, A. (2017). When do multinational companies consider corporate social responsibility? A multi-country study in sub-Saharan Africa. *Business and Society Review*, 122(2), 191–220.

Hamann, R., & Kapelus, P. (2004). Corporate social responsibility in mining in Southern Africa: Fair accountability or just greenwash? *Development*, 47(3), 85–92.

Holmes, S. L. (1976). Executive perceptions of corporate social responsibility. *Business Horizons*, 19(3), 34–40.

Idemudia, U. (2011). Corporate social responsibility and developing countries: Moving the critical CSR research agenda in Africa forward. *Progress in Development Studies*, 11(1), 1–18.

Idemudia, U. (2014). Corporate social responsibility and development in Africa: Issues and possibilities. *Geography Compass*, 8(7), 421–435.

İyigün, N. Ö. (2015). What could entrepreneurship do for sustainable development? A corporate social responsibility-based approach. *Procedia-Social and Behavioral Sciences*, 195, 1226–1231.

Jenkins, R. (2005). Globalization, corporate social responsibility and poverty. *International Affairs*, 81(3), 525–540.

Khan, M. S., & Haque, N. U. (1987). Capital flight from developing countries. *Finance and Development*, 24(1), 2.

Lensink, R., Hermes, N., & Murinde, V. (2000). Capital flight and political risk. *Journal of International Money and Finance*, 19(1), 73–92.

Mahmud, A., Ding, D., & Hasan, M. M. (2021). Corporate social responsibility: Business responses to coronavirus (COVID-19) pandemic. *SAGE Open*, 11(1), 2158244020988710.

Muthuri, J. N. (2013). Corporate social responsibility in Africa: Definition, issues and processes. In *Management in Africa* (pp. 110–131). Routledge.

Muthuri, J. N., & Gilbert, V. (2011). An institutional analysis of corporate social responsibility in Kenya. *Journal of business Ethics*, 98(3), 467–483.

Ndikumana, L., & Boyce, J. K. (2003). Public debts and private assets: Explaining capital flight from sub-Saharan African countries. *World Development*, 31(1), 107–130.

Ndikumana, L., Boyce, J. K., & Ndiaye, A. S. (2014). Capital flight from Africa. *Capital Flight from Africa: Causes, Effects, and Policy Issues*, 15.

Nyuur, Richard Benon-be-isan, Ofori, D. F., & Debrah, Y. (2014). Corporate social responsibility in sub-Saharan Africa: Hindering and supporting factors. *African Journal of Economic and Management Studies*, 5(1), 93–113.

Ocheje, P. D. (2006). The extractive industries transparency initiative (EITI): Voluntary codes of conduct, poverty and accountability in Africa. *Journal of Sustainable Development in Africa*, 8(3), 222–239.

Popkova, E., DeLo, P., & Sergi, B. S. (2021). Corporate social responsibility amid social distancing during the COVID-19 crisis: BRICS vs. OECD countries. *Research in International Business and Finance*, 55, 101315.

Raimo, N., Rella, A., Vitolla, F., Sánchez-Vicente, M.-I., & García-Sánchez, I.-M. (2021). Corporate social responsibility in the COVID-19 pandemic period: A traditional way to address new social issues. *Sustainability*, 13(12), 6561.

Ramlall, S. (2012). Corporate social responsibility in post-apartheid South Africa. *Social Responsibility Journal*, 8(2), 270–288.

Sachs, J. D., & Warner, A. M. (2001). The curse of natural resources. *European Economic Review*, 45(4-6), 827–838.

Sadiq, M., Nonthapot, S., Mohamad, S., Ehsanullah, S., & Iqbal, N. (2021). Does green finance matter for sustainable entrepreneurship and environmental corporate social responsibility during COVID-19? *China Finance Review International*, 12(2), 317–333.

Silberhorn, D., & Warren, R. C. (2007). Defining corporate social responsibility: A view from big companies in Germany and the UK. *European Business Review*, 19(5), 352–372.

Thomasnet. (2019). A brief history of corporate social responsibility (CSR). https://www.thomasnet.com/insights/history-of-corporate-social-responsibility/

Tiba, S., & Frikha, M. (2019). The controversy of the resource curse and the environment in the SDGs background: The African context. *Resources Policy*, 62, 437–452.

United national Conference on Trade and Development (UNCTAD). (2020). World investment report 2020: International production beyond the pandemic. United Nations, New York.

Visser, W. (2010). The age of responsibility: CSR 2.0 and the New DNA of business. *Journal of Business Systems Governance and Ethics*, 5(3). 10.15209/jbsge.v5i3.185

Vizcaíno, F. V., Martin, S. L., Cardenas, J. J., & Cardenas, M. (2021). Employees' attitudes toward corporate social responsibility programs: The influence of corporate frugality and polychronicity organizational capabilities. *Journal of Business Research*, 124, 538–546.

Wood, D. J. (1991). Corporate social performance revisited. *The Academy of Management Review*, 16(4), 691–718. 10.2307/258977

Yin, G. K. (2001). Getting serious about corporate tax shelters: Taking a lesson from history. *SMU Law Review*, 54(1), 209.

9 The Application of TPB Concepts in Building Innovative African Entrepreneurs, and Effective Entrepreneurship Education in Africa: A Way Forward for Africa to Post-Covid-19 Economic Sustainability

Ekene Francis Okagbue, Ujunwa Perpetua Ezeachikulo, and Sayibu Muhideen

Introduction

Africa is seen, in the world of business exchange, as the world's second emerging market, following China (Frese et al., 2014). It is a continent endowed with numerous natural resources, mineral deposits, and human resources, if properly managed and applied into producing of other commodities and products for exports will practically change the economic conditions of Africa, and makes it one of the most prosperous continents in the globe (Egerová et al., 2017). However, the inability to convert these opportunities for the greater good of the continent leads to an increase in hunger, unemployment, social crises, poverty, etc, (Chae & Goh, 2020). For Africa to come out of the aforementioned social challenges, it requires a practical and strategic application of entrepreneurship education to bring a new direction for a progressive Africa (Adeleye & Eboagu, 2019). Effective application of entrepreneurship education in educational activities in African schools will help to raise confident entrepreneurs with the necessary entrepreneurial skills and entrepreneurial intention (EI) to solve the current challenges Africa is facing, and therefore improve the living conditions of the people (Opute et al., 2021). One advantage of entrepreneurship education is the ability to impact individuals with courage, critical ideas on how to tackle issues, and an entrepreneurial mindset to become successful entrepreneurs (Asongu et al., 2017). The benefit such as entrepreneurial mindset and intention can be triggered by the concept of the theory of planned behaviour (TPB) (K. Srivastava & Thomas, 2017). Ma et al. (2020)

DOI: 10.4324/9781003216469-9

opine that the TPB in connection with entrepreneurship education can cause entrepreneurship behaviour and intention which are referred to as the core element for an individual to perform an entrepreneurial action. From TPB elements, the factors that influence the entrepreneurship intention for an entrepreneurial action to occur are said to be attitude, subjective norm, and PBC (perceived behavioural control).

The TPB provides the reasons why people start businesses or have the desire to start a new venture which is attributed to the attitude and intention. TPB is considered a critical element in entrepreneurship education for nurturing post-Covid-19 African entrepreneurs for long-term sustainability (Ahmed et al., 2020). Due to the obvious prevalence of the Covid-19 outbreak and its effects on Africa's entrepreneurship education and entrepreneurship, this project aims to assess (1) the conditions of entrepreneurship education in Africa, (2) the obstacles and challenges affecting the progress of entrepreneurship education and entrepreneurship, (3) the impact of TPB on the effective development of EI and attitude in entrepreneurship education, entrepreneurship and African entrepreneurs, and (4) offer recommendations to governments and policymakers on what to do to promote effective entrepreneurship education across schools in Africa. Several scholars have addressed the following questions: (1) what plans does Africa have to push their continent forward?, (2) how can effective entrepreneurship education be promoted across the continent in consideration of TPB?, (3) how does entrepreneurship education help to improve entrepreneurial activity in Africa in the post-Covid-19 era?

Entrepreneurship education is considered to be the appropriate tool to steer Africa to the right pathways for a new era (Akpan et al., 2012; Henry, 2013; K. Srivastava & Thomas, 2017; Velentzas, 2017), at the same time arms the potential future entrepreneurs with the knowledge to exploit greater height in wealth creation, generation of idealistic views for proactive entrepreneurship (Nowiński & Haddoud, 2019). In the argument of (Aja-Okorie Onele Adali, 2013; Gabadeen & Raimi, 2012; Ogbari et al., 2018; Olorundare & Kayode, 2014), they opined that entrepreneurship education is not limited only to fostering business attitude and EIs but also entails building up futuristic dreams of the students and coaching them to make a wise career decision (Adeleye & Eboagu, 2019).

In the same vein, entrepreneurship education embodies holistic concepts of creating a successful business environment, career coaching for self-development, advancement of technology in all aspects of life, education development, etc (Naudé, 2021). This study suggests that all African governments and policymakers should invest in entrepreneurship education, and also introduce effective policies that can anchor strategic teaching and training programmes for entrepreneurial activities across all schools on the continent.

Literature review

Conceptual framing of TPB and entrepreneurship

The TPB has become a focal point of the concept network of predictive attitudes and behaviour across time. TPB elements with entrepreneurship education provide the needed qualities for a transformative change to happen in an environment. Icek Ajzen (1991) visualises the TPB as the agent to stimulate effective entrepreneurship behaviour in the African continent (Jena, 2020). Effective entrepreneurship behaviour according to Icek Ajzen (1991) is the possibility of the TPB to create willingness in an individual to act. In furtherance, subjective norms PBC, and attitude remain the crucial factors for EI, behaviour, and entrepreneurship. TPB is the degree of intentions and behaviours, which is expected in educational entrepreneurship (Handayati et al., 2020). TPB in the literature on entrepreneurship education accentuated on knowledge of the discipline sets oneself on a predictive innovation with connected norms, attitudes, and behaviours (Lortie & Castogiovanni, 2015). Many scholars on entrepreneurship discourse agreed on the principle that is fundamental for a novelty of growing a business to rely on TPB (behaviours are related to entrepreneurship) (Almeida et al., 2021). Secundo, De Beer, Fai, and Schutte 2019 alluded that TPB helps in nurturing entrepreneurship mindset and intention as the key factors to improve economic and environmental conditions (Ruiz-Rosa et al., 2020). To comprehend the role of entrepreneurship intention alongside TPB, Küttim et al. (2014) argued that it has no distinct and straightforward definition, and varies in different domains. However, in the paradigm of TPB, for entrepreneurial activity to occur depends on an intention of an individual to cognitively intend to engage in the behaviours of opportunity recognition, venture conception, and venture development (Krueger et al., 2000).

Moreover, the fusion of TPB application on entrepreneurship education influences people's intentions and behaviours causing them to harbour clear entrepreneurship PBC (Küttim et al., 2014). Research has shown that TPB has been an influential resource for efficient entrepreneurship education on the borderline of intention as a means of possessing a burning desire, passion, and orientation toward establishing a business and education reforms (Gelderen et al., 2008). Intention as the mediating factor for entrepreneurship behaviour, Kuttim et al. (2014) views on Ajzen's (2002) definition of entrepreneurship intention conforms to Icek Ajzen's TPB, which is linked to attitude, and attitude is the predictor of strategic behaviour and action (Netemeyer & Ryn, 1991). The benefits of applying TPB concepts in entrepreneurship are to create an attitude of wise decision-making, cognitive thinking, and opportunity identification (Gelderen et al., 2008).

For further elaboration on TPB, extant literature expresses the similarity and difference of TPB dimensions on human behaviour of Ajzen 1988, 1991 and Shapero and Sokol 1982 studies on subjective norms, PBC, and attitude for Ajzen. And perceived feasibility, desirability, and intuition to act for Shapero, and Sokol. These established factors from these two great scholars are modelled as precursors for triggering innate strength to pursue set goals (Gelderen et al., 2008).

In order to harness the innate intention and bring forth desired action that will cause a change in the entrepreneurship environment, entrepreneurs ought to acquire the elements of TPB established by Icek Ajzen, and Shapero and Sokol (Ahmed et al., 2020), which can help entrepreneurs to make a wise decision (Higgins & Elliott, 2011). Studies on TPB have emphasised its effects on entrepreneurship education, and entrepreneurship, especially on human attitudes such as motivation, resilience, and determination to build a successful business enterprise (Barba-Sánchez & Atienza-Sahuquillo, 2018; Oosterbeek et al., 2010; Vaicekauskaite & Valackiene, 2018).

The remainder of this article is arranged as follows: section 2.2 describes entrepreneurship education, entrepreneurship, and entrepreneur, 2.3 the emergence and concept of entrepreneurship, and so on; section 3 briefly explains ICT and entrepreneurship education in Africa, followed by the challenges of entrepreneurship education development in Africa, and its benefits; section 4 is the conclusion and recommendation, and section 5 provides the study's limitations and future research directions, and finally, section 6 illustrates policy implication of the study. Innovation, organisation, risk-taking, and vision are the key elements of entrepreneurship education and entrepreneurship, and they are completely detailed in section 2.3.

Entrepreneurship education, entrepreneurship, and entrepreneur

Teaching entrepreneurship education in nexus with the TPB to promote the spirit of entrepreneurship, and produce intentional African entrepreneurs will change the trajectory of African society (Ratten & Jones, 2021). This section focuses on providing a clear understanding of three distinct terms that have been extensively investigated by many scholars; entrepreneurship education, entrepreneurship, and entrepreneur. According to Martin et al. (2013), entrepreneurship education promotes the development of human capital and skill acquisition. They discuss entrepreneurship education in relation to human capital theory, offering comprehensive knowledge that can develop a survival mindset (Ployhart & Moliterno, 2011).

Entrepreneurship education, according to the global entrepreneurship monitor 2010 defines it as a discipline that teaches the fundamentals for entrepreneurship practices, business operations, and techniques to run successful business enterprises (Remeikiene et al., 2013). Isaacs et al., 2007 describe EE as a means of intervention to learners for easy navigation of life in the future (Isaacs et al., 2007). Application of TPB in EE instructions gives rise to innovative mindsets, entrepreneurial competence, self-efficacy, and pragmatic behaviour (Gabadeen & Raimi, 2012), thereby encouraging individuals to take reasonable actions by engaging in entrepreneurship.

Entrepreneurship, the definition of entrepreneurship is often juxtaposed with the description of entrepreneurship education. Gabadeen and Raimi (2012) defined entrepreneurship as an approach to discovering and grabbing opportunities that have not yet been discovered and commercialising those opportunities into financial gains. Most significantly, entrepreneurship is described as the creation of business and financial opportunities, and the provision of services to the public, including the production and procession of goods and commodities for public consumption and the subjective well-being of individuals (Amjad et al., 2020). Iwu et al. (2021) consider entrepreneurship as the agent that causes the rise of entrepreneurial traits and behaviours. The benefit of effective teaching entrepreneurship education, and practising entrepreneurship is the ability to train and raise charismatic entrepreneurs that have transformative ideas (Cui et al., 2021). As Cui et al. (2021) describe entrepreneurship education as a means of breeding pragmatic entrepreneurs, it is pertinent to explore the understanding of who is an entrepreneur from the existing scholarship. Gartner (2014) interprets the word entrepreneur from different perspectives and elaborates further on the two contrasting terms entrepreneurs and non-entrepreneurs on the premise of character, personality, behaviour, and motivation. He posits that an entrepreneur is an individual with the personality, behaviour, motivation, and character to take calculated risks and start a business, while non-entrepreneurs do not. Nonetheless, Gartner's (2014) description of an entrepreneur corroborates with the definitions of the three famous authors, for example, Brockhaus (1980) defines an entrepreneur as a job creator who has never worked for anybody else. Cole (1959) opines it as a collection of people who produce services and profit from them; Collins and Moore (1970) see it as workers in organisations that engage in entrepreneurial activities to advance the financial trajectory of the company (Gartner, 2014).

In these three concepts (entrepreneurship education, entrepreneurship, and entrepreneur), one common recurring factor is the individual intention to perform a given behaviour by engaging in entrepreneurship, and TPB explains that intentions are transformed into a given behaviour when the individual critically assesses the external factors that might affect his or her decision. The external factors such as social pressures, individuals' knowledge of entrepreneurship, and the ability to succeed as an entrepreneur (Karimi et al., 2016). Once the individual identifies the factors that might affect his entrepreneurial decisions, the self-motivation, and resilience to surmount the perceived factors become the propelling force to attain his entrepreneurial desires. For that, TPB elements are considered the determinants of entrepreneurship education in raising intentional entrepreneurs (Laguía et al., 2019). And also they inspire an opportunity-seeking attitude toward wealth creation (Stephan & El-Ganainy, 2007). Developing the attitude to create wealth through entrepreneurship by entrepreneurs, first, have to understand the principles of the TPB (Tornikoski, 2019), which originally centres on the intentions that can be determined by the subjective norm (SN), and one's tendency to take actions (personal attitude) (Yurtkoru et al., 2014). And the personal attitude from the theoretical model is considered as the behavioural intention (BI). Behavioural intention is one of the components of TPB, Wilson et al. (2007) stress that BI measures an individual's ability to make entrepreneurial decisions, they further stated that entrepreneurship education inspires the behavioural intention of an individual in understanding the subjective norms.

Entrepreneurship education defines behavioural intention as EI and considers the reagent for a non-entrepreneurs to decide to become an entrepreneur (Yurtkoru et al., 2014). One way a non-entrepreneur develops entrepreneurship intention to become an entrepreneur depends on the entrepreneurship training and education received (Küttim et al., 2014), the knowledge of it gives rise to the EI that a novice entrepreneur would be determined and resilient to succeed in his or her embarked entrepreneurial activities.

In furtherance, TPB is the fulcrum that entrepreneurship education depends on to train serious-minded entrepreneurs with a positive attitude to acquire entrepreneurship skills (Ma et al., 2020). From this explanation, we can deduce that effective entrepreneurship education, successful entrepreneurship, and intentional entrepreneurs are the products of the strategic application of the TPB. Entrepreneurship thrives smoothly when the recipients (entrepreneurs) of EE are groomed through the practical comprehension of TPB models, they tend to be cognisant of the PBC concept (Jena, 2020). For entrepreneurship to reach the apogee of generating income for the society, the entrepreneurs who are the implementers of the entrepreneurial ideas acquired from entrepreneurship education ought to apply PBC (Gelderen et al., 2008).

The PBC can be understood as the confidence and trust one has in his or her ability to take action. This also entails an individual trusting his capability to perform a certain behaviour under investigation, and believing to have control over the behaviour (Ajzen, 2002). Fayolle et al. (2006) assert that there is a close relationship between behavioural feasibility and PBC, indicating that an individual adopts a behaviour that he or she perceives and feels can control and master. This implies that entrepreneurship education instils confidence in potential entrepreneurs to control their fears and take substantive action. PBC as the element of TPB encourages entrepreneurs to have the right attitude in indulging in entrepreneurship (Alvarez et al., 2006). Entrepreneurship is an act to master and learn, an individual that wants to be an entrepreneur has to learn and master the required attitude and behaviour for entrepreneurship (Kakouris & Georgiadis, 2016). This behaviour determines the success tendency of the individual. Bandura's (1982) study on self-efficacy theory, shows the homogeneity of self-efficacy and PBC. Self-efficacy theory and PBC share a similar definition of an individual's ability to execute a task.

In a nutshell, the TPB model will play a significant role in teaching EE in African academic institutions to generate EI in the students' engagement in entrepreneurship. It impacts students to possess a positive attitude. TPB theory also stipulates that when an individual shows a positive attitude toward a certain behaviour, the stronger the intention to make a tangible decision, the more positive one's subjective norms, the stronger the intention, the better the PBC, the stronger the intention to take an action (Ma et al., 2020). The perfect individuals to transfer the elements of TPB to the individuals such as positive attitude, EI, confidence, or self-efficacy start from the instructors of EE to raise sound entrepreneurs that internalised the concepts of TPB and have the behavioural intention to engage in productive entrepreneurship (Barba-Sánchez & Atienza-Sahuquillo, 2018) (Figure 9.1).

Various authors defined an entrepreneur as a risk-taker, manager, innovator (Aljuwaiber, 2020; Jůvová et al., 2017; Remeikiene et al., 2013), leader, idea creator (Gartner, 2014), business coach, team player, business investor (Van Ness et al., 2020), a problem solver or solution finder, etc., (Deloitte, 2018; Fayolle & Gailly, 2008; Michelacci & Schivardi, 2020).

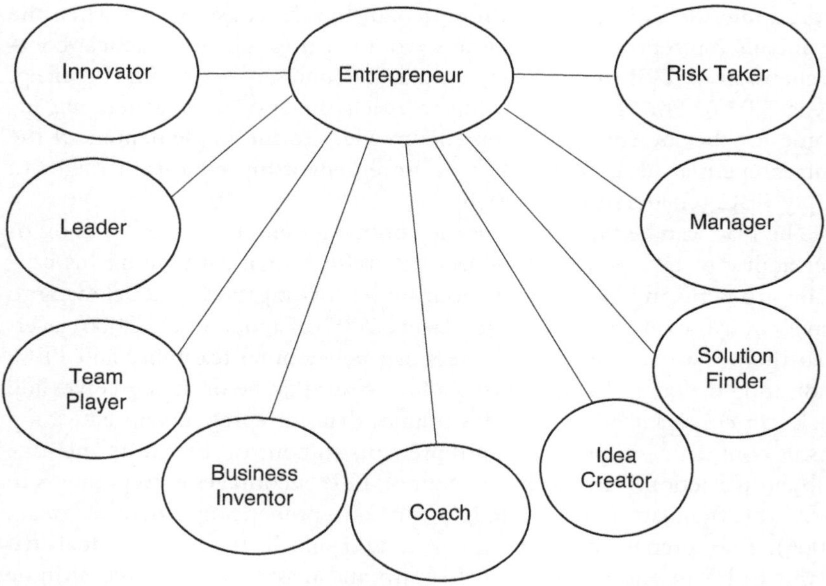

Figure 9.1 Summarises the understanding of different scholars' views on entrepreneurs.
Source: Summarised by the Author.

Emergence and concept of EE

The concept of entrepreneurship education originally began with entrepreneurial activities around the 1970s (Kuratko, 2005). The emergence of business firms, companies, and business ventures in the United States with the economic revenues from the business transactions led to the American Universities adopting EE in their learning curriculum in 1947 (Katz, 2003). The first induction of the entrepreneurship concepts into the learning programme was done by the Californian Southern University titled MBA (Master of Business of Administration) in 1971; subsequently, up to three hundred universities adopted entrepreneurship and business-related courses in their curriculum. Between the actual emergence of EE in the 1980s to the 1990s, more than fifty schools integrated it as a learning course in their respective schools (Kuratko, 2005).

As a field of study, its significant aims will be adequately highlighted. The conceptual dimension of EE is focused on the teaching methods learning contents, and who are the targeted learners (Hatt & Hatt, 2018). However, being a system of learning that is discovered from the business interactions; therefore the quest to understand the principles and theories to run a successful business enterprise and intentions to improve the economic returns becomes the pivotal motivation for the creation of entrepreneurship learning programmes. Initially, the difficult questions raised were the teachability of entrepreneurship education, such as "what should be taught" (the contents) and "how it should be taught" (teaching approach or methodology) (Kuratko, 2005).

The primary concerns of effective entrepreneurship education are what should be taught, and how it should be taught to teach. What areas of entrepreneurship education should be taught, according to Kuratko (2005), should focus on the underlined points in Table 9.1.

Promoting entrepreneurial skills in learning institutions, teacher training, and professional development programmes is quintessential in grooming capable entrepreneurs, especially in Africa (Laguía et al., 2019). For the question, who should entrepreneurship education be taught to? Countries like Australia, China, the United States of America, and New Zealand initiated entrepreneurship education from the basic level to empower the students for future challenges.

Core elements of entrepreneurship education and entrepreneurship

The possible core elements of Entrepreneurship education and entrepreneurship are perceived to be (1) innovation, (2) risk-taking, (3) organisation, and (4) vision. Olorundare and Kayode (2014) expressed that entrepreneurship education can inherently equip individuals with innovation consciousness and ideas to create services and products for well-being and monetary gains.

Table 9.1 Learning concepts and explanation

Learning concepts	*Explanation*	*Authors*
Strategy of Entrepreneurship	It entails the possession of pragmatic entrepreneurship behaviour, mindset, and attitude, knowledge to run successful enterprises.	(Sexton, 2001)
Ethics of Entrepreneurship	It teaches the procedures, principles, and ethos to manage entrepreneurship investments.	(Kuratko et al., 2004)
Management Dimension	The systematic process of managing business, career, skills, organisation, and institutions in achieving the desired aims and objectives.	(Ireland et al., 2003)
Venture Finance	Financial decisions on business investments and establishing financial property. Having sufficient knowledge on loss and gains concept in entrepreneurship.	(Zacharakis & Shepherd, n.d.)
Corporate Entrepreneurship	It provides the teachings of understanding the concept of business establishment, investments, and creation of services.	(Miles & Covin, 2002)

In furtherance of this thought, innovation cannot be ascribed as the inventions of goods and services for financial purposes only but extends to building and developing human capital and career mentorships (Olorundare & Kayode, 2014). Idea creation, formulation, and execution of the ideas into actions are also referred to as innovation (Dou et al., 2019; Handayati et al., 2020; Ratten & Jones, 2021). Innovation, vision, and risk-taking are indispensable; nonetheless, vision spurs up risk-taking, and risk-taking provides the possibility for innovation (Ratten & Jones, 2021; Ratten & Usmanij, 2021).

One of the benefits of entrepreneurship education is the strategic thinking pattern, flexibility in visioning workable, and successful ways to carry out business purposes or ideas (González-Serrano et al., 2020). Inarguably, the force that propels a risk-taking attitude in entrepreneurial activities is thoughtful visions. The conviction of excelling in any entrepreneurial activity reduces the failure mindset and fear of the unknown. The essence of entrepreneurship education is to foster the willingness and entrepreneurship intentions to identify one capability quickly. Conversely, besides creating visible business enterprises, organisations, service delivery companies, careers, etc. And not understanding the organisational and managerial concepts leads to the collapse of the venture and self-development (Almeida et al., 2021). The Almeida et al. (2021) underpinnings corroborate the statement that entrepreneurship education leads to human capital development (Martin et al., 2013; Ployhart & Moliterno, 2011; Shirazi & Hajli, 2021).

Entrepreneurship education dimension during Covid-19 in Africa

Africa's education system witnessed a massive shock at the sudden outbreak of Covid-19. Education was paused for many months due to the ravaging impacts of the pandemic on human life (Liguori & Winkler, 2020). This event led to the closure of various schools across the continent that failed to provide continuous education learning platforms for students to continue their education in their respective homes (Amadasun, 2021). Ahmed et al. (2020) also delineated that the inability of almost 75% of schools in Africa to avail alternative means to engage students in the learning activity during the lockdown period was caused due to lack of ICT infrastructure in the school teaching system. In comparison to countries that swiftly switched to remote learning approach, for instance, China was known as the epicentre during the first virus outbreak, implemented a policy titled "close schools, but do not stop class" (Chen et al., 2020), this shows the readiness of China's government in providing the necessary resources to the schools. The United States of America, Canada, France, the Uk, etc, followed suit in adopting web-based learning systems. The shortage of standard technology devices in the education environment remains a challenge in enhancing entrepreneurship education in the African school system (UNESCO, 2020). Besides the effects of Covid-19 on Africa's education system, other entrepreneurial activities such as daily business transactions and related economic exchange were gravely affected (Devine & Kiggundu, 2016). The non-existence of digital business culture impeded the growth of financial activities (Crick et al., 2020).

Evidence of effective entrepreneurship education in society is the ability to provide sophisticated inventions and innovations in all spheres of life to promote people's subjective happiness (Ratten & Usmanij, 2021). The orientation of digital marketing, cryptocurrency, remote learning through software, ICT framework both in business, education, governance, advanced science, health sector, smart cities, etc, in a country is an indicator of an effective entrepreneurship education influences on the environment with a progressive thought (Internet Society, 2017). Peterman and Kennedy (2003) asserted effective adoption of entrepreneurship education is the only precursor to turn things around in African society (Peterman & Kennedy, 2003).

ICT and entrepreneurship education in Africa

Entrepreneurial operations cannot grow in this era without an information and communication technology infrastructure. Informatization and digitisation are important in all aspects of society (Deloitte, 2018). The evidence of students being unable to participate in schooling programmes at their respective homes during the lockdown time of the initial epidemic of Covid-19 suggests a lack of an information and communication technology framework in Africa's educational environment (Butcherr & Association for the Development of Education in Africa, 2014). As a result, learners felt rejected because there were no other tools provided by the government and school leadership to enforce continuous learning as other advanced countries did (Shirazi & Hajli, 2021). This incident demonstrates that digital online learning platforms are not present in Africa's educational design (Farber, 2013). One of the facilitators of entrepreneurial education is digital distant learning (Hamburg, 2021).

To improve entrepreneurship education to benefit Africa's financial growth, economic sustainability, rise in industrialisation, job creation, and poverty eradication, the usual conventional attitude, mindset, and practice of business exchange have to change (Crawford et al., 2020; Eze, Chinedu-Eze, Okike, & Bello, n.d.; Guthrie & McCracken, 2010). The traditional method of education, teaching behaviour, learning materials, and course contents must be modified to spark cognitive agility in learners (Jůvová et al., 2017).

While the issue of a digital divide is present in Africa, even though ICT consciousness and digital technology awareness are present, Africa represents the least number of individuals using technology to resolve social issues (Dsv et al., 2016). This divide has dampened the entrepreneurship strive due to the difficulty in assessing ICT networks devices, broadband connectivity, and affordable internet (Blackburn & Kovalainen, 2009; Frese et al., 2014; Išoraitė & Gulevičiūtė, 2021; A. Srivastava, Singh, Srivastava, & Sinha, n.d.) (Figure 9.2).

Despite the digital divide and the near-impossibility of using technology advancements to solve Africa's challenges, a report from the International Telecommunication Union (ITU) shows that one-third of African citizens in Sub-Saharan and North Africa are active internet users. This is obvious

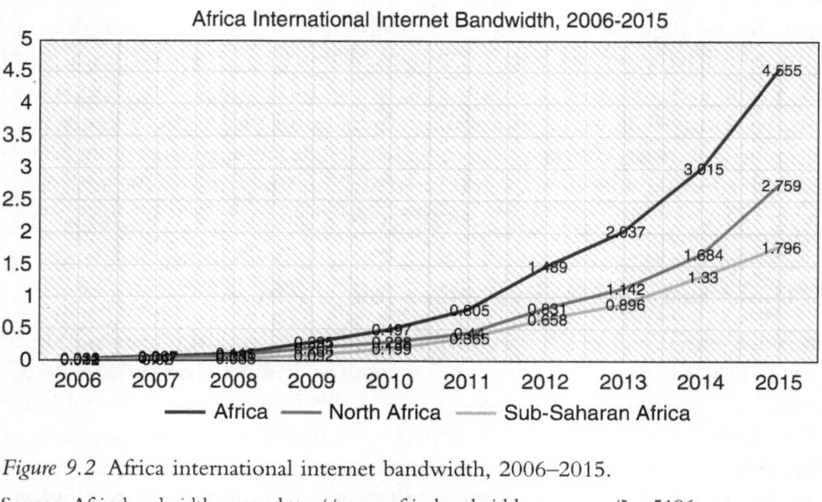

Figure 9.2 Africa international internet bandwidth, 2006–2015.

Source: Africabandwidth maps, http://www.africabandwidthmaps.com/?p=5186.

evidence that information and communication technology is progressively gaining some traction throughout Africa. The graph illustrates a significant growth in internet users from 2006 to 2015, with an improved bandwidth to about 4.5 terabits in 2015. It is predicted to keep getting better as it progresses with time (Internet Society, 2017). Countries like Nigeria, South Africa, Kenya, Rwanda, Egypt, Zambia, Ghana, Angola, and Zimbabwe have initiated sustainable goals initiatives for overhaul transformation achievements in the countries with the ICT application (Asongu et al., 2017).

This validation from International Telecommunication Union surveys, on the other hand, does not indicate that Africa's ICT ecosystem is without difficulties. Notably, entrepreneurship education will have a predicted positive impact in Africa if ICT and its characteristics are broadly accessible to all citizens (Unwin, 2015). Figure 9.3 below shows that Africa has a low number of internet and information communication technology users.

Challenges of entrepreneurship education development in Africa

Following the establishment of the important characteristics of entrepreneurship education in the preceding sections (Adeleye & Eboagu, 2019), iterates that a complete inclusion of entrepreneurship-related courses across African learning institutions will boost the human capital development index and produce a capable human resource that will strategically run and manage the economy. Nonetheless, various obstacles have hampered the success and profits that entrepreneurship knowledge would have

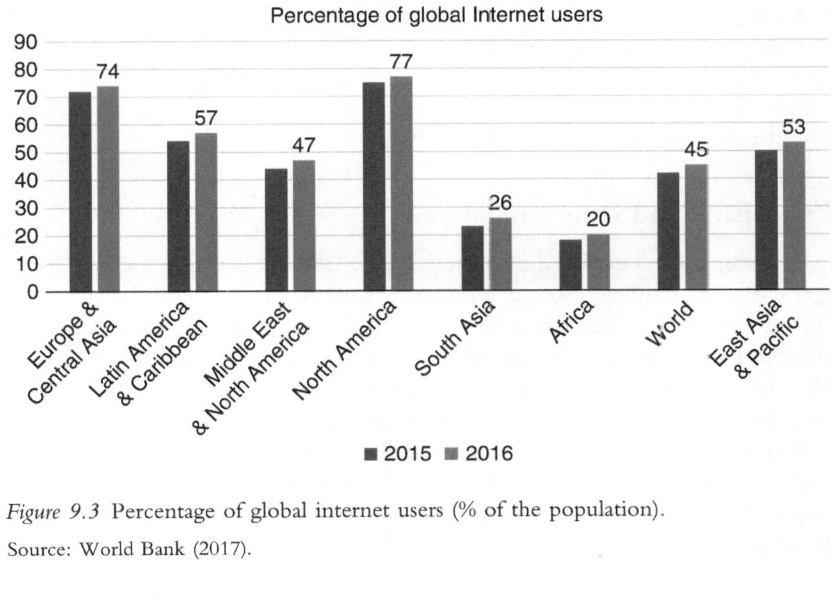

Figure 9.3 Percentage of global internet users (% of the population).

Source: World Bank (2017).

provided (Counted & Arawole, 2015). The most significant impediment to EE growth is a lack of an updated learning curriculum (Oosterbeek et al., 2010). Pedagogical practices shape entrepreneurial attitudes and culture. As a result, teaching entrepreneurship at the primary, secondary, and tertiary levels can reduce challenges and promote consistent innovation for long-term development (Hermann & Bossle, 2020). Aside from the lack of a strategic entrepreneurship education curriculum, Ict and In (2008) stated that internet access and ICT teaching equipment will strategically shape entrepreneurial activities and education; however, most academic institutions do not have the planned behaviours. A digitally conscious society changes societal dynamics (Higgins et al., 2013). Poor educational policies, according to Soriano and Montoro-Sanchez (2011), are the most repellent forces drowning out the possibilities of entrepreneurship education in most African countries. Nonetheless, social insecurity has an impact on entrepreneurship and entrepreneurship education, as well as poverty and illiteracy (Soriano & Montoro-Sanchez, 2011). According to Asongu and Odhiambo (2019), entrepreneurship education promotes digital literacy and understanding of the technicalities of digital entrepreneurship, digital marketing, and remote learning. Nonetheless, due to ineffective EE, a lack of ICT skills has refuted many African millennials the ability to compete in this trend (Aljuwaiber, 2020).

Policies are regarded as the engines of substantive development in a country; effective educational policies modify the dynamics of education in society (Herrington & Coduras, 2019). Furthermore, bad education policies contribute to the backward position of Africa's entrepreneurial education and education system in general (Kakouris & Georgiadis, 2016). Finally, the high prevalence of corruption impairs the sustainability of entrepreneurship and the dramatic improvements that effective entrepreneurship education may bring to Africa. Also, corruption reduces students' possibility of putting their talents and knowledge to use in developing things that can drive society forward and cut down on the ambition of achieving greatness (Devine & Kiggundu, 2016) (Table 9.2).

Conclusion and recommendation

In general, it has been demonstrated that entrepreneurship education is an agent of the socio-economic transformation of Africa (Ruiz-Rosa et al., 2020). The TPB is considered an element that will trigger entrepreneurial behaviours in Africans to change the economic situation of the continent (Handayati et al., 2020). The assured means through which entrepreneurial behaviours are acquired is through the effective application of entrepreneurship education across the academic institutions on the continent (Laguía et al., 2019). Extant scholarships deduced that TPB theory fosters pragmatic entrepreneurial traits in an individual which propels entrepreneurial actions (Fayolle & Gailly, 2008).

Table 9.2 Benefits of entrepreneurship education

Themes	*Descriptions*	*Authors*
Job Creation and financial generation	Entrepreneurship education provides sufficient knowledge for creating jobs and employment, simultaneously providing financial returns and gains.	(Adeleye & Eboagu, 2019; Alvarez et al., 2006; Ferreira et al., 2017; Iwu et al., 2021)
Cognitive Development	The stimulation of cognitive ability and skills from entrepreneurship courses significantly impacts an individual's perceptions, views, and entrepreneurial attitudes.	(Alvarez et al., 2006; Ferreira et al., 2017; Jena, 2020; Meyer et al., 2014)
Entrepreneurial attitude and intentions	Organised and coordinated entrepreneurship behaviour in identifying new ideas and opportunities and taking practical action to fulfil them is one of the elements of entrepreneurship education.	(Dou et al., 2019; Ajike, Kelechi, Akinlabi, Onyia, & Kwarbai, 2015; Jena, 2020; Ma et al., 2020; Ratten, 2020)
Self-Efficacy	Entrepreneurship instils confidence and willingness to trust one decision-making in business venturing, investment, or choosing a career path.	(Egerová et al., 2017; Jůvová et al., 2017; Remeikiene et al., 2013; Van Ness et al., 2020)
Skill Mastery	An essential gain of entrepreneurship education is skill acquisition. It exposes students to master different skills both for technology and handcraft.	(Alvarez et al., 2006)
Problem Solving	The knowledge of entrepreneurship education provides ideas and approaches to existing problems that affect society and humans	(Hermann & Bossle, 2020; Jůvová et al., 2017; Peschl et al., 2021)

In order to build entrepreneurial attitudes in African society, effective entrepreneurship education should be encouraged at all levels of education in Africa (Pittaway & Cope, 2007). Classroom instructors with an in-depth understanding of the TPB concept would be preferable in breeding and grooming the students to possess the qualities of potential entrepreneurs. One of the challenges that might affect the instruction of entrepreneurship education is finding teachers with adequate knowledge of TPB. A teacher with a grasp of TPB concepts and having the skills and approach on how to drive positive attitudes in the learners to muster the courage to delve into entrepreneurship is highly quintessential. This will dissipate the doubts in the individuals and learners as they consider the effects of subjective norms in making their entrepreneurial decisions. Note that subjective norm is the pressure on an individual to consider whether to act on the intention or not to act in becoming an entrepreneur or take the route of entrepreneurship (Gelderen et al., 2008).

Another important TPB element in ensuring effective EE, entrepreneurship, and intelligent entrepreneur is the PBC. PBC is highlighted in section 2.2 as one of the crucial factors that can stir a positive attitude in an individual to trust one's ability. Ma et al. (2020) review that PBC influences behavioural intention (EI), also entrepreneurial attitude influences EI by perceived control. The PBC creates the conviction in oneself that he or she is capable to perform a certain action with maximum behavioural control. When an individual trusts his ability to perform a particular behaviour he becomes competent to take more risks with positive attitudes and absolute confidence to achieve success. PBC and entrepreneurship attitude can be indicators to assess the sustainability tendency of the entrepreneurs who are into entrepreneurship, other elements of PBC are perseverance, and knowing when to perform a certain behaviour (entrepreneurial behaviour). Ajzen's (1991) TPB delineates three elements that determine the intention and behaviour of an individual centre on (1) attitude, (2) social norms, and (3) PBC.

For Africa to attain a significant economic milestone, its citizens must be taught TPB elements of attitude which entails the extent someone has a favourable and unfavourable assessment of certain behaviour. This also indicates individual perception toward a behaviour. When there is a positive perception toward a certain behaviour, a more favourable attitude and stronger intention to indulge in the activity (Almeida et al., 2021). When entrepreneurship education provides relatable knowledge and information, it creates a trust for learners to have a positive attitude toward entrepreneurship. Subjective norm is referred to as the perceived social pressure that influences the individual's belief in making a decision for example; either to take action or not to, in African society this is prevalent. There are numerous social pressures that influence an individual to go into entrepreneurship or not, which could be the fear of the unknown, external factors like policy, crisis, lack of adequate finances, family pressure, etc. These become barriers to entrepreneurship and for entrepreneurs to thrive in Africa. PBC means one has the ability to take action regardless the pressure, and fear. The application of this theory in EE, and entrepreneurship will definitely produce entrepreneurs with transformative attitudes and intentions (Cunningham & Menter, 2021).

Finally, this article suggests to African policymakers implement actionable policies that will improve the teaching and learning of entrepreneurship education in the African continent for economic sustenance through innovation, and entrepreneurship. Establishing training grounds for entrepreneurship programmes such as how to create a business, service delivery, innovate things, and turn ideas into a tangible means to solve social issues in Africa is paramount in building human capital that will transform unprogressive Africa into a progressive continent. The lessons and experiences of the Covid-19 outbreak should awaken the consciousness of the leadership of Africa to take action now to prevent the future incident from happening again. One of the crucial areas ministries of education in Africa should also consider in building effective entrepreneurship education in schools is designing a 21st-century education curriculum that meets the demands of the 21st-century society that will bring strategic development to Africa's society (Iwu et al., 2021). As previously said, TPB concepts in entrepreneurship education and practical entrepreneurship training will inculcate in African entrepreneurs the entrepreneurial mindset, behaviour, and intentions (Malebana, 2021).

Limitations and future research directions

The authors agreed that this current study did not capture all the possible angles of TPB in influencing entrepreneurship education, entrepreneurship, and entrepreneur. TPB is believed to trigger EI and behaviour from the three antecedents (1) attitude, (2) subjective norm, and (3) PBC (Almeida et al., 2021). These elements are considered to be precursors for entrepreneurship education, entrepreneurship, and entrepreneurs to prevail. However, this study failed to cover the possible impact of TPB on entrepreneurship and entrepreneurs that are facing challenges (such as environmental and political challenges). We also consider the methodology used in this article as one of the limitations of this paper, as the study adopted a critical literature review as the methodology. For that reason, the authors suggest that more quantitative studies are still needed on this discourse, especially in the African context.

We suggest that future research should therefore address the above-mentioned limitations of the study. For instance, it may be thoughtful for future research to explore the impact of TPB on struggling entrepreneurship and entrepreneurs touching on the most significant and practical areas on how TPB can turn around entrepreneurship, facing numerous social pressures to strive, and how it can impact entrepreneurs not to give up.

Another area, this study recommends for future studies to consider is how can instructors of EE apply the TPB model to trigger innovative mindsets and ideas in African students. In this study, PBC from the TPB model has a direct impact on the behaviour, that is to say, that EE can impact learners of EE to possess entrepreneurial behavioural traits including the confidence and self-efficacy to be actively involved in entrepreneurial activities. This statement is made in connection to section 2.4 on the EE dimension during Covid-19 in Africa, the incidence of the pandemic reveals the importance of TPB as the right model to drive innovation and economic development of Africa beyond its present state, also given the challenges that affect EE, entrepreneurship which one factor out of the many ones is ICT problem in Africa, in this time and age lack of ICT can affect the development of entrepreneurship and teachings of entrepreneurship education for that reason, future research should also consider expanding knowledge on this with TPB elements.

An updated entrepreneurship course content and teaching curriculum with TPB concepts can bring forth an EI and positive attitude in African entrepreneurs and students to be able to identify issues in the community and take action to solve them. This area also calls for further studies to explore the possibility of course content and curriculum alongside TPB elements influencing the entrepreneurial attitude and intention of African entrepreneurs.

Additionally, there is a need for education stakeholders, and ministries of education to look into the entrepreneurship education curriculum, the course components, and curriculum content of the schools in the continent ensuring that they can have a significant impact on EI, attitude, and ability to act. Further research can explore how the education stakeholders and policymakers are working to develop EE, and entrepreneurship in the continent for a productive economy and subjective wellbeing of the citizens.

Conclusively, future studies should explore beyond the conceptualisation of this study and adopt advanced research designs such as meta-analysis, systematic and bibliometric analysis can also be adopted to explore the application of TPB in developing entrepreneurship both in the academic institutions, and corporate society this will bring a holistic understanding of TPB.

6.0 Policy implication

Entrepreneurship education with the TPB concept is claimed to foster EIs to promote entrepreneurship development (Bohlmann, 2017). Many academics acknowledged that including TPB concept in entrepreneurship education is critical for cultivating an entrepreneurship culture that can encourage an individual to pursue entrepreneurial activities (Ireland et al., 2003). To compete with other continents on a global scale, Africa's entrepreneurship education and entrepreneurship styles must be redefined. Failures in company establishments, poor marketing campaigns, a lack of innovative ideas, and possibly erroneous career choices owing to a lack of proper understanding of how to be successful entrepreneurs can result if this programme is not adequately implemented in the education curriculum (Dai et al., 2019). As a result, Africa's entrepreneurship education provides proactive answers to Africa's high unemployment rate, hunger, poverty, corruption, bad education system, and climate change challenges (Chimucheka, 2014). To do this, the government and the leaders of various academic institutions should work together to ensure that the required resources are available for Africa's new dimension. This is accomplished through advanced entrepreneurship training.

Finally, the importance of this paper rests on the fact that education stakeholders, appropriate agencies, and education policymakers must ensure that everyone receives entrepreneurship training. This admonition may be formal or casual. This is for the benefit of their respective nations. Second, provide a standardised entrepreneurship education curriculum that may suit the needs of African society and spur innovation. Third, qualified teachers with a practical understanding of the discipline must be employed to optimise the sufficiency of entrepreneurship education and learning content. Students should be mentored and trained for the future. Finally, the government should provide financial incentives and develop individuals with novel ideas capable of venturing into any entrepreneurial dimension of their own businesses.

References

Adeleye, N., & Eboagu, C. (2019). Evaluation of ICT development and economic growth in Africa.

Ahmed, T., Chandran, V. G. R., Klobas, J. E., Liñán, F., & Kokkalis, P. (2020). Entrepreneurship education programmes: How learning, inspiration, and resources affect intentions for new venture creation in a developing economy. *International Journal of Management Education*, 18(1), 100327. 10.1016/j.ijme.2019.100327

Aja-Okorie Onele Adali, U. (2013). Achieving youth empowerment through repositioning entrepreneurial education in Nigerian Universities: Problems and prospects. *European Scientific Journal*, 9(28), 1857–7881.

Ajike, E. O., Kelechi, N. G., Akinlabi, B. H., Onyia, V. A., & Kwarbai J. D. (2015). Entrepreneurship education and entrepreneurial intentions: The role of theory of planned behaviour. *International journal of advanced research in social engineering and development strategies*, 3(1), 118–135.

Ajzen, I. (1991). The theory of planned behavior. *Organisational Behavior and Human Decision Processes*, 50(2), 1–63.

Ajzen, I. (2002). Perceived behavioral control, self-efficacy, locus of control, and the theory of planned behavior. *Journal of Applied Social Psychology*, 32(4), 1–20.

Akpan, E. I., Effiong, S. A., & Ele, A. A. (2012). Entrepreneurship education policy: An intervention strategy for economic development in Nigeria. *Business & Entrepreneurship Journal*, 1(1), 101–110.

Aljuwaiber, A. (2020). Entrepreneurship research in the Middle East and North Africa: Trends, challenges, and sustainability issues. *Journal of Entrepreneurship in Emerging Economies*, 13(3), 380–426. 10.1108/JEEE-08-2019-0123

Almeida, J., Daniel, A. D., & Figueiredo, C. (2021). The future of management education: The role of entrepreneurship education and junior enterprises. International Journal of Management Education, 19(1), 100318. 10.1016/j.ijme.2019.100318

Alvarez, R. D., DeNoble, A. F., & Jung, D. (2006). Educational curricula and self-efficacy: Entrepreneurial orientation and new venture intentions among University Students in Mexico. In International Research in the Business Disciplines, 5. 10.1016/S1074-7877(06)05019-7

Amadasun, S. (2021). COVID-19 pandemic in Africa: What lessons for social work education and practice? *International Social Work*, 64(2), 246–250. 10 1177/0020872820949620

Amjad, T., Abdul Rani, S. H. B., & Sa'atar, S. B. (2020). Entrepreneurship development and pedagogical gaps in entrepreneurial marketing education. *International Journal of Management Education*, 18(2), 100379. 10.1016/j.ijme.2020.100379

Asongu, S. A., Le, S., & Biekpe, N. (2017). Technological forecasting & social change enhancing ICT for environmental sustainability in sub-Saharan Africa. *Technological Forecasting & Social Change*, (September), 1–8. 10.1016/j.techfore.2017.09.022

Asongu, S. A., & Odhiambo, N. M. (2019). How enhancing information and communication technology has affected inequality in Africa for sustainable development: An empirical investigation. *Sustainable Development*, 27, 647–656.

Bandura, A., Reese, L., & Adams, N. E. (1982). Microanalysis of action and fear arousal as a function of differential levels of perceived self-efficacy. *Journal of Personality and Social Psychology*, 5, 5–21.

Bandura, A. (1982). Self-efficacy mechanism in human agency. *American Psychologist*, 37, 122–147.

Barba-Sánchez, V., & Atienza-Sahuquillo, C. (2018). Entrepreneurial intention among engineering students: The role of entrepreneurship education. *European Research on Management and Business Economics*, 24(1), 53–61. 10.1016/j.iedeen.2017.04.001

Blackburn, R., & Kovalainen, A. (2009). Researching small firms and entrepreneurship: Past, present, and future. *International Journal of Management Reviews*, 11(2), 127–148. 10.1111/j.1468-2370.2008.00254.x

Bohlmann, D. (2017). University of Valencia: The business culture chair and entrepreneurship training for university lecturers. 10.1007/978-3-319-55547-8_14

Brockhaus, R. H. (1980). Risk Taking Propensity of Entrepreneurship, *Academy of Management Journal*, 23, 3.

Butcher, N., & Association for the Development of Education in Africa. (2014). Technological infrastructure and use of ICT in education in Africa: An overview.

Chae, B. (Kevin), & Goh, G. (2020). Digital entrepreneurs in artificial intelligence and data analytics: Who are they? *Journal of Open Innovation: Technology, Market, and Complexity*, 6(3). 10.3390/JOITMC6030056

Chen, T., Peng, L., Jing, B., Wu, C., Yang, J., & Cong, G. (2020). The impact of the COVID-19 pandemic on user experience with online education platforms in China. *Sustainability (Switzerland)*, 12(18). 10.3390/SU12187329

Chimucheka, T. (2014). Entrepreneurship education in South Africa. *Mediterranean Journal of Social Sciences*, 5(2), 403–416. 10.5901/mjss.2014.v5n2p403

Counted, A. V., & Arawole, J. O. (2015). 'We are connected, but constrained': Internet inequality and the challenges of millennials in Africa as actors in innovation. *Journal of Innovation and Entrepreneurship*, 5(1), 1–22. 10.1186/s13731-015-0029-1

Cole, A. H. (1959). Business enterprise in its social setting. Cambridge: Harvard University Press.

Collins, O. F., & Moore, D. G. (1970). The organization makers: A behavioral study of independent entrepreneurs. New York: Appleton-century-crofts (Meredith Corp.).

Crawford, J., Henderson, K. B., Rudolph, J., Malkawi, B., Glowatz, M., Burton, R., … Lam, S. (2020). Journal of applied learning & teaching COVID-19: 20 countries' higher education intra-period digital pedagogy responses. *Journal of Applied Learning & Teaching*, 3(1), 1–20.

Crick, J. M., Crick, D., & Chaudhry, S. (2020). Entrepreneurial marketing decision-making in rapidly internationalizing and de-internationalizing start-up firms. *Journal of Business Research*, 113(November), 158–167. 10.1016/j.jbusres.2018.11.033

Cui, J., Sun, J., & Bell, R. (2021). The impact of entrepreneurship education on the entrepreneurial mindset of college students in China: The mediating role of inspiration and the role of educational attributes. *International Journal of Management Education*, 19(1), 1–16. 10.1016/j.ijme.2019.04.001

Cunningham, J. A., & Menter, M. (2021). Transformative change in higher education: Entrepreneurial universities and high-technology entrepreneurship. Industry and Innovation, 28(3), 343–364. 10.1080/13662716.2020.1763263

Dai, S., Wang, Y., & Liu, Y. (2019). The emergence of Chinese entrepreneurs: Social connections and innovation. *Journal of Entrepreneurship in Emerging Economies*, 11(3), 351–368. 10.1108/JEEE-02-2018-0021

Deloitte. (2018). Data science transforming the ICT domain. 24.

Devine, R. A., & Kiggundu, M. N. (2016). Entrepreneurship in Africa: Identifying the frontier of impactful research. *Africa Journal of Management*, 2(3), 349–380. 10.1080/23322373.2016.1206802

Dou, X., Zhu, X., Zhang, J. Q., & Wang, J. (2019). Outcomes of entrepreneurship education in China: A customer experience management perspective. *Journal of Business Research*, 103(xxxx), 338–347. 10.1016/j.jbusres.2019.01.058

Dsv, I. I., Cunningham, M., & Dsv, I. I. (2016). Ficloicte a. 1–23. 10.1002/j.1681-4835.2016.tb00526.x

Egerová, D., Eger, L., & Mičík, M. (2017). Does entrepreneurship education matter? Business students' perspectives. *Tertiary Education and Management*, 23(4), 319–333. 10.1080/13583883.2017.1299205

Eze, S. C., Chinedu Eze, V. C. A., Okike, C. K., & Bello, A. O. (n.d.). Factors influencing the use of e-learning facilities Institution (HEI) in a developing economy. *Humanities and Social Sciences Communications*, (2020), 1–15. 10.1057/s41599-020-00624-6

Farber, R. S. (2013). Distance education and teaching online: My journey from mystery to mastery. *Occupational Therapy in Health Care*, 27(3), 272–279. 10.3109/07380577.2013.809180

Fayolle, A., & Gailly, B. (2008). From craft to science: Teaching models and learning processes in entrepreneurship education. *Journal of European Industrial Training*, 32(7), 569–593. 10.1108/03090590810899838

Fayolle, A., Gailly, B., & Lassas-Clerc, N. (2006). Assessing the impact of entrepreneurship education programmes: a new methodology. *Journal of European Industrial Training*, 30(9), 701–720.

Ferreira, J. J., Fernandes, C. I., & Ratten, V. (2017). The influence of entrepreneurship education on entrepreneurial intentions. 10.1007/978-3-319-47949-1_2

Frese, M., Rousseau, D. M., & Wiklund, J. (2014). The emergence of evidence-based entrepreneurship *Entrepreneurship: Theory and Practice*, 38(2), 209–216. 10.1111/etap.12094

Gabadeen, W. O., & Raimi, L. (2012). Management of entrepreneurship education in Nigerian higher institutions: Management of entrepreneurship education in Nigerian higher institutions: Issues, challenges, and way forward. *Abuja International Journal of Education and Management Sciences*, 2(January), 1–26.

Gartner, W. B. (2014). Is an entrepreneur?" Is the wrong question. (July). 10.1177/104225878801200401

Gelderen, M. V., Brand, M., Praag, M. V., Bodewes, W., & Gils, A. V. (2008). Theory of planned behavior Explaining entrepreneurial intentions by means of the theory of planned behavior. 10.1108/13620430810901688

González-Serrano, M. H., Sanz, V. A., & González-García, R. J. (2020). Sustainable sports entrepreneurship and innovation: A bibliometric analysis of this emerging field of research. *Sustainability (Switzerland)*, 12(12). 10.3390/su12125209

Guthrie, K. L., & McCracken, H. (2010). Making a difference online: Facilitating service-learning through distance education. *Internet and Higher Education*, 13(3), 153–157. 10.1016/j.iheduc.2010.02.006

Hamburg, I. (2021). Social measures and disruptive innovations in entrepreneurship education to cope with COVID-19. *Advances in Social Sciences Research Journal*, 8(1), 70–80. 10.14738/assrj.81.9561

Handayati, P., Wulandari, D., Soetjipto, B. E., Wibowo, A., & Narmaditya, B. S. (2020). Does entrepreneurship education promote vocational students' entrepreneurial mindset? *Heliyon*, 6(11), e05426. 10.1016/j.heliyon.2020.e05426

Hatt, L., & Hatt, L. (2018). Threshold concepts in entrepreneurship – the entrepreneurs' perspective Threshold concepts in entrepreneurship – the entrepreneurs' perspective. 10.1108/ET-08-2017-0119

Henry, C. (2013). Entrepreneurship education in HE: Are policymakers expecting too much? *Education and Training*, 55(8–9), 836–848. 10.1108/ET-06-2013-0079

Hermann, R. R., & Bossle, M. B. (2020). Bringing an entrepreneurial focus to sustainability education: A teaching framework based on content analysis. Journal of Cleaner Production, 246(xxxx), 119038. 10.1016/j.jclepro.2019.119038

Herrington, M., & Coduras, A. (2019). The national entrepreneurship framework conditions in sub- Saharan Africa: A comparative study of GEM data/National Expert Surveys for South Africa, Angola, Mozambique, and Madagascar. *Journal of Global Entrepreneurship Research*, 9(1), 1– 24. 10.1186/s40497-019-0183-1

Higgins, D. & Elliott, C. (2011). Learning to make sense: What works in entrepreneurial education? *Journal of European Industrial Training*, 35(4), 345–367. 10. 1108/03090591111128324

Higgins, D., Smith, K., & Mirza, M. (2013). Entrepreneurial education: Reflexive approaches to entrepreneurial learning in practice. *Journal of Entrepreneurship*, 22(2), 135–160. 10.1177/0971355713490619

Hytti, U., & Gorman, C. O. (2001). What is "enterprise education"? An analysis of the objectives and methods of enterprise education programmes in four European countries. 10.1108/00400910410518188

Internet Society. (2017). Internet for education in Africa. (May), 47.

Ireland, R. D., Hitt, M. A., Sirmon, D. G., & Hitt, M. A. (2003). A model of strategic entrepreneurship: 10.1016/S0149-2063

Isaacs, E., Visser, K., Friedrich, C., & Brijlal, P. (2007). Entrepreneurship education and training at the Further Education and Training (FET) level in South Africa. *South African Journal of Education*, 27(4), 613–629. 10.4314/saje.v27i4.25136

Išoraitė, M., & Gulevičiūtė, G. (2021). A study of online entrepreneurship education under conditions of a pandemic. *Entrepreneurship and Sustainability Issues*, 8(3), 179–192. 10.9770/jesi.2021.8.3(10)

Iwu, C. G., Opute, P. A., Nchu, R., Eresia-Eke, C., Tengeh, R. K., Jaiyeoba, O., & Aliyu, O. A. (2021). Entrepreneurship education, curriculum, and lecturer-competency as antecedents of student entrepreneurial intention. *International Journal of Management Education*, 19(1), 0–1. 10.1016/j.ijme.2019.03.007

Jena, R. K. (2020). Measuring the impact of business management Student's attitude towards entrepreneurship education on entrepreneurial intention: A case study. Computers in Human Behavior, 107. 10.1016/j.chb.2020.106275

Jůvová, A., Čech, T., & Duda, O. (2017). Education for entrepreneurship – A challenge for school practice. *Acta Educationis Generalis*, 7(3), 63–75. 10.1515/atd-2017-0024

Kakouris, A., & Georgiadis, P. (2016). Analyzing entrepreneurship education: A bibliometric survey pattern. *Journal of Global Entrepreneurship Research*, 6(1). 10.1186/s40497-016-0046-y

Karimi, S., Biemans, H. J. A., Lans, T., Chizari, M., & Mulder, M. (2016). The impact of entrepreneurship education: A study of Iranian students' entrepreneurial intentions and opportunity identification. *Journal of Small Business Management*, 54(1), 187–209. 10.1111/jsbm.12137

Katz, J. A. (2003). The chronology and intellectual trajectory of American entrepreneurship education: 1876–1999. *Journal of Business Venturing*, 18, 283–300. http://dx.doi.org/10.1016/S0883-9026(02)00098-8

Kuratko, D. F. (2005). The emergence of entrepreneurship education - Luratko, 2005. *Entrepreneurship: Theory and Practice*, 29(5), 577–597. Retrieved from https://journals.sagepub.com/doi/abs/10.1111/j.1540-6520.2005.00099.x?journalCode=etpb

Kuratko, D. F., Hornsby, J. S., & Goldsby, M. G. (2004). Sustaining corporate entrepreneurship modeling perceived implementation and outcome comparisons at organizational and individual levels, *The International Journal of Entrepreneurship and Innovation*, 5(2), 77–89. 10.5367/000000004773863237

Krueger, N. F. J., Reilly, M. D., & Carsrud, A. L. (2000). Competing models of entrepreneurial intention. *Journal of Business Venturing*, 15(5-6), 411–432.

Küttim, M., Kallaste, M., Venesaar, U., & Kiis, A. (2014). Entrepreneurship education at university level and students' entrepreneurial intentions. *Procedia - Social and Behavioral Sciences*, 110, 658–668. 10.1016/j.sbspro.2013.12.910

Laguía, A., Moriano, J. A., & Gorgievski, M. J. (2019). A psychosocial study of self-perceived creativity and entrepreneurial intentions in a sample of university students. *Thinking Skills and Creativity*, 31, 44–57. 10.1016/j.tsc.2018.11.004

Liguori, E., & Winkler, C. (2020). From offline to online: Challenges and opportunities for entrepreneurship education following the COVID-19 pandemic. *Entrepreneurship Education and Pedagogy*, 3(4), 346–351. 10.1177/2515127420916738

Lortie, J., & Castogiovanni, G. (2015). The theory of planned behavior in entrepreneurship research: What we know and future directions. *The International Entrepreneurship and Management Journal*, 11(4), 935–957.

Ma, L., Lan, Z., & Tan, R. (2020). Influencing factors of innovation and entrepreneurship education based on the theory of planned behavior. *International Journal of Emerging Technologies in Learning*, 15(13), 190–206. 10.3991/ijet.v15i13.15345

Malebana, M. J. (2021). Relationship between entrepreneurial support, business information seminars, and entrepreneurial intention. *Journal of Entrepreneurship Education*, 24(1), 1–15. Retrieved from https://lavasalibrary.remotexs.in/scholarly-journals/relationship-between-entrepreneurial-support/doc view/2513612577/se-2?accountid=38885

Martin, B. C., McNally, J. J., & Kay, M. J. (2013). Examining the formation of human capital in entrepreneurship: A meta-analysis of entrepreneurship education outcomes. *Journal of Business Venturing*, 28(2), 211–224. 10.1016/j.jbusvent.2012.03.002

Meyer, M., Libaers, D., Thijs, B., Grant, K., Glänzel, W., & Debackere, K. (2014). Origin and emergence of entrepreneurship as a research field. *Scientometrics*, 98(1), 473–485. 10.1007/s11192-013-1021-9

Michelacci, C., & Schivardi, F. (2020). Are they all like Bill, Mark, and Steve? The education premium for entrepreneurs. *Labour Economics*, 67(May). 10.1016/j.labeco.2020.101933

Miles, M. P., & Covin, J. G. (2002). Exploring the practice of corporate venturing: Some common forms and their organizational implications. *Entrepreneurship theory and practice*, 26(3), 21–40. 10.1177/104225870202600302

Naudé, W. (2021). Entrepreneurship, education and the Fourth Industrial Revolution in Africa. *SSRN Electronic Journal*. 10.2139/ssrn.2998964

Netemeyer, R., & Ryn, M. Van. (1991). The theory of planned behavior.

Nowiński, W., & Haddoud, M. Y. (2019). The role of inspiring role models in enhancing entrepreneurial intention. *Journal of Business Research*, 96(June 2018), 183–193. 10.1016/j.jbusres.2018.11.005

Ogbari, M. E., Olokundun, M. A., Uzuegbunam, J., Isiavwe, D. T., Ilogho, J. E., Obi, J. N., & Moses, C. L. (2018). Data on entrepreneurship education and entrepreneurial performance of aspiring entrepreneurs in selected Nigerian universities. *Data in Brief*, 20, 108–112. 10.1016/j.dib.2018.07.044

Olorundare, S., & Kayode, D. J. (2014). Entrepreneurship education in Nigerian universities: A tool for. *Asia Pacific Journal of Educators and Education*, 29, 155–175.

Oosterbeek, H., van Praag, M., & Ijsselstein, A. (2010). The impact of entrepreneurship education on entrepreneurship skills and motivation. *European Economic Review*, 54(3), 442–454. 10.1016/j.euroecorev.2009.08.002

Opute, A. P., Iwu, C. G., Kalu, K. I., & Adeola, O. (2021). Steering sustainable economic growth: Entrepreneurial ecosystem approach. 10.1177/23939575211024384

Peschl, H., Deng, C., & Larson, N. (2021). Entrepreneurial thinking: A signature pedagogy for an uncertain 21st century. *International Journal of Management Education*, 19(1), 100427. 10.1016/j.ijme.2020.100427

Peterman, N. E., & Kennedy, J. (2003). Enterprise education: Influencing students' perceptions of entrepreneurship. *Entrepreneurship Theory and Practice*, 28(2), 129–144. 10.1046/j.1540-6520.2003.00035.x

Pittaway, L., & Cope, J. (2007). Entrepreneurship education: A systematic review of the evidence. *International Small Business Journal*, 25(5), 479–510. 10.1177/0266242607080656

Ployhart, R., & Moliterno, T. (2011). The emergence of the human capital resource: A multilevel model. *Academy of Management Review*, 36(1), 127–150. 10.5465/amr.2009.0318

Ratten, V. (2020). Coronavirus (Covid-19) and the entrepreneurship education community. *Journal of Enterprising Communities*, 14(5), 753–764. 10.1108/JEC-06-2020-0121

Ratten, V., & Jones, P. (2021). Entrepreneurship and management education: Exploring trends and gaps. *International Journal of Management Education*, 19(1), 100431. 10.1016/j.ijme.2020.100431

Ratten, V., & Usmanij, P. (2021). Entrepreneurship education: Time for a change in research direction? *International Journal of Management Education*, 19(1), 100367. 10.1016/j.ijme.2020.100367

Remeikiene, R., Startiene, G., & Dumciuviene, D. (2013). Explaining entrepreneurial intention of university students: The role of entrepreneurial education. Management, Knowledge and Learning International Conference 2013, 299–307.

Ruiz-Rosa, I., Gutiérrez-Taño, D., & García-Rodríguez, F. J. (2020). Social entrepreneurial intention and the impact of COVID-19 pandemic: A structural model. *Sustainability (Switzerland)*, 12(17), 9–12. 10.3390/SU12176970

Secundo, G., De Beer, C., Fai, F. M., & Schutte, C. S.L. (2019). Increasing university entrepreneurialism: qualitative insights from the technology transfer office. *Measuring Business Excellence*, 23(3), 253–268. https://doi.org/10.1108/MBE-02-2019-0015

Sexton, D. L. (2001). Guest editors introduction to the special issue strategic entrepreneurship: Entrepreneurial strategic for wealth creation. *Strategic Management Journal*, 491, 479–491. 10.1002/smj.196.

Shirazi, F., & Hajli, N. (2021). IT-enabled sustainable innovation and the global digital divide. *Sustainability (Switzerland)*, 13(17), 1–24. 10.3390/su13179711

Soriano, D. R., & Montoro-Sanchez, M. A. (2011). Introduction: The challenges of defining and studying contemporary entrepreneurship. *Canadian Journal of Administrative Sciences*, 28(3), 297–301. 10.1002/CJAS.217

Srivastava, A., Singh, V., Srivastava, P., & Sinha, R. (n.d.). Innovation Incubation and Entrepreneurship in Biotechnology. *In Ijtra.Com*, 4. Retrieved from https://www.ijtra.com/view/innovation-incubation-and-entrepreneurship-in-biotechnology-review.pdf

Srivastava, K., & Thomas, P. (2017). Promoting entrepreneurship in higher educational institutions: The role of entrepreneurial methodologies. *In Entrepreneurship Education: Experiments with Curriculum, Pedagogy and Target Groups*. 10.1007/978-981-10-3319-3_14

Stephan, P. E., & El-Ganainy, A. (2007). The entrepreneurial puzzle: Explaining the gender gap. *Journal of Technology Transfer*, 32(5), 475–487. 10.1007/s10961-007-9033-3

Tornikoski, E. (2019). Isbj critical reflections – the theory of planned behaviour: An interview with Icek Ajzen with implications for entrepreneurship research. 10.1177/0266242619829681

UNESCO. (2020). The futures of education after COVID-19: Regional dialogue. 1–24.

Unwin, T. (2015). Towards a framework for the use of ICT in teacher training in Africa. 20(2), 113– 129. 10.1080/02680510500094124

Vaicekauskaite, R., & Valackiene, A. (2018). The need for entrepreneurial education at university. *Journal of Teacher Education for Sustainability*, 20(1), 82–92. 10.2478/jtes-2018-0005

Van Ness, R. K., Seifert, C. F., Marler, J. H., Wales, W. J., & Hughes, M. E. (2020). Proactive entrepreneurs: Who are they and how are they different? *Journal of Entrepreneurship*, 29(1), 148–175. 10.1177/0971355719893504

Velentzas, P. G. (2017). University-based entrepreneurship centers: How they address the learning needs of entrepreneurs. *ProQuest Dissertations and Theses*, 164. Retrieved from https://search.proquest.com/docview/1957414191?accountid=26642%0Ahttp://link.periodicos.capes.gov.br/sfxlcl41?url_ver=Z39.882004&rft_val_fmt=info:ofi/fmt:kev:mtx:dissertation&genre=dissertations+%26+theses&sid=ProQ:ProQuest+Dissertations+%26+Theses+Globa

Wilson, F., Kickul, J., & Marlino, D. (2007). Gender, entrepreneurial self-efficacy, and entrepreneurial career intentions: Implications for entrepreneurship education. *Entrepreneurship Theory & Practice*, 31(3), 2007, 387–406.

World Bank (2017). World development indicators, World Bank. Available at: https://openknowledge.world bank.org/handle/10986/26447 (accessed 18 December, 2018).

Yurtkoru, E. S., Kuşcu, Z. K., & Doğanay, A. (2014). Exploring the antecedents of entrepreneurial intention on Turkish University students. *Procedia - Social and Behavioral Sciences*, 150, 841–850. 10.1016/j.sbspro.2014.09.093

Zacharakis, A. L., & Shepherd, D. A. (n.d.). The nature of information and overconfidence in venture capitalists decision making. *Journal of Business Venturing*, 16(4), 311– 332. 10.1016/S0883-9026(99)00052-X.

10 Informal Entrepreneurship in Africa

Elona N. Ndlovu-Hlatshwayo and Alufheli Edgar Nesamvuni

Introduction

Entrepreneurship is an active process that involves taking risks to create or seize opportunities (Luger & Koo, 2005). It is described as an economic driver and a process that consists of an entrepreneur maximising their creative and unique perspectives in seizing opportunities (Landstrom, 2007; Yetisen et al., 2015). Entrepreneurship serves a critical purpose as it has the potential to boost living standards and alleviate poverty not only for the entrepreneur but for their community and other connected businesses (Laing et al., 2021). Entrepreneurship has been identified as an economic driver and a means of reducing poverty and creating employment (Bu & Cuervo-Cazurra, 2020; Schutte & Direng, 2019; van der Spuy, 2019). This need is even more significant in developing countries where poverty alleviation and employment opportunities are critical needs (Karim, 2017; Rogerson, 2015; Schutte & Direng, 2019). The urgency for entrepreneurship is timely in South Africa and many African countries that continue to experience economic shrinkage and high unemployment since the COVID-19 outbreak (Dludla, 2021).

There are two broad types of entrepreneurship: informal and formal entrepreneurship. Both forms of entrepreneurship exist in different versions of the economy: formal and informal economy (Laing et al., 2021; Omri, 2020). The informal economy is a huge space of economic activities and businesses that are not registered and protected by state laws (Adu-Gyamfi et al., 2022; Fredström et al., 2021). Initially, informal economy was used synonymously with self-employment, but it is now noted as any form of paid work/business that is not government recognised and protected (Galdino et al., 2018). The formal economy are businesses, and economic activities that are registered and protected by the government – they pay taxes on all earned incomes and taxpaying activities (Thai & Turkina, 2014). Formal entrepreneurs are registered and are compliant with all relevant government regulations. Whereas formal arrangements do not adequately cover informal entrepreneurs due to legislation or practice, such as proper registration and tax responsibilities (Bu & Cuervo-Cazurra, 2020; Laing et al., 2021).

DOI: 10.4324/9781003216469-10

Informal entrepreneurs are essentially survivalist or entrepreneurships who are spontaneously responding to a need in their community or frustrated by an inability to get a formal job (Adele et al., 2015; Adom, 2014; Ranyane, 2015). However, this is an incorrect representation because informality and necessity are two distinct aspects of a complex process (Choto et al., 2014). Informal entrepreneurship is broader than just survival. There are many motivations for informal entrepreneurs like poverty, high unemployment rates, testing market gaps and opportunities, and increasing autonomy (Adele et al., 2015; Adom, 2014; Dell'Anno, 2021; Ladan & Williams, 2019). Choto et al. (2014) conceptualised survivalist entrepreneurs as those who operate on a small scale mainly to sustain family needs as they seek formal employment or means of economic survival. Adele et al. (2015) highlight that informal entrepreneurship has been viewed as a sign of underdevelopment. Although this has largely been disputed, it is widely true for developed economies where survival is not the motivator for venturing into entrepreneurship (Adele et al., 2015; Laing et al., 2021). It is important to understand that, in the African context, most informal entrepreneurs are necessity-driven or survivalists (Choto et al., 2014; Iwu & Opute, 2019; Ranyane, 2015).

Informal entrepreneurship operates within the informal economy for various reasons, such as avoiding the structural costs needed for registering the business, government regulatory taxes and policies costs (labour law) (Galdino et al., 2018). Informal entrepreneurship is prevalent in low-income countries (Crush & McCordic, 2017; Kok, 2019; Laing et al., 2021). There is no universal form in which informal entrepreneurs operate and how they are addressed. Some examples of informal enterprises include street markets where food and clothing are sold, neighbourhood car washes, electrical repairs, taxi services, and short-distance delivery services. The goal of this chapter is to examine how applicable the theories are to informal entrepreneurship in Africa. This chapter explores definitions of informal entrepreneurship, and provides a theoretical appraisal, looking at the applicability of these theories in the African informal entrepreneurship sector. Further, it makes recommendations on the key elements needed for informal entrepreneurship to thrive in Africa.

Defining informal entrepreneurship

Informal entrepreneurship has been conceptualised through the lens of various theoretical perspectives. One of the most prominent is the institutional theory by North (1991) who argues that institutions are regulations and structures set up to manage how humans interact politically, socially, and economically. Institutions are part of informal and formal environments and often include personal values and beliefs, public organisations, and legal and regulatory bodies. This theory posits that institutions are necessary to regulate and control the players in the economy.

In the context of entrepreneurship, institutions are there to control and create rules of engagement for entrepreneurs with co-operation from the political, financial, and legal regulators (Nwajiuba et al., 2020).

Accordingly, informal entrepreneurship as currently framed consists of "non-legitimate" institutions as they are unregistered and largely unregulated (Bruton et al., 2010; Fredström et al., 2021). Informal entrepreneurship is seen as the polar opposite of modernisation, indicating underdevelopment and backwardness (Ladan & Williams, 2019). According to the modernisation theory, informal entrepreneurship is an obsolete manner of doing business, and that informal entrepreneurs are gradually dwindling (Williams & Gurtoo, 2012). The structuralist theory thinks of informal entrepreneurship as an inherent aspect of a capitalist society where informal entrepreneurs tend to be subcontractors of bigger, formal, and established enterprises (Ladan & Williams, 2019). For the neoliberalist theorists, informal entrepreneurship is described as rational economic participants who make a conscious decision to conduct their firms informally and without governmental rules for various reasons (Dawson, 2021; Dell'Anno, 2021; Laing et al., 2021). Similarly, poststructuralist theory portrays informal entrepreneurs as rational individuals who make reasonable judgements to operate their enterprises informally, while their motivations differ from those of neoliberals (Ladan & Williams, 2019).

> *Despite the different definitions and techniques for defining and conceptualising informal entrepreneurship outlined above, there is a growing understanding that there is no one-size-fits-all theory that can accommodate the global heterogeneity of the informal entrepreneurship* (Dell'Anno, 2021; Williams & Shahid, 2014*). As a result, the purpose of this research is to identify the elements that exist in the African informal entrepreneurship sector, as well as the applicability of the above theories to the African setting.*

Theoretical appraisal

The entrepreneurial ecosystem theory

Entrepreneurial ecosystems are a collection of interdependent agents and elements that work together to support profitable entrepreneurship in a given area (Isenberg, 2010). This systemic view of entrepreneurship has been researched since the late 1980s (Dubini, 1989, as cited in Alvedalen & Boschma, 2017). The entrepreneurial ecosystem theory by Isenberg (2014) presents entrepreneurship as a multifaceted and interrelated character. The entrepreneurship ecosystem refers to the several domains that contribute to the facilitation or impediment of entrepreneurial activity (Isenberg, 2016). It can also be viewed as the system through which entrepreneurs interact with a variety of stakeholders (public, private, and non-profit actors) in such a way that their activities are influenced (Isenberg, 2014). Culture, markets, human capital, finance, supports, and policy are the six domains that make up this ecosystem (Isenberg, 2010). When evaluating an ecosystem, Isenberg (2016) emphasises the importance of understanding how a natural ecosystem functions to assess how the entrepreneurial ecosystem can function optimally.

As governments, universities, corporations, and communities recognise the importance of an holistic and integrated approach to foster regional entrepreneurial activity and enable innovation, entrepreneurial ecosystems are becoming increasingly popular in public and private institutions globally (Fredin & Lidén, 2020; Spigel, 2016). Figure 10.1 below depicts the six domains of entrepreneurial ecosystems (Isenberg, 2016). This framework

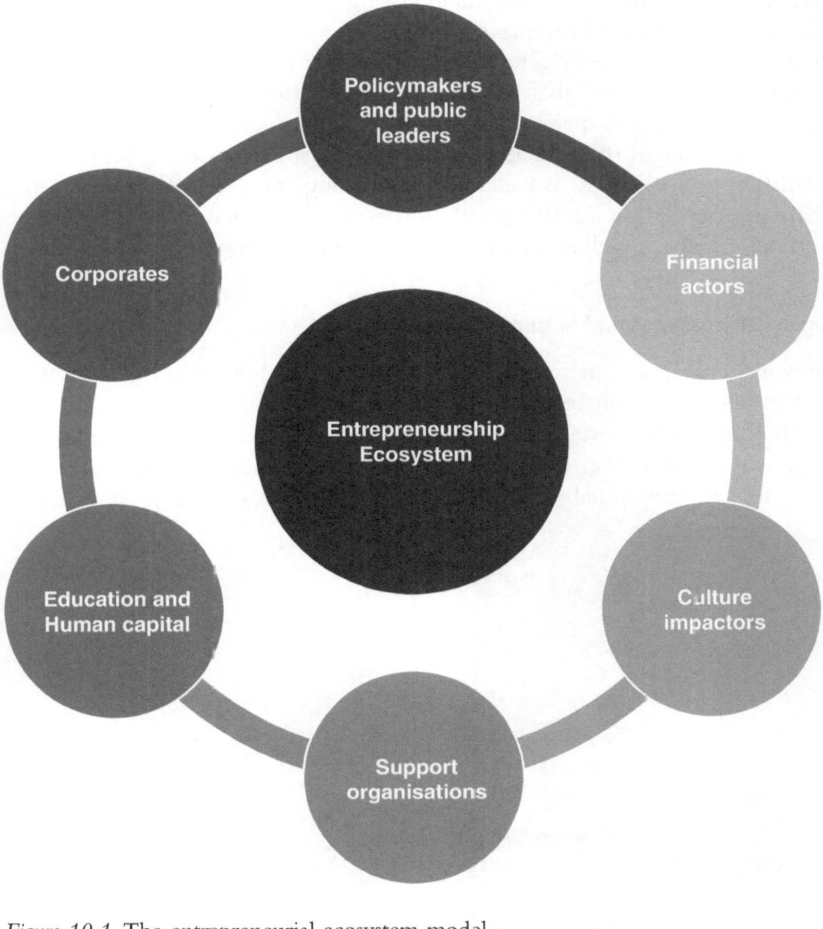

Figure 10.1 The entrepreneurial ecosystem model.

Source: Adapted from Isenberg (2016).

gives an overview of the support structures available to entrepreneurs. Nonetheless, it is obvious that the framework is more geared toward formal entrepreneurs than informal entrepreneurs, who encounter several problems in gaining access to the facilities. Thus, understanding the ecosystem requirements of informal entrepreneurs is critical for bridging the gap between exclusion from formal institutional assistance.

The eclectic theory

The eclectic theory focuses on addressing the rationale of why informal entrepreneurs opt to enter a business. According to this theory, a firm decision to go into business is inspired by two advantages – ownership and location advantages (Dunning, 1995). Ownership advantages can be described as the resources of a firm. These may include tangible assets, patent designs, trademarks, production techniques, entrepreneurial skills, and return to scale (Dunning, 1995). The eclectic theory argues that location-specific advantages include the raw materials from the selected location in which the business operates, low wages, special taxes or tariffs, and government incentives.

The advantages of the eclectic theory in Africa include the location and availability of resources, as well as good exchange rate control. Furthermore, there are ownership advantages like expertise and experience in supporting and delivering, as well as technological capabilities (Figure 10.2).

Informal entrepreneurship and the eclectic theory

Informal entrepreneurships are common in low and developing economies, but as the economic grows, informal entrepreneurships are quickly relegated. Informal entrepreneurship is propelled by a culture that is socially supportive and aware. Informal constraints like culture, shape human interaction as individuals and organisations. Informal entrepreneurship is

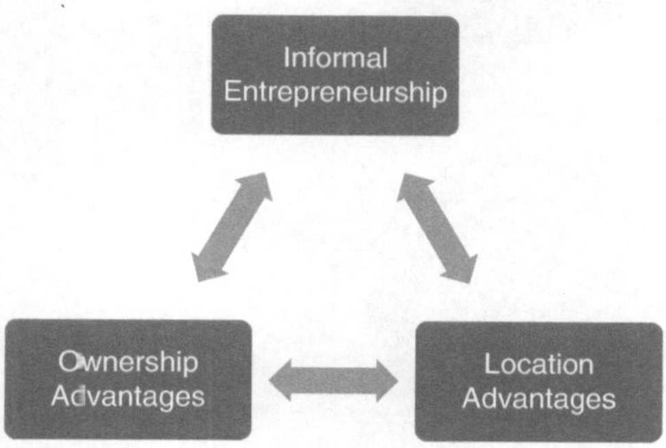

Figure 10.2 Informal entrepreneurship adopted eclectic theory.

Source: Adapted from several authors (Dunning, 1995; Shaheen et al., 2021).

mainly starting up a business, participating in the production, marketing and sales of the goods and services. Informal entrepreneurships are legal and trade legitimate goods and services except that they are not registered, regulated, or protected by government policies (Williams & Nadine, 2010). Although informal entrepreneurships operate mainly informally, they serve a massive part of the society (Webb et al., 2009). A large part of a country's entrepreneurial activities are informal, which makes this sector crucial. A country could advance in its entrepreneurial development by encouraging start-ups (ownership) even when they are informal; these start-ups can then be guided from this informal space to the formal sector where they are effectively regulated and protected by state laws.

Lean start-up methodology

A lean start-up is basically opening a business or creating a new product for an established business (Bortolini et al., 2018). A key strategy in the lean start-up concept is ensuring that the new product or business is already being demanded by the customers – the buyers of the product must have been identified before the product is made available (Bocken & Snihur, 2020). The lean start-up is a business concept that is focused on continuous learning. It outlines a new methodology for entrepreneurs, as well as the behaviours they should adopt to boost their chances of success (Bortolini et al., 2018). While the notion works best in a technology or Internet setting, it may be applied to any business (Ávalos et al., 2019). It simply states that rather than spend years improving your product, you should rather send it to market to gain instant input from customers. You use a "just do it" attitude while being structured and testing your concept on a regular basis. The lean start-up teaches you to focus on whether your product should be produced rather than whether it can be built (Bocken & Snihur, 2020).

There have also been some criticisms of this strategy. One may argue that there are not enough success stories of start-ups that have adopted this practice (Bortolini et al., 2018). The lean start-up is a helpful method for getting your idea to the market, but it must be seen in context. The size of the business, following the lean start-up methodology without contextual adaptation, can be detrimental to the business (Yordanova, 2022). It is important to understand the lean start-up methodology in the context of the African Informal entrepreneurship sector. Figure 10.3.

Informal entrepreneurship in Africa

Having defined informal entrepreneurship from various perspectives and explored the three theoretical approaches – the entrepreneurial ecosystem, the eclectic theory, and the lean start-up methodology, we now look at the types of businesses in this sector, their challenges, and their needs.

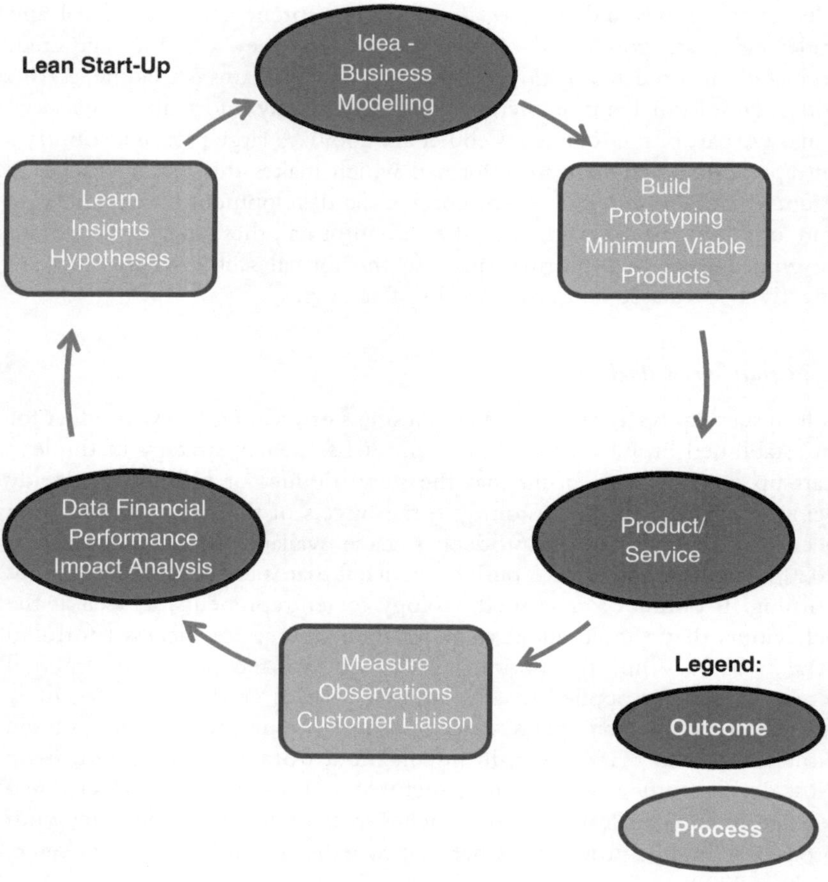

Figure 10.3 Lean start-up methodology.

Source: Adapted from several authors (Bocken & Snihur, 2020; Bortolini et al., 2018; Welter et al., 2021).

Types of businesses in Africa's informal sector

The informal sector is a chunk of the economies of developing countries (Crush & McCordic, 2017). For example, in South Africa, the informal sector was responsible for 5.2% of the nation's GDP for 2015; in 2016 (Statistics South Africa, 2015). There are various levels of GDP contribution from the different countries across the African continent, with differing reports on the exact percentage of GDP contribution. Galdino et al. (2018) maintain that the informal sector makes up 90% of the job provision in low-income countries like the Central African Republic and the Democratic Republic of Congo. Moreover, informal entrepreneurship accounts for 52% of North Africa and 66% of Sub-Saharan Africa's employment provision (Galdino et al., 2018). Table 10.1 below

Table 10.1 Estimates of informal output as a percentage of official GDP

Economy	*2010*	*2011*	*2012*	*2013*	*2014*	*2015*	*2016*	*2017*	*2018*
Algeria	31,8	32,4	32,2	31,9	31,8	32,0	31,8	31,7	31,3
Angola	44,1	44,3	43,6	44,2	43,5	43,2	43,4	43,4	43,3
Benin	51,8	51,5	51,2	50,4	49,4	50,3	49,8	48,7	47,5
Botswana	31,4	31,0	30,8	30,3	30,4	30,4	29,9	30,0	30,1
Burkina Faso	39,9	39,6	39,5	39,5	39,2	39,3	39,0	38,7	38,2
Burundi	39,1	39,1	39,2	39,0	38,8	39,4	40,1	40,2	40,4
Cabo Verde	35,5	35,0	34,4	34,4	35,2	35,5	34,9	35,2	34,6
Cameroon	32,2	32,6	32,5	32,3	31,6	31,4	31,0	30,4	30,2
Central African Republic	39,0	38,0	37,8	45,1	45,1	44,5	44,0	43,5	43,0
Chad	43,5	44,8	44,0	44,3	42,6	42,4	44,0	44,5	43,9
Comoros	38,9	38,4	37,9	37,2	37,5	38,3	37,5	36,9	36,5
Congo, Dem. Rep.	47,9	47,6	47,7	46,6	45,5	45,7	44,5	43,6	43,0
Congo, Rep.	44,2	44,4	44,2	43,9	42,8	42,1	43,9	45,3	44,9
Cote d'Ivoire	44,1	44,5	43,8	42,9	42,0	40,6	39,7	39,8	38,7
Egypt, Arab Rep.	33,5	34,4	34,5	34,8	35,0	34,7	34,1	33,0	31,6
Equatorial Guinea	31,9	31,7	31,6	32,1	32,6	33,3	33,9	33,9	33,7
Eritrea	39,3	38,7	40,8	41,2	40,8	41,2	41,2		
Eswatini	40,5	40,2	39,3	38,8	39,2	39,3	39,5	39,4	38,9
Ethiopia	36,0	36,0	35,4	35,3	34,9	34,7	34,8	34,5	34,1
Gabon	52,0	51,3	51,7	51,5	51,0	51,0	51,2	51,1	50,1
The Gambia	43,3	47,6	46,0	46,6	48,9	49,6	49,3	48,2	46,8
Ghana	39,3	40,6	39,5	38,9	39,1	38,8	38,2	37,6	37,6
Guinea	39,6	39,6	39,4	39,7	39,5	39,5	38,0	36,9	36,5
Guinea-Bissau	37,8	37,1	38,3	37,7	39,5	38,6	37,9	37,3	36,8
Kenya	32,4	32,0	31,7	31,4	30,9	30,5	29,8	29,4	29,2
Lesotho	30,5	29,6	29,9	29,0	29,6	29,1	29,0	30,0	30,0
Liberia	43,9	43,8	43,5	43,8	43,7	43,8	44,5	44,5	44,6
Libya	33,3	37,2	35,2	36,6	37,2	36,5	36,8		
Madagascar	42,7	43,3	43,4	43,8	43,7	43,6	43,0	42,7	41,7
Malawi	38,3	38,2	38,5	38,5	37,7	37,9	37,9	37,6	37,6
Mali	39,6	40,4	40,2	40,4	40,2	40,7	40,4	40,0	39,6
Mauritania	34,2	33,9	33,7	33,4	33,3	33,7	33,5	33,4	33,4
Mauritius	21,7	21,5	21,4	21,8	21,7	21,6	21,6	21,4	21,3
Morocco	34,3	34,6	34,8	34,5	34,7	34,1	34,2	34,2	34,1
Mozambique	38,5	38,6	38,5	38,6	39,0	38,7	38,8	38,5	38,1
Namibia	30,7	29,8	29,7	29,8	29,7	29,1	29,1	29,0	29,2
Niger	41,3	41,9	40,0	39,8	39,5	40,3	39,6	38,9	37,8
Nigeria	56,8	56,2	55,6	54,9	55,1	54,6	55,9	55,8	56,2
Rwanda	37,3	36,7	36,7	36,5	36,7	36,1	35,7	35,1	34,4
Senegal	45,0	46,1	45,5	45,5	44,7	43,6	42,9	42,1	41,1
Sierra Leone	45,0	44,5	43,6	41,3	40,2	43,8	44,0	42,7	41,7
South Africa	27,7	27,4	27,6	27,5	27,7	27,7	28,0	28,1	28,3
Uganda	40,7	41,0	40,0	40,0	39,6	39,6	39,3	39,7	40,3
Zambia	47,1	46,8	46,5	46,5	47,0	47,4	48,0	46,4	46,2
Zimbabwe	62,4	61,8	60,5	60,1	60,3	60,1	60,0	60,1	58,7

Source: Data extracted from Elgin, Kose, Ohnsorge, & Yu (2021).

provides a distribution of the GDP of the informal sector across Africa from the period of 2010 to 2018. Despite the different sources of data, the consensus is that the informal sector is a significant contributor to the African economy.

Challenges faced by Informal businesses in Africa

Generally, entrepreneurs face several challenges on their journey like access to funding, access to the market, access to training, access to skills for their human capital, and active competition from established entities (Dubihlela & Van Schaikwyk, 2014; Mazanai & Fatoki, 2011; Worku, 2016). Entrepreneurs in the formal economy are also faced with barriers. However, those in the informal economy who do not receive the same institutional support as their formal counterparts face more challenges and obstacles to growth and formalising. One of the significant challenges confronting Africa's informal entrepreneurs is their vulnerability to microeconomic and macroeconomic trends (Braha, 2012). For example, the 2020 COVID-19 pandemic negatively impacted street vendors' market share (Zutshi et al., 2021). There is a general lack of government aid for informal businesses, and there are no uniform policies in place to assist these entrepreneurs (Adu-Gyamfi et al., 2022; Dawson, 2021; Laing et al., 2021). Informal entrepreneurs have limited access to external finance, owing mostly to financing institutions and programmes failing to fully recognise the economic value that this segment provides especially as they are not often supported by financial statements (Omri, 2020; Santos et al., 2020). For example, banks and other financiers do not appear to assist organisations that do not have predicted or previous financial records. Other hurdles include the legal and regulatory environment, acquiring managerial expertise, access to relevant technology, and quality basic business infrastructure in disadvantaged areas (Igwe et al., 2020; Urban & Ndou, 2019).

Scholarly work that has paid attention to necessity-oriented entrepreneurs (those who enter entrepreneurship as a means of survival) is minimal. The attention has mainly turned to opportunity-oriented entrepreneurs (those who enter entrepreneurship based on the identification of opportunities); they are adjudged as providing better structures for dynamism and development (growth) (Ranyane, 2015; Tengeh & Choto, 2015). The drift here is that many entrepreneurs who began on the necessity-drive side gradually metamorphose into opportunity-driven entrepreneurs. It would be a mistake and lack of vision to dismiss informally functioning necessity entrepreneurs as undeserving of support.

Although unemployment is a typical motivation for informal entrepreneurs, this does not infer that the majority of informal entrepreneurs are unemployed (Laing et al., 2021). However, the findings of Viljamaa et al. (2018) point to starting-up enterprise owners that can be in full-time formal work and negotiate both parts of the economy (formal and informal) as a "risk reduction strategy". When their informal entrepreneurship begins to grow and they become sufficiently self-employed, they leave their employment in the formal sector.

Informal entrepreneurs survive by being innovative and creative to remain relevant in the context in which they operate. Although they may largely be excluded from the formal entrepreneurship ecosystem, they have been known to successfully improvise. An enabling environment is required for entrepreneurship to thrive in an economy (Stats SA, 2019; Urban & Ndou, 2019). The informal entrepreneurs are largely excluded from accessing the support facilities that are provided in the entrepreneurship ecosystem (Dawson, 2021). In South Africa, this was recently evident when many entrepreneurs were unable to access business rescue packages during the COVID-19 lockdown due to non-compliance – running informal entrepreneurship.

However, across the continent, there are some instances where informal entrepreneurs have received decent support. Kebede (2018) presents that social capital (SC) is one of the ways entrepreneurs in Addis Ababa rely on to supplement the lack of formal support structures. Again, Kebede (2018) argues that social networks are critical in the informal economy to substitute what the informal entrepreneurs lack in the formal economy. This phenomenon is not unique to the Ethiopian context and applies to other African contexts (Bakengela Shamba & Gasse, 2019; Dawson, 2021). Some contexts may be more predisposed to an informal economy, such as Ibadan, Nigeria. Small enterprises in Nigeria are largely funded by informal financiers as opposed to formal capital markets (Adele et al., 2015). In like manner, South African informal entrepreneurs also resort to collectivist means of business funding like stokvels.[1] In most of Sub-Saharan Africa, relationships emphasise values, such as collective support, and are favourable for informal agreements and entrepreneurial practices (Afreh et al., 2019a). In the case of rural youth from Ghana, Afreh et al. (2019b) found that the youth utilised the relational ties they have to develop their entrepreneurial skills, and gather the required resources to launch their informal businesses.

In the Ethiopian context, Kebede (2018) posits that the collective values in the society are care and social security. Based on these values, entrepreneurs often get support from family and friends for entrepreneurial support as formal institutional support is lacking. In South Africa, Crush and McCordic (2017) highlight that the informal sector is comprised of South African citizens and refugees. Their findings explain the local context where there is a larger proportion of refugee immigrants in the informal economy than in South African businesses. However, the differences are that the refugee immigrants make use of their social capital to raise the required resources for their entities and grow faster than their South African counterparts who operated in silos.

Recommendations for informal entrepreneurship in Africa

Starting and sustaining a business can be risky, but the lean start-up method can help reduce start-ups' chances of failing and making the business venture less difficult. Some of the risk reduction mechanisms include collecting pre-orders from clients and taking time to understand their markets before creating unneeded products (Bortolini et al., 2018). The lean start-up methodology ensures that founders thoroughly assess the risk involved in their business and ensure that it is a worthy venture before they proceed. This methodology has been praised for its strength in enabling entrepreneurs the chance to experiment with or test their novel ideas as they do product or service development (Bocken & Snihur, 2020). This aspect is essential today where the market is highly competitive or seemingly saturated and can help entrepreneurs identify a gap and differentiate themselves.

Lean start-up as a customer segment creation can assist informal entrepreneurs in understanding their target market and serving them better. Founders look at the target audience in-depth to learn what they need and acquire their perceptions about the business or product generated. It involves extensive testing, with the results being used by the start-up to improve their service or product. This is essential for business growth and improving its competitive edge. It enables entrepreneurs to research and understand their buyer personas; this helps start-ups build customer-centric services and products (Figure 10.4).

The lean start-up methodology encourages innovation. The founders must create a minimum valuable product as the method foresees the need to innovate to remain relevant. The technique also encourages creativity in start-ups because investors are attracted to creative business ideas, placing them in a better position for development and growth opportunities. The lean start-up process supports innovation and embeds creativity in founders. Entrepreneurs experiment, monitor, and iterate more on results because this methodology permits thinking outside the box and the introduction of new ideas. In addition to entrepreneurs making use of the lean start-up methodology in Africa, we propose an adapted entrepreneurial ecosystem with the following recommendations.

Policymakers and public leaders

African governments are advised to have ministries responsible for entrepreneurship development/small business development. It is recommended that legislation should be enacted to allow informal entrepreneurs trade without registration, which will aid in removing barriers to trade for the informal entrepreneurs, if they adhere to by-laws regarding trading spaces. Revenue offices should halt requirements for registration until the income exceed a threshold of $16 000.

Financial sector

To be inclusive of the informal sector, it is recommended that banks prioritise the ease of opening low-interest and services bank accounts.

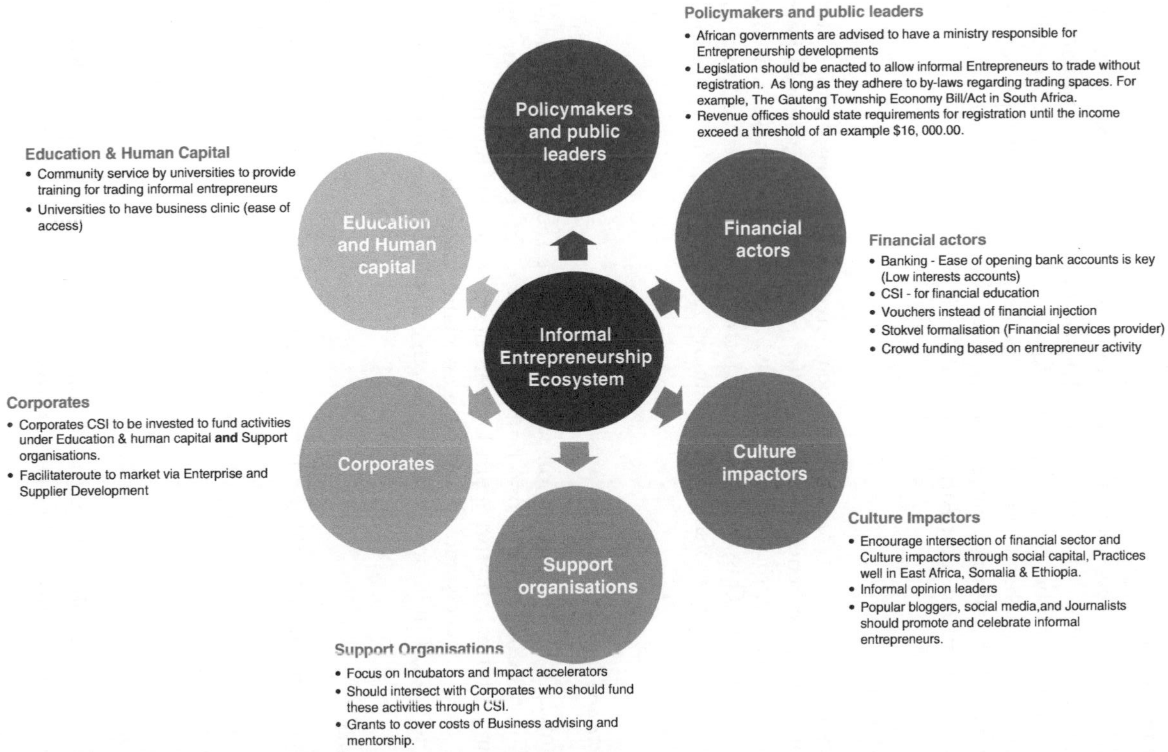

Figure 10.4 Proposed African informal entrepreneurship ecosystem.

Source: Researcher's adaptation.

Banks' Corporate Social Investment (CSI) should be in the form of financial education for informal entrepreneurs. To ensure governance of funds donated, we recommend the use of vouchers redeemable at service providers instead of cash injection. There should be formalisation or recognition of informal financial systems such as stokvels and other social forms of crowdfunding.

Culture impactors

In addition to existing systems, there should be an intersection of the financial sector and cultural impactors. The advocacy for social capital has been evinced to be beneficial for the informal sector in collectivist communities. This has been shown to aid in bridging the entrepreneurial support gap that informal entrepreneurs face. As mentioned above, this practice works well in East Africa, Somalia, and Ethiopia.

Support organisations

In terms of support organisations, a focus on incubators and impact accelerators would be beneficial for the informal sector. There should be a collaboration with corporates (f below) who should fund these activities through their CSI. This could be in the form of grants to cover costs of business advising, mentorship, skills training, and supply chain development.

Education and human capital

In alignment with the integration stated above, we recommend that educational institutions embark on community service by providing training for trading informal entrepreneurs. Universities should have business clinics that are easy to access and in the business clinic, there should be opportunities to upskill the informal entrepreneurs and link them to markets.

Corporates

Similarly, corporates should use their CSI to fund programmes related to education and human capital, as well as support organisations. Furthermore, when the informal entity is ready to upscale, this assistance may extend to enterprise supplier development.

Conclusion

This research has shed light on informal entrepreneurship in Africa through various theoretical perspectives. The components of the entrepreneurial ecosystem illustrate the needs of entrepreneurs which demonstrates the gap for informal entrepreneurs as they are institutionally excluded from most of the support in the ecosystem. The eclectic theory is a holistic way, it evaluates the complete connections and interactions of a business's multiple components. The theory sets out a plan for increasing operations through foreign direct investment. The goal is to see if a certain approach has a greater overall value than other national or international possibilities for manufacturing goods or services. When applied to informal entrepreneurship, the approach that the lean start-up methodology presents is the norm in African informal entrepreneurship. One of the important conclusions, which is in line with the existing research, is that a comprehensive, supportive ecosystem is vital for informal entrepreneurship to thrive, as well as understanding how to evaluate opportunities through iterations with their product development and when deciding on expansion.

African informal entrepreneurs often use their meagre resources in starting and sustaining their ventures. The expansion of informal entrepreneurs should go beyond the assistance provided by the government and its agencies. Numerous significant players, including large businesses, banks, chambers of commerce, and community associations, should acknowledge the significance of growing informal entrepreneurs. Informal entrepreneurs should be given options for capital mobilisation in micro-grants and loans. Various government assistance programmes may consider implementing credit guarantee schemes in collaboration with big banks to provide capital to informal enterprises. Informal entrepreneurs should have access to business development services, leading to their formalisation.

Against this backdrop, informal entrepreneurs that leverage their social capital appear to outperform those that take an individualistic approach (e.g., Pakistani and South African family businesses that seem to take an individualistic rather than a collectivist strategy). Informal entrepreneurs, like other economic segments, use a lean start-up process. For example, they run simple tests on their products/services. However, due to the nature of the informal sector, this procedure is not institutionalised. What needs to be seen is the future of informal entrepreneurship in Africa should include the applicability of a lean start-up strategy.

Note

1 Stokvels are a small group of people who come together for the purpose of investing in the financial growth of one another. Members contribute fixed sums of money usually monthly to an account. The total sum is given to a member to invest in their business or interests. All members in the group get a turn. There can also be stokvels for purchasing groceries or even books. It is really about a collaborative approach to lessening individual burdens.

References

Adele, H., Oyedokun, J. A., Oyerinde, A. J., & Ayodele, A. Y. (2015). An examination of factors motivating informal entrepreneurship in Ibadan, south-west Nigeria. *European Journal of Business and Management*, 7, 18–30. https://citeseerx.ist.psu.edu/viewdoc/download?doi=10.1.1.734.7821&rep=rep1&type=pdf

Adom, K. (2014). Beyond the marginalization thesis: An examination of the motivations of informal entrepreneurs in sub-Saharan Africa. *The International Journal of Entrepreneurship and Innovation*, 15(2), 113–125. 10.5367/ijei.2014.0144

Adu-Gyamfi, R., Kuada, J., & Asongu, S. A. (2022). An Integrative framework for formal and informal entrepreneurship research in Africa. *Journal of African Business*, 1–21. 10.1080/15228916.2022.2042102

Afreh, B., Rodgers, P., Vershinina, N., & Williams, C. C. (2019a). Varieties of context and informal entrepreneurship. *International Journal of Entrepreneurial Behavior & Research*, 25(5), 996–1013. 10.1108/ijebr-02-2018-0109

Afreh, B., Rodgers, P., Vershinina, N., & Williams, C. C. (2019b). Varieties of context and informal entrepreneurship: Entrepreneurial activities of migrant youths in rural ghana. *International Journal of Entrepreneurial Behavior & Research*, 25(5), 996–1013. 10.1108/ijebr-02-2018-0109

Alvedalen, J., & Boschma, R. (2017). A critical review of entrepreneurial ecosystems research: Towards a future research agenda. *European Planning Studies*, 25(6), 887–903. 10.1080/09654313.2017.1299694

Ávalos, C., Pérez-Escoda, A., & Monge, L. (2019). Lean Startup as a learning methodology for developing digital and research competencies. *Journal of New Approaches in Educational Research*, 8(2). 10.7821/naer.2019.7.438

Bakengela Shamba, P., & Gasse, Y. (2019). Social capital and new forms of informal entrepreneurship in Africa- an exploratory analysis. https://papers.ssrn.com/sol3/papers.cfm?abstract_id=3470235

Bocken, N., & Snihur, Y. (2020). Lean Startup and the business model: Experimenting for novelty and impact. *Long Range Planning*, 53(4). 10.1016/j.lrp.2019.101953

Bortolini, R. F., Nogueira Cortimiglia, M., Danilevicz, A. d. M. F., & Ghezzi, A. (2018). Lean startup: A comprehensive historical review. *Management Decision*, 59(8), 1765–1783. 10.1108/md-07-2017-0663

Braha, D. (2012). Global civil unrest: contagion, self-organization, and prediction. *PLoS One*, 7(10), e48596. 10.1371/journal.pone.0048596

Bruton, G. D., Ahlstrom, D., & Li, H. L. (2010). Institutional theory and entrepreneurship: Where are we now and where do we need to move in the future? *Entrepreneurship Theory and Practice*, 34(3), 421–440. 10.1111/j.1540-6520.2010.00390.x

Bu, J., & Cuervo-Cazurra, A. (2020). Informality costs: Informal entrepreneurship and Innovation in Emerging economies. *Strategic Entrepreneurship Journal*, 14(3), 329–368. https://doi.org/10.1002/sej.1358

Choto, P., Tengeh, R. K., & Iwu, C. G. (2014). Daring to survive or to grow? The growth aspirations and challenges of survivalist entrepreneurs in South Africa. *Environmental Economics*, 5(4), 93–101.

Crush, J., & McCordic, C. (2017). Comparing refugee and south African migrant enterprise in the urban informal sector. *AHMR*, 3(Special Issue).

Dawson, H. J. (2021). "Making plans through people": The social embeddedness of informal entrepreneurship in urban south Africa. *Social Dynamics*, 47(3), 389–402. 10.1080/02533952.2021.1909949

Dell'Anno, R. (2021). Theories and definitions of the informal economy: A survey. *Journal of Economic Surveys*. 10.1111/joes.12487

Dubihlela, J., & Van Schaikwyk, P. J. (2014). Small business incubation and the entrepreneurial business environment in South Africa: A theoretical perspective. *Mediterranean Journal of Social Sciences*, 5(23), 264. https://www.mcser.org/journal/index.php/mjss/article/view/4524

Dubini, P. (1989). The influence of motivations and environment on business start-ups: Some hints for public policies. *Journal of Business Venturing*, 4(1), 11–26. https://doi.org/10.1016/0883-9026(89)90031-1

Dunning, J. H. (1995). Reappraising the eclectic paradigm in an age of alliance capitalism. *Journal of International Business Studies*, 26(3), 461–491.

Fredin, S., & Lidén, A. (2020). Entrepreneurial ecosystems: Towards a systemic approach to entrepreneurship? *Geografisk Tidsskrift-Danish Journal of Geography*, 1–13. 10.1080/00167223.2020.1769491

Fredström, A., Peltonen, J., & Wincent, J. (2021). A country-level institutional perspective on entrepreneurship productivity: The effects of informal economy and regulation. *Journal of Business Venturing*, 36(5). 10.1016/j.jbusvent.2020.106002

Galdino, K. M., Kiggundu, M. N., Jones, C. D., & Ro, S. (2018). The informal economy in pan-Africa: Review of the literature, themes, questions, and directions for management research. *Africa Journal of Management*, 4(3), 225–258. 10.1080/23322373.2018.1517542

Igwe, P. A., Odunukan, K., Rahman, M., Rugara, D. G., & Ochinanwata, C. (2020). How entrepreneurship ecosystem influences the development of frugal innovation and informal entrepreneurship. *Thunderbird International Business Review*, 62(5), 475–488. 10.1002/tie.22157

Isenberg, D. J. (2010). How to start an entrepreneurial revolution. *Harvard Business Review*, 1–11. [Online], https://hbr.org/2010/06/the-big-idea-how-to-start-an-entrepreneurial-revolution June 2010.

Isenberg, D. J. (2014). What an entrepreneurship ecosystem actually is. *Harvard Business Review, [online]*. https://hbr.org/2014/05/what-an-entrepreneurial-ecosystem-actually-is

Isenberg, D. J. (2016). Applying the ecosystem metaphor to entrepreneurship. *The Antitrust Bulletin*, 61(4), 564–573. 10.1177/0003603x16676162

Iwu, C. G., & Opute, A. P. (2019). Eradicating poverty and unemployment: Narratives of survivalist entrepreneurs. *Journal of Reviews on Global Economics*, 8, 1438–1451. 10.6000/1929-7092.2019.08.127

Karim, I. U. (2017). Typology on entrepreneurship support in emerging markets. *Journal of Entrepreneurship and Management*, 6(3), 52–78.

Kebede, G. F. (2018). Social capital and entrepreneurial outcomes: Evidence from informal sector entrepreneurs in Ethiopia. *The Journal of Entrepreneurship*, 27(2), 209–242. 10.1177/0971355718781250

Kok, J. D., & Berrios, M. (2019). Small matters: Global evidence on the contribution to employment by the self-employed, micro-enterprises and SMEs. *Geneva: International Labour Organization (ILO)*. https://www.ilo.org/wcmsp5/groups/public/---dgreports/---dcomm/---publ/documents/publication/wcms_723282.pdf

Ladan, U., & Williams, C. C. (2019). Evaluating theorizations of informal sector entrepreneurship: Some lessons from Zamfara, Nigeria. *Journal of Developmental Entrepreneurship*, 24(04). 10.1142/s1084946719500225

Laing, E., van Stel, A., & Storey, D. J. (2021). Formal and informal entrepreneurship: A cross-country policy perspective. *Small Business Economics*. 10.1007/s11187-021-00548-8

Landstrom, H. (2007). Pioneers in entrepreneurship and small business research. *What do we mean by Entrepreneurship*(Page 10) 8.

Luger, M. I., & Koo, J. (2005). Defining and tracking business start-ups. *Small Business Economics*, 24(1), 17–28.

Mazanai, M., & Fatoki, O. (2011). The effectiveness of business development services providers (BDS) in improving access to debt finance by start-up SMEs in South Africa. *International Journal of Economics and Finance*, 3(4), 208–216. https://citeseerx.ist.psu.edu/viewdoc/download?doi=10.1.1.880.9174&rep=rep1&type=pdf

North, D. C. (1991). Institutions. *Journal of economic perspectives*, 5(1), 97–112. https://pubs.aeaweb.org/doi/pdf/10.1257/jep.5.1.97?source=post_page

Nwajiuba, C. A., Igwe, P. A., Binuomote, M. O., Nwajiuba, A. O., & Nwekpa, K. C. (2020). The barriers to high-growth enterprises - what do businesses in Africa experience? *European Journal of Sustainable Development*, 34(5), 358–367.

Omri, A. (2020). Formal versus informal entrepreneurship in Emerging economies: The roles of governance and the financial sector. *Journal of Business Research*, 108, 277–290. 10.1016/j.jbusres.2019.11.027

Ranyane, K. A. (2015). Survivalist entrepreneurship: An income generating alternative for the unemployed populace. *Mediterranean Journal of Social Sciences*. 10.5901/mjss.2015.v6n4p301

Rogerson, C. M. (2015). South Africa's informal economy: reframing debates in national policy. *Local Economy: The Journal of the Local Economy Policy Unit*, 31(1-2), 172–186. 10.1177/0269094215613505

Santos, E., Fernandes, C. I., Ferreira, J. J., & Lobo, C. A. (2020). What is the impact of informal entrepreneurship on venture capital flows? *Journal of the Knowledge Economy*. 10.1007/s13132-020-00701-w

Schutte, F., & Direng, T. (2019). Incubation of entrepreneurs contributes to business growth and job creation - Botswana case study. *Academy of Entrepreneurship Journal*, 25(3).

Shaheen, N., Ahmad, N., Hussain, S., & Hussain, B. (2021). An eclectic theory of entrepreneurship - three level analysis for developing entrepreneurship policy in Pakistan. *Journal of Contemporary Issues in Business and Government*, 27(6), 1066–1080. 10.47750/cibg.2021.27.06.090

Spigel, B. (2016). Developing and governing entrepreneurial ecosystems: The structure of entrepreneurial support programs in Edinburgh, Scotland. *International Journal of Innovation and Regional Development*, 7(2). 10.1504/ijird.2016.077889

Statistics South Africa 2015. https://www.statssa.gov.za/publications/Report-02-11-02/Report-02-11-022015.pdf

Stats SA (2019). *Stats SA*.

Tengeh, R. K., & Choto, P. (2015). The relevance and challenges of business incubators that support survivalist entrepreneurs. *Investment Management and Financial Innovations*, 12(2), 150–161.

Thai, M. T. T., & Turkina, E. (2014). Macro-level determinants of formal entrepreneurship versus informal entrepreneurship. *Journal of Business Venturing*, 29(4), 490–510. 10.1016/j.jbusvent.2013.07.005

Urban, B., & Ndou, B. (2019). Informal entrepreneurship: A focus on south African township entrepreneurs. *Journal of Developmental Entrepreneurship*, 24(04). 10.1142/s1084946719500213 van der Spuy, S. J. H. (2019). The state of business incubation in the northern cape: A service spectrum perspective. *The Southern African Journal of Entrepreneurship and Small Business Management*, 11(1). 10.4102/sajesbm.v11i1.271

Viljamaa, A., Varamäki, E., & Joensuu-Salo, S. (2018). Best of both Worlds? Persistent hybrid entrepreneurship. *Journal of Enterprising Culture*, 25(04), 339–359. 10.1142/s0218495817500133

Webb, J. W., Tihanyi, L., Ireland, R. D., & Sirmon, D. G. (2009). You say illegal, I say legitimate: Entrepreneurship in the informal economy. *Academy of Management Review*, 34(3), 492–510. https://doi.org/10.5465/amr.2009.40632826

Welter, C., Scrimpshire, A., Tolonen, D., & Obrimah, E. (2021). The road to entrepreneurial success: Business plans, lean startup, or both? *New England Journal of Entrepreneurship*, 24(1), 21–42. 10.1108/neje-08-2020-0031

Williams, C. C., & Gurtoo, A. (2012). Evaluating competing theories of street entrepreneurship: Some lessons from a study of street vendors in Bangalore, India. *International Entrepreneurship and Management Journal*, 8(4), 391–409. 10.1007/s11365-012-0227-2

Williams, C. C., & Shahid, M. S. (2014). Informal entrepreneurship and institutional theory: Explaining the varying degrees of (in)formalization of entrepreneurs in Pakistan. *Entrepreneurship & Regional Development*, 28(1-2), 1–25. 10.1080/08985626.2014.963889

Williams, C. C., & Nadin, S. (2010). Entrepreneurship and the informal economy: An overview. *Journal of Developmental Entrepreneurship*, 15(04), 361–378. 10.1142/s1084946710001683

Worku, Z. (2016). Barriers to the growth of small, micro and medium-sized business enterprises in the Vaal Triangle region of South Africa. *African Journal of Science, Technology, Innovation and Development*, 8(2), 134–141. https://doi.org/10.1080/20421338.2015.1128135

Yetisen, A. K., Volpatti, L. R., Coskun, A. F., Cho, S., Kamrani, E., Butt, H., Khademhosseini, A., & Yun, S. H. (2015). Entrepreneurship. *Lab Chip*, 15(18), 3638–3660. 10.1039/c5lc00577a

Yordanova, Z. B. (2022). Lean Startup method hampers breakthrough innovations and company's innovativeness. *Emerging Issues and Trends in Innovation and Technology Management*, 1–20. 10.1142/9789811247729

Zutshi, A., Mendy, J., Sharma, G. D., Thomas, A., & Sarker, T. (2021). From challenges to creativity: Enhancing SMEs' Resilience in the context of COVID-19. *Sustainability*, 13(12). 10.3390/su13126542

11 Entrepreneurship Education and Productive Entrepreneurship

A.P. Opute, I.K. Kalu, K.C. Mezieobi, C.G. Iwu, S.B. Hagos, and D.O. Obor

Introduction

For several decades, the criticality of entrepreneurship in propelling economic growth and improving well-being has been reiterated in academic discourse (e.g., Ferreira et al., 2019; Opute, 2020; Opute et al., 2021b). Elaborating this criticality, Ferreira et al. (2019) note that entrepreneurship boosts regional economies, drives technology development, increases added value, creates new jobs, and steers innovation, while Opute (2020), reinforcing the innovation plausibility, posits that productive entrepreneurship would steer a snowballing economic growth impact. Concurring to this impact foundation, further literature underlines the need for intensified effort towards strategically steering entrepreneurship activity (e.g., Iwu & Opute, 2019; Opute et al., 2021a; Valencia-Arias et al., 2021). Reinforcing that pertinence, scholars emphasise that more jobs should be created to combat increasing unemployment rates (Valencia-Arias et al., 2021) and in particular in the sub-Saharan Africa setting (Iwu & Opute, 2019; Iwu et al., 2020b).

Entrepreneurship would aid sustainable development through creating employment opportunities, enhancing well-being and boosting competitiveness (Hernandez-Lopez et al., 2018). The United Nation, in its central governmental position, has often underlined in its United Nations Economic Programme (UNEP) policy guidelines the pertinence for strategic mechanisms for achieving the sustainability goal. Showcasing that importance, the UN in its blueprint for achieving a sustainable future for all by 2030, forwards the United Nations Sustainable Development Goals model that draws attention to critical sustainable economic growth indicators such as poverty (goal 1), zero hunger (goal 2), and decent work and economic growth (goal 8), amongst others.

Thus, researchers, as well as government quarters and policy makers recognise this important role of entrepreneurship to sustainable economic growth, and the pertinence for more research. Little wonder, therefore, that much research attention is increasingly given to illuminate various domains of entrepreneurship activity, for example, small and medium entrepreneurships

DOI: 10.4324/9781003216469-11

(e.g., Opute, 2020; Opute et al., 2020a), family entrepreneurships (e.g., Igwe et al., 2020; Opute et al., 2021a), ethnic minority entrepreneurships (e.g., Hagos et al., 2019; Opute et al., 2020a). Additional to other domains that have been considered in entrepreneurship discourse, a theoretical premise that has gained predominant mention recently relates to entrepreneurial ecosystem. An entrepreneurship theme that sits within the entrepreneurial ecosystem foundation and has equally gained increasing mention in the academic discourse is entrepreneurship education. Scholars rationalise this increasing attention on the plausibility that entrepreneurship education is a critical component in the strive for productive entrepreneurship that drives and sustains economic growth and combats unemployment and poverty (e.g., Iwu & Opute, 2019; Iwu & Opute, 2021; Madichie & Gbadamosi, 2017; Opute et al., 2021b). Embracing plausibility and research pertinence, entrepreneurship education is the premise of this chapter. To contribute to this theoretical premise, this chapter gives particular attention to the sub-Saharan Africa setting that has been repeatedly noted to be plagued by high unemployment, poverty, and under-utilisation of resources (e.g., Iwu & Opute, 2019; Iwu et al., 2020b; Opute, 2020). While Igwe et al. (2020) reinforce the notion of high unemployment in the African setting and underline youth unemployment as a highly worrying development, Iwu and his colleagues (Iwu & Opute, 2019; Iwu et al., 2020b) describe entrepreneurship in the African setting as highly survivalist natured.

The chapter is structured thus: First, the theoretical framing is explained highlighting the underlying theoretical foundation. Building on the underlying theoretical foundation, the importance of entrepreneurship to economic growth is summarised towards further rationalising the importance of the theoretical premise of entrepreneurship education. Thereafter, entrepreneurship education is explained showing clearly the conceptualisation in this chapter and justification. In this chapter, the conceptualisation of entrepreneurship education takes an all-inclusive viewpoint that recognises the criticality of proactiveness, strategic marketing, entrepreneurship marketing, and innovation, as well as the importance of research to productive entrepreneurship. The critical entrepreneurship education challenges in Africa are then pinpointed. To conclude, recommendations towards strategic entrepreneurship education for achieving productive entrepreneurship are offered and future research directions flagged.

Conceptual framing of this chapter

The strategic role of entrepreneurship in steering sustainable economic growth and enhancing well-being has been reinforced in the literature (e.g., Opute, 2020; Opute et al., 2021b). Given that strategic role, researchers have lauded the pertinence for studies that enhance the ecosystem perspective of entrepreneurship literature (e.g., McAdam et al., 2018; Opute et al., 2021b). In a recent publication, Opute et al. (2021b) conceptualise ecosystem viewpoint for steering sustained economic development (contextualised to include sustained economic growth, employment creation and combating poverty). Spurned by that contextualisation, this chapter gives particular attention to the African setting characterised (1) by high levels of unemployment (e.g., Iwu & Opute, 2019; Iwu et al., 2020b; Zachary, 2020) and (2) passive and survivalist natured entrepreneurship (e.g., Iwu & Opute, 2019; Iwu et al., 2020b). Conceptually, this chapter forwards the thesis that sustainable and productive entrepreneurship can be achieved if entrepreneurship education is strategically delivered (e.g., Amjad et al., 2020; Opute et al., 2021b). Within that focus, the important role of entrepreneurship to economic development is underlined next. The entrepreneurship education premise in this chapter is explained next.

Entrepreneurship education

Entrepreneurship education is a critical tool for stimulating entrepreneurial intention and drive (e.g., Iwu & Opute, 2021; Iwu et al., 2020c; Opute et al., 2021b). Global sustainability agenda is increasingly becoming a driving force of global activities. Consequently, entrepreneurship discourse has focused significant attention on how economic sustainability impact of entrepreneurship can be optimised (e.g., Opute, 2020; Opute et al., 2021b: Tengeh et al., 2015). Equally driven by that sustainability focus, the need for a strategic and all-embracing entrepreneurship approach (Opute, 2020) that integrates marketing (e.g., Gbadamosi, 2020; Nwankwo, 2020; Opute, 2020) and management (e.g., Ivanova & Rimanoczy, 2022, forthcoming; Ratten & Jones, 2020) foundations has been emphasised. Recognising that pertinence, and aligning to the responsible entrepreneurship education viewpoint (Igwe et al., 2020), the conceptualisation of entrepreneurship education in this chapter follows the all-embracing approach. In that conceptualisation approach, this chapter follows the notion that to impact behaviour, the mindset has to shift (Ivanova & Rimanoczy, 2022, forthcoming). Thus, the conceptualisation in this chapter is premised on the foundation that to achieve productive entrepreneurship, learners (future entrepreneurs) should be trained to imbibe a sustainability mindset.

Ratten and Jones note that entrepreneurship education has been defined in different ways. From the entrepreneurship education viewpoint, Kakouris and Liargovas (2021) conceptualise human learning as "a broad term pertaining to the process of acquiring (or advancing) knowledge and knowledge structures, skills, attitudes (along with values, beliefs, habits and others depending on the holistic nature of learning" (p. 4). In line with the sustainability mindset proposed in this chapter, entrepreneurship education conceptualisation in this chapter draws from two critical definitions. First, Linan (2004, p. 166) defines entrepreneurship education as

> the whole set of education and training activities – within the education system or not – that try to develop in the participants the intention to perform entrepreneurial behaviours, or some of the elements that affect that intention, such as entrepreneurial knowledge, desirability of the entrepreneurial activity or its feasibility.

Reinforcing the entrepreneurial learning, as well as the proactive attitude importance, Iacobucci and Micozzi (2012, p. 678, cited in Ratten & Jones, 2020, p. 2) conceptualise entrepreneurship education as "the process of providing individuals with the ability to recognise commercial opportunities and the insight, self-esteem, knowledge and skills to react on them". Recognising these entrepreneurial learning and proactive attitude importance, entrepreneurship education conceptualisation in this chapter builds off four of six critical principles for management education specified by PRME: purpose, values, methods, and research.

From the point of *purpose*, entrepreneurship education should be strategically focused at developing the capabilities of learners to position them as productive entrepreneurs that drive economic growth and contribute to sustainable economic development. Similarly, entrepreneurship education should be organised in a way that academic activities, curricula, and practices impact in learners' (future entrepreneurs) *values* of responsibility and commitment to economic growth (creating jobs and combating unemployment). As a third component, entrepreneurship education delivery *method* should involve educational frameworks, processes, and mechanisms that enable effective learning experience (including experiential learning) that would enable learners to be equipped with relevant skill sets for productive entrepreneurship. Also, entrepreneurship education should be designed to impact in learners' (future entrepreneurs) understanding of the importance of *research* as a critical tool in the drive for proactive entrepreneurial orientation that would facilitate and sustain productive entrepreneurship that contributes to sustainable economic development.

Within that strategic focus of ensuring entrepreneurship education that is underpinned by the aforementioned management education principles, the entrepreneurship education conceptualisation in this chapter recognises the importance of entrepreneurship education curricula that incorporate taught and experiential learning components. The criticality of that approach has been documented in entrepreneurship discourse (e.g., Iwu et al., 2020c; Lv et al., 2021; Valencia-Arias et al., 2021). Entrepreneurship education curricula should contain critical components that would enable learners (future entrepreneurs) obtain substantial understanding of entrepreneurship dynamics (e.g., Iwu et al., 2020c; Nchu et al., 2015). Equally documented in entrepreneurship discourse is the plausibility that entrepreneurship education could also motivate entrepreneurial intention (e.g., Iwu et al., 2020a). Towards achieving active entrepreneurship for steering economic growth, scholars have underlined the need to incorporate experiential learning components into the entrepreneurship education curricula (e.g., Iwu & Opute, 2021; Iwu et al., 2020c; Lv et al., 2021). The plausibility of that advocacy has been lauded in further literature on the notion that the experiential learning component of entrepreneurship education is a significant predictor of active entrepreneurship. For example, documenting the benefits of experiential learning in building critical skill sets and driving entrepreneurial thinking among college students, Gibson and Tavlaridis (2018) note that experiential learning pedagogy could draw from diverse knowledge domains thereby allowing business education to permeate entrepreneurship education. Lloyd et al. (2019) enhance that viewpoint and comment that the experiential learning component boosts the entrepreneurial, business, and technical skill sets of learners.

Within the experiential learning foundation of entrepreneurship education, critical tools have been categorised to include trainings (Bhatti et al., 2021; Opute et al., 2021b), discussions, problem-solving, case studies, role-play sessions (e.g., Wiederman, 2015), business plan competitions (e.g., Lv et al., 2021), and entrepreneurial practice support (e.g., Lv et al., 2021). Further literature that reinforces the importance of experiential learning component of training document that such entrepreneurial training tools enable students to acquire essential business and technical skills (Lloyd et al., 2019) and multiple skills, abilities, and interdisciplinary perspective for optimal value creation (Lombardi et al., 2017). On their part, Bhatti et al. (2021) add that training programmes as constituent part of entrepreneurship education would enhance psychological attributes, self-confidence, innovativeness, and achievement motivation of students. Emphasising that entrepreneurial skills can be taught and learnt, Farouk et al. (2014) categorise such skills to include business management know-how, growth analysis skills, ethical awareness, and skills relating to identifying and exploiting business opportunities.

From a strategic viewpoint, therefore, entrepreneurship education should motivate entrepreneurship intention (e.g., Iwu et al., 2016; Iwu et al., 2020a; Madichie et al., 2020) and equip learners with values, mindset, and skill sets to steer active and productive entrepreneurship (e.g., Iwu & Opute, 2021; Iwu et al., 2020c). This chapter conceptualises a holistic perspective of entrepreneurship education that recognises the need to ensure a strategical entrepreneurship curriculum that combines adequate measures of taught and experiential components towards effectively motivating entrepreneurship intention and equipping learners with a futuristic entrepreneurship mindset. Within that focus, core elements considered in this chapter include entrepreneurship intention, pro-activity, strategic marketing, and innovation.

Entrepreneurship intention

Entrepreneurship education is "the collection of formalised teachings that inform, train and educate learners who are interested in setting up a business"

(Ramayah et al., 2012, p. 69). The theory of planned behaviour (TPB) is one central theory that has been utilised in understanding new business creation processes (e.g., Iwu et al., 2016; Iwu et al., 2020a; Lortie & Castogiovanni, 2015). Based on that foundation, entrepreneurship intention could be innate. Extending the viewpoint, Kirby and Ibrahim (2011) contend that entrepreneurship may not only be intentional but pre-planned.

In the entrepreneurship discourse, it has been argued that entrepreneurial intention, which implies an individual's conscious determination to start a new business venture, can be facilitated by entrepreneurship education content and mode of delivery (e.g., Iwu et al., 2020c; Karimi et al., 2016; Liñán et al., 2011). Reinforcing that substance, recent research (Yousaf et al., 2021) documents an influence of entrepreneurial education on entrepreneurial intention, and notes that entrepreneurship education enables the self-efficacy perception of potential entrepreneurs towards developing a positive attitude to starting a new business. By that notion, if entrepreneurship education is strategically implemented, that would steer a zeal for entrepreneurial uptake.

Proactive mindset

A central thread in the entrepreneurship discourse suggests that entrepreneurship education would equip learners (future entrepreneurs) with essential competencies for discovering opportunities and exploiting such opportunities (e.g., Ferreira et al., 2018; Opute et al., 2021b). Extending that theoretical foundation, Amjad et al. (2020) suggest non-entrepreneurial career as a consequence of inadequate Entrepreneurship Education (EE) curricula while Opute et al. (2021b) contend that strategically designed EE curricula would steer productive entrepreneurship. Entrepreneurship curricula should be carefully designed to provoke a proactive mindset in learners (future entrepreneurs). This will enable them to keep a futuristic mindset that seeks new ways of maximising value creation.

Entrepreneurship marketing

Entrepreneurship marketing is a critical component that should be given due consideration in entrepreneurship education in the drive to instil a sustainability mindset in the learners (e.g., Gbadamosi, 2020; Opute, 2020). The American Marketing Association (AMA) (2017) defines marketing thus: "Marketing is the activity, set of institutions, and processes for creating, communicating, delivering, and exchanging offerings that have value for customers, clients, partners, and society at large".[1]

Thus, marketing is an activity and involves a set of institutions (practices and mechanisms used in the marketing role), which implies that marketing involves carrying out some tasks towards achieving a goal – creating value (creating and or developing products or services that meets the needs of the market). From a sustainability point, entrepreneurs must incorporate this marketing logic in their entrepreneurial activities. Effectively achieving that value creation requires that entrepreneurs effectively identify problems in their market (or entrepreneurial) space and endorse innovation and strategic marketing practices and mechanisms (Opute, 2020; Opute et al., 2020b).

In entrepreneurship discourse, critical qualities attributed to entrepreneurship include creativity, flexibility, risk taking, leveraging opportunity, ability to find novel solutions, proactiveness, innovativeness, and value creation (e.g., Opute, 2020). Entrepreneurship marketing, which is an intersection between marketing and entrepreneurship, is described as external and customer-focused approach to marketing towards creating value for customers. The focus in entrepreneurship marketing is to proactively utilise opportunities through innovative strategies (e.g., Gbadamosi, 2020; Opute, 2020). As noted by Miles and Darroch (2006), entrepreneurial marketing processes augment marketing's customer focus and embraces proactive and innovative initiatives to effectively create superior value propositions for future and current customers (see also Opute, 2020).

In the literature (e.g., Gbadamosi, 2020; Opute, 2020), the central entrepreneurship marketing characteristics include:

- Proactiveness
- Innovativeness
- Utilising an opportunity
- Risk taking
- Value creation

Innovativeness

According to the OECD, innovation is "the implementation of a new or significantly improved product (good or service), or process, a new marketing method, or a new organizational method in business practices, workplace organization or external relations" (OECD & Eurostat, 2005, p. 46). As the global challenge to create more jobs towards reducing ever-increasing unemployment rate (e.g., Opute, 2020; Valencia-Arias et al., 2021), entrepreneurship activity must be more productively steered to achieve its critical facilitating role in generating sustainable development through job creation and snowballing economic growth impact (Hernandez-Lopez et al., 2018; Opute, 2020). Achieving these performance targets of productive entrepreneurs requires entrepreneurs with the operational mindset that recognises the critical importance of innovative strategies. As documented by Opute (2020), such innovative mindset, expressed through marketing strategies innovation and products-based (or services) innovation, would not only enable entrepreneurs to compete more effectively in their market domains but also to make a global market entry. Entrepreneurship education must effectively play its facilitating role towards enabling learners and future entrepreneurs to acquire skills that aid that innovative mindset.

Utilising an opportunity

A critical entrepreneurship attitude that would essentially enable the innovative strategy and performance impact described above relates to the willingness and ability of the entrepreneur to utilise opportunity (e.g., Madichie & Gbadamosi, 2017; Opute, 2020). The entrepreneur must be futuristic minded and should identify and utilise opportunities in the market. The extent to which entrepreneurial attitude would reflect such operational mindset would depend on the entrepreneur's skill sets. Therefore, entrepreneurship education curriculum must be strategically contextualised to aid learners (future entrepreneurs) identify and utilise opportunities.

Risk taking

Another critical point relating to entrepreneurship education relates to risk taking. Initiating the move to utilise identified opportunities is a critical step. This usually involves some measure of risk and entrepreneurs must possess reasonable level of boldness to take risks when they identify opportunities (Opute, 2020). Being risk-averse would significantly impede the entrepreneur's ability to compete effectively in his/her market. Entrepreneurship education must therefore be tailored towards enabling learners (future entrepreneurs) to have a good understanding of how to effectively evaluate their operational environment to ensure wise risk taking.

Value creation

Achieving productive entrepreneurship requires entrepreneurial mindset that recognises the centrality of value creation in entrepreneurial activity. Value creation should be a central focus in entrepreneurship marketing, and entrepreneurship education curricula must be designed to incorporate taught and experiential components that enable learners (future entrepreneurs) to build a mindset that recognises the value creation importance.

Entrepreneurship education in the African setting: critical challenges

Entrepreneurship education discourse has gained increasing importance in the African setting over the last decade (e.g., Iwu et al., 2020a; Iwu et al., 2020c; Nchu et al., 2015; Tengeh et al., 2015). While that trend is commendable, entrepreneurship activity in sub-Saharan Africa remains relatively unproductive, a direct consequence of which is stagnancy in the level of economic growth and extendedly higher unemployment and poverty levels (e.g., Iwu & Opute, 2019; Iwu et al., 2020b). Fayolle et al. (2006, p. 702) conceptualise entrepreneurship education to consist of "any pedagogical program or process of education for entrepreneurial attitudes and skills". Leveraging that importance of pedagogical programme and education process, three critical categories of factors that contribute to the inadequacy of entrepreneurship education in driving economic growth impacting entrepreneurship in the sub-Saharan Africa (SSA)setting are identified:

1 Lecturer mindset-related factors
2 Curricular-related elements
3 Research and entrepreneurship

Lecturer mindset-related factors

A critical factor that significantly explains why entrepreneurship in the African setting is predominantly survivalist and lacks the orientation to make meaningful contribution to economic growth and combatting major economic malaise of high unemployment and poverty in the African setting finds its bearing in lecturer-related deficiencies. In a recent study, Iwu et al. (2020c) reported a highly positive association of perceived competence of lecturing team to student entrepreneurial intention. Elaborating, Iwu et al. (2020c) suggest that 1% increase in the competence of lecturing team will propel 0.66% increase in student entrepreneurship intention. This measure of positive impact would also be expected on the way entrepreneurship activities are operationalised if learners (future entrepreneurs) are exposed to entrepreneurship education where the lecturing team is competent and grounded in core curricular for steering productive entrepreneurship. In the African setting, the lecturing team seems not to be adequately skilled and therefore do not teach future entrepreneurs key foundations on proactiveness, futuristic orientation and innovativeness. It must also be mentioned that teaching in the African setting is largely tailored towards producing job seekers and not graduates equipped with a mindset towards taking bold approach and delving into entrepreneurship.

Curricula-related elements

Entrepreneurship discourse has stressed the importance of entrepreneurship education towards motivating entrepreneurial intention (e.g., Ferreira et al., 2017; Iwu et al., 2020c). Equally, these scholars emphasise the role of strategically focused entrepreneurship education in stimulating critical thinking in entrepreneurial students. In particular, Iwu et al. (2020c), which explored the entrepreneurship education perception of students as well as the facilitating impact of curriculum content on entrepreneurial intention, found that although participating students perceive the suitability of academic programme and delivery components (entrepreneurship education curricula) would motivate entrepreneurial uptake (descriptive evidence), significant evidence was not found. Consequently, Iwu et al. (2020c) reinforce prior literature (Bechard & Gregoire, 2005) and suggest a purposefully designed and implemented entrepreneurship curricula involving also systematic teaching approaches towards optimising the gains of entrepreneurship education. In the African setting, entrepreneurship education is lopsided and predominantly based on taught components. Entrepreneurship students are rarely skilled for critical thinking and being futuristic minded. Entrepreneurship students in the African setting are rarely exposed to cross-disciplinary training that would enable them leverage critical productive entrepreneurship practices such as problem identification, proactive mindset, entrepreneurship marketing, entrepreneurship – marketing interface, innovative, value creation, entrepreneurial ecosystem, amongst other.

Further on the point of poor entrepreneurship training, there is a significant disconnect of entrepreneurship pedagogy in the African setting from contemporary trends in industrialised settings. Entrepreneurship education delivery in the African setting is not strategically focused towards enhancing critical productive entrepreneurship mindset through the use of hands-on-deck mechanisms like training, internship, field work, role plan, business plan initiatives, etc. In that regard too, a critical point worth mentioning relates to the poor management skills of entrepreneurs, a problematic that can be attributed to improper training of entrepreneurs. It has been documented that entrepreneurship in the African setting is relatively survivalist natured (e.g., Iwu & Opute, 2019; Iwu et al. 2020b), leading consequently to unproductive entrepreneurship. As reinforced by these scholars, most entrepreneurs lack the management know-how for effectively navigating their entrepreneurial activities in a way that they can contribute meaningfully to the economic wheel. Owing to these management skills, handicap entrepreneurs are not able to pursue a customer-focused and entrepreneurial marketing strategy, critical strategies for driving entrepreneurial ventures, and meeting customers' product or service needs and expectations (e.g., Opute, 2020; Opute et al., 2020c). These management skills shortcomings could be effectively addressed through strategic entrepreneurship education.

Entrepreneurship discourse has lauded the association of entrepreneurial networking to entrepreneurial orientation (e.g., Opute et al., 2020a; Opute et al. 2021a), futuristic entrepreneurial marketing and market penetration (e.g., Opute, 2020), and economic growth impacting entrepreneurship (e.g., Opute, 2020; Opute et al., 2021b; McAdam et al., 2018). Besides recent conceptual mention in the literature (e.g., Opute, 2020; Opute et al., 2021b), not much is known about entrepreneurial networking dynamics in the Africa setting. While this gap undoubtedly reflects failure to recognise the critical importance for leveraging networks embedded goodwill, it also underlines the entrepreneurship education training failures in the African setting. This gap thus suggests that entrepreneurship training in that setting does not adequately incorporate entrepreneurship marketing elements into the curricula towards underlining the importance of the networking strategy.

Digitisation has become a constituent part of modern-day society. The unprecedented consequences of COVID-19 pandemic have not only intensified this trend but indeed have ushered in a new norm that organisations aiming to compete in the marketspace must embrace (e.g., Opute, 2022; Opute et al. 2020b). Digitisation processes and digital platforms are critical media for driving entrepreneurial activity and leveraging networks innovation strategies for achieving active entrepreneurship that steers economic growth. From the point of leveraging digitisation processes, more effort is required in the African setting to sensitise this importance and train future entrepreneurs. Entrepreneurship education curricula in the African setting need to be upgraded to ensure that learners and future entrepreneurs are equipped with relevant digital awareness for effectively steering their entrepreneurial activities.

Research and entrepreneurship

Failure to fully leverage the research tool in driving change. Unlike in the Western context where research is utilised as a critical tool for understanding entrepreneurial problems and challenges and consequently necessary change strategies, this criticality in understanding these core elements seems yet to have eluded practitioners and policy makers in the African setting. For example, in the Western context, the government and corporate bodies instrumentally drive research by providing much needed funding. In the African setting, measure of support remains relatively lacking. Given that shortcoming, students (future entrepreneurs) lack the awareness of this research importance in steering active entrepreneurship. The collaborative working between the government, corporate institutions, and academic institutions that offer entrepreneurship education should be improved.

Recommendations

The importance of strategic initiatives and actions that align with the Sustainable Development Goals (SGDs) is ever intensifying for global economies. Higher education institutions, in their role as critical actors in the drive for equipping the next generation of entrepreneurs must enforce entrepreneurial training strategies that align to the sustainability focus.

Behavioural discourse contends that culture is a critical programming feature of individual mindset (e.g., Opute, 2017; Opute et al., 2020c; Opute et al., 2021a). As a consequence, how individuals process decision and judgement making hinges on the cultural artefacts that condition their mindset. Concurring to that theoretical substance, this chapter contends that if the mindset of entrepreneurs is strategically programmed from the entrepreneurship perspective, and through entrepreneurship education, this will empower them with vintage entrepreneurial skill sets to effectively steer their entrepreneurship efforts and achieve productive entrepreneurship towards boosting economic growth, and combating unemployment and poverty. Thus, this chapter contends that while motivating entrepreneurship intention is important (e.g., Iwu et al., 2016; Iwu et al., 2020a), of more importance is a strategically curriculumed entrepreneurship education that equips students with entrepreneurship knowledge set to steer productive entrepreneurship. Figure 11.1 summarises the conceptual framework forwarded in this chapter.

Critical to achieving productive entrepreneurship that steers sustainable economic development (contributes to economic growth, combats unemployment and poverty) is entrepreneurship education that fully fulfils its facilitating function in training and equipping entrepreneurs with pertinent skill sets for productive entrepreneurship orientation. The literature has documented a tendency for entrepreneurship in the African setting to be predominantly survivalist natured (e.g., Iwu & Opute, 2019; Iwu et al., 2020b). Entrepreneurship education must therefore be geared towards addressing the passivity and survivalist entrepreneurship focus, as well as the multiple entrepreneurial challenges in the African setting. A critical starting

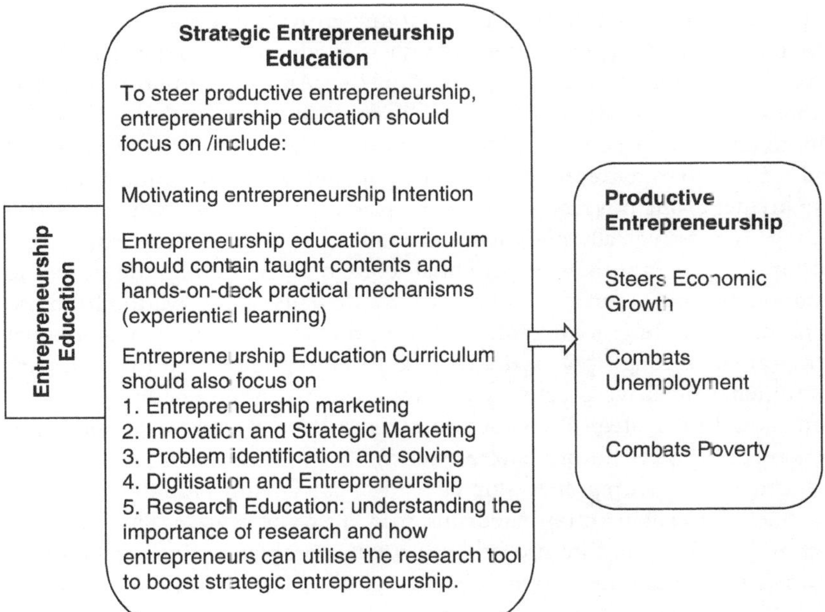

Figure 11.1 Entrepreneurship education for productive entrepreneurship.

Source: Authors.

step to achieving that is to ensure that entrepreneurship educators are technically equipped to strategically train entrepreneurs and empower them with entrepreneurial skills and mindset to steer sustainable economic development impacting productive entrepreneurship. This chapter recommends adequate training of entrepreneurship educators (e.g., Iwu et al., 2020c) to enable them effectively fulfil their pivotal role as motivators of not only entrepreneurship intention (e.g., Iwu et al., 2020a) but also productive entrepreneurship (e.g., Iwu & Opute, 2021; Opute et al., 2021b).

Entrepreneurship education must embrace a curriculum that is strategically tailored to turn out sustainability goals anchored entrepreneurs that are equipped with knowledge and skill sets that position them to act proactively and innovatively to action the SDGs. Academics in their roles as lecturers and critical actors in the drive for optimum economic growth impacting entrepreneurship orientation must demonstrate strategic and goal-oriented teaching. Of central importance in that focus is a teaching curriculum that delivers improved students' learning and experience (e.g., Iwu et al., 2020c). Entrepreneurship education should go beyond the model, concept, and techniques approach but should also include more critically an experiential component that enables learners (entrepreneurs) to fundamentally shift their position and take meaningful actions towards value delivery and exploiting market opportunities. In particular, the experiential input in the entrepreneurship training is of critical importance towards achieving entrepreneurship that contributes to economic growth. Entrepreneurships can generate snowballing economic growth if productive entrepreneurship is maximised (Opute et al., 2021b). For the African setting where entrepreneurship activity remains largely survivalist natured (e.g., Iwu & Opute, 2019; Iwu et al., 2020b), a critical pathway towards a turnaround and productive entrepreneurship that would help in combating unemployment and poverty – two core plagues in the sub-Saharan Africa setting, is a strategically designed and implemented entrepreneurship education that incorporates experiential components. While the teaching components of the curriculum drives entrepreneurship motivation from the point of uptake (e.g., Iwu et al., 2020a; Iwu et al., 2020c), the experiential components through practical exposure to entrepreneurship dynamics are instrumental in driving active entrepreneurship. Entrepreneurship education should be strategically structured to instil and nurture a sustainability mindset in learners (future entrepreneurs).

Furthermore, entrepreneurship education curriculum should incorporate practices that enable entrepreneurship students to be strategically trained to identify problems and be proactive in solving problems. Entrepreneurship education programme should be strategically contextualised to expose students to sound understanding of entrepreneurial marketing. To thrive in today's highly competitive marketplace and contribute to economic growth, entrepreneurships should embrace entrepreneurial marketing, an entrepreneurship knowledge that position entrepreneurs to embrace strategic marketing and innovative processes (marketing and products/services) towards effectively navigating entrepreneurial challenges and creating value for customers (e.g., Opute, 2020; Opute et al., 2020b).

To fully optimise the gains of entrepreneurship education towards sustainable economic development, it is important to recognise the role that research plays. Entrepreneurship education curriculum should be designed to take into consideration this importance, and learners and future entrepreneurs should be trained to leverage the research tool in understanding the challenges they face and how to overcome them.

Finally, the COVID-19 pandemic that has and continues to have unprecedent global impact has compelled organisations to embrace proactive response initiatives to survive. One thing that has become glaringly evident as a consequence of COVID-19 is the digitisation development that has become a constant part of daily life. Digitisation has become the new norm (e.g., Opute, 2022) and organisations that fail to recognise this shift would perish (Opute et al., 2020b). To cope with this shift, entrepreneurs in the African setting would need to upgrade their processes and ensure adequate digitisation relevant for productive entrepreneurship. Consequently too, entrepreneurship education in the African setting would need to incorporate digitisation into the entrepreneurial curriculum to enable learners (future entrepreneurs) to understand the digitisation importance and how digitisation can be utilised to drive entrepreneurial value creation.

Future research directions

To steer entrepreneurship productively towards achieving sustainable economic development in the African setting where entrepreneurship is currently predominantly survivalist oriented (e.g., Iwu & Opute, 2019; Iwu et al., 2020b), a strategic approach for steering entrepreneurship education that stimulates productive entrepreneurship is critical. Within that strategic entrepreneurship education approach is the recognition of the important role that research plays in knowledge development, capacity building, and as a lubricator of the inter-link between the core actors in the entrepreneurial ecosystem. In line with the conceptual framing of this chapter, critical research directions are flagged towards progressing the drive for productive entrepreneurship that would contribute to economic growth and alleviating the unemployment and poverty situations in the African setting.

The first critical step in this regard relates to entrepreneurship educators in their role as major facilitators of entrepreneurship intention and drive. Critical questions that researches should seek to explore include but are not limited to: (1) Are entrepreneurship educators adequately trained to strategically to empower future learners and future entrepreneurs with critical skills set (e.g., problem identification, proactiveness, entrepreneurship marketing, innovation, risk taking, amongst others) for productive entrepreneurship? (2) Are entrepreneurship educators provided adequate hands-on-deck support to enable strategic entrepreneurship content that recognises the need to integrate both taught and experiential elements? and (3) Are entrepreneurship educators exposed to modern teaching methods and bespoke productive entrepreneurship impacting teaching modes from the point of teaching contents?

Also, more research should be undertaken to document the transition of learners to entrepreneurial actors, and the transition experiences from the point of challenges faced pre- and post-start-up. Equally important in that research drive is the understanding of the success or failure stories of the entrepreneurs and steps taken (or anticipated) towards responding to failure episodes. Further on the point of understanding the entrepreneurship experience of entrepreneurs, future research should also seek to illuminate the proactive, innovative, strategic marketing, problem solving, and digitisation dynamics in the entrepreneurial activities.

Finally, and from the entrepreneurial ecosystem foundation, future research should also explore the practices of entrepreneurs in utilising the tools of entrepreneurial networking and research to drive productive entrepreneurship. The government being a critical entrepreneurial ecosystem actor and facilitator of productive entrepreneurship (e.g., Iwu & Opute, 2019; Opute et al. 2021b), future should also shed light on the extent to which the government is effectively facilitating productive entrepreneurship.

Note

1 https://www.marketingstudyguide.com/amas-definition-marketing/

References

Amjad, T., Abdul Rani, S. H. B., & Sa'atar, S. B. (2020). Entrepreneurship development and pedagogical gaps in entrepreneurial marketing education. *International Journal of Management Education*, 18, 100379.

Bechard, J., & Gregoire, D. (2005). Entrepreneurship education research revisited: The case of higher education. *The Academy of Management Learning and Education*, 4(1), 22–43.

Bhatti, M. A., Al Doghan, M. A., Mat Saat, S. A., Juhari, A. S., & Alshagawi, M. (2021). Entrepreneurial intentions among women: Does entrepreneurial training and education matters? (Pre- and post-evaluation of psychological attributes and its effects on entrepreneurial intention). *Journal of Small Business and Enterprise Development*. 10.1108/JSBED-09-2019-0305AQ:9

Farouk, A., Ikram, A., & Boudabbous, S. (2014). The influence of individual factors on entrepreneurial intention. *International Journal of Managing Value and Supply Chains*, 5(4), 47–57.

Fayolle, A., Gailly, B., & Lassas-Clerc, N., (2006). Assessing the impact of entrepreneurship education programmes: A new methodology. *Journal of European Industrial Training*, 30(9), 701–720.

Ferreira, J. J., Fayolle, A., Ratten, V., & Raposo, M. (Eds.). (2018). *Entrepreneurial universities*. Cheltenham, United Kingdom: Edward Elgar Publishing.

Ferreira, J. M., Fernandes, C. I., & Kraus, S. (2019). Entrepreneurship research: Mapping intellectual structures and research trends. *Review of Managerial Science*, 13, 181–205. 10.1007/s11846-017-0242-3

Ferreira, J. J. M., Fernandes, C. I., & Ratten, V. (2017). The influence of entrepreneurship education on entrepreneurial intentions. 10.1007/978-3-319-47949-1_2. book chapter.

Gbadamosi, A. (2020). The entrepreneurship marketing environment. In S. Nwankwo & A. Gbadamosi (Eds.), *Entrepreneurship marketing: Principles and practice of SME Marketing*. London: Routledge Publishers.

Gibson, D., & Tavlaridis, V. (2018). Work-based learning for enterprise education? The case of Liverpool John Moores University 'live' civic engagement projects for students. *Higher Education, Skills and Work-Based Learning*, 8(1), 5–14.

Hagos, S., Izak, M., & Scott, J. M. (2019). Objective institutionalised barriers and subjective performance factors of new migrant entrepreneurs. *International Journal of Entrepreneurial Behaviour & Research*, 25(8), 842–858.

Hernandez-Lopez, D. M., Moncada-Toro, J. F., & Henao-Colorado, L. C. (2018). Intencion emprendedora de los empleados del sector privado de la ciudad de Medellın y su Area Metropolitana [Entrepreneurial intention of employees in the private sector in Medellın and its metropolitan area Diana Milena]. *Revista CEA*, 4(8), 13–33. 10.22430/24223182.1045

Igwe, P. A., Okolie, U. C., & Nwokoro, C. V. (2020). Towards a responsible entrepreneurship education and the future of the workforce. *The International Journal of Management Education*. 10.1016/j.ijme.2019.05.001

Ivanova, E., & Rimanoczy, I. (2022, forthcoming). Revolutionising sustainability education: Stories and tools of mindset transformation. *The principles for responsible management series*. New York: Routledge. ISBN 9781032135330

Iwu, C. G., Eze, I., Opute, A. P., Dongo, G., & Dongo, O. W. (2020b). Scavenging for survival and its health implications. The nexus between unemployment and Ill-health. *WSEAS Transactions on Environment and Development*, 17(1), 1–18.

Iwu, C. G., Ezeuduji, I., Eresia-Eke, C., & Tengeh, R. (2016). The entrepreneurial intention of university students: The case of a university of technology in South Africa. *Acta Universitatis Danubius*. Œconomica, 12(1), 164–181.

Iwu, C. G., & Opute, A. P. (2019). Eradicating poverty and unemployment: Narratives of survivalist entrepreneurs. *Journal of Reviews on Global Economics*, 1438–1451. 10.6000/1929-7092.2019.08.127

Iwu, C. G., & Opute, A. P. (2021). Steering productive entrepreneurship activities in emerging markets: The role of the university. In *The role of universities and their entrepreneurial ecosystems in advocating sustainability*, Chapter 14 in *Universities, entrepreneurial ecosystems and sustainability* (edited by C. Fernandes, M. Ramírez-Pasillas, J. J. Ferreira). De Gruyter Studies in Knowledge Management and Entrepreneurial Ecosystems. Walter De Gruyter GmbH, Berlin/Boston. ISBN 9783110670165.

Iwu, C. G., Opute, A. P., Nchu, R., Babatunde, A. A., Iwu, C. H., & Eze, I. F. (2020a). The antecedents of university students' entrepreneurship intention. The theory of planned behaviour viewpoint. *Harvard Deusto Business Research*, IX(2), 221–240.

Iwu, C. G., Opute, A. P., Nchu, R., Eresia-Eke, C., Tengeh, R. K., Jaiyeoba, O., & Aliyu, O. A. (2020c). Entrepreneurship education, curriculum and lecturer – competency as antecedents of student entrepreneurial intention. *International Journal of Management Education*. doi.org/10.1016/j.ijme.2019.03.007

Kakouris, A., & Liargovas, P. (2021). On the about/for/through framework of entrepreneurship education: A critical analysis. *Entrepreneurship Education and Pedagogy*, 4(3), 396–421. 2515127420916740.

Karimi, S., Biemans, H. J., Lans, T., Chizari, M., & Mulder, M. (2016). The impact of entrepreneurship education: A study of Iranian students' entrepreneurial intentions and opportunity identification. *Journal of Small Business Management*, 54(1), 187–209.

Kirby, D. A., & Ibrahim, N. (2011). Entrepreneurship education and the creation of an enterprise culture: Provisional results from an experiment in Egypt. *International Entrepreneurship and Management Journal*, 7(2), 181–193.

Liñán, F. (2004). Intention-based models of entrepreneurship education. *Piccola Impresa / Small Business*, 11–35.

Liñán, F., Rodríguez-Cohard, J. C., & Rueda-Cantuche, J. M. (2011). Factors affecting entrepreneurial intention levels: A role for education. *International Entrepreneurship and Management Journal*, 7(2), 195–218.

Lloyd, R., Martin, M. J., Hyatt, J., & Tritt, A. (2019). A cold call on work-based learning: A 'live' group project for the strategic selling classroom. *Higher Education, Skills and Work-Based Learning*, 9(3), 329–346.

Lombardi, R., Lardo, A., Cuozzo, B., & Trequattrini, R. (2017). Emerging trends in entrepreneurial universities within mediterranean regions: An international comparison. *EuroMed Journal of Business*, 12(2), 130–145.

Lortie, J., & Castogiovanni, G. (2015). The theory of planned behaviour in entrepreneurship research: What we know and future directions. *International Entrepreneurship and Management Journal*, 11(4), 935–957.

Lv, Y., Chen, Y., Sha, Y., Wang, J., An, L., Chen, T., Huang, X., Huang, Y., & Huang, L. (2021). How entrepreneurship education at universities influences entrepreneurial intention: Mediating effect based on entrepreneurial competence. *Frontiers in Psychology*, 12, 655868. 10.3389/fpsyg.2021.655868

Madichie, N. O., & Gbadamosi, A. (2017). The entrepreneurial university: An exploration of "value-creation" in a non-management department. *Journal of Management Development*, 36(2), 196–216. 10.1108/JMD-06-2016-0098

Madichie, N. O., Ibrahim, M., Adam, D. R., & Ustarz, Y. (2020). Entrepreneurial intentions amongst African students: A case study of the university of education, Winneba, Ghana. In *Entrepreneurial universities* (pp. 169–190). Cham: Palgrave Macmillan.

McAdam, M., Harrison, R. T., & Leitch, C. M. (2018). Stories from the field: Women's networking as gender capital in entrepreneurial ecosystems. *Small Business Economics*, 53, 459–474. 10.1007/s11187-018-9995-6

Miles, M. P., & Darroch, J. (2006). Large firms, entrepreneurial marketing processes, and the cycle of competitive advantage. *European Journal of Marketing*, 40(5/6), 485–501.

Nchu, R. M., Tengeh, R. K., & Hassan, L. S. (2015). High school learners' perception of the efficacy of entrepreneurship education: A case study of selected high schools in South Africa. *Socioeconomica – The Scientific Journal for Theory and Practice of Socio-economic Development*, 4(8), 507–526.

Nwankwo, S. (2020). Contemporary issues in entrepreneurship marketing, sustainability, ethics and social responsibility. In S. Nwankwo & A. Gbadamosi (Eds.), *Entrepreneurship marketing: Principles and practice of SME marketing*. London: Routledge Publishers.

OECD & Eurostsat (2005). Guidelines for collecting and interpreting innovation data. OECD Report, 1–166.

Opute, A. P. (2017). Exploring personality, identity and self-concept among young consumers (Chapter 5). In *Young consumer behaviour: A research companion*. London: Routledge (Taylor and Francis). ISBN: 978-0-415-79008-6 (hbk).

Opute, A. P. (2022, forthcoming). Virtual teams: The new work norm for the post Covid-19 era (Chapter 10). In *Digital service delivery in Africa*. Switzerland: Springer. 10.1007/978-3-030-83909-3

Opute, A. P., Irene, B N., & Iwu, C. G. (2020a). Tourism service and digital technologies: A value creation perspective. *African Journal of Hospitality, Tourism and Leisure*, 9(2). ISSN:223-814X.

Opute, A. P., Iwu, C. G., Adeola, O., Mugobo, V., Okeke-Uzodike, O. E., Fagbola, S., & Jaiyeoba, O. (2020b). The Covid-19 pandemic and implications for businesses: Innovative retail marketing viewpoint. *Retail Marketing Review*, 16, SE.

Opute, A. P. (2020c). Small and medium enterprises marketing: Innovation and sustainable economic growth perspective. In S. Nwankwo & A. Gbadamosi (Eds.), *Entrepreneurship marketing: Principles and practice of SME marketing*. London: Routledge Publishers. https://doi.org/10.4324/9780429505461

Opute, A. P., Iwu, C. G., Khosa, R. M., Eresia-Eke, C., Hagos, S. B., & Irene, B. N. O. (2021a). African immigrant entrepreneurship in the UK: The hidden hand of family influence on entrepreneurial orientation. *Harvard Deusto Business Research*, X (1), 53–79.

Opute, A. P., Kalu, K. I., Adeola, O., & Iwu, C. G. (2021b). Steering sustainable economic growth: Entrepreneurial ecosystem approach. *Journal of Entrepreneurship and Innovation in Emerging Economies*, 7(2), 1–30.

Opute, A. P., Madichie, N. O., Hagos, S. B., & Ojra, A. (2020c). Entrepreneurship behaviour of African minorities in the UK: 'Demystifying cultural influence'. *International Journal of Entrepreneurship and Small Business*, 44(3), 298–322.

Ramayah, T., Ahmad N. H., & Fei, T. H. C. (2012). Entrepreneur education: Does prior experience matter? *Journal of Entrepreneurship Education*, 15, 65.

Ratten, V., & Jones, P. (2020). Entrepreneurship and management education: Exploring trends and gaps. *The International Journal of Management Education*. 10.1016/j.ijme.2020.100431

Tengeh, R. K., Iwu, C. G., & Nchu, R. M. (2015). Embeddedness of entrepreneurship education in the curricula of non-business university programmes: Preliminary evidence from South African universities of technology. *Socioeconomica – The Scientific Journal for Theory and Practice of Socio-economic Development*, 4(7), 111–126.

Valencia-Arias, A., Arango-Botero, D., & Sanchez-Torres, J. A. (2021). Promoting entrepreneurship based on university students' perceptions of entrepreneurial attitude, university environment, entrepreneurial culture and entrepreneurial training. *Higher Education, Skills and Work-based Learning*. 10.1108/HESWBL-07-2020-0169

Wiederman, M. (2015). Active learning and learner-centered instruction, University of South Carolina School of Medicine Greenville. Available at: https://www.sc.edu/study/colleges_schools/medicine_greenville/internal/documents/learner_centered_strategies.pd

Yousaf, U., Ali, S. A., Ahmed, M., Usman, B., & Sameer, I. (2021). From entrepreneurial education to entrepreneurial intention: A sequential mediation of self-efficacy and entrepreneurial attitude. *International Journal of Innovation Science*. 10.1108/IJIS-09-2020-013

Zachary, D. (2020). What is the future of poverty in Africa? Institute for security studies. https://issafrica.org/iss-today/what-is-the-future-of-poverty-in-africa

12 Productive Entrepreneurship: Entrepreneurial Networking Perspective and Research Agenda

A.P. Opute, O. Chukwuma-Nwuba, C.G. Iwu, A.A. Eniola, J. Ojra, and J. Irene

Introduction

Entrepreneurship discourse has remained a persistent feature in academic literature within the last three decades. Given its criticality in steering economic development, increasing effort is devoted towards enhancing the understanding of diverse entrepreneurship domains, for example, small- and medium-sized enterprises (SMEs) (e.g., Opute, 2020; Opute et al., 2021a), informal entrepreneurships (Galdino et al., 2018; Laing et al., 2021), women entrepreneurship (e.g., Irene et al., 2022; Lipoko et al., 2021), entrepreneurial ecosystem (e.g., Fernandes & Ferreira, 2021; Iwu & Opute, 2021; Opute et al., 2021b; Stam & Spigel, 2017; Theodoraki et al., 2022), amongst others. On that economic development association rationality, there is a plausibility to expect a growing focus on entrepreneurship in academic discourse in the future. As a matter of fact, given the pressure to achieve sustainability goals, the need to enhance the understanding of entrepreneurial ecosystems is a central focus to academics, governments and policy makers (e.g., Iwu & Opute, 2021; Opute et al., 2021b; Theodoraki et al., 2022).

Driven by that sustainability goal, this chapter is purposed to contribute to the understanding of entrepreneurship and in particular towards steering productive entrepreneurship in the African setting that is plagued by high levels of unemployment (G.E.M., 2015; Iwu & Opute, 2019) and predominantly survivalist natured entrepreneurship (Iwu & Opute, 2019; Iwu et al., 2021).

Aiming to contribute to entrepreneurship discourse in general and entrepreneurial ecosystem in particular, this chapter sensitises entrepreneurial networking. Towards achieving that conceptual focus, this chapter is organised further thus: Firstly, the conceptual framing of the chapter is summarised. Following that, the concept of entrepreneurial ecosystem is explained and the central entrepreneurial ecosystem focus of the chapter underlined. Subsequently, entrepreneurial networking is elaborated highlighting the networks and interaction processes that entrepreneurships can leverage to achieve pro-active, strategic marketing and innovative processes

DOI: 10.4324/9781003216469-12

on which productive entrepreneurship thrives. In the productive entrepreneurship, the impacting role of such networking on entrepreneurial capital (social, human and financial) is also explained. Thereafter, digitisation is explained showcasing its networking and productive entrepreneurship association. To conclude, relevant recommendations are offered to enable entrepreneurs in the African setting to effectively ensure networking processes that would positively impact their entrepreneurship activities. Also, core research directions are flagged towards knowledge development.

The conceptual framing of this chapter

Feeding off the sustainability foundation, this chapter is grounded on the rationality that strategically oriented entrepreneurship or productive entrepreneurship (e.g., Opute et al., 2021b; Pankov et al., 2021; Stam & Spigel, 2017) would boost sustainable economic development. The term "entrepreneur", which was first used by Richard Cantillon (1755), is conceptualised to imply the organiser and manager of production or trade. This act of organising and managing production or trade encompasses multiple actions. Leveraging the entrepreneurial ecosystems foundation (e.g., Iwu & Opute, 2021; Opute et al., 2021b), this chapter conceptualises a networking perspective. Taking that viewpoint, this chapter builds off the social-embeddedness logic (e.g., Opute et al., 2020b; Opute et al., 2021a) and illuminates how entrepreneurial networking can be strategically actioned to achieve productive entrepreneurship that is anchored on proactive, strategic marketing and innovative processes.

The first mention of the term "productive entrepreneurship" in entrepreneurship literature was in Baumol's (1996) seminal work "Entrepreneurship: Productive, Unproductive, and Destructive". Conceptually, this chapter invokes productive entrepreneurship definition in Lucas and Fuller (2017, p. 45): "Productive entrepreneurship is that which contributes to societal well-being, including the introduction of new products or new production processes". Reinforcing that viewpoint, Opute et al. (2021b) add that productive entrepreneurship is one that drives snowballing economic growth.

Entrepreneurial ecosystem: definition, and conceptual premise in this chapter

Driven by the sustainable economic development relevance, the advocacy for due attention on entrepreneurial ecosystems towards optimising productive entrepreneurship has intensified recently (e.g., Fernandes & Ferreira, 2021; Iwu & Opute, 2021; Opute et al., 2021b; Theodoraki et al., 2022). Stam and Spigel (2017, p. 1) defined entrepreneurial ecosystems as "a set of interdependent actors and factors coordinated in such a way that they enable productive entrepreneurship within a particular territory", while Spigel (2017, p. 49) conceptualises it as "the union of localized cultural outlooks, social networks, investment capital, universities, and active economic policies that create environments supportive of innovation-based ventures".

According to domain discourse, if the actors in the ecosystem interact and relate effectively, and play their facilitating roles effectively, that would propel active and productive entrepreneurship for sustaining economic growth (e.g., Iwu & Opute, 2021; Opute et al., 2021b; Pankov et al., 2021; Theodoraki et al., 2018).

In the networking viewpoint of entrepreneurial ecosystems, the focus is on understanding the interactions within the ecosystems. Thus, the entrepreneurial ecosystem is perceived as a social network involving the various actors that hold multiple values in the ecosystem (Hayter et al., 2018; Theodoraki et al., 2018). Value creation is of critical importance as ecosystem members share a common fate (Theodoraki & Messeghem, 2017). Networking is a critical entrepreneurial ecosystem element (Opute et al., 2021b; Theodoraki et al., 2018) and in particular in the sustainability focus (Opute et al., 2021b; Theodoraki et al., 2022). Recognising that criticality, this chapter focuses on entrepreneurial networking bearing in mind that three core attributes, namely structural, cognitive (cultural) and relational, can be utilised to analyse entrepreneurial ecosystem (Spigel, 2017). Specifically, this chapter focuses on networking as a tool for leveraging structural, social-embeddedness and collaboration-related gains towards achieving sustainable economic growth impacting entrepreneurship.

Entrepreneurial networking: definition and productive entrepreneurship

The critical association of intra-organisational (e.g., Opute, 2014; Opute & Madichie, 2017) and inter-organisational (e.g., Alexiev et al., 2016; Drummond et al., 2022; Schruijer, 2020) collaboration to performance enhancement of organisation has been reiterated in academic discourse. In entrepreneurship discourse, a theoretical foundation that connects to that logic relates to entrepreneurial networking. Situated in the broad entrepreneurship domain of entrepreneurial ecosystem, entrepreneurial networking relates to the networks that exist between entrepreneurial actors. Entrepreneurial networks imply the relationships or ties that exist between entrepreneurships.

According to social-embeddedness literature (e.g., Opute et al., 2020b; Opute et al., 2021b), the networks of organisations are critical facilitators of entrepreneurial success. Thus, entrepreneurships can leverage networks-embedded goodwill to strategically position themselves in their marketspace. As elaborated by Opute et al. (2020b), entrepreneurships that optimise this goodwill utilisation would command a strong competitive edge in the market. Offering a gender perspective, McAdam et al. (2018) reinforce the social-embeddedness viewpoint. According to that study, entrepreneurial networks play a significant role in entrepreneurial ecosystems. Through their networking, women entrepreneurs generate gender capital that enables them to participate actively in the entrepreneurial ecosystem. That financing impact of entrepreneurial networking is reinforced by Opute et al. (2020b) who found that ethnic minority entrepreneurships access vitals finance through their socially embedded networks.

As argued by further literature (e.g., Opute et al., 2021a; Opute et al., 2021b), if entrepreneurs effectively leverage their networks in the ecosystem and collaborate effectively, they would generate vital resource towards offsetting the shortcomings (financial, human or infrastructural) that the individual entrepreneurs may have. Social goodwill emerges when entrepreneurships leverage their relationships or ties to drive their entrepreneurship operations. These networks enable entrepreneurships to collaborate and "overcome innate resource limitations of individual SMEs" (McAdam et al., 2016, p. 1317). Within the SMEs domain, a critical resource that is generated through networking among entrepreneurs relates to human capital. When entrepreneurs form effective networks, that could be leveraged to offset human capital limitations (e.g., Opute et al., 2020b; Opute et al., 2021a). Opute et al. (2021a) extend this human capital impact and argue that collaborative efforts of this nature enable SMEs entry into new markets, an insight that connects to innovative marketing viewpoint (e.g., Opute, 2020; Stam, 2015). This innovative marketing contention is further reinforced by Turkina et al. (2019), who, in their explanation of the interactionist dynamics in entrepreneurial ecosystem, emphasise that networking, coexistence and leveraging of ties spark innovation, as organisations strive to compete profitably (see also, McAdam et al., 2016).

In the tripartite viewpoint of social-embeddedness foundation embraced in this chapter, it is noted that networking also enables entrepreneurs to offset shortcomings of infrastructural nature. In their social capital viewpoint, Theodoraki et al. (2018) distil three dimensions, which include, among others, the structural dimension that is made up of links, configuration and stability. Entrepreneurs share one common goal – profitably steering their entrepreneurial activities, and entrepreneurs can leverage their networks and collaborations to enable them overcome their individual structural deficits (Opute, 2020; Theodorakis et al., 2018). Accessing such structural benefits through their networks would enable active and productive entrepreneurship that would impact sustainable economic growth.

A crucial part in the leveraging of entrepreneurial ecosystems goodwill involves utilising inherent social networks to overcome the shortcomings that individual entrepreneurs may have. Networking in the entrepreneurial ecosystem offers entrepreneurs multiple resource which they could leverage to enable active entrepreneurship that would contribute to sustainable economic growth. As competition intensifies, inter-organisational networking and collaboration offer critical competitive option (Kofler et al., 2018; Opute, 2020). Entrepreneurs who engage in social networking and collaboration would more adequately respond to market opportunities through their marketing and product (service)-based innovative strategies. Consequently, these entrepreneurships would create wealth and drive economic growth (Opute, 2020; Stam, 2015).

Digitisation, networking and productive entrepreneurship

Connecting the foundation that networking goodwill would aid entrepreneurial success to entrepreneurial marketing, Opute (2020) adds that organisations can leverage such network goodwill to effectively solve problems and enforce pro-active initiatives that aid innovative and market penetration processes. Problem-solving attitude and pro-active mindset are critical entrepreneurship components for achieving productive entrepreneurship that would steer sustainable economic development snowballing impact (Opute et al., 2021a).

Extending that viewpoint, this chapter forwards a conceptualisation that recognises the criticality of digitisation in global dynamics (e.g., Opute, 2017; Opute, 2022; Opute et al., 2020a). Digital technologies are vital tools for communication, content management, networking (Sousa & Rocha, 2019) and customer engagement (Opute et al., 2020a; Opute et al., 2020c). In a study that explored entrepreneurships in Uganda, Kimuli et al. (2021) underline the importance for firms in the developing context to integrate digital technologies in their operations. This chapter re-echoes that call. Understanding this digitisation criticality is a *sine qua non* in the post-COVID-19 pandemic era (Opute et al., 2020b; Ratten & Jones, 2020). This criticality is supported by recent research on SMEs during COVID-19 (Papadopoulos et al., 2020): digital technologies aid access to markets and advertising of entrepreneurship activities (locally and internationally). This chapter therefore recognises the pertinence for entrepreneurship to incorporate digitisation in their entrepreneurial processes to enable them optimise networking goodwill towards finding solutions to their marketing challenges. Building on Opute (2020), we suggest in this chapter that doing that would enable entrepreneurships stay innovative, both from the product (or service) point as well as from marketing options (including also internationalisation prospects).

Digital technology and social media in particular are critical tools that organisations can utilise to strategically drive marketing (Drummond et al., 2022; Enyinda et al., 2021). Digital technologies are key resource for enabling inter-organisational networks. For example, social media are used by collaborating entrepreneurial network to enable interaction between inter-organisational network actors (Drummond et al., 2022). Prior research (Olanrewaju et al., 2020) supports that utility substance and suggests that social media are used as market platform to enable information search and business networking of small businesses. As documented further in the literature, social media are critical to developing and maintaining inter-organisational relationships in a collaborative network (Drummond et al., 2018), and also for enabling network embeddedness in internationalisation processes (Fraccastoro et al., 2021).

Another support of the strategic use of enterprise social media (SM) is provided by Enyinda et al. (2021) who note that SM platforms such as Facebook, LinkedIn, Twitter, YouTube, amongst others, enable organisations keep track of their entrepreneurial networks, the extended networks of their networks, and what and how they do what they do. These media could also be utilised to capture intelligence that would enable entrepreneurs to identify other entrepreneurs and businesses, locally and internationally, of strategic operational importance to them.

Entrepreneurs must give due attention to the interface between entrepreneurship and marketing (Opute, 2020). Leveraging entrepreneurship marketing knowledge is critical for corporate success. Beyond the network enabling utility towards driving marketing, a further vital utility of digital technology relates to its market enablement impact from the point of responding to consumers' stimuli (Opute, 2017; Opute et al., 2020c) and marketing strategy implementation (including also tracking consumer behaviour) (Enyinda et al., 2021; Opute, 2020). Technological evolution has transformed life massively (Spencer & Sutton-Brady, 2020) and marketers, willingly or not, are accepting the reality of a paradigm shift from the point of marketing mix element of "place". In today's marketplace, place is no longer physical but reasonably virtual as consumers increasingly endorse e-commerce. The unprecedented implications of COVID-19 have also alarmed societies globally of the pertinence for digital technology endorsement. Endorsing digital technologies is also a critical option for entrepreneurs given its relevance in enabling engagement with customers (Opute et al., 2020a).

Conclusions to the chapter, recommendations and research agenda

While entrepreneurial endeavours increasingly drive economic growth in Western societies (e.g., Acs et al., 2018; Audretsch et al., 2018), a stagnant trend has been reported about the sub-Saharan Africa setting (e.g., Iwu & Opute, 2019; Iwu et al., 2021). Recent entrepreneurship discourse has strongly underlined the importance of networking approach to productive entrepreneurship activity (e.g., McAdam et al., 2014; McAdam et al., 2015; Opute, 2020).

Entrepreneurial networking discourse (e.g., Opute, 2020; Opute et al., 2021b) distils two core levels: networking between entrepreneurs and partners (suppliers and partners that aid the entrepreneurial activity) and networking between entrepreneurs in similar domain. Premised in the latter context, this chapter forwards a conceptual framework of entrepreneurial networking (see Figure 12.1) that can be leveraged to achieve productive entrepreneurship in the African setting.

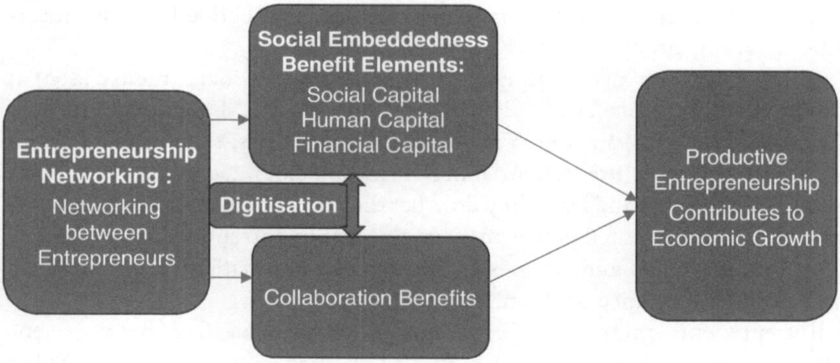

Figure 12.1 Conceptual framework of entrepreneurship networking towards driving economic growth.

Source: Author.

The framing of this chapter supports the notion that effective networks would enhance the quantity of entrepreneurial activity (density), as well as entrepreneurial activity (which extendedly aids fluidity; McAdam et al., 2018; Opute et al., 2021b). Conceptually, this chapter forwards that if entrepreneurs leverage the inherent goodwill in their networks, this will drive productive entrepreneurship that over time (Opute et al., 2021b) would yield snowballing economic growth. The framework forwards a networking conceptualisation that considers social embeddedness components as well as collaboration aspects between entrepreneurs. Within the focus of steering productive entrepreneurship that significantly drives economic growth, and bearing in mind the pertinence for embracing digital technology in the post-COVID-19 era (Opute, 2022), digitisation is underlined as critical in the optimisation of the networking benefits.

Recommendations

Building on relevant literature (e.g., Motoyama & Watkins, 2014; Turkina, 2018), Iwu and Opute (2021) emphasise that "utilising social networks and support institutions would facilitate business growth through reduction of transaction cost, business opportunities creation, knowledge sharing, and research and training" (p. 289). That substance connects logically with Stam and Spigel's (2017) viewpoint which conceptualises that entrepreneurial ecosystem constitutes a set of actors that are interdependent and interact and function to enable productive entrepreneurship. The networking foundation and its entrepreneurship boosting substance is forwarded in this chapter. Specifically, this chapter argues that if the entrepreneurial actors in an ecosystem leverage their socially embedded networks, this would enable productive entrepreneurship.

SMEs and entrepreneurships in general, which effectively leverage the networking benefits, acquire useful resources that enable them outplay their competitors in the market. This chapter points entrepreneurs in the African setting to two central networking-based aspects for achieving that competitive advantage. The first aspect finds its bearing in the social-embeddedness foundation (e.g., Opute et al., 2020b; Opute et al., 2021a), and relates to the bonding impact and goodwill that emerges when entrepreneurs network. Such networking enables entrepreneurs to harness financial, social and human capital opportunities that exist in socially embedded networks. For entrepreneurs in this setting where financial handicap and lack of facilitating support from the government are known to be major challenges (e.g., Iwu & Opute, 2019; Iwu et al., 2021), such networks offer critical resource for offsetting financial challenges (e.g., Opute et al., 2020b; Opute et al., 2021a). Such networks could also be leveraged for staff sourcing (e.g., Opute et al., 2021a).

The second aspect relates to innovation and marketing strategy notions (e.g., Opute, 2020). Ensuring economic growth requires that entrepreneurships are customer focused. Entrepreneurs in the African setting must embrace entrepreneurship marketing approach that prioritises strategic marketing orientation that drives customer focus. Through entrepreneurial networking, entrepreneurs can put themselves in vintage position to enhance their customer orientation focus from the point of exploring initiatives improving their product (or service) offers. Such networking opportunities could be leveraged for mutually benefiting collaboration between the entrepreneurs that could usher in innovative strategies product-wise. When organisations engage in close networking, a learning experience takes place and that experience can be leveraged to drive innovative agenda. As extended by Opute (2020), such networking opportunity can also be leveraged to break into new markets and also for globalising entrepreneurial operations.

To achieve the aforementioned dual networking-based competitive advantage, entrepreneurs in the African setting are reminded of the pertinence for digital literacy. Technological evolution has tremendously transformed daily life. Businesses globally are increasingly recognising that pertinence and are embracing digital technologies towards improving their competitive options (e.g., Opute et al., 2020a, Opute et al., 2020c). More so, the consequences of the COVID-19 pandemic have further reinvigorated the critical importance of digital technology to contemporary marketing (Opute et al., 2020c). Digital technologies are of contemporary importance to organisations as they enable content generation, review and use for marketing implementation (Akpan et al., 2020; Enyinda et al., 2021). Digital literacy is essential towards utilising digital technology to embrace innovation and enabling networking towards providing adequate solutions to existing customers and also penetrating new markets. Networking with other entrepreneurs and collaborating effectively with them will enable them to effectively pull their resources, leverage inherent benefits towards boosting product-based innovation as well as market-penetration strategies (Opute, 2020). Beyond these networking-based benefits, embracing digital technologies will enable entrepreneurs in the African setting to achieve effective marketing implementation (e.g., Opute, 2020), consumer behaviour tracking (e.g., Opute et al., 2020a; Enyinda et al., 2021) and competing effectively (e.g., Opute, 2020).

Research agenda

Regrettably, SMEs have largely failed to assume the desired role of critical economic growth drivers in sub-Saharan Africa, a reality that poses a major concern to policy makers and governments in this region where unemployment and poverty are major challenges. Purpose-driven strategic efforts must be made to drive necessary change towards ensuring that entrepreneurships in the sub-Saharan African region become active contributors to sustainable economic growth. Aiming to contribute to this change drive, this chapter forwards an entrepreneurship approach that would galvanise successful entrepreneurship activity. Specifically, towards ensuring SMEs that profitably satisfy customers and actively play the role of employers and active economic growth drivers, this chapter proposes a networking approach that is anchored on social-embeddedness foundation. Within that focus, this chapter recognises the growing pertinence for organisations to align their operational strategy with digital technology evolution. Embracing that digital-technology-aligned operational strategy is critical to overcoming the COVID-19 pandemic consequences and thriving in the post-COVID-19 era (Opute, 2022).

The framework forwarded in this chapter offers useful directions for achieving productive entrepreneurship in the African setting. A further contribution from this chapter relates to the research directions that emerge from the conceptualised focus of this chapter. Research is a critical tool for driving change. Future research should aim to illuminate the nature of entrepreneurial networking within and beyond the social-embeddedness viewpoint, inherent challenges and performance implications.

Further on the implication aspect, this chapter builds on prior literature (e.g., Kandemir et al., 2006; Karami & Tang, 2019; Opute, 2020; Opute et al., 2021a) to draw attention to further core directions for knowledge development that undoubtedly would enable the drive for sustainable economic growth impacting productive entrepreneurship in the African setting. Prior literature notes that strategic networks and alliances promote organisational learning (e.g., Drummond et al., 2022; Opute, 2020) and enable productive innovation (e.g., Kandemir et al., 2006; Opute, 2020). Further literature underscores the critical role of networks and inter-organisational cooperation on timely positioning of new products to the market (e.g., Karami & Tang, 2019) and also penetrating new markets (e.g., Opute et al., 2021a). Researchers in the African domain could seek to illuminate the validity of these notions in the African setting.

Finally, this chapter has focused on entrepreneurial networking between entrepreneurs in same or close entrepreneurship domain. Future research could extend entrepreneurial networking discourse by illuminating the levels of networks between entrepreneurs and the multi-partner levels and how such networks could be strategically optimised for productive entrepreneurship.

References

Acs, Z. J., Estrin, S., Mickiewicz, T., & Szerb, L. (2018). Entrepreneurship, institutional economics, and economic growth: An ecosystem perspective. *Small Business Economics*, 51(2), 501–514.

Akpan, I. J., Udoh, E. A. P., & Adebisi, B. (2020). Small business awareness and adoption of state-of the-art technologies in emerging and developing markets, and lessons from the COVID-19 pandemic. *Journal of Small Business and Entrepreneurship*, 34(2), 123–140.

Alexiev, A. S., Volberda, H. W., & Van den Bosch, F. A. J. (2016). Interorganizational collaboration and firm innovativeness: Unpacking the role of the organizational environment. *Journal of Business Research*, 69, 974–984.

Audretsch, D. B., Belitski, M., & Desai, S. (2018). National business regulations and city entrepreneurship in Europe: A multilevel nested analysis. *Entrepreneurship Theory and Practice*, 4, 6.

Baumol, W. J. (1996). Entrepreneurship: Productive, unproductive, and destructive. *Journal of Business Venturing*, 11(1), 3–22.

Cantillon, R. (1755). *Essai sur la nature du commerce en général*. London: Fletcher Gyles [Paris].

Drummond, C., McGrath, H., & O'Toole, T. (2018). The impact of social media on resource mobilisation in entrepreneurial firms. *Industrial Marketing Management*, 70, 68–89. 10.1016/j.indmarman.2017.05.009

Drummond, C., O'Toole, T., & McGrath, H. (2022). Social media resourcing of an entrepreneurial firm network: Collaborative mobilisation process. *Journal of Business Research*, 145, 171–187.

Enyinda, C. I., Opute, A. P., Fadahunsi, A., & Mbah, C. H. (2021). Marketing-sales-service interface and social media marketing influence on B2B sales process. *Journal of Business & Industrial Marketing*, 36(6), 990–1009.

Fernandes, A. J., & Ferreira, J. J. (2021). Entrepreneurial ecosystems and networks: A literature review and research agenda. *Review of Managerial Science*. 10.1007/s11846-020-00437-6

Fraccastoro, S., Gabrielsson, M., & Chetty, S. (2021). Social media firm specific advantages as enablers of network embeddedness of international entrepreneurial ventures. *Journal of World Business*, 56(3), Article 101164. 10.1016/j.jwb.2020.101164

Galdino, K. M., Kiggundu, M. N., Jones, C. D., & Ro, S. (2018). The informal economy in pan-Africa: Review of the literature, themes, questions, and directions for management research. *Africa Journal of Management*, 4(3), 225–258. 10.1080/23322373.2018.1517542

G.E.M. (2015/2016). *Global report*. Available online at: https://www.gemconsortium.org/report/49480 (accessed June 23, 2017).

Hayter, C. S., Nelson, A. J., Zayed, S., & O'Connor, A. C. (2018). Conceptualizing academic entrepreneurship ecosystems: A review, analysis and extension of the literature. *The Journal of Technology Transfer*, 43(4), 1039–1082. 10.1007/s10961-018-9657-5

Irene, B. N. O., Opute, A. P., & Murithi, W. (2022). An empirical insight into the factors affecting the oscillation of women between self and paid employment in South Africa. In *The Palgrave handbook of African entrepreneurship*. Switzerland: Palgrave Macmillan.

Iwu, C. G. (2021). COVID-19 lessons for mitigation and future SME Prospects. In *Handbook of research on strategies and interventions to mitigate COVID-19 impact on SMEs* (pp. 74–100). IGI Global.

Iwu, C. G., & Opute, A. P. (2019). Eradicating poverty and unemployment: Narratives of survivalist entrepreneurs. *Journal of Reviews on Global Economics*, 8, 1438–1451.

Iwu, C. G., & Opute, A. P. (2021). Steering productive entrepreneurship activities in emerging markets: The role of the university (Chapter 14). In C. Fernandes, M. Ramírez-Pasillas, & J. J. Ferreira (Eds.), *Universities, entrepreneurial ecosystems and sustainability*. De Gruyter studies in knowledge management and entrepreneurial ecosystems. Walter De Gruyter GmbH, Berlin/Boston. ISBN 9783110670165.

Iwu, C. G., Opute, A. P., Eze I. F., Dongo, U. G., & Dongo, O. W. (2021). Scavenging for survival and its health implications. *The nexus between unemployment and ill-health*, 17, 1–18. WSEAS Transactions on Environment and Development, ISSN:1790-5079.

Kandemir, D., Yaprak, A., & Cavusgil, S. T. (2006). Alliance orientation: Conceptualization, measurement, and impact on market performance. *Journal of the Academy of Marketing Science*, 34, 324. 10.1177/0092070305285953

Karami, M., & Tang, J. (2019). Entrepreneurial orientation and SME international performance: The mediating role of networking capability and experiential learning. *International Small Business Journal: Researching Entrepreneurship*, 37(2), 105–124.

Kimuli, S. N. L., Sendawula, K., & Nagujja, S. (2021). Digital technologies in micro and small enterprise: Evidence from Uganda's informal sector during the COVID-19 pandemic. *World Journal of Science, Technology and Sustainability Development*. 10.1108/WJSTSD-02-2021-0017

Kofler, I., Marcher, A., Volgger, M., & Pechlaner, H. (2018). The special characteristics of tourism innovation networks: The case of the regional innovation system in South Tyrol. *Journal of Hospitality and Tourism Management*, 37, 68–75.

Laing, E., van Stel, A., & Storey, D. J. (2021). Formal and informal entrepreneurship: A cross-country policy perspective. *Small Business Economics*. 10.1007/s11187-021-00548-8

Lipoko, D. U. D., Iwu, C. G., & Opute, A. P. (2021). Gender discrepancy in economic participation: The case of young women in the Democratic Republic of Congo. EUREKA: Social and Humanities, Number 6. 10.21303/2504-5571.2021.002121

Lucas, D. S., & Fuller, C. S. (2017). Entrepreneurship: Productive, unproductive and destructive – relative to what? *Journal of Business Venturing Insight*, 7, 45–49.

McAdam, M., Harrison, R. T., & Leitch, C. M. (2018). Stories from the field: Women's networking as gender capital in entrepreneurial ecosystems. *Small Business Economics*, 53, 459–474. 10.1007/s11187-018-9995-6

McAdam, M., McAdam, R., Dunn, A., & McCall, C. (2014). Development of small and medium-sized enterprise horizontal innovation networks: UK agri-food sector study. *International Small Business Journal*, 32, 830–853.

McAdam, M., McAdam, R., Dunn, A., & McCall, C. (2015). Regional horizontal networks within the SME agri-food sector: An innovation and social network perspective. *Regional Studies*. 50(8), 1–14.

McAdam, M., McAdam, R., Dunn, A., & McCall, C. (2016). Regional horizontal networks within the SME agri-food sector: An innovation and social network perspective. *Regional Studies*, 50(8), 1316–1329.

Motoyama, Y., & Watkins, K. K. (2014). *Examining the connections within the start-up ecosystem: A study of St. Louis*. Kauffman Foundation.

Olanrewaju, A.-S.-T., Hossain, M. A., Whiteside, N., & Mercieca, P. (2020). Social media and entrepreneurship research: A literature review. *International Journal of Information Management*, 50, 90–110. 10.1016/j.ijinfomgt.2019.05.011

Opute, A. P. (2014). Cross-functional bridge in dyadic relationship: Conflict management and performance implications. *Team Performance Management*, 20(3/4), 121–147.

Opute, A. P. (2017). Exploring personality, identity and self-concept among young consumers (Chapter 5). In *Young consumer behaviour: A research companion*. London: Routledge (Taylor and Francis). ISBN: 978-0-415-79008-6 (hbk).

Opute, A. P. (2020). Small and medium enterprises marketing: Innovation and sustainable economic growth perspective (Chapter 2). In *Entrepreneurship marketing: Principles and practice of SME marketing*. London: Routledge Publishers.

Opute, A. P. (2022). Virtual teams: The new work norm for the post Covid-19 era (Chapter 13). In *Digital service delivery in Africa*. 10.1007/978-3-030-83909-3

Opute, A. P., & Madichie, N. (2017). Accounting-marketing integration dimensions and antecedents: Insights from a frontier market. *Journal of Business and Industrial Marketing*, 32(8), 1144–1158.

Opute, A. P., Irene, B. N., & Iwu, C. G. (2020a). Tourism service and digital technologies: A value creation perspective. *African Journal of Hospitality, Tourism and Leisure*, 9(2). ISSN:223-814X. https://www.ajhtl.com/2020-early-volume.html

Opute, A. P., Iwu, C. G., Adeola, O., Mugobo, V., Okeke-Uzodike, O. E., Fagbola, S., & Jaiyeoba, O. (2020c). The Covid-19-pandemic and implications for businesses: Innovative retail marketing viewpoint. *Retail Marketing Review*, 16, SE

Opute, A. P., Iwu, C. G., Khosa, R. M., Eresia-Eke, C., Hagos, S. B., & Irene, B. N. O. (2021a). African immigrant entrepreneurship in the UK: The hidden hand of family influence on entrepreneurial orientation. *Harvard Deusto Business Research*. X(1), 53–79.

Opute, A. P., Kalu, K. I., Adeola, O., & Iwu, C. G. (2021b). Steering sustainable economic growth: Entrepreneurial ecosystem approach. *Journal of Entrepreneurship and Innovation in Emerging Economies*, 7(2), 1–30.

Opute, A. P., Madichie, N. O., Hagos, S. B., & Ojra, J. (2020b) Entrepreneurship behaviour of African minorities in the UK: 'Demystifying cultural influence'. *International Journal of Entrepreneurship and Small Business*, 44(3), 298–322.

Pankov, S., Velamuri, V. K., & Schneckenberg, D. (2021). Towards sustainable entrepreneurial ecosystems: Examining the effect of contextual factors on sustainable entrepreneurial activities in the sharing economy. *Small Business Economics*, 56(3), 1073–1095. 10.1007/s11187-019-00255-5

Papadopoulos, T., Baltas, K. N., & Balta, M. E. (2020). The use of digital technologies by small and medium enterprises during COVID-19: Implications for theory and practice. *International Journal of Information Management*, 55, 102192.

Ratten, V., & Jones, P. (2020). Entrepreneurship and management education: Exploring trends and gaps. *The International Journal of Management Education*. 10.1016/j.ijme.2020.100431

Schruijer, S. G. L. (2020). Developing collaborative interorganizational relationships: An action research approach. *Team Performance Management*, 26(1/2), 17–28. 10.1108/TPM-11-2019-0106

Sousa, M. J., & Rocha, A. (2019). Skills for disruptive digital business. *Journal of Business Research*, 94, 257–263.

Spencer, R., & Sutton-Brady, C. (2021). Interactions, relationships and networks in a digital era, *Journal of Business & Industrial Marketing* Call for Papers. https://hi-in.facebook.com/Marketingscholars/posts/iinteractions-relationships-and-networks-in-a-digital-eraspecial-issue-of-the-jo/3276179845828359/

Spigel, B. (2017). The relational organization of entrepreneurial ecosystems. *Entrepreneurship Theory and Practice*, 41(1), 49–72. 10.1111/etap.12167

Stam, E. (2015). Entrepreneurial ecosystems and regional policy: A sympathetic critique. *European Planning Studies*, 23(9), 1759–1769. 10.1080/09654313.2015.1061484

Stam, E. & Spigel, B. (2017). Entrepreneurial ecosystems. In R. Blackburn, D. De Clercq, J. Heinonen, & Z. Wang (Eds.), *Handbook for entrepreneurship and small business*. London: SAGE Publications.

Theodoraki, C., Dana, L-P., & Caputo, A. (2022). Building sustainable entrepreneurial ecosystems: A holistic approach. *Journal of Business Research*, 140, 340–360.

Theodoraki, C., & Messeghem, K. (2017). Exploring the entrepreneurial ecosystem in the field of entrepreneurial support: A multi-level approach. *International Journal of Entrepreneurship and Small Business*, 31(1), 47–66. 10.1504/IJESB.2017.083847

Theodoraki, C., Messeghem, K., & Rice, M. P. (2018). A social capital approach to the development of sustainable entrepreneurial ecosystems: An explorative study. *Small Business Economics*, 51(1), 153–170. 10.1007/s11187-017-9924-0

Turkina, E. (2018). The importance of networking to entrepreneurship: Montreal's artificial intelligence cluster and its born-global firm element AI. *Journal of Small Business and Entrepreneurship*, 30(1), 1–8.

Turkina, E., Oreshkin, B., & Kali, R. (2019). Regional innovation clusters and firm innovation performance: An interactionist approach. *Regional Studies*, 53(8), 1193–1206.

Index